CIPS Study Matters

Level 6

Graduate Diploma in Purchasing and Supply

Legal Aspects in Purchasing and Supply

Patricia Elliot
Thetes Group

THE
CHARTERED INSTITUTE OF
PURCHASING & SUPPLY

Published by

The Chartered Institute of Purchasing and Supply
Easton House, Easton on the Hill, Stamford, Lincolnshire PE9 3NZ
Tel: +44 (0) 1780 756 777
Fax: +44 (0) 1780 751 610
Email: info@cips.org
Website: CIPS: http://www.cips.org

Technical reviewer: Margaret Griffiths, University of Glamorgan

Instructional design and publishing project management by Wordhouse
Ltd, Reading, UK

Content management system, instructional editing and pre-press by
Echelon Learning Ltd, London, UK

Index prepared by Indexing Specialists (UK) Ltd, Hove, UK

ISBN 1-86124-164-X
ISBN 978-186124-164-1

Contents

Introduction

This course book has been designed to assist you in studying for the CIPS Legal Aspects in Purchasing and Supply unit in the level 6 Graduate Diploma in Purchasing and Supply. The book covers all topics in the official CIPS unit content document, as illustrated in the table beginning on page xi.

It is becoming increasingly important for procurement professionals to keep abreast of legal developments relevant to their role of purchasing and supply within an organisation whether that be public or private sector.

Although there is emphasis within the course book on contractual issues and sale of goods legislation, the content is wide ranging and includes other areas of law such as agency, tendering, aspects of outsourcing, competition, intellectual property, electronic trading and international trade.

The aim of the course book is to provide purchasing and supply professionals with the necessary knowledge and resources to undertake and, where studied in depth, achieve success in their assessment for this unit. However, it can also act as a helpful and practical resource for the procurement professional in his or her everyday work.

How to use this book

The course book will take you step by step through the unit content in a series of carefully planned 'study sessions' and provides you with learning activities, self-assessment questions and revision questions to help you master the subject matter. The guide should help you organise and carry out your studies in a methodical, logical and effective way, but if you have your own study preferences you will find it a flexible resource too.

Before you begin using course this book, make sure you are familiar with any advice provided by CIPS on such things as study skills, revision techniques or support and how to handle formal assessments.

If you are on a taught course, it will be up to your tutor to explain how to use the book – when to read the study sessions, when to tackle the activities and questions, and so on.

If you are on a self-study course, or studying independently, you can use the course book in the following way:

1   Scan the whole book to get a feel for the nature and content of the subject matter.

2   Plan your overall study schedule so that you allow enough time to complete all 20 study sessions well before your examinations – in other words, leaving plenty of time for revision.

3   For each session, set aside enough time for reading the text, tackling all the learning activities and self-assessment questions, and the revision question at the end of the session, and for the suggested further reading. Guidance on roughly how long you should set aside for studying each session is given at the beginning of the session.

Now let's take a look at the structure and content of the individual study sessions.

Overview of the study sessions

The course book breaks the content down into 20 sessions, which vary from three to six or seven hours' duration each. However, we are not advising you to study for this sort of time without a break! The sessions are simply a convenient way of breaking the syllabus into manageable chunks. Most people would try to study one or two sessions a week, taking one or two breaks within each session. You will quickly find out what suits you best.

Each session begins with a brief **introduction** which sets out the areas of the syllabus being covered and explains, if necessary, how the session fits in with the topics that come before and after.

After the introduction there is a statement of the **session learning objectives**. The objectives are designed to help you understand exactly what you should be able to do after you've studied the session. You might find it helpful to tick them off as you progress through the session. You will also find them useful during revision. There is one session learning objective for each numbered subsection of the session.

After this, there is a brief section reproducing the learning objectives and indicative content from the official **unit content document**. This will help you to understand exactly which part of the syllabus you are studying in the current session.

Following this, there are **prior knowledge** and **resources** sections if necessary. These will let you know if there are any topics you need to be familiar with before tackling each particular session, or any special resources you might need, such as a calculator or graph paper.

Then the main part of the study session begins, with the first of the numbered main subsections. At regular intervals in each study session, we have provided you with **learning activities**, which are designed to get you actively involved in the learning process. You should always try to complete the activities – usually on a separate sheet of your own paper – before reading on. You will learn much more effectively if you are actively involved in doing something as you study, rather than just passively reading the text in front of you. The feedback or answers to the activities are provided at the end of the session. Do not be tempted to skip the activity.

We also provide a number of **self-assessment questions** in each study session. These are to help you to decide for yourself whether or not you have achieved the learning objectives set out at the beginning of the session. As with the activities, you should always tackle them – usually on a separate sheet of paper. Don't be tempted to skip them. The feedback or answers are again at the end of the session. If you still do not understand a topic having attempted the self-assessment question, always try to re-read the relevant passages in the textbook readings or session, or follow the advice on further reading at the end of the session. If this still doesn't work, you should contact the CIPS Membership and Qualification Advice team.

For most of the learning activities and self assessment questions you will need to use separate sheets of paper for your answers or responses. Some of the activities or questions require you to complete a table or form, in which case you could write your response in the study guide itself, or photocopy the page.

At the end of the session are three final sections.

The first is the **summary**. Use it to remind yourself or check off what you have just studied, or later on during revision.

Then follows the **suggested further reading** section. This section, if it appears, contains recommendations for further reading which you can follow up if you would like to read alternative treatments of the topics. If for any reason you are having difficulty understanding the course book on a particular topic, try one of the alternative treatments recommended. If you are keen to read around and beyond the syllabus, to help you pick up extra points in the examination for example, you may like to try some of the additional readings recommended. If this section does not appear at the end of a session, it usually means that further reading for the session topics is not necessary.

At the end of the session we direct you to a **revision question**, which you will find in a separate section at the end of the course book. Feedback on the questions is also given.

Reading lists

CIPS produces an official reading list, which recommends essential and desirable texts for augmenting your studies. This reading list is available on the CIPS website or from the CIPS Bookshop. This course book is one of the essential texts for this unit. In this section we describe the main characteristics of the other essential text for this unit, which you are strongly urged to buy and use throughout your course.

The other essential text is:

Legal Aspects of Purchasing and Supply Chain Management by Ian Longdin, published by Liverpool Academic Press in 2005.

The main strength of this book is that it provides another aspect and view of legal principles relating specifically to purchasing and supply professionals. It covers all the unit content of the study guide. Like the course book the text makes legal issues accessible to those with no previous legal experience being written in an approachable style. Reading this text as well as the course book gives the student the best possible chance of success in the examination.

There is no particular weakness other than the fact that the book takes account of the law up to the date of publication. As new laws, rules and regulations come into force on a regular basis it is recommended that students keep abreast of such changes by sourcing as up to date information as possible. This is made easier in this technological age with the development of the world wide web.

Prior knowledge of law

This course book assumes that you have been introduced to basic concepts in law at an earlier stage in your studies. The content of this book builds upon this basic knowledge of law, which might have been acquired while studying the CIPS Level 4 'Developing Contracts in Purchasing and Supply' unit ('Developing Contracts' for short) or an equivalent level course or textbook with similar content. You will therefore find helpful references to the 'Developing Contracts' course book throughout this book, and wherever possible you should refer back to that course book, or to similar sections of an equivalent textbook used in your earlier studies.

Unit content coverage

In this section we reproduce the whole of the official CIPS unit content document for this unit. The overall unit characteristics and learning outcomes for the unit are given first. Then, in the table that follows, the learning objectives and indicative content are given in the left hand column. In the right hand column are the study sessions, or subsections, in which you will find coverage of the various topics.

Unit Characteristics

This unit seeks to familiarise students with the law that regulates the purchasing function.

The purchasing and supply professional needs to understand where legal issues may impact on the organisation and when to take action to avoid risk. They should also be able to recognise situations when the appropriate action would be to seek legal expertise.

The content provides an essential overview of different legal issues with particular emphasis on contractual issues and sale of goods legislation. Other areas covered include the legal aspects of outsourcing, competition law, intellectual property law, electronic trading and international trade. It is designed to assist professionals who work in either the public or private sector.

Learning Outcomes

On completion of this unit, students will be able to:

- Analyse the process of contract formation and assess the validity of a range of contract clauses.
- Distinguish between the statutes relating to sale of goods and the supply of goods and services in specific circumstances and apply those rules to given practical situations.
- Judge when it would be appropriate for legal action to be taken against a third party.
- Diagnose the impact of specific UK and EU regulations on the purchasing and supply function.
- Examine those intellectual property rights that are registerable and those that are un-registerable.
- Examine the impact of e-trading on traditional contract law.
- Predict the legal issues that need to be addressed when entering into an international contract for the purchase of goods.

Learning objectives and indicative content

1.0 Contract law. (Weighting 35%)

1.1 Develop knowledge of the process of contract formation to be able to subject this to analysis of the problems of reconciling the buyer's terms and conditions with those of the seller when faced with the battle of the forms.   Study session 1
   - Offer and acceptance
   - Consideration
   - Intention to create legal relations
   - Battle of the forms
   - When a contract is formed in cyberspace

1.2 Distinguish between expressed and implied terms and apply the principles relating to specific types of contractual clauses in a practical setting and in particular in relation to the sale and supply of goods and services.   Study session 2
   - Expressed and implied terms
   - Conditions,warranties and innominate terms.
   - Exclusion and limitation clauses
   - Force Majeure clauses
   - Penalty and liquidated damages clauses
   - Retention of title clauses.

1.3 Determine the factors that may vitiate consent to a contract.   Study session 3
   - Duress
   - Repudiation
   - Misrepresentation
   - Mistake
   - Undue influence

1.4 Critically evaluate the different common law methods by which a contract is terminated, and the remedies available to either party should a contract be breached.   Study session 4
   - Performance
   - Frustration
   - Agreement including variation of a contract
   - Breach
   - Assessment of unliquidated damages

1.5 Critically evaluate the alternative methods of resolving commercial disputes.   Study session 5
   - Litigation
   - Arbitration
   - Mediation
   - Conciliation
   - Adjudication
   - International arbitration

2.0 Sale and supply of goods and services, including third party rights and obligations. (Weighting 30%)

2.1 Distinguish between the statutes relating to the sale of goods and the supply of goods and services in specific circumstances and apply those rules to given practical situations.
Study session 6
- Sale of Goods Act 1979 (as amended)
- Supply of Goods and Services Act 1982
- Contracts for the sale of goods
- Contracts for work and materials

2.2 Recognise the protection provided by implied conditions and warranties contained in the Sale of Goods Act 1979 (as amended) and the Supply of Goods and Services Act 1982.
Study session 7
- S12 – S15 Sale of Goods Act
- Part one and Part two Supply of Goods and Services Act

2.3 Differentiate between ownership, risk, delivery and acceptance of goods and examine when each passes under the Sale of Goods Act 1979.
Study session 8
- S16 - S20 Sale of Goods Act
- S30 Delivery
- S31 Instalment deliveries
- S34 - S35 Acceptance of goods

2.4 Analyse the rules relating to the passing of title by a non-owner under legislation and the exceptions to these rules.
Study session 9
- The Nemo dat rule
- Romalpa clauses
- Estoppel
- Sale by a merchantile agent
- Sale under a voidable title
- Sale by a seller in possession
- Sale by a buyer in possession
- Sale of a motor vehicle on hire purchase
- Sale under a court order

2.5 Evaluate the various methods for circumventing the problems created by privity of contract.
Study session 10
- Collateral contracts and warranties
- Negligence
- Indemnity clauses
- Agency arrangements
- Consumer Protection Act 1987 part one
- Contract (Rights of Third Parties) Act 1999
- Assignment and novation of rights and obligations to a third party

2.6 Test the legal principles that apply to agency and bailment in a given situation.
Study session 11
- Creation of agency
- Rights and duties of agents and principals
- Relationship of principal /agent with third parties
- Responsibilities that arise from a bailment relationship.

3.0 Specific UK and EU regulations affecting the purchasing function. (Weighting 25%)

3.1 Determine the collateral legal obligations that arise from a   Study session 12
tendering process (including e-tendering) and distinguish
between those obligations that arise before the tender is awarded
and those that arise after the tender is awarded.

- Legal status of the tender bid
- Open and closed tenders
- Duty to consider all compliant tenders
- Equal and timely access to information
- Fair treatment and good faith
- Post award negotiations
- Letters of intent
- Avoidance of the battle of the forms

3.2 Critically assess the responsibilities of public procurement staff   Study session 13
resulting from the EU Public Sector Directive 2004/18/EC
(including the Utilities Directive).

- Thresholds, time limits, advertising
- Award criteria
- Right to feedback
- Framework agreements
- Open, restricted, negotiated and competitive dialogue
  procedure
- E-procurement mechanisms
- Central purchasing bodies
- Social and environmental considerations

3.3 Critically evaluate the impact of the Freedom of Information   Study session 14
Act 2000 on the procurement function.

- Right to request information
- Absolute exemptions
- Qualified exemptions
- Partial disclosure

3.4 Predict whether outsourcing a service or operation is compliant   Study session 15
with legal requirements.

- TUPE
- Consultation
- Redundancy law
- Alternatives to redundancy

3.5 Examine the laws that regulate anti-competitive behaviour and
abuse of a dominant market position in both the UK and the
EU.

- Competition Act 1998
- Article 81 EC Treaty
- Article 82 EC Treaty
- Enterprise Act 2002

**4.0 Intellectual property rights and international trade.
(Weighting 10%)**

4.1 Distinguish between those intellectual property rights that are   Study session 17
registerable and those that are unregisterable.
  • Patents
  • Trade marks
  • Design rights
  • Copyright
  • IPR protection through contractual clauses

4.2 Explain and apply the common law rules relating to   Study session 18
confidentiality and the protection of trade secrets in English
law.
  • Tort of passing-off
  • Breach of confidence
  • Restraint of trade clauses

4.3 Predict the legal issues that need to be addressed when entering   Study session 19
into an international contract for the purchase of goods.
  • Incoterms including CIF, FOB, EXW, DDP and FAS.
  • Bill of Lading
  • Contracts of Carriage
  • Jurisdiction
  • The Uniform Law on International Sales Act 1967 (Hague
    Convention)

4.4 Propose the most appropriate means of payment and explain the   Study session 20
appropriate documentation involved in a transaction for the sale
of goods in an international context.
  • Letters of credit (or documentary credits)
  • Shipping documents

Contract law – the application

Introduction

'I'm going to make him an offer he can't refuse.'
Don Corleone, *The Godfather* (1972)

This course is designed to assist you as a purchasing and supply professional, whether you work in the public or private sector, in the application of contract law. You should already have studied contract in Level 4, Developing Contracts, study sessions 4 – 6, or as part of an equivalent course. We recommend that you revisit these sessions to refresh your memory on contract. In this study session you will be looking at the essential elements to formation of a contract, how to avoid the battle of the forms, and with the ever-increasing use of electronic communication what to consider when entering into an e-contract.

Session learning objectives

After completing this session you should be able to:

1.1 Describe the elements of offer and acceptance.
1.2 Explain the principles of consideration.
1.3 Explain intention to create legal relations.
1.4 Explain what is meant by the battle of the forms.
1.5 Describe contracts in cyberspace (e-contracts).

Unit content coverage

This study session covers the following topics from the official CIPS unit content document:

Learning outcome

Analyse the process of contract formation and assess the validity of a range of contract clauses.

Learning objective

1.1 Develop knowledge of the process of contract formation to be able to subject this to analysis of the problems of reconciling the buyer's terms and conditions with those of the seller when faced with the battle of the forms.
- Offer and acceptance
- Consideration
- Intention to create legal relations
- Battle of the forms
- When a contract is formed in cyberspace

1

Prior knowledge

Level 4, Developing Contracts, study sessions 4 – 6, or equivalent studies.

Timing

You should set aside about 6 hours to read and complete this session, including learning activities, self-assessment questions, the suggested further reading (if any) and the revision question.

1.1 The elements of offer and acceptance

Learning activity 1.1

Write the essential elements of a contract with a brief explanation of each.

Feedback on page 14

Contract law has a vital role to play in the life of procurement professionals.

To gain the most benefit from this study guide it is important to understand the basic legal principles of contract law. Before doing the above learning activity you will hopefully have revisited Level 4, Developing Contracts, study sessions 4 and 5, or an equivalent book, and reflected on the history of contract law from the 18th and 19th centuries to the present day.

Contract law was established by judges in relevant cases and followed according to the rules of **judicial precedent**. More information on the doctrine of judicial precedent and the hierarchy of courts can be found in the Level 4 course book. For ease of reference, a diagram of the hierarchy of courts is shown in figure 1.1. Read more about the courts in Smith and Keenan (2003).

Figure 1.1: The hierarchy of courts

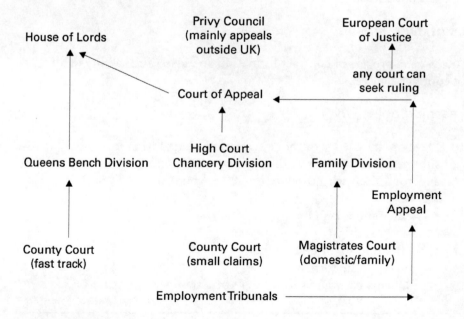

Significant changes were and continue to be made through parliamentary intervention with primary (statutes) and secondary (statutory instruments and regulations) legislation. Further changes continue through the UK's entry into the European Economic Community (EEC) (now known as the European Union (EU)).

Look again at the definition of contract: a contract is an agreement, enforceable by law, between two or more persons to do, or to abstain from doing, some act or acts.

To decide if there is a contract, the courts examine each situation objectively to see if the essential elements of a contract exist. An overview of the contractual process is provided in figure 1.2.

Figure 1.2: Overview of the contractual process

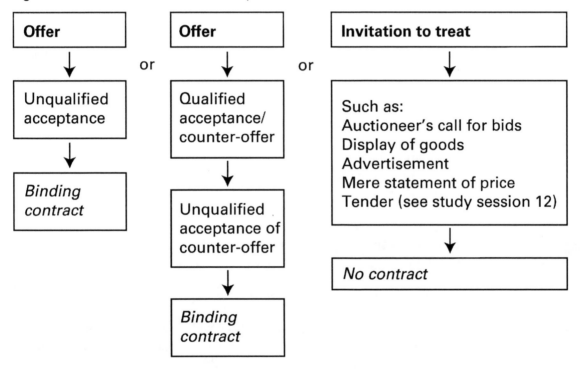

Offer

An offer is an expression of willingness to contract made with the intention that it shall become binding on the offeror as soon as it is accepted by the offeree. An offer to be capable of acceptance must be communicated to the offeree.

A genuine offer is different from what is known as an invitation to treat. An invitation to treat is where a party is merely inviting offers that can be accepted or rejected.

Examples of invitation to treat

Auctions

When an auctioneer calls for bids this is an invitation to treat or a request for offers. The person or bidder who makes a bid is the party making an offer that the auctioneer can either accept or reject. The bidder may retract his bid before is it accepted. See the case of *British Car Auctions Ltd* v *Wright* [1972], which involved the sale of an un-roadworthy car. The court decided that the auctioneer invites people present to make offers. The bidders then make offers and acceptance is usually by fall of the gavel (see Level 4, Developing Contracts, section 4.2).

Display of goods

The courts have decided that display of goods with a price ticket in a shop window or supermarket shelf is not an offer to sell but an invitation for customers to make an offer to buy. See *Fisher* v *Bell* [1960] where a shopkeeper displayed a flick knife for sale in his shop window. The court held this was an invitation to treat.

Advertisements

These are normally interpreted as invitations to treat. However, they may be construed as offers if they are unilateral, that is open to the entire world to accept. See *Carlill* v *Carbolic Smoke Ball Co* [1893]. In this case the defendants were makers of a health product. They published newspaper advertisements promising to pay £100 to anyone who contracted flu after buying one of their smoke balls and using it as directed. The advertisements also said that they had deposited £1,000 in a named bank to show their sincerity in this matter. The plaintiff bought a smoke ball and used it as directed but still caught flu. She sued for the £100 promised. The Court of Appeal held that the advertisement in this case was an offer to the whole world, the wording of the advertisement clearly showed an intention to be bound to anyone accepting this offer. The plaintiff had accepted the offer by her actions.

Mere statements of price or supply of information

A mere statement at which a party may be willing to sell will not amount to an offer. See *Harvey* v *Facey* [1893] where the claimants sent a telegram to the defendants stating 'Will you sell us Bumper Hall Pen? Telegraph lowest cash price.' The defendants telegraphed in reply 'Lowest price for Bumper Hall Pen £900.' The claimants then telegraphed 'We agree to buy Bumper Hall Pen for £900 asked by you. Please send us your title deeds in order that we may get early possession'. The defendants made no reply. The Supreme Court of Jamaica granted the claimants a decree of specific implement which meant that title deeds were to be sent to them. However, on appeal the Privy Council held that there was no contract. The second telegram was not an offer but was a mere price indication and in the nature of an invitation to treat at a minimum price of £900. The third telegram could not therefore be an acceptance resulting in a contract. There was no contract.

Tenders

Where goods are advertised for sale by tender, the statement is not an offer but an invitation to treat. It is a request by the owner of the goods for offers to purchase them (see study sessions 12 and 17).

The process of competitive tendering came under scrutiny in *Harvela Investments* v *Royal Trust Co of Canada* [1985]. Two parties were invited to bid secretly for a block of shares on the understanding that the shares would be sold to the highest bidder. The plaintiff bid $2,175,000 while the other party bid '$2,100,000 or $10,000 more than any other cash bid whichever is higher' (that is, a referential bid). The House of Lords held that the referential bid was ineffective and that the plaintiff's cash bid should have been accepted. The use of referential bids, they said, defeated the whole purpose of confidential competitive tendering and was not to be encouraged. Tendering is dealt with in study session 12.

See also *Blackpool and Fylde Aero Club* v *Blackpool Borough Council* [1990]. In this case the plaintiff and six other parties were invited to submit tenders for the concession to run pleasure flights from Blackpool Airport. The plaintiff submitted a tender in due form, complying with all requirements but their tender was not considered owing to council staff failing to open the letterbox. The court held that the council was liable for breach of contract, holding that the plaintiff had a contractual right to have its tender considered as it had complied with all the requirements of the invitation to tender.

Acceptance

In your previous studies you should have learned that offers can be terminated in various ways, including rejection, acceptance, counter-offer, revocation and time. Revisit Level 4, Developing Contracts, section 4.4, or equivalent material, and refresh your memory on the difference between acceptance and counter-offer. See also the case of *Hyde* v *Wrench* [1840] where the defendant offered to sell his farm for £1,000. The claimant's agent made an offer of £950 and the defendant asked for a few days to think about it after which the defendant wrote saying he could not accept it. The claimant then wrote purporting to accept the offer to sell at £1,000. The defendant did not consider himself bound by this and the claimant sued for specific performance. The court held that the claimant could not enforce this acceptance because his counter-offer of £950 was an implied rejection of the original offer to sell at £1,000.

When an acceptance is final and unqualified or unconditional then the offer is terminated. It means that an agreement then exists. For a contract to be legally binding the offeree must accept all the terms of the offer. However, in certain circumstances a binding contract may exist without a matching offer and acceptance. This depends on the method of communication of acceptance. You will have studied this in Level 4, Developing Contracts, section 4.5 under communication of acceptance.

You saw earlier that an offer must be communicated to the offeree. The same applies to acceptance. For acceptance to be effective it must be communicated. The exception to this is the postal rule, which is discussed below (see also Level 4, Developing Contracts, section 4.5).

Acceptance is often communicated in writing or verbally but situations involving silence or conduct may also arise (see Level 4, Developing

Contracts, section 4.5). Instant communication, such as telex, fax, telephone or the internet, follows the general rule and the acceptance must be received by the offeror.

Acceptance involving silence or conduct can be seen in various cases below.

Silence: see *Felthouse* v *Bindley* [1862] where the courts held that 'mental' acceptance or silence did not constitute contractual acceptance.

Conduct: see *Brogden* v *Metropolitan Railway Company* [1877] where there was an annual written contract. A new contract was amended, amounting to a counter-offer and returned but this was never returned. However, the deliveries of coal continued to be accepted. The court held that the new contract had been accepted by silent conduct.

Unilateral offers: this is an exception to the communication rule. See *Carlill* v *Carbolic Smoke Ball Co* [1893] where the court held that the offeror waived the right for acceptance to be communicated.

Where the courts have had difficulty in identifying the separate elements of offer and acceptance the judges have been prepared to hold that a contract has come into existence. See *Trentham Ltd* v *Archital Luxfer* [1993] where Trentham were building and engineering contractors who were engaged as main contractors in a building contract. They negotiated with Archital Luxfer for Archital to install aluminium windows, doors and screens in the premises. Work commenced before negotiations were complete although both parties clearly intended to create an agreement and work was paid for. Trentham alleged that there were defects in the windows and claimed damages for breach of contract. Archital denied liability stating that no contract had been concluded. The Court of Appeal held that a binding contract existed and came into existence during the performance of the contract even if it could not precisely analyse the terms of offer and acceptance.

You have seen above that unilateral offers are an exception to the communication rule. The 'postal rule' is another exception to the general rule. Where acceptance is posted the acceptance is deemed communicated when you put your letter of acceptance into the post even if it never arrives and the offeror does not receive actual notice of your acceptance. This could cause problems if the offeror is unaware that you have validly accepted the offer. See *Adams* v *Lindsell* [1818]: the defendant wrote to the plaintiff offering to sell some wool and asked for a reply in course of post. This offer was delayed two days in the post, and consequently the plaintiff's acceptance was late in coming back. On the day before it arrived (but after it had been expected), the defendant sold the wool elsewhere. The court held that the plaintiff was entitled to damages as his acceptance was complete when his letter was posted before the wool was sold to the third party.

Postal rule

The postal rule applies to communications by cable or telegram but not the instant methods of telephone, telex or fax.

Self-assessment question 1.1

Read the following statements and answer true/false.

1 An offer must always be communicated in writing.
2 The display of goods in a shop window is an invitation to treat.
3 An auctioneer selling a car at an auction is making an offer.
4 A revocation is effective from time of posting.
5 A qualified acceptance can also be known as a counter-offer.
6 If an offeree rejects the offer no agreement is made.
7 If an offer is unconditionally accepted by the offeree a contract is formed.
8 In *Carlill* v *Carbolic Smoke Ball Co Ltd* the courts held that the advertisement was only an invitation to treat.

Feedback on page 15

1.2 The principles of consideration

Learning activity 1.2

Review previous studies in relation to consideration and explain with reference to appropriate case law the technical rules that have been developed by the courts. It is recommended that you revisit and reflect on Level 4, Developing Contracts, section 5.1.

Feedback on page 15

As you saw from the previous session consideration is one of the essential elements of a contract. If there is no consideration there can be no contract. As you will have studied in Level 4, Developing Contracts, section 5.1, consideration carries with it the idea that in a contract, a bargain is struck.

In the case of *Currie* v *Misa* [1875] the judge defined consideration as 'some right, interest, profit or benefit accruing to one party, or some forbearance, detriment, loss or responsibility given, suffered or undertaken by the other'. Consideration must be of some value but the courts have consistently refused to look at its adequacy.

Let us look at the rules of consideration. Remember to revisit Level 4, Developing Contracts, section 5.1 on this.

Consideration must be sufficient but need not be adequate. It is important to know the distinction between sufficiency and adequacy. Within the context of contract law sufficient consideration means the type that the law recognises as being capable of having value. The most obvious type is money. Adequacy is about the amount of consideration. The law is not interested on how good a deal you have made as long as it is clear you made a deal.

Sometimes the courts will find that there is 'no valuable' consideration, for example where you are already obliged to do something because of an existing public duty. See the case of *Collins* v *Godefroy* [1831] where the defendant Godefroy offered to pay Collins the sum of six guineas to give evidence in a court case. Collins had actually been subpoenaed to attend court and therefore was under a public duty to attend. His action to recover the six guineas failed for lack of consideration; or where you are already obliged to do something under an existing contractual duty. See the cases of *Stilk* v *Myrick* [1809] where the plaintiff was employed as a sailor. He was under contract to man a ship of which the defendant was the captain. During the voyage two seamen deserted the ship and the captain promised the remaining crew that if they manned the ship home shorthanded then he would divide the wages of the two who had deserted between those remaining. The captain then refused to do this and was sued. The court held that the defendant did not need to pay as the remaining crew were already contractually bound to man the ship back home and had not provided any consideration for the promise of the extra money. See also *Hartley* v *Ponsonby* [1857]: this case was similar to the case of *Stilk* v *Myrick* but nearly half the crew deserted. This meant that the voyage was more hazardous for the remaining crew. The remaining crew sued for recovery of £40 per man that they had been promised for bringing the ship home. The court held that they were entitled to receive the additional money as the nature of the voyage had altered drastically as it had become more hazardous. This meant that the original contract had effectively terminated leaving them free to make a new contract on different terms. This point is also covered in *Atlas Express Ltd* v *Kafco (Importers) Ltd* [1989], which was a case of economic duress. In this case the plaintiff company, Atlas, contracted with the defendants, Kafco, to transport cartons of basketware for them to retail premises nationwide. The agreed rate was £1.10 per carton with the plaintiff's expectations being that each load would consist of 400–600 cartons. The first load contained only 200 cartons and the plaintiffs refused to carry any more loads unless the defendants agreed to a minimum price of £440 per load. The defendants were unable to find alternative carriers and therefore reluctantly agreed to pay the new rate. Subsequently they refused to pay the new rate and the plaintiffs sued to enforce the new agreement. The court held that the pressure applied by the plaintiffs to force the defendants to renegotiate the contract was economic duress and this vitiated the contract.

The courts also consider there is 'no valuable' consideration where there is part payment of a debt. When you only pay part of a debt it cannot usually be considered as sufficient. See the case of *D & C Builders* v *Rees* [1965]. D & C were a small company who did work for Rees. Rees owed them £482.13s.1d. There was no dispute at first about the work done but Rees did not pay D & C. The claimants wrote to Rees for the money and received no reply. Later Mrs Rees (Mr Rees was ill) telephoned the claimants and complained about the workmanship. Mrs Rees told them 'My husband will offer you £300 in settlement. That is all you will get. It is to be in satisfaction.' D & C were in financial difficulties and faced bankruptcy. Therefore they offered to take the £300 and allow Rees one year to find the balance. Mrs Rees replied 'No, we will never have enough money to pay the balance, £300 is better than nothing.' The claimants responded by stating that they had no choice but to accept. Mrs Rees paid by cheque and insisted on a receipt in completion of the account. The claimants later brought an action against Rees to recover the balance. The defendants claimed poor workmanship and that there had been a binding settlement. The Court of Appeal held that a smaller sum in cash could be no settlement of a larger sum and no sensible distinction could be drawn between payments of a lesser sum by cash and the payment of it by cheque. In this case Mrs Rees had held the creditors to ransom and there was no reason why the claimants should not enforce the full amount of the debt. This case also illustrates the need for equality of bargaining power between the parties.

Past consideration is generally unacceptable. The consideration must be clearly associated with the promise. When consideration relates to past actions the law will not enforce a promise. See the case *Re McArdle* [1951] where Mr McArdle left his house to his widow for her lifetime and thereafter to his children. During his widow's lifetime one of the children and his wife moved into the house and did some renovation work costing £448. Subsequently all the children signed a document agreeing to reimburse the wife when the deceased's estate was distributed finally. They failed to reimburse the wife and she sued to enforce the promise. The Court of Appeal held that she could not enforce it as it was made after the work had been done. The consideration was in the past and did not support the promise. There was no contract. See also the more recent case of *Pao On* v *Lau Yui Long* [1980] where this rule has been re-formulated: this case recognised that duress could be economic duress. The basis of economic duress is that it must always amount to a coercion of will which vitiates consent.

Consideration must also move from the promisee. This is in line with the principle of privity of contract where only someone who is a party to the contract can sue or be sued on it. You will study this topic and the changes made by the Contract (Rights of Third Parties) Act 1999 in study session 10 or you should revisit Level 4, Developing Contracts, section 5.3.

Self-assessment question 1.2

Answer the following short questions.

1   Does consideration have to be sufficient and adequate to be recognised by the law?
2   Is consideration in part payment of a debt considered by the courts to be sufficient consideration?
3   Will the law enforce a promise when the consideration is related to past actions?
4   Can someone who provides consideration for the contractual promise enforce the contract?

(continued on next page)

1

5   Give an example of consideration which is capable of having value.

Feedback on page 15

1.3   Intention to create legal obligations

Domestic agreements between a husband and wife living together as one household are presumed not to be intended to be legally binding, unless the agreement states to the contrary. Refer to the case of *Balfour* v *Balfour* [1919]. In this case the husband and wife came home from Ceylon to England together. However, the husband returned to Ceylon alone as the wife remained in England on her doctor's advice. Before the husband left for Ceylon he agreed to pay his wife £30 per month as maintenance but he failed to do so. She sued but the court held that there was no enforceable contract because the parties did not intend to create legal relations. However, the case would be different where the husband and wife were separated. However, the presumption will not apply where the spouses are not living together. See the case of *Merritt* v *Merritt* [1969]. In this case the husband and wife were not living together when he agreed to pay £40 per month maintenance. The court held that as the husband and wife were separated at the time the agreement was made, it was enforceable. Agreements between parent and child are considered in the same way. See the case of *Simpkins* v *Pays* [1955] where the defendant and the defendant's granddaughter made an agreement with the claimant who was a paying boarder that they should submit a weekly coupon in the defendant's name to a newspaper competition. On one occasion a forecast by the grandmother was correct and the defendant received a prize of £750. The claimant sued for her share of the sum. The court held that there was an intention to create legal relations. Far from being a friendly domestic arrangement, the evidence showed that it was a joint enterprise and that the parties expected to share in any prize money.

Social agreements are presumed not to create legal obligations. Examples include inviting a friend for a meal. The courts have applied this to other situations such as sharing petrol costs where a person is given a lift to work. See the case of *Coward* v *Motor Insurers' Bureau* [1963] where an offer to share the cost of petrol used on a journey was not an intention to create legal relations.

On the other hand, in commercial agreements, there is a strong presumption that the parties intend to create legal relations and to be legally bound. The courts will consider whether the words are clear and unambiguous. The burden of rebutting contractual intent is an onerous one. The burden is on the party wishing to rely on it.

Learning activity 1.3

You studied this topic in Developing Contracts, Level 4. You should revisit Level 4, Developing Contracts, study session 5 and refresh your memory before attempting this learning activity. Now think of some activities you

(continued on next page)

Learning activity 1.3 (continued)

have been doing over the past few days. These might include going out with a friend for dinner, or arranging to meet your brother or sister at the theatre, or buying a bus ticket to go to work, or negotiating a contract at work. List these activities under appropriate headings of whether you consider them to be domestic/social or commercial/business and briefly explain why.

Feedback on page 16

The courts will not enforce any contract unless it is clear that the parties intended to be legally bound by their agreement. It is presumed that this is the intention in normal commercial contracts, and that it is not the intention in respect of domestic and social agreements. This presumption can be rebutted and it depends on each case. See the case of *Balfour* v *Balfour* [1919] where the courts held that this was an agreement between husband and wife and that the parties never intended they might be sued upon it. The intention to be bound must be clear and complete. See the case of *Guthing* v *Lynn* [1831] where P bought a horse for £63 and promised D an extra £5 'if the horse was lucky'. The court held that the promise was too vague to be a legally enforceable contract.

In the case of *Walford* v *Miles* [1992] two groups negotiating the sale of a business agreed that so long as AA provided a bankers letter by a certain date, RR would not negotiate with any third party and would continue negotiations with AA in good faith. The House of Lords (HL) held that the agreement was unenforceable for lack of certainty. However, gaps in a contract can be filled by the use of 'implied terms' such as under Sale of Goods Act 1979 (SGA) and Supply of Goods and Services Act 1982 (SOGAS). You will be studying these later on in study session 2. Before answering the self-assessment question, it is recommended that you revisit and reflect on Level 4, Developing Contracts, section 5.2.

Self-assessment question 1.3

Read the following statements and answer true/false with reference to appropriate case law.

1 Bob agrees to pay his wife Margaret £50 per week housekeeping. Bob fails to pay any money to his wife. Margaret successfully sues Bob.
2 An advertisement by Brushup in a newspaper states that the hair restore lotion is 'the best in the world'. This advertisement is an advertising puff.
3 In the case of *Simpkins* v *Pays* [1955] the courts held that there was no intention to create a legal obligation.
4 The plaintiff in the case of *Carlill* v *Carbolic Smoke Ball Co* [1892] successfully rebutted the claim that the advertisement was a mere puff.
5 A social arrangement is legally enforceable.
6 'Ex gratia' negates the existence of a contract.

Feedback on page 16

1

1.4 The battle of the forms

Having studied the essential elements of a valid contract this section examines different types of standard form contracts and how to avoid a 'battle of the forms' situation.

Learning activity 1.4

Reflect on previous studies and explain the procedures to avoid the battle of the forms situation arising. It is recommended that you revisit and reflect on Level 4, Developing Contracts, section 6.1 to refresh your memory. You may also wish to consider the tendering process in your organisation.

Feedback on page 16

You are now aware of the essential requirements of a valid contract. You should reflect on the session on the essential elements. Now look at these in relation to standard form contracts. Some standard documents include an order form, enquiry, tender invitation, acknowledgement, confirmation, despatch note, delivery note and invoice. Each of these will or may frequently contain terms and conditions of the originating party. Let us take a scenario of the buyer making an offer on their order form (offer). The response is an acknowledgement by the seller containing their terms that contradict the buyer's terms. This is a counter-offer. Reflecting on your previous studies, you know that a counter-offer kills off the original offer. This situation can continue with forms back and forward. So what do you do to avoid this? Employ a tendering process.

Self-assessment question 1.4

Answer the following with a brief explanation.

1   In what way does a standard form contract differ from a normal contract?
2   List three advantages to a business using standard form contracts as a way of setting contractual terms.
3   List two disadvantages to a consumer dealing with a business on the business' standard contract form.

Feedback on page 18

1.5 Contracts in cyberspace (e-contracts)

Learning activity 1.5

Reflect on previous studies on formation of contract and Level 4, Developing Contracts, section 6.4 on e-contracts. Apply the general principles governing formation of contracts to contracting over the internet.

Feedback on page 18

You have studied the essential elements for contract formation and know that if all the necessary requirements are present then a contract is legally binding. Since oral contracts are enforceable in court even though they may be more difficult to prove there is no reason why the general principles that produce this result should not apply to contracts evidenced by digital communication. You also know from previous studies that an offer can be accepted by conduct. Taking this approach the legal effect of clicking an 'accept' button on a website is accepting by conduct. This is similar to the case of *Thornton* v *Shoe Lane Parking* [1971], which involved a driver of a car entering a car park having had the opportunity to read, but not having read, the terms and conditions of entry. The court held that a binding contract had been created.

The major exceptions to this approach under English law are contracts relating to land, contracts where there is no consideration and specific exceptions under legislation such as those in the Consumer Credit Act 1974.

The common law of contract is 'technology neutral' and has been for several years. The difficulty was in relation to admissibility of evidence and this was addressed by the Civil Evidence Act 1995. Computer-generated and computer-stored information in civil proceedings is allowed. It is best practice for businesses to be able to produce technical evidence to show why their computer records are trustworthy. Giving evidence in court should be included in an IT manager's job description.

Article 9 of the E-Commerce Directive required EU Member States to ensure that their legal system allows contracts to be concluded by electronic means. This is the case in most situations in English law.

The most important thing to consider when entering into an e-contract is the information on the website. You must also remember that the 'battle of the forms' situation could arise in e-contracts where contracts are made using emails and you must take the same care with e-contracts as you would do with non e-contracts. Suppliers who have a web site can ensure that their standard terms and conditions must apply to any contract and can avoid the battle of the forms situation arising.

You have already studied the Electronic Communications Act 2000 (see Level 4, Developing Contracts, section 6.4) which permits contractual negotiations and documents to be exchanged by email and permits the electronic signature to be used to confirm that the email is authentic.

Self-assessment question 1.5

Identify the essential elements of the e-contract and analyse what happens when you enter into a contract in cyberspace.

Feedback on page 18

Revision question

Now try the revision question for this session on page 311.

1

Summary

Now that you have studied the essential elements of the formation of a contract, which include the offer and acceptance, the rules of consideration, the intention to create legal obligations and e-contracts, you will now be studying the different types of contractual clause. It is hoped that you have also reflected on the recommended Level 4, Developing Contracts, study sessions 4 – 6, or equivalent material, to refresh your memory.

Suggested further reading

Griffiths and Griffiths (2002). You should read the chapter on contract formation, part I, chapter 1.

Smith and Keenan (2003), part 2, chapters 6 and 7.

Dobson (1997), chapter 1.

Stone (2000), chapters 1 and 2.

Feedback on learning activities and self-assessment questions

Feedback on learning activity 1.1

You were recommended in the introduction to this study session to revisit Level 4 to refresh your memory of contract law. Having done so, you should have found no difficulty in completing this learning activity. You should have written the following terms and brief explanations.

Agreement

This is at the heart of every contract. It has been referred to as a 'meeting of the minds' or the **consensus in idem.** It is important to know that an agreement alone is not legally enforceable at English law. An agreement is formed when one party (offeror) makes an offer that is accepted by another party (offeree) (see Level 4, Developing Contracts, section 4.2). A contract also contains these other essential elements.

Consideration

Both parties must have provided consideration: that is, each side must promise to give or do something for the other party (see sections 1.2 and Level 4, Developing Contracts, section 5.1).

Intention to create legal relations

The parties must have intended their agreement to have legal consequences. The law will not concern itself with purely domestic or social agreements (see sections 1.3 and Level 4, Developing Contracts, section 5.2).

Formalities

Normally no formalities are required to make contracts. In general they do not have to be in writing to be valid. Contracts may be made orally, by conduct or in writing. Some statutes specify several types of contract must be in writing, for example, consumer credit agreements. It is also desirable, although not a legal requirement, for commercial contracts to be in writing as there will be a written record of the terms and conditions agreed by the parties (see Level 4, Developing Contracts, study session 4).

Capacity

The parties must be legally capable of entering into a contract (see Level 4, Developing Contracts, study session 5).

Consent

The agreement must have been entered into freely. Consent may be vitiated by duress or undue influence (see sections 1.3 and Level 4, Developing Contracts, section 5.2).

Legality

The purpose of the agreement must not be illegal or contrary to public policy (see Level 4, Developing Contracts, study sessions 5 and 3).

Feedback on self-assessment question 1.1

1 False.
2 True.
3 False.
4 False.
5 True.
6 True.
7 True.
8 False.

Feedback on learning activity 1.2

Having reviewed Level 4 you should include in your answer the following technical rules.

Consideration must be sufficient but need not be adequate. The circumstances where the courts will find that there is no 'valuable consideration' and therefore no contract because consideration is insufficient include: performance of existing public duties; performance of existing contractual duties; part payment of a debt. Past consideration is no consideration; consideration must move from the promisee, which follows the principle of privity (see Level 4, Developing Contracts, sections 5.3 and study session 10).

Feedback on self-assessment question 1.2

1 The answer is no. Consideration must be sufficient but need not be adequate.
2 The answer to this question is no. This was decided in the case of *D & C Builders* v *Rees* [1965] where the defendant made a part payment in cash but this was held to be insufficient to settle the debt.

3   The answer is no. The law will not enforce a promise when the consideration is related to past actions.
4   The answer is yes. This relates to the doctrine of privity of contract whereby only the parties to the contract can enforce it.
5   An example is money.

Feedback on learning activity 1.3

Your list of activities might include those mentioned in learning activity 1.2 and of course others, such as buying a newspaper, a friend getting married, your mum and dad making arrangements to go to the pictures, buying electrical goods, purchasing desks for the office, and so on. The reason you have chosen an activity to be regarded as domestic/social or business/commercial should be to do with the intention of the parties to the activity wanting to create legal obligations. For example if you invite a friend round for a meal and they do not turn up did you intend this to be such an agreement that you could sue them? Of course not. The same applies with domestic agreements between say your mother and father, husband and wife. On the other hand, if you purchased desks for your office you would intend that there is a legal obligation to be bound to fulfil the agreement by delivering the desks.

Feedback on self-assessment question 1.3

1   False: this can be explained in the case of *Balfour* v *Balfour* [1919]. Agreements between a husband and wife living together as one household are presumed not to be intended to be legally binding.
2   True: where the advertisers make flamboyant claims about their products the law assumes there is no legal intention to be bound. They are mere puffs to puff up the product.
3   False: in this case the defendant, her granddaughter and the plaintiff who was a lodger all lived together in the defendant's house. They regularly entered into a competition with the entry being in the defendant's name. All paid towards the competition. The parties won and the defendant refused to pay the lodger claiming there was no intention to create a legal relationship. The court found that there was sufficient mutuality in the arrangements to establish a legally binding commitment.
4   True: the court held that the defendant did show legal intention to be bound.
5   False: social arrangements such as arranging to meet someone for dinner are not legally enforceable. If you fail to turn up you cannot be sued.
6   False: see the case of *Edwards* v *Skyways* [1964] where the courts held that the words 'ex gratia' did not negate the existence of a contract.

Feedback on learning activity 1.4

As the term 'battle of the forms' suggests, it is not just about 'forms' going backwards and forwards, but battling to see who wins. Your answer should include there being often a common business process of sending an order, that is, an offer, subject to their own standard pre-printed conditions, which is in itself not a major problem. The problem arises when the second party accepts the offer on its own standard form acceptance. This often means that the terms of the offer and the acceptance do not meet and may even contradict each other. Sometimes both sets of conditions state that in the event of a dispute its terms will rule. Frequently the terms of the contract will be those of the party who 'fired the last shot'. This follows the traditional approach that the submission of each standard form is like a counter-offer and therefore the last one submitted contains the final contractual terms. It is not always as clear-cut and each case will be decided on its own merits. You should refer to the foundation case of *Butler Machine Tool Co* v *Ex-Cell-O Corporation* [1979]. The plaintiff offered to sell a machine to the defendants on certain fixed terms including a price variations clause which were said to prevail over any other terms in the buyers' order. The defendant replied by placing an order on their standard order form in which some of the terms were significantly different and there was no price variation clause. The order form incorporated a tear-off slip which read 'We accept your order on the terms and conditions stated thereon' and this was signed and returned by the plaintiffs. The Court of Appeal held that the defendant's order on different terms constituted a counter-offer which was accepted by the plaintiffs when they returned the tear-off slip without further amendment. When there is a 'battle of the forms', said Lord Denning, it will be found in most cases that the contract is complete as soon as the last form is sent and received without objection being taken to it. The battle of the forms is dealt with later on in this study session. To avoid this 'battle' you need to ensure careful documentation and contracts management (see figure 1.3).

Figure 1.3

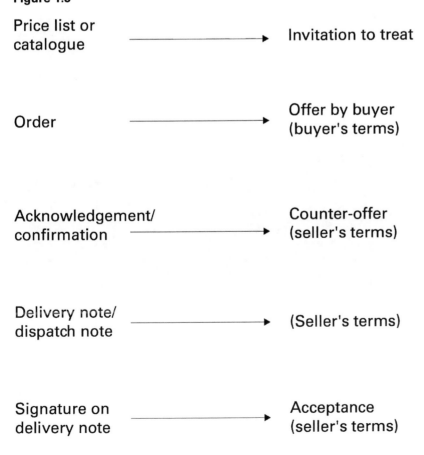

Price list or catalogue	⟶	Invitation to treat
Order	⟶	Offer by buyer (buyer's terms)
Acknowledgement/ confirmation	⟶	Counter-offer (seller's terms)
Delivery note/ dispatch note	⟶	(Seller's terms)
Signature on delivery note	⟶	Acceptance (seller's terms)

Feedback on self-assessment question 1.4

1 The main difference is that in a standard form contract, the contracting party can dictate the terms of the contract to the other. This can mean that the parties are not of equal bargaining power.
2 One advantage is time saving. It means that the business will not need to negotiate the terms of the contract to every new customer. Another advantage is that it is a standard form and a junior member of staff can use the forms. Having a standard form can also mean that the business person designing the form can include terms that are advantageous to it.
3 The consumer is in a weaker position and may not be able to do anything about it. They may have to accept the terms that are advantageous to the business. Also, standard forms may have more technical information that the consumer may not understand.

Feedback on learning activity 1.5

You should explain the essential elements of offer, acceptance, intention to create legal relations and consideration in contract law and that they are sufficiently flexible to deal with most technical developments. They have already been applied to telex and fax communications. This provides the guidelines to the likely legal position for email and online communication using a web server.

Feedback on self-assessment question 1.5

You should identify that the essential elements of an e-contract are the same as non-e-contracts.

Common law and statutory contractual terms

'To include or not to...that is the question.'
Anon.

Introduction

In this session you will be studying the distinction between express and implied terms, and the principles relating to specific types of contractual clauses at common law and under statute with particular emphasis on the sale and supply of goods and services. It is recommended that you revisit Level 4, Developing Contracts, study sessions 9 – 12, or equivalent material, to refresh your memory.

Session learning objectives

After completing this session you should be able to:

2.1 Distinguish between express and implied terms.
2.2 Classify common law and statutory exclusion clauses.
2.3 Distinguish between penalties and liquidated damages.
2.4 Explain the meaning of retention of title.

Unit content coverage

This study session covers the following topics from the official CIPS unit content document:

Learning outcome

Analyse the process of contract formation and assess the validity of a range of contract clauses.

Learning objective

1.2 Distinguish between express and implied terms and apply the principles relating to specific types of contractual clauses in a practical setting and in particular in relation to the sale and supply of goods and services.
   • Express and implied terms
   • Conditions, warranties and innominate terms
   • Exclusion and limitation clauses
   • Force Majeure clauses
   • Penalty and liquidated damages clauses
   • Retention of title clauses

Prior knowledge

Level 4, Developing Contracts, study sessions 9 – 12, or equivalent material.

2

Timing

You should set aside about 6 hours to read and complete this session, including learning activities, self-assessment questions, the suggested further reading (if any) and the revision question.

2.1 The difference between express and implied terms

Learning activity 2.1

You may wish to revisit and refresh your memory of express and implied terms in Level 4, Developing Contracts, study sessions 9 and 10, or equivalent material, before attempting this learning activity. Now explain the distinction between express and implied terms.

Feedback on page 31

You have already studied the essential elements required to form a contract. In the course of negotiating a contract various statements, promises and stipulations may be made. They can be grouped together under the word 'terms'. These terms may be express or implied. It is the terms of a contract that determine the extent of the rights and duties of each party and the remedies available if the terms are broken.

Statements made by parties in the course of negotiations leading up to the formation of the contract are classified by the court as either representations or terms. A representation is a statement that induces the contract but does not form part of it. A term is a promise or undertaking that is part of the contract. If a representation does become part of the contract then the Misrepresentation Act 1967 will apply. This is discussed in study session 3 on vitiating factors.

Whether a statement is a representation or a term is primarily a question of intention. Several situations can be considered.

If the parties have indicated that a statement is to be regarded as a term, then the court will implement their intention. It also depends on the manner in which it is made and the timing. See the case of *Ecay* v *Godfrey* [1947] where one party made a statement asking the other party to check out a boat, have it surveyed. In this case, the statement was held not to be a term. However, in the case of *Schawel* v *Reade* [1913] a horse seller told the buyer that he need not look for anything, the horse was perfectly sound. The statement was held to be a term of the contract as it was made to prevent the other party from finding a defect.

Timing of the statement: where there is a long interval between making the statement and concluding the contract this may indicate that the parties did not intend that the statement become a term of the contract.

Importance of the statement: where a statement is of such importance that the contract would not have been entered into, it is likely to be a term.

Special knowledge and skill: where one party has superior knowledge and skill relating to the subject matter of the contract, the court may hold that any statement made by such a person is a term. See the case of *Dick Bentley Productions Ltd* v *Harold Smith (Motors) Ltd* [1965] where a car dealer gave a false statement as to the mileage. The court held that this statement was a term.

Collateral contracts: where a contract is entered into on the basis of a statement made by one of the parties, there can be a collateral contract based on the statement. The collateral contract must have all the essential requirements of a contract. The collateral contract may also be used to evade the privity rule. See the case of *Shanklin Pier Ltd* v *Detel Products Ltd* [1951] in which a contract existed between the plaintiff and a contractor for the painting of a pier. The plaintiff, relying on representations made by the defendant paint manufacturer, insisted that the defendant's paint should be used for the job. The contractor purchased the paint which proved unsatisfactory and did not match up to specification. The court held that the plaintiff was entitled to recover damages from the defendant manufacturer of the paint on the basis of a collateral contract. Privity is also discussed in study session 10.

Express terms

On the matter of importance, not all the terms of a contract are of equal importance. The law has classified them into conditions, warranties and innominate terms. The definitions of conditions and warranties came from the Sale of Goods Act 1893 (now SGA 1979) but came to be applied by the courts to other types of contract. The classification is based on the examination of the contract itself to ascertain the intention of the parties. It has a bearing also on the remedy for breach of contract, whether termination or damages (see below).

Conditions

This is the term used to describe an important term of a contract. The breach of a condition will entitle the injured party to discharge themselves from the contract and sue for damages.

Warranties

This is a contractual term of lesser importance. If this term is breached the injured party has the right to claim damages but not to discharge themselves from the contract.

Whether the term is a condition or warranty depends on the intention of the parties. It is not conclusive even if they have described a term in the contract as a 'condition'. See the case of *Poussard* v *Spiers* [1876] where the opera singer's obligation to sing on the first night of a three-month series of concerts was held to be a condition. In the case of *Bettini* v *Gye* [1876] the singer's obligation to attend all the rehearsals was held to be a warranty.

Innominate term (also known as intermediate term)

This came about when the courts started to look at the effect a breach had on the injured party. Only when the true nature of the breach is

2

considered do the courts classify the term as 'innominate'. See the case of *Hong Kong Fir Shipping Co Ltd* v *Kawasaki Kisen Kaisha Ltd* [1962] where the defendants chartered a ship from the plaintiffs for 2 years. The engines were old and staff incompetent. This resulted in 20 lost weeks. The defendants repudiated the charter alleging breach of a 'condition' to provide a seaworthy ship. The plaintiffs brought an action for wrongful repudiation arguing that their breach did not entitle the defendants to terminate the contract, but only to a claim for damages. The appeal court held that as the defendants had not been deprived of the whole benefit under the contract the breach did not justify termination. So it is possible to have an innominate term where the remedy for the breach would depend on the nature of the breach.

Implied terms

Terms may be implied into a contract by the court, by statute or by custom.

Implied by the court (by law): where a term is not expressly stated but is one that the courts consider that one of the parties must have intended to include for business efficacy, the term may be implied into the contract by the court. It must be so obvious it goes without saying. See the case of *The Moorcock* [1889]: AA were the owners of a wharf and agreed that it should be used by R's ship for loading cargo. The ship grounded and was damaged because of the condition of the river bed which was not under AA's control. The court held that AA were liable for this damage as it was an implied term that they had taken reasonable steps to ensure the river bed adjacent to their wharf was safe.

Other terms that are implied by law relate to certain types of contract such as landlord and tenant. See the case of *Liverpool CC* v *Irwin* [1977] where the courts held that it was an implied term in a tenancy agreement of a council flat that the landlord should take reasonable care to keep lifts and staircases in a reasonable state of repair.

Implied by statute: many implied terms are incorporated into contracts by statute, for example, Sale of Goods Act (SGA) 1979 and Supply of Goods and Services Act (SOGAS) 1982. The implied terms cover title, description, fitness for purpose and satisfactory quality and sale by sample. This is discussed in more detail in study session 7.

Implied by custom: where the contract is silent terms are implied by looking at local custom or trade usage. A custom will not be implied if it is contrary to the express terms in the contract.

Exclusion clauses

These are discussed in section 2.2 below.

Other clauses

It is worthwhile mentioning other clauses that can be and are often inserted into contracts. These include a Romalpa clause, which is discussed later on in this session. Briefly, it is a clause inserted to retain title, also known as retention of title clause.

A clause inserted to provide for a specific remedy is known as a force majeure clause. It is often included in a contract that has an international dimension.

Force majeure clause

A force majeure clause is a clause expressly inserted into a contract by the contracting parties in an attempt to provide for a specific remedy in the event that something happens that is beyond their control and affects the performance of the contract. It differs from frustration, which is discussed in study session 3.

Force majeure is a more flexible way of dealing with problems raised by unforeseen events. The major advantages of a force majeure clause are that the parties can insert other events into their clause; the parties can provide for suspension of a contract rather than termination; and the clause can provide for allocation of expenses or losses rather than relying on the Law Reform (Frustrated Contracts) Act 1943, which is discussed in study session 3.

The parties are not limited as to what they include in a force majeure clause, but in a contract between UK parties the clause is subject to the reasonableness test under the Unfair Contract Terms Act 1977 (UCTA).

Self-assessment question 2.1

Give examples of condition, warranty and innominate terms using relevant case law.

Feedback on page 31

2.2 Common law and statutory exclusion clauses

Learning activity 2.2

Before attempting this learning activity you may wish to revisit Level 4, Developing Contracts, study session 13, or equivalent material, to refresh your memory of this topic. Now read the following two statements relating to liability and explain using relevant case law in what circumstances the clause will be binding.

1 Notice on the back of the bedroom door in a hotel stating 'Management accept no responsibility for guests' belongings left in the room'.
2 Terms limiting liability were on the back of an acknowledgement slip.

Feedback on page 32

In section 2.1 above you have studied express and implied terms. You are now going to be looking at exclusion clauses. The purpose of exclusion

2

clauses is that in the event of a breach of contract they limit or even exclude liability of one of the contracting parties. In the next session you will learn about penalty and liquidated damages clauses.

Exclusion clauses are inserted into a contract to exclude one party's liability for breach of contract, misrepresentation or negligence. The courts try to control the use of these clauses and they are governed by the Unfair Contract Terms Act 1977 and the Unfair Terms in Consumer Contracts Regulations 1999.

How exclusion clauses are interpreted is important. In earlier sessions you have learned that clauses in contracts should be clear and unambiguous. In practice, many written contracts in modern use are clear, unambiguous and free from jargon. Basic rules of interpretation have emerged to deal with problems. The starting point is to assume that parties say what they mean and mean what they say. Words are generally given their ordinary and natural meaning. If there is more than one interpretation the courts tend to favour the one that gives effect to the contract rather than the interpretation that might nullify it.

Where a contract contains a term which is unclear or ambiguous the term will be interpreted **contra proferentem**. This means that the clause will be interpreted against the party seeking to rely on it. This is particularly the case with exclusion clauses. Even if a contract term is clear it can never protect one party from the consequences of a total breach of contract. This is known as the doctrine of fundamental breach, which is discussed in study session 4. See the case of *Pollock* v *Macrae* [1922], which relates to the repugnancy rule. This is where an exclusion or exemption clause is struck out of the contract as it is in direct contradiction to the main purpose of the contract. In the Pollock case the defendants entered into a contract to build and supply marine engines. The contract contained an exclusion clause which was designed to protect the defendants from liability for defective materials and workmanship. In this case the engines supplied under the contract had so many defects that they could not be used. The House of Lords held that the exclusion clause be struck out as it was contradictory or repugnant to the main purpose of the contract. The claimant was awarded damages.

You will recall from your previous studies that before a party can claim a contract exists, there must be a 'meeting of minds' or 'consensus in idem' about the essential elements that make up the terms and conditions of the obligation. If you sign a document containing an exclusion clause, you have indicated your acceptance of it. Exceptions are rare and would not apply in a business context.

Where a document is not signed, for example the clause is in a delivery note, it will only be regarded as incorporate if reasonable efforts have been made to give notice of it to the other party. See ticket cases below and whether the parties have had regular dealings.

Sometimes one of the parties may have greater bargaining power from the other and will try to bring conditions into the contract of which the other party has no knowledge or does not understand or realise their significance.

In such a situation the party with the greater bargaining power might attempt to incorporate an exclusion clause, excluding or limiting their liability. The purpose is to limit liability particularly for negligence.

One thing is certain, additional conditions cannot be added after the contract has been formed unless there is the consent of both parties. See the case of *Olley* v *Marlborough Court Hotel Ltd* [1949] on page 34.

The position regarding exclusion clauses on tickets can be summarised as follows. An exclusion clause cannot usually be brought in through the use of a ticket if it is only a voucher or receipt. If it is more than a voucher or receipt, and the person knew that there were conditions but did not read them, then he will be bound by them subject to the UCTA):exclusion clauses. If the person has read them they will be bound by them subject to the Unfair Contract Terms Act (UCTA) 1977. If the person does not know about them, they will only be bound if they have been properly brought to their attention, for example, printed on the front or clear reference to them on the front where they are printed elsewhere.

If parties are both in business and they elect to sign contracts at arm's length then they will be bound by them subject to standard form contracts which require to be fair and reasonable under the UCTA.

The name of the UCTA is somewhat misleading as it does not cover all unfair contract terms. It only covers exclusion clauses. Certain exclusion clauses are declared void and others are subject to the test of whether they are 'fair and reasonable'. The Act only applies to liability by businesses, which include companies, partnerships, sole traders, professionals, local authorities and government departments. It does not include individuals who act in a personal or private capacity.

The Act also applies to certain types of contract: contracts in the course of business – these include consumer contracts and standard form contracts; contracts for the sale of goods – this includes goods bought under credit or hire purchase agreements; contracts for the hire of goods – this relates to moveable items but not to the lease of heritable property; contracts of employment – which includes contracts of apprenticeship.

The UCTA does not cover insurance contracts and contracts for the transfer of interest in land.

The main points of the UCTA can be summarised as follows.

It relates to contracts in the course of business: see above for more detail; liability for death or personal injury caused by negligence cannot be excluded; other exclusions must pass the 'reasonableness' test; the burden of proof is on the party inserting the exclusion clause to show that it is fair and reasonable in the particular circumstances of the case.

The impact of the EU Directive on Unfair Terms in Consumer Contracts was to increase the type of contracts covered by the UCTA. The new regulations cover all consumer contracts that are likely to be deemed unfair. A consumer can avoid a term in a contract for goods or services by

2

showing that it is unfair, contrary to good faith or causes imbalance that is detrimental to him.

Self-assessment question 2.2

Answer these short questions on exclusion clauses.

1 Why do exclusion clauses need to be controlled?
2 What conditions must be satisfied before an exclusion clause will be incorporated into an unsigned document?
3 What are the rules of interpretation used by the courts when interpreting exclusion clauses?

Feedback on page 33

2.3 The difference between penalties and unliquidated damages

Learning activity 2.3

Review previous studies in Level 4, Developing Contracts, study session 12, or equivalent material, and identify exclusion clauses and explain how the courts will interpret them.

Feedback on page 33

You have studied implied and express clauses in contracts as well as clauses that can exclude or limit liability. You are now going to be looking at clauses that are inserted into contracts as an attempt by contracting parties to provide for circumstances where a breach of contract arises. To understand these clauses and how they are interpreted, you are going to consider what these clauses are called by the parties inserting them into a contract.

Penalty clauses

Parties can agree at the outset of the contract how much will be paid as damages in the event of a breach taking place. This is particularly common in contracts involving building or contracting work, for example, to cover loss incurred through delays in completion. This form of damages is called liquidated damages. This is discussed below. Such a provision in a contract is often called a penalty clause. This is confusing because damages for breach of contract are intended to be compensatory not a penalty. What matters of course is not what a clause is called but what the actual effect of the clause is.

If it is clear that the clause is intended to punish rather than compensate, then it is invalid and unenforceable. In such a case, the court will have to assess damages using certain criteria.

Firstly, damages are never to be consider as a penalty or civil punishment. Damages are to compensate the innocent party for loss and to place them in the position they would have been in had the contract been fully performed in so far as money alone is capable of doing this. See the case of *Irving* v *Burns* [1915]. In this case Burns was secretary of a picture house company. Irving was engaged to carry out certain plumbing work. However, Burns had no authority to engage Irving. Irving carried out his part of the contract but received no payment as at that time the company was now insolvent. Irving then sued Burns for damages. Irving failed in his action as although he had suffered loss it was not due to Burns' breach of warranty of authority. Even if the contract had been properly formed Irving would not have received payment as the company was insolvent. The court held that Irving was no worse off as a result of Burns' conduct. Even if there is no actual loss, the court may award nominal damages to compensate for trouble and inconvenience.

Secondly, the innocent party is expected to take reasonable steps to minimise their loss. See the case of *Ireland* v *Merryton Coal Co* [1894]. In this case a wholesaler agreed to supply retail coal merchants with a large quantity of coal. The contract stated that they would deliver the coal over the next four months in 'average' or 'about equal' monthly quantities. By the end of the four-month period the wholesaler had only supplied about half of the total consignment. The retailers claimed damages on the basis of the market price ruling at the end of the four months. The price had risen over the period. The court held that the retailers had not taken all reasonable steps to minimise their loss which restricted their claim for damages. They do not need to take extraordinary steps.

Thirdly, quantum: this is the question of how damages are calculated. Damages are calculated on the principle that only loss that is a direct and foreseeable result of the breach of contract can be claimed. Such damages are known as general or ordinary.

The question of special damages may arise. Special damages arise where there are special or knock-on circumstances that lead to an unusual or special loss. The party in breach is not liable for special damages unless they know of the special circumstances at the time the contract was formed. The basic principle is often referred to as the rule in *Hadley* v *Baxendale* [1854]. In this case Hadley's (H) flourmill was unable to operate because the cast-iron crankshaft from a steam engine had fractured. The broken crankshaft had to be sent from the mill some distance to a Greenwich foundry to be used as a pattern for a replacement. The carrier, Baxendale (B), was engaged to transport the broken crankshaft to the foundry. B was told that the crankshaft was for a mill but he was not told that the mill was at a standstill because the crankshaft was broken. Most mills did keep a spare. B undertook to deliver the new crankshaft within two days. B was negligent and delayed in delivering the new crankshaft. B was in breach of contract because he failed to deliver within the two days. The court held that H was not entitled to special damages for the loss of profits when the mill was at a standstill as the special circumstances had not been explained to B when the contract was formed. Therefore the special loss of profit was beyond what the carrier, B, could have been expected to foresee.

See also the case of *Victoria Laundry (Windsor) Ltd* v *Newman Industries* [1949]. In this case Newman (N) agreed to supply a boiler to Victoria

2

Laundry (V). V required it to expand their business and to allow them to take up a large government contract. The boiler was delivered late and because of this V lost the government contract. As N had no way of knowing about the government contract when they agreed to supply the boiler the court held that they were only liable for ordinary or general damages for the foreseeable loss of business and not for any special damages in respect of the lost contract. The court held that the liability was for ordinary or general damages for the foreseeable loss of business and not for any special damages in respect of the lost government contract about which N had no way of knowing.

In a more recent case of *Balfour Beatty Construction (Scotland) Ltd* v *Scottish Power plc* [1994] B were constructing a concrete aqueduct to carry the Union Canal over a bypass. This required a continuous pour of concrete. Work on the first stage was almost complete when the electricity supply failed. As a result, the first stage had to be entirely demolished. B claimed special damages of over a quarter of a million pounds against S. B lost their case. The House of Lords held that it would have required a high degree of technical knowledge of the construction industry on the part of S for them to have foreseen the result of an interruption of the electricity supply.

Let us look now at the distinction between liquidated damages and unliquidated damages.

Liquidated damages

These represent a genuine attempt by the contracting parties to estimate their likely losses in the event of a contractual breach. You have already read above that parties often confusingly refer to this clause as a penalty clause. The courts will be guided by such estimates as long as they reflect actual losses rather than a penalty.

In distinguishing between penalty clauses and liquidated damages clauses, the courts have regard to the principles set out in *Dunlop Pneumatic Tyre Co* v *New Garage and Motor Co* [1915]. In this case the appellants, manufacturers of motor tyres, supplied goods to the respondents under a contract which provided that the respondents would not sell tyres at less than the appellants' list price. It was further provided that if the respondents did sell a tyre in breach of this agreement then they would pay the appellants £5. The court held that this sum would be regarded as liquidated damages and not as a penalty. The principles set out in this case can be summarised as follows.

1   The use of the words penalty or liquidated damages is not conclusive in itself.
2   A penalty punishes whereas liquidated damages is a genuine pre-estimate of loss.
3   Whether a sum is a penalty or liquidated damages is a question judged at the time of the formation of the contract not at the time of the alleged breach.
4   If a sum is clearly a penalty it will be deemed unenforceable.
5   If the same single lump sum is payable on the occurrence of several different situations, it will be presumed to be a penalty.

The advantage to a buyer of inserting such clauses in the contract is that they do not need to sue for their loss, they simply deduct the liquidated damages from the contract price before payment and leave the seller to argue about the deduction later.

The advantage for the seller is that it forms the top limit of their potential liability. Both parties know where they stand.

Unliquidated damages

This is where there is no agreed figure for the damages. In this situation the plaintiff will sue for unliquidated damages. This is the sum that the court or, in the case of arbitration, the arbiter, considers appropriate to compensate the injured party for the loss suffered as a result of the breach.

Self-assessment question 2.3

Explain three important points to note about damages. Refer to appropriate case law.

Feedback on page 33

2.4   Retention of title or Romalpa clause

In the previous sessions you have been studying express and implied terms. You have seen how exclusion clauses can be inserted into a contract and a special force majeure clause where the parties attempt to provide for a specific remedy in the event of something happening outside their control. Parties can also insert a clause which provides for retention of ownership of the goods until certain conditions are satisfied.

A retention of title clause can be expressly inserted into the contract. Where there is no such clause the matter is governed by the passing of title and risk in ss16–20 Sale of Goods Act 1979 (SGA) which is discussed in study sessions 8 and 9.

The retention of title clause expressly inserted into a contract became known as Romalpa because of the case of *Aluminium Industrie Vaasen* v *Romalpa Aluminium Ltd* [1976]. In this case the plaintiff was a Dutch company which sold some aluminium foil to an English company. The contract contained a retention of title clause which retained to the seller the ownership of any unmixed foil in the possession of the buyer until the seller had been paid all sums due to them. Furthermore if the foil was used to manufacture any other items then the seller's retention of title would transfer to the manufactured items and the buyer should hold them as **'fiduciary'** (in trust) for the seller as well as any proceeds of sale of such manufactured items. The buyer went into liquidation while in possession of some unmixed foil. He had also sold some unmixed foil to another buyer. The seller sought to have the retention of title clause enforced. The Court of Appeal held that the plaintiff seller was able to recover the unmixed foil

2

in the buyer's possession as well as the proceeds of the sales by the buyer. In later cases the approach taken by the courts depended on the state of the goods, whether in their original state or not. In the case of *Clough Mill Ltd* v *Martin* [1984] the courts held that a retention of title clause can be enforced when the goods in the buyer's possession have not been altered, that is, in their original form.

Where the contract depends on a condition being satisfied, which is usually payment for the goods by the buyer; it is in the seller's interest to insert a retention of title clause. Such a clause also gives the seller preferential treatment over other creditors in the event of the buyer's liquidation.

Learning activity 2.4

Having read the above and revisited Level 4, Developing Contracts, study session 14, or equivalent material, on special clauses and the Romalpa case to refresh your memory you can now try this learning activity. Explain what happens where no Romalpa clause exists.

Feedback on page 33

As you have learned from the learning activity, the Romalpa clause is concerned with the seller retaining title to goods until some condition is satisfied. The matter of title is discussed later on in study sessions 8 and 9. These sessions cover passage of title and risk, which are governed by ss16–20 Sale of Goods Act 1979.

Self-assessment question 2.4

Analyse the following case study and advise on the legal position.

Resico supplied resin to Timberkit for incorporation into chipboard. Resico's retention of title clause stated that they retained ownership of any unmixed resin in the possession of Timberkit until Resico had been paid all sums due to them by Timberkit. If the resin was used to manufacture chipboard or similar items, Resico's retention of title clause would transfer to the chipboard and other items. Timberkit would hold them as 'fiduciary' for Resico as well as any proceeds of sale of such manufactured goods. Timberkit went into liquidation. They still had some resin and had sold some chipboard. Advise Resico whether they will be able to recover the resin and the proceeds of the chipboard.

Feedback on page 34

Revision question

Now try the revision question for this session on page 311.

Summary

Having completed this study session you now know that various terms and clauses can be inserted into contracts either expressly by the parties or implied by statute or common law. You should know the difference in importance between conditions, warranties and innominate terms. You learned that exclusion clauses can be inserted under statute or common law as well as other clauses such as a force majeure clause which is inserted into a contract to provide for a specific remedy; also a retention of title or Romalpa clause. You also know that parties can insert a damages clause into the contract in an attempt to provide for circumstances where a breach of contract may arise. However, you also studied how such clauses are interpreted as to whether they are considered a penalty or unliquidated damages clause.

Suggested further reading

Griffiths and Griffiths (2002). You should read the chapters on contract formation, part I, chapters 1 and 2.

Smith and Keenan (2003), part 2, chapters 6 and 7.

Feedback on learning activities and self-assessment questions

Feedback on learning activity 2.1

You should include a brief explanation on each of the terms. Express terms can take two forms. They are those that are formally written into your contract. These are the standard forms and conditions referred to in the previous session on 'battle of the forms' and standard contracts. Express terms can also be those verbally agreed between the parties. These verbal terms must be expressly agreed.

Implied terms are those that are never written into the contract but are implied by the law. These terms can be implied by the courts or implied by statute such as under the Sale of Goods Act 1979 (SGA) (as amended) and Supply of Goods and Services Act 1982 (SOGAS) which are discussed in study sessions 6 and 7 inclusive of this study guide.

Feedback on self-assessment question 2.1

A condition is a term used to describe an important term of the contract. If such a term is breached then it entitles the injured party to treat the contract as discharged and a right to sue for damages. See the case of *Poussard* v *Spiers* [1876] where an actress P agreed to play the leading role in an opera to be produced by the defendants. Owing to illness she could not attend the last rehearsal or the first four performances and when she offered to take her part in the fifth performance the defendants refused. P sued for wrongful dismissal, but the court held that her participation in the first four

2

performances was a condition fundamental to the contract and its breach by her entitled the defendants to treat the contract as terminated.

A warranty is of lesser importance and in the event of a breach entitles the injured party to seek damages only. They cannot discharge themselves from the contract. See the case of *Bettini* v *Gye* [1876] in which a singer, the plaintiff, agreed to perform for the defendant and the contract stipulated that he should arrive six days before the first performance for rehearsals. Owing to illness the plaintiff missed the first three rehearsals and the defendant refused to proceed. The court held that this was not a fundamental condition and that the defendant could not terminate the contract although he was entitled to damages.

Innominate term is also known as an intermediate term. This is because the courts will wait to see what the true effects of the breach have on the contract and decide on the remedy accordingly. See the case of *Hong Kong Fir Shipping Co Ltd* v *Kawasaki Kisen Kaisha Ltd* [1962]: the defendants chartered a ship that was to be in every way fitted for ordinary cargo service but which in fact was in a poor state of repair and incompetently crewed. The defendants sought to terminate the contract but the Court of Appeal held that this was a warranty rather than a condition and the proper remedy was an award of damages.

Feedback on learning activity 2.2

1   This relates to the case of *Olley* v *Marlborough Court Hotel Ltd* [1949] where a hotel guest signed in and went to her room. On the back of the door there was a notice stating that the management accept no responsibility for guests' belongings left in the room. Her fur coat was stolen and she sued. The court held that as the notice had not been brought to her attention when she entered the contract then it could not be incorporated into the contract. She was entitled to claim. She would not have succeeded if the notice had been displayed at the reception desk. This point also raises the questions of previous dealings. In a commercial case where the parties had regular past dealings, the exclusion clause may be binding even if not explicitly stated in the contract.

2   This relates to cases where the clause is not contained in a signed document such as an acknowledgement slip or a delivery note then it will only be regarded as incorporated into the contract if reasonable efforts are taken to give notice of it to the other party. See the case of *Interfoto Picture Gallery Ltd* v *Stiletto Visual Programmes Ltd* [1988]. This case relates to constructive communication and whether a term in the contract will be applied or not. In this case Stiletto needed photographs from the 1950s for an advertising presentation to a client. Interfoto sent some transparencies to Stiletto to enable it to make a selection. The delivery note, which is a contractual document, contained a clause which stated that if the transparencies were not returned within 14 days then Stiletto would pay £5 per day for each transparency retained after that. Stiletto delayed in returning the transparencies for 3 weeks. This resulted in them running up a bill of £3,783. Interfoto sued Stiletto for this sum. The court held that

the sum could not be recovered by Interfoto as the clause had not been specifically drawn to the attention of Stiletto. Although the court refused to apply the clause they still awarded damages of £3.50 per transparency.

Feedback on self-assessment question 2.2

1   Exclusion clauses need to be controlled because they are considered to be unfair in some situations. The main problem arises where the parties are not in an equal bargaining situation and the exclusion clause is forced on to the weaker party by the party in the stronger position.
2   The clause will only be regarded as incorporated into the contract if reasonable efforts have been made to give notice of it to the other party. This notice must be given before the contract was made or at the same time as the contract is made.
3   Exclusion clauses are interpreted using the contra proferentem rule. Also the courts tend to favour the approach which gives effect to the contract rather than that which might make it null.

Feedback on learning activity 2.3

You should refer to the exclusion clauses that you have studied and explain how they are interpreted by the courts. This will include reference to clauses that not only attempt to exclude but limit liability of one party in some way for something they would otherwise be liable for. This is concerned with whether one party has in the contractual terms excused themselves from that liability. You should mention that a party to a contract can never exclude liability for death or personal injury. When they do insert an exclusion clause it will be interpreted in a strict sense, and using the contra proferentem rule. Refer to some of the case law mentioned above.

Feedback on self-assessment question 2.3

You should identify that damages are never to be considered as a penalty or civil punishment. The innocent party is expected to take reasonable steps to minimise their loss. You can refer to the case of *Ireland* v *Merryton Coal Co* [1894]. You should include how damages are assessed; known as the quantum and that it is calculated on the principle of only considering loss that is a direct and foreseeable result of the breach of contract. The matter of special damages should be discussed and you should refer to the basic rule known as the rule in *Hadley* v *Baxendale* [1854].

Feedback on learning activity 2.4

You should include an explanation of the Romalpa case. This is the case of *Aluminium Industrie Vaasen BV* v *Romalpa Aluminium Ltd* [1976]. The Court of Appeal recognised the retention of title clause in this case and since then such clauses are quite usual in commercial contracts. The retention of title clause protects the seller against the liquidation of the buyer and gives the seller preferential treatment over other creditors. So it is in the seller's interest to retain title to the goods until some condition is satisfied.

2

The usual condition is payment for the goods. Where there is no Romalpa clause, s19 Sale of Goods Act 1979 will cover this situation. If the seller feels it is desirable to reserve title then an express clause is required.

Feedback on self-assessment question 2.4

The advice to Resico will be that it will depend on the wording of their clause and whether the courts will look to the case of Romalpa under judicial precedent or the later cases of Clough where the goods require to be in their original state. You should refer to the Romalpa case and the decision in that case. You should also refer to other decisions that have not been as favourable to the seller. These cases distinguish between goods in their original form and those which have been mixed or altered identity through the manufacturing process. Such cases include *Clough Mill Ltd* v *Martin* [1984]] and *Borden (UK) Ltd* v *Scottish Timber Products Ltd* [1981]. In the latter case Borden (B) supplied resin to Scottish Timber (S) which S used in making chipboard. B inserted a retention of title clause in the contract. The clause stated that goods supplied by the company shall be at the purchaser's risk immediately on delivery to the purchaser or into custody on behalf of the purchaser whichever is the sooner...The seller tried to claim a portion of the chipboard but the court held that this must fail as the resin had lost its identity.

Vitiating factors

'Only painters and lawyers can change white to black.'
Japanese proverb

Introduction

In the previous sessions you have been studying how a contract can be formed and what clauses can be inserted into a contract. In this session you will study vitiating factors. These are factors that can render a contract faulty or defective. The factors are duress, undue influence, misrepresentation and mistake. You will also study the legal rules and remedies when a contract is affected by such factors. You will study the difference between void and voidable.

Session learning objectives

After completing this session you should be able to:

3.1 Distinguish between duress and undue influence.
3.2 Distinguish between misrepresentation and mistake.
3.3 Describe the effects of misrepresentation and mistake.
3.4 Explain the legal rules and remedies when a contract is affected by vitiating factors.

Unit content coverage

This study session covers the following topics from the official CIPS unit content document:

Learning outcome

Analyse the process of contract formation and assess the validity of a range of contract clauses.

Learning objective

1.3 Determine the factors that may vitiate consent to a contract.
  • Duress
  • Repudiation
  • Misrepresentation
  • Mistake
  • Undue influence

Prior knowledge

Study sessions 1 and 2.

3

Timing

You should set aside about 5 hours to read and complete this session, including learning activities, self-assessment questions, the suggested further reading (if any) and the revision question.

3.1 Distinguish between duress and undue influence

In this section we look at various types of duress, explanations of economic duress and undue influence. Repudiation is discussed in study session 7.

In this part of the study session you will look at the difference between duress and undue influence. As a starting point it is worthwhile considering a definition of each. Duress is a common law concept and was originally restricted to actual violence or threats of violence made to the contracting party or those close to them and where they had to be frightened of loss of life or bodily harm. Duress is now extended to economic duress which is considered later on in this study session.

Undue influence occurs where one party influences the mind of the other party. This usually happens where there is a close relationship between the parties. It may exist where there is no such relationship but it would then have to be proved by the person seeking to avoid the contract on the grounds of undue influence. In certain relationships undue influence is presumed. These are relationships such as doctor and patient, solicitor and client.

Learning activity 3.1

Consider the two short scenarios and explain whether they fall within duress or undue influence and why.

Scenario one: Jeanette is 89 years old and lives on her own. She owns her house, which is mortgage-free. She takes in a lodger, Peter. She comes to trust Peter and allows him to manage all her financial affairs. After a year she transfers the house into Peter's name so that her nephew, Kenneth, cannot put Peter out of the house. However, Peter sells the house to Alan. Jeanette now wants the house to be transferred back into her name.

Scenario two: Anne owns her own house worth about £70,000. Her brother George, who does not live with her, is a gambler and has run up substantial gambling debts. Anne has always been frightened of her brother who has a violent temper. George frequently borrows money from Anne, albeit small sums. He has now come to her threatening to burn down her house unless she agrees to be guarantor to a loan to cover his debts. Anne agrees to be guarantor. George defaults on the loan and the lenders are taking action against Anne as guarantor.

Feedback on page 51

3

Duress and undue influence are two of the vitiating factors that affect contracts. Vitiate means to render defective. You know from your previous study that the basis of a valid contract is the voluntary agreement of both parties. If one party is forced to enter into the contract as a result of violence or threatened violence to themselves or their immediate family they could ask the court to set aside the contract on grounds of duress. See the case of *Skeate* v *Beale* [1840]. In this case a tenant owed £19 10s in old money and agreed to pay £3 7s 6d immediately with the remaining amount of £16 2s 6d within one month if his landlord would withdraw a writ of distress under which he was threatening to sell the tenant's goods. The tenant later disputed what he owed and the landlord tried to use the agreement and sued for the remaining amount. The court held that the landlord was entitled to the remaining sum of £16 2s 6d under the agreement because it was not affected by the duress as the threat was to sell the tenant's goods. The courts have moved away from this view that threats to property cannot invalidate a contract. The threat had to be to the person and not the goods. However, since the case of *Pau On* v *Lau Yiu Long* [1979] the effect of duress is to make the contract **voidable**. In this case P threatened to break a contract unless they were given an indemnity to cover the loss arising as a result of entering into the contract. There was no duress or coercion of the will involved. The court held that the guarantee was not vitiated by duress. Lord Scarman said that in determining whether there was coercion of the will such that there was no consent, it is material whether the person alleged to have been coerced:

1   did or did not protest
2   at the time did or did not have an alternative course open to him such as an adequate legal remedy
3   was independently advised
4   after entering the contract took steps to avoid it.

All these matters are required to be taken into account in considering whether the plaintiff acted voluntarily or not. This means that the injured party has the option to continue with the contract if they want. The new rule applies to cases of personal violence and has been extended to cases involving economic duress, that is, commercial pressure.

For duress to be actionable the court takes into account a range of factors. These include: did the victim of the duress complain at the time; did the victim intend to repudiate the agreement (see repudiation in study session 7); has there been an actual or threatened breach of contract; did the person allegedly exerting the pressure act in good or bad faith; did the victim have any realistic alternatives; and did the victim affirm the contract?

One form of duress is economic duress. This concept was established in the case of *Atlas Express Ltd* v *Kafco (Importers and Distributors) Ltd* [1989] where it was said that duress requires coercion of the will to vitiate consent and that mere commercial pressure is not sufficient. In this case the defendants entered into an agreement to supply their imported basketware to Woolworth shops and they contracted with the plaintiffs to deliver the goods. Before the contract was concluded the plaintiff's depot manager had seen a sample of the defendants' goods at their warehouse and calculated the price on the basis of transporting a minimum of 400 cartons on each trailer.

3

The first load, however, contained only 200 cartons. The plaintiffs' manager told the defendants that they could not carry any more cartons unless the defendants agreed to pay a minimum price of £440 per load. They were very dependent on this contract and could not find another carrier so they agreed to this minimum price. Later however they refused to pay the new rate. The court dismissed the plaintiffs' claim as the defendants' consent to the new terms was vitiated by economic duress. In any event there was no consideration for the new agreement. Of course, remember that each case is decided on its merits.

Another definition of duress was provided in the case of *DSND Subsea Ltd* v *Petroleum Geo-Services ASA* [2000]. The factual background to this case is complicated and concerned the development of a floating production storage and off-take vessel (FPSO) in the Banff sector of the North Sea. PGS Offshore Technology AS (PGS) contracted with DSND Subsea Limited (DSND) to provide subsea work required to hook up the FPSO to an underwater wellhead. The agreement was formalised in a number of documents. The first of these was the heads of agreement. There was no dispute about the terms of this agreement. Subsequently, the parties entered into a further document, the memorandum of understanding (MOU). PGS later alleged inter alia that this agreement was entered into as a result of economic duress. DSND had refused to continue work on the FPSO until PGS had agreed to provide:

1 assurances as to their insurance cover and an indemnity, and
2 a reimbursable basis of payment.

PGS were under severe financial pressure from their employer and were at risk of substantial damages for delay. PGS agreed to these terms. They claimed later that they had done so under duress. In this case it was decided that for duress to be actionable there must be pressure:

1 whose practical effect is that there is compulsion on or a lack of practical choice for the victim;
2 which is illegitimate; and
3 which is a significant cause inducing the claimant to enter into the contract.

In deciding on whether there is duress it is important to look at the relationship between the parties. In all relationships where one person is in a position of dominance over the other they have a duty not to take unfair advantage of the other. The dominant party must show that they have not exercised undue influence over the other party or the contract will be set aside. The presumption of undue influence can be rebutted if the dominant person can show that the victim was able to freely exercise independent will.

Self-assessment question 3.1

Complete the blanks in the following paragraph and then list examples of relationships where the courts will presume undue influence and ones where there is no presumption. Some are discussed above but can you think of others?

(continued on next page)

Self-assessment question 3.1 (continued)

'Duress is a _____ law concept. It used to make a contract _____ and applied to threats to the person rather than to _____. However since the case of *Pau On* v _____ [1979] duress now renders a contract _____ and has been extended to cases involving _____ duress, that is, commercial _____. The narrow scope of the doctrine of duress also led to the development of the doctrine of undue _____. This doctrine applied where the improper _____ did not amount to duress at common law. Cases of undue influence fall into two categories. Where there is no special _____ relationship or where such a relationship exists. The presumption of undue influence is established if there is a fiduciary relationship where one party is _____ and the transaction is actually disadvantageous to the _____ party.'

Feedback on page 52

3.2 Distinguish between misrepresentation and mistake

In the last part you looked at two of the vitiating factors: duress and undue influence. You are now going to study the difference between misrepresentation and mistakes, which are also vitiating factors. You will be studying the different types of both these factors as this has a bearing on the type of remedy that can be claimed. Remedies are studied later on.

Let us look briefly at misrepresentation and mistake. A misrepresentation is not part of the contract but it is an untrue statement of fact that induces a party to enter into a contract.

However, mistakes may occur in negotiations leading up to the formation of the contract. As you will see later on in this session mistakes are not all treated the same. There are common mistakes, mutual mistakes and unilateral mistakes and they have different effects on the contract.

Learning activity 3.2

Think about some of the things you have done over the years. For example, have you gone on holiday? Or purchased something from a brochure? Or become a customer of a certain bank? Or approached a new doctor to sign on as a patient? Do you remember why you booked that particular holiday, or bought the item, or became a customer of that bank, or signed as a patient for that doctor's practice?

Feedback on page 52

From study of previous sessions and Developing Contracts in Level 4, or equivalent, you will recall that representations are pre-contractual statements of fact made in the negotiation stage. Despite a representation not being a term of the contract it is still one of the reasons that induce a party to enter into the agreement. The person making the representation is known as the representor and the person to whom it is made is known as the representee.

3

The statement must be a statement of fact and relate to either some past fact or a present fact. A statement of opinion does not constitute a representation and will not amount to a misrepresentation should it turn out that it was wrong.

Misrepresentations can result in civil and criminal consequences. The Trade Descriptions Act 1968 and the Property Misdescriptions Act 1991 created offences relating to certain types of misrepresentation in the course of business.

A misrepresentation is an untrue statement of fact, not law. It must be material and induce a party to enter into the contract. There must be a statement of some kind. However, a representation need not always be verbal: for example, payment by cheque implies a representation that the bank will honour the cheque. Mere silence cannot constitute misrepresentation even when it is obvious that the other party is mistaken as to the facts.

Where the contract requires utmost good faith, known as **uberrimae fidei**, the party must disclose all material facts. Contracts of this type include insurance, or where a company sells shares. We recommend that you revisit the definition of undue influence in section 3.1 above. Remember that where one party is in a stronger position good faith is required.

If a party makes a representation on a particular matter, the statement must be full and frank and silence must not be used to distort the positive representation. See the case of *Curtis* v *Chemical Cleaning and Dyeing Co* [1951] where an assistant in a dry cleaners told a customer that a certain exclusion clause limited liability for damage to sequins. This statement was held to be a misrepresentation as the exclusion clause referred to by the assistant actually limited liability for all forms of damage.

The categories of misrepresentation are: fraudulent, negligent and innocent.

Fraudulent misrepresentation

This occurs when a party makes a false statement without honestly believing it to be true. It may be a deliberate lie or it may be a statement made recklessly. In such cases an innocent party may affirm the contract and claim damages for consequential loss and sue under the law of tort of deceit; or the innocent party can repudiate the contract and claim damages and/or rescission. The effects are discussed again in the next session. See the case of *Derry* v *Peek* [1889]. This case is one of the most famous in the area of misrepresentation. In the case the directors of the Plymouth, Devonport and District Tramways Company issued a share prospectus stating that the company had the right to use steam power in its trams. D bought shares in the company on the strength of that statement. In fact, the company was only entitled to use steam power if it was issued with a Board of Trade certificate. The Board declined to issue such a certificate. D raised an action against for damages against the directors of the now insolvent company but the action failed. The court held that the statement had been made in the honest belief that it was true, even although the directors had not taken all reasonable care to check their statements. The law on company prospectuses was changed by statute shortly after this and is now governed by the Companies Act 1985, although in this case the action in deceit failed as D had honestly believed that the necessary consent from the Board of Trade would be forthcoming.

Negligent misrepresentation

This occurs when a false statement is made by a person having a duty of care. There have been some views that the phrase 'by a person having a duty of care' is not necessary and that everyone owes everyone else such a duty. However, it is now clear that some proximity or relationship must exist. Proximity is clearly present between the parties to a contract, so the aggrieved party can take two lines of action, contract and tort. See the cases of *Hedley Byrne* v *Heller* [1963] and *Esso Petroleum* v *Mardon* [1976] In the former case HB were advertising agents. They were asked by Easipower Ltd to arrange their advertising. HB enquired into the financial soundness of E by requesting their own bank to write to H & P who were E's bankers. H & P stated that E were financially stable enough to honour the contract. The letter from H & P was headed 'confidential for your private use and without responsibility on the part of this Bank'. Relying on this information HB placed advertisements. Shortly afterwards E went into liquidation leaving HB with substantial losses. It was clear from subsequent enquiries that E had been in considerable financial difficulties when H & P had made their statement. HB sued H & P for damages on the grounds of negligent misrepresentation. The case established that bankers do owe a duty of care in answering such enquiries where it is clear that recipients rely on them. The court held that no damages were payable in this instance because of the express provision that the information was given 'without responsibility'.

Before considering *Esso Petroleum* v *Mardon* [1976] it is important to note that the case of *Hedley Byrne & Co Ltd v Heller & Partners* dealt with the civil wrong or delictual aspects of negligent misrepresentation. The basic principle in the Hedley case was extended to contract matters in the Esso case. In the latter case, M wished to take the tenancy of a filling station owned by EP. An experienced sales representative of EP stated that by the third year of operation, the throughput of petrol should be around 200,000 gallons a year. M relied on this information and entered into the tenancy agreement. He did not make the profit anticipated. When EP sued him for sums due, M counter-claimed on the grounds that EP's negligent misrepresentation had induced him to enter the contract. M's counter-claim was successful. The court held that EP owed M a duty of care. The remedies of rescission and damages in the tort of negligence are discussed later.

Innocent misrepresentation

This occurs when neither fraudulent nor negligent misrepresentation applies and the misrepresentation was made without any fault. The remedies are discussed in the next section.

Mistake

You are still looking at the negotiations, the pre-contractual stage in the contract process. In such negotiations various mistakes may occur. There are three different kinds of mistake. Sometimes it can be confusing as these kinds of mistake are given different names and classifications. The categories discussed here are common mistake; mutual mistake and unilateral mistake.

Common mistake

This occurs when both parties make the same mistake: for example, as to the ownership of goods, or to the existence of goods or the nature of the goods). Common mistake can be subdivided into two further categories.

Common mistake that renders the contract void: This occurs where the subject matter at the time of the contract no longer exists or never existed. See the case of *Couturier* v *Hastie* [1856]. In this case a cargo of corn en route to London had to be sold at a port of refuge as it had begun to ferment. Unaware of this the parties entered into a contract for the sale of corn in London. The House of Lords held that the contract was void because of the non-existence of its subject matter. This principle has been codified in relation to a proposed sale of specific goods by s6 of the Sale of Goods Act 1979. You will look at the Sale of Goods Act in more detail later on in study sessions 6 and 7.

Common mistake such as to the quality of goods: This does not invalidate a contract. See the case of *Bell* v *Lever Brothers* [1932]. In this case Bell, an employee of Lever Brothers, entered into an agreement to terminate his employment under which he was paid £30,000 compensation. It was later discovered that Bell could have been dismissed without compensation due to certain breaches of contract by him and about which he had forgotten. The House of Lords treated this as a common mistake as to quality but held the contract to be valid.

Mutual mistake

This occurs when each party is mistaken as to the intentions of the other party in respect of the contract. You will recall that for a valid contract to exist there must be a 'meeting of minds'. Clearly if each is mistaken as to the intentions of the other then there is no meeting of minds, no consensus in idem and therefore no contract. See the case of *Raffles* v *Wichelhaus* [1864], also known as *The Peerless*: the case of two ships with the same name *Peerless*. This case illustrates mutual mistake. In this case the defendants agreed to buy cotton from the plaintiffs from the ship '*Peerless*' from Bombay. Two ships of that name were due to leave Bombay. The defendants had in mind the ship leaving in October and the plaintiffs had in mind the ship leaving in December. The court held that the transaction was too ambiguous to be enforced as a contract. The court held the contract as void due to mutual mistake.

Unilateral mistake

This occurs where just one party is mistaken as to the identity or intention of the other party or as to the nature of the document being signed. This kind of mistake may be the result of misrepresentation or may be a mere error by the mistaken party. The remedy is discussed later on. However, at common law, in the absence of misrepresentation, a unilateral mistake does not invalidate a contract. In the interest of equity when reaching a decision the courts will look at whether the other party took unfair advantage of the mistaken party.

3

Mistaken identity

Also falling within the category unilateral mistake is the case of mistaken identity. This occurs where one party makes a unilateral mistake as to the identity of the other because of deliberate deception. There are stringent tests imposed to protect an innocent third party to whom goods have been resold. The party wanting to avoid the contract must show that they intended to contract with a particular person other than the one with whom they contracted; the other party must be aware of this intention; the party claiming the mistake must regard the matter of identity as being of crucial importance; and that they took reasonable steps to verify the other's identity. See the cases of *Cundy* v *Lindsay* [1878] and *Phillips* v *Brooks* [1919]. The former case relates to mistake as to identity. In this case the plaintiffs received an order for linen from a rogue, Blenkarn, who gave his address as 37 Wood Street, Cheapside. In the correspondence he imitated the signature of a reputable firm, Blenkiron and Co, known to the plaintiffs. The plaintiffs were therefore fraudulently induced to send goods to Blenkarn's address where he took possession of them and disposed of them to the defendants, who were innocent purchasers. The court held that the contract between the plaintiffs and Blenkarn was void due to mistake as the plaintiffs intended to deal only with Blenkiron and Co. No title in the goods passed to Blenkarn as the contract was void. Therefore no title passed to the defendants.

In the latter case, a rogue called North entered the plaintiff's shop and having selected some jewellery, wrote a cheque and announced himself as Sir George Bullough of St James's Square, a man of means of whom the plaintiff had heard. The plaintiff, having checked this address in a directory, allowed North to take away a ring. North then pledged the ring with the defendants who were not aware of the fraud. The plaintiffs raised an action to recover the ring. The court held that the contract between the plaintiffs and North was not void due to mistake because the plaintiffs intended to contract with the person in the shop whoever he was. The only mistake was as to creditworthiness not identity of the person. However the contract was voidable because of the fraud but as the defendants had acquired the ring in good faith before the contract was set aside they acquired a good title. Remember that it depends on the facts of each case and identity in certain circumstances may be held to be crucial. See the case of *Ingram v Little* [1961]. In this case identity of the person was held to be crucial. The plaintiffs, elderly ladies, advertised their car for sale. A rogue calling himself PGM Hutchinson of an address in Caterham offered to buy the car. The plaintiffs would only accept a cheque once they had verified from a directory that there was such a person at the address. The cheque turned out to be worthless and the rogue disposed of the car to the defendant. The defendant took the car in good faith. The court held that the contract between the plaintiffs and the rogue was void because of the mistake as to identity.

The wrong document

Another situation involving mistake is where one party signs the wrong document. This is known as **non est factum**. In the case of *L'Estrange* v *Graucob* [1934] the Court of Appeal confirmed the general rule that any person who signs a document is taken to have agreed to its terms whether

3

they have actually read it or not. Where the person signing wants to have the contract invalidated they must show that it is not their document, that it is radically different and that the mistake was not due to their own carelessness. Miss L'Estrange owned and ran a café in Llandudno. She decided to buy one of Graucob's cigarette-vending machines. One of Graucob's representatives produced a form which was headed 'Sales Agreement'. The sales representative inserted on the form details of Miss L'Estrange's sale and she signed it. The document stated that the agreement was 'on the terms stated below'. One of the terms in small print stated 'this agreement contains all the terms and conditions under which I agree to purchase the machine specified above, and any express or implied conditions, statement or warranty, statutory or otherwise not stated herein is hereby excluded'. The machine was delivered and installed but within a few days it jammed and was unable to be operated. After a month, Miss L'Estrange sought to terminate the contract, have the machine removed and her payment to be returned. The court held that Miss L'Estrange was bound by the contract as she had signed the document and there had been no fraud or misrepresentation by the sales representative.

Self-assessment question 3.2

Read the following statements and identify to which category of misrepresentation or mistake each statement belongs. Refer to relevant case law where appropriate.

1 Bill contracted to purchase a cargo of seeds which unknown to either party had already been sold.
2 To sell his car, George told the prospective purchaser that it had only done 5,000 miles on the clock.
3 Hans agreed to buy some silk from India believing that it was being transported on the ship *Indonia*. The seller believed that the cargo was being transported on the ship *Indonia*. Unknown to either party, there were two ships of that name and both were sailing at different times.

Feedback on page 52

3.3 The effects of misrepresentation and mistake

You have been studying the different types of vitiating factors that affect a contract. Now you will study what remedies are available when misrepresentation and mistake affect the contract.

Learning activity 3.3

You have already studied fraudulent and negligent misrepresentation in section 3.2 above of this study session. You may wish to revisit it and refresh your memory before attempting this learning activity. Recall the facts of

(continued on next page)

Learning activity 3.3 *(continued)*

the following two legal cases, which relate to fraudulent and negligent misrepresentation.

Discuss the cases of *Derry* v *Peek* [1889] and *Hedley Byrne* v *Heller* [1963].

Feedback on page 53

3

From the above learning activity you have looked at the legal cases which laid down the common law rules for fraudulent and negligent misrepresentation. You will also see later on how the onus of proof in the *Hedley Byrne* case was changed by the Misrepresentation Act 1967. You are now going to look at the effects of misrepresentation on contracts and what remedies are available in the different types of misrepresentation.

Misrepresentation

You have already looked at the different categories of fraudulent, negligent and innocent misrepresentation. The remedy will depend on the type of misrepresentation which induced the party to enter the contract.

In general the effect of actionable misrepresentation is to make the contract **voidable**. This gives the innocent party the right to rescind the contract and/or claim damages.

Fraudulent misrepresentation gives rise to a remedy of **rescission** and **damages** (see below) in the tort of deceit.

Negligent misrepresentation gives rise to two possible ways of claiming, depending on whether the negligent misrepresentation is at common law or under statute.

In negligent misrepresentation at common law the remedies are rescission (subject to exceptions which are discussed later) and damages in the **tort of negligence**. The House of Lords held that in certain circumstances damages may be recoverable in tort for negligent misrepresentation causing financial loss. See the case of *Hedley Byrne* v *Heller* [1963]. Success depends on the proof of a special relationship existing between the parties. Such a relationship can arise in a commercial relationship where the representor has or purports to have some special skill or knowledge and knows that the representee will rely on it. See the case of *Esso Petroleum* v *Mardon* [1976].

In negligent misrepresentation under the Misrepresentation Act 1976the remedy is the same as in fraudulent misrepresentation unless the person making the representation discharges the burden of proof. In particular, damages will be based on the tort of deceit rather than the tort of negligence.

In innocent misrepresentation the remedy is rescission or damages in lieu of rescission at the court's discretion under s2(2) Misrepresentation Act 1967.

Rescission

This means setting aside the contract. This is a possible remedy in all cases of misrepresentation. The aim is to put the parties back to their original

3

position as though the contract had never been made. The injured party may rescind the contract by giving notice to the representor but this is not always necessary. It can be any act of repudiation such as notifying the authorities. Under the Misrepresentation Act 1976 rescission is at the discretion of the court.

The injured party may lose the right to rescind the contract in certain circumstances. These circumstances are where they affirm the contract; by lapse of time; where restitution or restoration is impossible; where a third party acquires rights in the goods; or where the courts exercise their discretion under the Misrepresentation Act 1967 and award damages in lieu of rescission.

Affirmation of the contract occurs where the injured party with the full knowledge of the misrepresentation expressly states that they intend to continue with the contract or if they act in such a way that this is implied.

Lapse of time: the right to rescind is lost if the injured party does not take action within a reasonable time. Time runs from the date of the contract except in the case of fraudulent misrepresentation where the time period starts when the fraud could, with reasonable diligence, have been discovered.

Restitution or restoration: if substantial restoration is impossible then the injured party cannot rescind the contract.

Where a third party acquires rights in the property in good faith and for value the right to rescind is lost.

Damages

In fraudulent misrepresentation the claim for damages is based on the tort of deceit. The purpose of damages is to restore the victim to the position they were in before the representation was made. The test of remoteness in deceit is that the injured party may recover all the direct loss incurred as a result of the fraudulent misrepresentation regardless of foreseeability. See the cases of *Doyle* v *Olby (Ironmongers) Ltd* [1969] and *Smith New Court Securities* v *Scrimgeour Vickers* [1996]. Damages may include lost opportunity costs such as loss of profits. In the former case, the plaintiff had been induced by the fraudulent misrepresentation of the defendant to buy an ironmonger's business for £4,500 plus stock at a valuation of £5,000. Shortly after the purchase, he discovered the fraud and started the action. But despite this he had to remain in occupation: 'he had burned his boats and had to carry on with the business as best he could'. After three years, he managed to sell the business for £3,700, but in the meantime he had incurred business debts. The court held that he was entitled to damages because of the fraudulent misrepresentations and in considering the measure of damages Lord Denning MR said that: 'The defendant is bound to make reparation for all the actual damage directly flowing from the fraudulent inducement…It does not lie in the mouth of the fraudulent person to say that they could not have been reasonably foreseen.'

The plaintiff in the latter case had acquired property by relying on a fraudulent misrepresentation made by the defendant. This case was complicated as there were two frauds involved. The first fraud was the fraudulent misrepresentation made by Roberts on behalf of Citibank which induced Smith to buy Ferranti shares. The second fraud was the fraud by Guerin on Ferranti. The fraud by Guerin was unknown to Citibank, Smith or Ferranti. Smith bought Ferranti shares with a view to holding them on its books over a comparatively long period to be sold on later. The court held that Smith would not have bought the shares if it had not been for the Roberts fraud. The House of Lords had to decide on the correct measure of damages where a plaintiff acquired property in reliance on a fraudulent misrepresentation made by the defendant.

In negligent misrepresentation the injured party may claim damages for negligence at common law and the test of remoteness in the tort of negligence is that the injured party may only recover foreseeable loss. See the case of *Esso Petroleum* v *Mardon* [1976]. The alternative is to claim damages under s2 Misrepresentation Act 1967. This course reverses the burden of proof and lays the burden on the representor. Damages are assessed on the basis of direct consequences as in fraudulent misrepresentation not reasonably foreseeable as in negligent.

In innocent misrepresentation cases, the court is given discretion under Misrepresentation Act 1967 where the injured party can rescind or claim damages in lieu. The injured party cannot claim damages as such; the damages can only be awarded by the court.

Exclusion or limitation of liability

What about the situation where one party wants to exclude or limit liability for misrepresentation or limit the remedy? It is recommended that you revisit and refresh your memory on exclusion clauses. A term of a contract that excludes liability for misrepresentation or restricts the remedy available is subject to the test of reasonableness under s3 Misrepresentation Act 1967. The question of reasonableness is a matter for the court to decide in all the circumstances.

Mistake and the remedies

You should revisit and refresh your memory on mistake and the different kinds. Whether the contract will be void or voidable depends on the type of mistake.

In common mistake where both parties make the same error relating to a fundamental fact the contract will be void at common law: for example if the subject matter of the agreement is non-existent. See the case of *Couturier* v *Hastie* [1856]. Another situation is where the party makes a contract to purchase something that they already own: the contract is void. See the case of *Cooper* v *Phibbs* [1867]. In this case, Cooper agreed to take a lease of a fishery from Phibbs, his uncle's daughter, who became apparent owner of it on her father's death. Unknown to either party the fishery already belonged to Cooper. This arose because of a mistake made by Cooper's uncle as to how the family land was held. The uncle innocently thought that he owned the fishery and before he died he told Cooper this but in fact it was already owned by Cooper. Cooper raised an action to have the lease set aside. The court held that the lease must be set aside on the grounds of common or identical bilateral mistake but Phibbs had a lien on the fishery for the improvements she had made to it during the time she believed she owned it. The lien could be discharged by Cooper giving Phibbs the value of the improvements.

Where the mistake relates to the quality of the subject matter, whether the contract is rendered void depends on the circumstances of each case, for example if both parties make the mistake and it relates to the existence of some quality without which the thing becomes something completely different. Remember the basic principle of contract law that for the contract to be valid there has to be consensus in idem.

Where a contract is void because of identical mistake, the court will decide on the appropriate remedy by using the principle of equity and justice. The remedies can range from refusing **specific performance**; rescinding any contract between the parties; imposing terms between the parties in order to do justice.

The circumstances where the right to rescind is lost are the same as in misrepresentation (see above).

In the case of unilateral mistake, the remedy depends on the types of mistake. Where one party is mistaken as to the nature of the contract and the other party is aware of the mistake, the contract is void. The courts will follow the principle of equity and will either rescind a contract affected by unilateral mistake or refuse specific performance.

Where there is a mistake as to identity, the law distinguishes between contracts where the parties are physically present or not. Where they are face to face, the presumption is that the mistaken party intends to deal with the person who is present. Where they have not met but have been dealing by correspondence then the contract will be void if one party intends to deal with some identifiable third party and the mistake relates to identity and not just attributes of the other party.

In the case of mutual mistake where both parties fail to understand each other the test applied by the courts is an objective one and whether a 'reasonable man' would take the agreement to mean what one party understood it to mean or the other party understood it to mean. If the conclusion of the test is that the contract could be understood in one sense only, both parties will be bound by the contract in that sense. If the transaction is totally ambiguous then the contract will be void. You will know the reason for this as there being no consensus in idem.

Specific performance

This is discussed in more detail in the next section. However, in short, specific performance is where the courts hold that the contract must be carried out. If the contract is void at law on the ground of mistake, the courts will follow the principle of equity and will refuse specific performance. The contract will be rescinded. If the contract is valid at law, specific performance will be refused if it would cause hardship.

Self-assessment question 3.3

Provide brief answers to the following questions.

1 What is the legal definition of misrepresentation?
2 When would a misrepresentation be fraudulent?
3 What remedy is available for all types of misrepresentation?
4 When can damages be claimed and in what types of misrepresentation?
5 Is it true to say that common mistake does not affect the validity of the contract? Explain.
6 Has unilateral mistake no effect on a contract?

Feedback on page 53

3.4 The equitable remedies of specific performance in injunctions

In section 3.3 above you have looked at the effect that vitiating factors have on contracts and depending on these factors different remedies are available. It is recommended that you revisit the section again and reflect on the different types of vitiating factor and the effect they have on the different types of remedy.

There are two categories of remedy: normal and equitable. You have already studied the remedy of damages above, which is the normal remedy. You are now going to look at the equitable remedies of specific performance and injunctions.

The distinction between damages and equitable remedies is that damages are awarded to the innocent party as of right. Equitable remedies are awarded at the discretion of the courts with the innocent party having no right to insist on them.

Learning activity 3.4

You have already studied vitiating factors above and this learning activity is to get you to think about such factors in a practical setting. Think of your organisation. Have you ordered goods from a supplier from whom you regularly order? Perhaps the order is for 30 items of stationery every month. Has there ever been a mistake, for example a typographical error in the order? Have you increased the order to 300 by mistake? Did the supplier insist on you taking 300 items? If so, what do you think the courts would do?

Feedback on page 54

You are now going to be looking in turn at the different types of equitable remedy: specific performance and injunctions.

Specific performance

This requires the defendant to perform his/her contractual obligations according to the terms of the contract. The order is at the discretion of the court and will only be awarded when the court considers it equitable and just to do so. The court follows certain criteria when considering specific performance as a remedy. The remedy of damages must be inadequate and specific performance must be available to both parties. The courts must also be able to supervise the order so it is unlikely that specific performance would be awarded in personal contracts such as employment contracts.

Injunction

This is the opposite of specific performance. It is where a person is ordered to refrain from doing something.

Repudiation is the act of one party to a contract expressing or implying that he/she is not going to perform it. This conduct entitles the other party to treat the contract as at an end and claim damages. See also study session 7.

Rescission has been discussed above. To summarise, it is the termination of a contract by the parties or by one of them. It can be done by agreement, or by repudiation, or by material default of another, or by misrepresentation or by fraud. Rescission takes effect by proceedings to have the contract judicially set aside or by one party giving notice to the other party of their intention to treat the contract at an end.

Self-assessment question 3.4

Having completed this study session on vitiating factors and their effects on contracts and what remedies are available complete the sentences below by filling in the blanks.

'When advertisements are shown on television can you identify what adverts would be considered advertising _____ from the serious statements about a _____ that you are intended to _____ in. A representation is _____ a part of a contract. It is a _____ that is made during the _____ stage. The purpose of misrepresentation is to _____ the party to enter into the contract. What are the three types of misrepresentation? _____, _____, _____. The victim of misrepresentation can claim _____ and _____. However, the remedy of _____ is only claimed in _____ and negligent misrepresentation. The courts have discretion under _____ Act to award _____ in lieu of rescission. Where one party tries to exclude or restrict liability or the remedies this is known as an _____ clause. This clause is subject to the _____ test. The principles for fraudulent misrepresentation are laid down in the case of _____ v *Peek*

(continued on next page)

Self-assessment question 3.4 (continued)
[1889]. It was held that a misrepresentation is not fraudulent if the person who made it _____ believed it to be true.'

Feedback on page 54

Revision question

Now try the revision question for this session on page 312.

Summary

This study session was all about the vitiating factors of duress, undue influence, misrepresentation and mistake. You learnt that such factors can render a contract faulty or defective. You looked at the difference between void and voidable. You then studied the different remedies available depending on the vitiating factor. You are now going on to look at ways in which contracts can be terminated and the remedies available on breach of contract.

Suggested further reading

Griffiths and Griffiths (2002). You should read the chapters on contract formation, part I, chapter 3.

Feedback on learning activities and self-assessment questions

Feedback on learning activity 3.1

In scenario one the question is whether Peter had exerted undue influence over Jeannette. Although they were not in a close family relationship Peter was in a position of trust and confidence which raised the presumption of undue influence. This scenario is based on the case of *Hodgson* v *Marks* [1970] where the court held that there was a presumption of undue influence because Mr Evans was in a position of trust and confidence. In this case Mrs Hodgson had taken in Mr Evans as a lodger and after a while trusted him enough to allow him to look after her financial affairs. She also put her house in Mr Evans' name to avoid her nephew putting him out of the house. Mr Evans sold the house to Mr Marks without telling Mrs Hodgson. Mrs Hodgson then sought to get her house back from Mr Marks. The lower court held that there was a presumption of undue influence as Evans had a relationship of trust and confidence. However, in the lower court Mrs Hodgson lost the case for other reasons, namely, because the Land Registration Act 1925 protected Mr Evans. The case went to appeal and the Court of Appeal held that Mrs Hodgson should get her house back as the purchaser must pay heed to the possibility of the rights of all occupiers. Mrs Hodgson was obviously in occupation with Mr Evans and the purchaser should have made enquiries as to her rights.

In scenario two, the elements for duress do exist. First of all George has coerced Anne into agreeing to be guarantor and the pressure exerted is illegitimate as being the unlawful act of burning her house down if she does not agree to act as guarantor. Anne can seek to have the guarantor agreement set aside as duress had vitiated the contract.

Feedback on self-assessment question 3.1

Duress is a common law concept. It used to make a contract void and applied to threats to the person rather than to goods. However, since the case of *Pau On* v *Lau Yui Long* [1979] duress now renders a contract voidable and has been extended to cases involving economic duress, that is, commercial pressure. The narrow scope of the doctrine of duress also led to the development of the doctrine of undue influence. This doctrine applied where the improper pressure did not amount to duress at common law. Cases of undue influence fall into two categories. Where there is no special fiduciary relationship or where such a relationship exists. The presumption of undue influence is established if there is a fiduciary relationship where one party is dominant and the transaction is actually disadvantageous to the weaker party.

Relationships where the courts will presume undue influence and which are given in the above text include: solicitor and client; doctor and patient.

Other such relationships could also include: guardian and ward; trustee and beneficiary; parent and child.

Examples of relationships where undue influence will not be presumed: banker and customer; husband and wife.

Feedback on learning activity 3.2

The purpose of this learning activity is to get you thinking about statements that are made by people or in brochures that lead you to book that holiday or buy that item from the brochure. Other situations include buying a house, buying shares, buying a business, buying goods for your organisations. Were you induced into the contract by these statements or were they just opinions?

You might be thinking of a time when you booked the holiday because the brochure or the holiday agent said that it was a five star accommodation, only to find that it was very poor accommodation and was opposite a building site. What did you do about it? Was it a genuine mistake; was it negligent or fraudulent misrepresentation? Did a friend tell you what an excellent service the bank gives? When you find that the service is below standard what do you do? Was your friend's remark just her opinion? Now read on to find out what you can do about different kinds of statements and opinion.

Feedback on self-assessment question 3.2

1   This relates to common mistake where the contract concerns subject matter that no longer exists. You could refer to the case of *Couturier* v *Hastie* [1856].

2   This is fraudulent misrepresentation if George knew it was not true whether it was a lie or was just reckless. You could refer to the case of *Derry* v *Peek* [1889].

3   This is a case of mutual mistake. You should refer to there having to be a meeting of the minds of the parties before a contract exists. There would be no contract in this situation. You could refer to the case of *Raffles* v *Wichelhaus* [1864].

Feedback on learning activity 3.3

You should include the fact that the principles of fraudulent misrepresentation are laid down in the case of *Derry* v *Peek*. In this case the company issued a prospectus which stated that the company was entitled to use steam power to run trams. Because of this statement the plaintiff purchased shares in the company. It turned out that the statement was false but the company had believed it to be true as they believed they would get permission from the Board of Trade to use steam power. The House of Lords held that the mere fact that the statement was inaccurate was not sufficient for it to be fraudulent.

The common law rule for negligent misrepresentation is laid down in the case of Hedley Byrne. You should include the definition of negligent misrepresentation, which is where a false statement is made without dishonesty but the person making it has no reasonable grounds for believing it is true. In *Hedley Byrne* the plaintiffs were advertising agents who were going to do some work for Easipower. They were to be liable if Easipower defaulted, so they asked Easipower's banker for a credit reference. As this was favourable, the plaintiffs acted on it. Easipower went into liquidation and this cost the plaintiffs a lot of money. It turned out that the reference was given negligently. The onus of proof was on the plaintiffs to prove negligent misrepresentation.

Feedback on self-assessment question 3.3

1   A misrepresentation is an untrue statement of fact, not law. It must be material and induce a party to enter into the contract.

2   Misrepresentation is fraudulent when it is proved that a false representation has been made knowingly or without belief in its truth or recklessly

3   The remedy which is available for all types of misrepresentation is rescission, the effect being to put the parties as far as possible back to the position they would have been in had the contract never been made. You may wish to look at the situations where the right to rescind is lost.

4   Damages can be claimed for fraudulent and negligent misrepresentation and under s2 Misrepresentation Act 1967. In the case of innocent misrepresentation the courts have discretion to award damages in lieu of rescission under s2 of this Act.

5   Common mistake does not affect the validity of the contract unless it affects the subject matter.

6   Unilateral mistake will render the contract invalid if the mistake is fundamental to the agreement. Remember there has to be consensus in idem for the contract to be valid.

3

Feedback on learning activity 3.4

This activity was to get you thinking about errors or mistakes. In the example above it was a 'typo'. In this situation you should identify that it is a unilateral mistake. You should also explain that in view of the regular dealings it is highly unlikely that you would have increased your order to that extent. The courts would not allow the supplier to insist upon this contract as they would consider the supplier to have noticed the difference and check the accuracy.

You should describe what a unilateral mistake is, namely, that it occurs where just one party is mistaken as to the identity or intention of the other party or as to the nature of the document being signed. This kind of mistake may be the result of misrepresentation or may be a mere error by the mistaken party. You can also explain that, at common law, in the absence of misrepresentation, a unilateral mistake does not invalidate a contract. In the interest of equity when reaching a decision the courts will look at whether the other party took unfair advantage of the mistaken party.

Feedback on self-assessment question 3.4

The blanks are: puffs, product, believe, not, statement, precontractual, induce, fraudulent, negligent, innocent, rescission, damages, fraudulent, Misrepresentation, damages, exclusion, reasonableness, Derry, honestly.

Study session 4
Termination of contract and remedies available

Introduction

In the previous sessions you have studied the essential elements for contract formation and various contractual terms. In study session 3 you looked at vitiating factors and the effect that pre-contractual statements have on a contract. You are now going to look at how contracts can be terminated and what remedies are available on breach of contract. You should also revisit Level 4, Developing Contracts, study sessions 11, 2 and 3, or equivalent material, to refresh your memory.

'In law, nothing is certain but the expense.'
Samuel Butler

4

Session learning objectives

After completing this session you should be able to:

4.1 Describe the different methods of termination of a contract.
4.2 Explain the legal effects of frustration on a contract.
4.3 Define breach of contract and explain the effects.
4.4 Explain how unliquidated damages are assessed.
4.5 Explain remedies for breach of a sale of goods contract.

Unit content coverage

This study session covers the following topics from the official CIPS unit content document:

Learning outcome

Analyse the process of contract formation and assess the validity of a range of contract clauses.

Learning objective

1.4 Critically evaluate the different common law methods by which a contract is terminated, and the remedies available to either party should a contract be breached.
   • Performance
   • Frustration
   • Agreement including variation of a contract
   • Breach
   • Assessment of unliquidated damages

Prior knowledge

Level 4, Developing Contracts, study sessions 11, 2 and 3, or equivalent material.

Timing

You should set aside about 5 hours to read and complete this session, including learning activities, self-assessment questions, the suggested further reading (if any) and the revision question.

4.1 Termination or discharge of contracts

Ways in which a contract is discharged, including by performance (this includes specific performance, substantial, part and staged contracts), agreement, frustration and where there is a breach.

In study session 3 you looked at the effect some statements have on a contract. These statements were those made in the negotiation or pre-contractual stage and rendered a contract void or voidable. You also studied how the remedy available depended on the type of vitiating factor. The remedy could be rescission, specific performance and/or damages.

You are now going to look at the ways in which a contract can be terminated or discharged. In general this means that the parties are freed from their mutual obligations. A contract can be discharged in four ways: performance, agreement, frustration and breach.

Performance

This is the most obvious way in which a contract comes to an end. This is when the contracting parties complete their obligations, that is, what they undertook to do under the contract. For the contract to be discharged or terminated the performance must be complete and unconditional. The doctrine of substantial performance and the use of staged contracts are discussed below.

Agreement

A contract can be terminated by agreement between the two contracting parties. This differs from agreement to vary.

Frustration

This occurs where a contract, which was feasible to perform when it was made, becomes impossible to perform due to a change in circumstances beyond the control of the contracting parties. You may wish to revisit study session 3 and refresh your memory of the case of *Couturier* v *Hastie* [1856] where the contract was held to be void due to common mistake. The doctrine of frustration is discussed in more detail below.

Breach of contract

This is where one party fails to fulfil or intimates that they do not intend to fulfil their obligations under the contract. The consequences of breach of a particular term have already been discussed in study session 2. The normal remedy for breach of contract is damages. However, the court may consider that damages are not an adequate remedy and order that the party in breach perform the actual obligation. This is known as an order for specific performance, which is discussed below along with anticipatory breach.

4

Learning activity 4.1

Describe the principal ways in which a contract can be terminated.

Feedback on page 71

You may come across other terms such as acceptilation; novation; delegation; confusion; compensation; prescription. You are not required to study these in any more detail at this stage. Now you are going to consider in more detail the ways in which a contract can be terminated.

Performance of the contract

This can be divided into full performance, partial performance or performance of instalment contracts. Full performance is the most obvious way of bringing a contract to an end. This is where both parties successfully complete their contractual obligations according to the terms of the contract.

Partial performance depends on whether it is a minor or trifling matter still to be fulfilled or a substantial part of the contract. A minor or trifling matter does not count as performance as the law does not concern itself with this. Minor or trifling matters are not reasons for litigation or grounds for rescission.

The doctrine of substantial performance emerged to deal with situations where a substantial part of the contract has been fulfilled. In such situations a contract may be deemed concluded and the price would be paid less an appropriate amount for obligations not fulfilled. See the case of *Hoenig* v *Isaacs* [1952]. In this case the claimant was an interior decorator and furniture designer. The defendant engaged the claimant to decorate a one room flat owned by the defendant. The claimant was also to provide furniture. The terms of the contract regarding payment stated 'Net cash as the work proceeds and the balance on completion'. The defendant made two payments to the claimant. The claimant advised the defendant that he had completed the work and asked for the balance. The defendant asserted that the work was defective and faulty. However, the defendant sent part payment to the claimant and moved into the flat and used the furniture. The claimant then sued for the balance due to him. The work was assessed by an independent referee who found that generally it was properly done except for the wardrobe door which needed replacing. The defendant claimed that the contract was entire and had to be completely performed before the claimant could recover his money. The court held that the claimant was entitled to sums due less a sum to rectify the defects.

Part performance in instalment contracts: sometimes also known as divisible contracts. Where the contract is for delivery of goods in instalments, the supplier would be entitled to payment for instalments delivered even if the full contract was not performed.

Agreement

Just as parties agree to contract, they can also agree to terminate a contract. They may do this by having an express contractual term in the contract. It may be that the parties have agreed that the contract comes to an end after a fixed period. Agreement to terminate is not the same as agreement to vary the contract. The agreement to terminate the contract must satisfy the requirements of a binding contract, that is, consideration must be present. You should revisit study session 1 which dealt with consideration. Review the definition of consideration by Sir Frederick Pollock, which was adopted by the House of Lords in the case of *Dunlop* v *Selfridge* [1915]. In this case Dunlop supplied tyres to a third party, Dew & Co. There was a contractual term whereby the contracting parties would agree not to resell the goods at less than the prescribed resale price. Dew & Co then sold them to Selfridge who was also subject to this agreement. Selfridge then sold the tyres and breached the agreement. Dunlop tried to enforce it against them. The court held that Dunlop could not enforce this contractual term as they were not privy to the contract between Dew & Co and Selfridge. This was a strict application of the rule of privity. You will be looking at privity later in study session 10. In a bilateral agreement where neither party has completed their contractual obligation, the consideration provided by each party releasing them from further contractual performance is the promise to release them from the remaining obligations. Both benefit from this agreement. However, where only one party has completed performance of their obligations but the other party has not, then although they can agree to terminate the contract, the agreement to terminate must be in writing to be enforceable.

Frustration or impossibility

Frustration is where there may be a valid contract but the contract becomes impossible to perform due to subsequent or supervening events outside the control of both parties. The contract is deemed frustrated. Illegality will have the effect of bringing a contract to an end. The rule is simple. If a valid contract is formed but subsequently changes in the law or political circumstances such as the outbreak of war make performance illegal, then the contract is at an end. See the case of *James D Fraser & Co Ltd* v *Denny, Mott & Dickson* [1944]. This case involved a contract for the supply of pine timber. The contract was terminated. Stocks were still available but supply had become illegal due to wartime restrictions. The court held that the contract was at an end. The rule is that if a valid contract is formed but a subsequent change in the law or political circumstances such as the outbreak of war as in this case, makes performance of the contract illegal, then the contract is treated as at an end.

Self-assessment question 4.1

Describe how performance and agreement can bring a contract to an end.

Feedback on page 71

4.2 The legal effects of frustration on a contract

Learning activity 4.2

Referring to appropriate case law describe situations in which a contract might become frustrated.

Feedback on page 72

You now know that parties to a contract can agree to terminate it. They can vary clauses by accepting that the original contract comes to an end and is replaced with a new obligation. Another situation is where one party is replaced by another party. This occurs in novation or delegation. No further detail is required at this stage.

Doctrine of frustration

Frustration involves a combination of common law and statute. The common law rules are concerned with what amounts to frustration and the Law Reform (Frustrated Contracts) Act 1943 is concerned with the effects of frustration on the parties.

You already know that frustration occurs where an external event outside the control of either party to the contract renders further performance of the contract impossible or radically different from what the parties had contracted.

The parties of course can provide for the consequences of frustration in the contract by including a force majeure clause. You may wish to revisit study session 2 and refresh your memory on exclusion clauses and in what circumstances the courts give effect to them. For this session when discussing frustration, it is assumed that there are no such clauses in the contract.

Frustration must not be confused with initial impossibility. See the case of *Couturier* v *Hastie* [1856] where both parties made the same error relating to a fundamental fact and the contract was held to be void. See study session 3 under common mistake. Also s6 Sale of Goods Act 1979 provides that where there is a contract for the sale of specific goods and the goods, without the knowledge of the seller, have perished at the time the contract is made, the contract is void.

Frustration, on the other hand, occurs where it is possible to perform the contract at the time the contract is made but it subsequently becomes impossible to perform the contract in whole or in part. The doctrine of frustration was developed by the judges in the case of *Davis Contractors Ltd v Fareham UDC* [1956]. In this case a builder had agreed to construct 78 houses within eight months for a fixed sum. Owing to shortages of labour and material, bad weather and inflation the builder found himself substantially out of pocket. The contract took 22 months to complete. The plaintiffs claimed that the original contract had been frustrated and sought a **quantum meruit** payment over and above the contract price. A **quantum meruit** claim is a claim for reasonable remuneration and is distinct from an award of damages which is essentially compensation for loss. The House of Lords held that there had been no frustration as the contract had not become impossible to perform and the rise in costs was a risk that the plaintiffs must have accepted when making the contract. Most building contracts allow for rises in costs due to materials, wages or inflation. Without the fault of either party, there was such a change in the significance of the obligation that the thing undertaken would, if performed, be a different thing to that contracted for. The question to ask is whether the event that causes the frustration deprives one of the parties to the contract of the entire benefit of the contract. It helps to look at some examples in case law.

Common law approaches

The destruction of the specific object

You will recall the case of *Taylor* v *Caldwell* [1863] where the subject matter of the contract was destroyed. In this case a contract had been concluded between the parties for the plaintiff to hire a hall for a series of concerts. After the agreement was concluded but before the concerts started, the hall was destroyed by fire. The courts held that the contract was frustrated and that all future obligations were discharged and no monies paid could be recovered. This does seem unfair and the question of recovery of monies paid and compensation for benefits received before the frustrating event was decided on to some extent in the case of *Fibrosa Spolka Akcyjna* v *Fairbairn* [1943]. In this case an English company agreed to sell machinery to a Polish company. It was agreed that a deposit of one-third of the purchase price would be paid at the time of the agreement. Before any machinery was delivered, war broke out and the contract was frustrated. The House of Lords held that the Polish company were entitled to recover the deposit paid on the ground of a total failure of consideration. Money had been paid to secure performance and there had been no performance. The Law Reform (Frustrated Contracts) Act 1943 introduced further flexibility. In the case of *Davis Contractors Ltd* v *Fareham* [1956] the contract became radically different from what was intended by the parties. The courts held that although the contract would come to an end, with all future obligations ceasing, there may be some redistribution between the parties to take account of money, property or services which have been transferred before the frustrating event.

The non-occurrence of an event

Compare the above with the non-occurrence of an event as in the 'coronation' cases of *Krell* v *Henry* [1903] and *Herne Bay Steamship* v *Hutton*

[1903]. The contract was for the hire of a boat to tour the royal fleet to watch the King's review. The contract was held not to be frustrated when the review was cancelled as the fleet remained and it was still possible for the tour to go ahead.

Interference from the government

Frustration can also occur by interference from the government as in the case of *Metropolitan Water Board* v *Dick Kerr* [1918]. In this case DK contracted with MWB to build a reservoir within six years. After two years the Minister of Munitions required DK to cease work, remove and sell its plant. MWB claimed the contract subsisted on the basis of a contract provision allowing a time extension in the event of difficulties. The House of Lords held the contract to be frustrated because of the government action. The interruption was so serious that any resumption of the contract when it became possible would be fundamentally different from the contract originally envisaged.

Or see the case of *James D Fraser & Co Ltd* v *Denny, Mott and Dickson* [1944], where the contract concerned trade in timber which was made illegal in 1939 and consequently the whole contract was held to be frustrated. This is referred to as supervening illegality.

Unexpected delays

See the case of *Jackson* v *Union Marine Insurance* [1873]. In this case a ship was chartered to proceed from Liverpool to Newport to pick up a cargo of iron for San Francisco. On its way to Newport the ship grounded on a sandbank. It took several months to refloat her and carry out major repairs. The charterers repudiated the contract. The court held that while the express words of the exception might cover the interruption the length of the delay was beyond what the parties would have contemplated and frustrated the contract. Although it would still have been possible for the original ship to proceed the outcome would have been very different due to the long delay. As regards the exclusion clause, you should revisit [session2].

Limitations of the doctrine of frustration

You have studied how parties can insert clauses into a contract to provide for various events. The parties can also expressly provide for frustration within the contract. In such a case, depending of course on the validity of the express term, the doctrine of frustration cannot override the express contractual provision. In the case of *Pioneer Shipping* v *BTP Tioxide* [1982], a ship was chartered for six or seven voyages between Canada and Europe during a nine month period. However, a lengthy strike at the loading port in Canada reduced the maximum number of voyages to two. The House of Lords upheld the arbitrator's decision that the contract had been frustrated as the extent to which it was capable of being performed was so inordinately small compared with that contracted for. Lord Roskill said that the doctrine of frustration was not to be invoked lightly to relieve contracting parties of the normal consequences of imprudent commercial bargains.

A mere increase in expense or loss of profit does not amount to frustration. See the case of *Tsakiroglou & Co Ltd* v *Noblee Thorl GmbH* [1962]. In this

4

case the plaintiffs agreed to supply the defendants with 300 tons of Sudanese groundnuts to be shipped to Hamburg. A few weeks later the Suez Canal was closed by Israel's invasion of Egypt. The plaintiffs claimed that this frustrated the contract. The House of Lords held that as the route around the Cape of Good Hope was still open the contract was not frustrated. The fact that this route was longer and more expensive was irrelevant. This was a commercial risk taken by the shippers.

Self-induced frustration

A party may not self-induce frustration. See the case of *Maritime National Fish* v *Ocean Trawlers* [1935]. In this case the plaintiffs chartered a trawler from the defendants to use for otter fishing, knowing that they would need to obtain a licence for this use. They applied for five licences and were granted three, which they allocated to three other vessels. The plaintiffs claimed that the contract had been frustrated. The court held that their claim could not succeed as the lack of a licence for the chartered boat was a matter of the plaintiff's own choice and a party cannot rely on frustration that is wholly or partly self-induced. In the case of *The Super Servant Two* [1990] (the full name of this case is *J Lauritzen AS* v *Wijsmuller*) the ship owners operated two large barges built to carry heavy structures. They contracted to transport an oil rig. Before the contract could be performed one of the barges was lost. The court held that the contract had been frustrated by the loss of the barge. The court held that the plaintiff was entitled to sue for damages for the expense of alternative means of transport following the loss of the barge before the voyage. The Court of Appeal held that as the defendants chose to perform the other contract, the contract with the plaintiff was deemed to be self-induced frustration.

Foreseeability of the frustrating event

See the case of *Walton Harvey Ltd* v *Walker & Homfrays Ltd* [1931] where it was held that, if a party could have foreseen the extraneous event at the time the contract was made, that party could not rely on the doctrine of frustration. In this case, the defendant, knowing that there was some likelihood that its hotel would be compulsorily acquired and demolished, permitted the plaintiff to erect an advertising hoarding on its roof. Part way through the seven-year contract, the building was acquired for demolition and the sign removed. The plaintiff sued for damages. The defendant argued that the compulsory acquisition had frustrated the contract, and that they were, therefore, excused from further liability. It was held that the contract had not been frustrated. The defendant had been aware of the risk, but had entered into the contract despite it. No provision had been made in the contract to deal with the event of compulsory acquisition.

Effects of frustration: the Law Reform (Frustrated Contracts) Act 1943

The common law doctrine of frustration was inflexible where monies had been paid or benefits received before the frustrating event. So the Law Reform Act was passed to provide for a just apportionment of losses where a contract is discharged by frustration.

Monies paid: s1(2) provides three rules for recovery of monies paid. This section states that money paid before the frustrating event is recoverable;

money payable before the frustrating event is not recoverable where there is a total failure of consideration; and if the party to whom sums are paid or payable incurred expenses before the frustration, the court may award such expenses up to the limit of the money paid or payable before the frustrating event.

Benefit received: s1(3) provides for the situation where valuable benefit has been received. If one party has obtained valuable benefit because of anything done by the other party in performance of the contract, the court may order them to pay a sum in respect of that benefit. The court will have regard to all the circumstances in each case. See the case of *BP Exploration* v *Hunt* [1982].

Scope of the 1943 Act: s2(3) allows for contracting out; s2(4) provides that the Act does not apply where the wholly performed contractual obligations can be separated from those affected by the frustrating event; s2(5) provides that the Act does not apply to contracts containing a provision to cover frustration; charterparties (with some exceptions); contracts for carriage of goods by sea (see later on under International Law in study sessions 19 and 20); contracts of insurance; contracts for the sale of specific goods which perish before the risk has passed to the buyer (see later under section 4.5 below, Sale of Goods).

The 1943 Act is concerned with the effects of frustration and common law rules are concerned with what amounts to frustration. Therefore the 1943 Act can only apply if frustration is established under the common law.

Self-assessment question 4.2

Read the following short scenarios and identify the relevant case law to which they relate. Provide a brief explanation for your choice.

Jane had agreed to hire the local community hall for a series of concerts to raise money for charity. The concerts were due to start in November. However, at the end of October the local community hall was destroyed by fire. Advise Jane, who wants to recover the expenses she incurred in the run up to the concerts.

Jamie had a keen interest in sailing. He hired a boat to see the yachts that were taking part in the 'Round the World' yacht race. Owing to stormy weather, the start of the race was delayed. Advise Jamie who now wants to cancel the hire and claim his deposit back.

Eva had booked a cruise to the Indian Ocean. She was advised just a week before the ship was due to leave Southampton that because of the outbreak of war, the ship was now going to sail to the Caribbean. Advise Eva, who wants to cancel her trip.

Feedback on page 72

4.3 Breach of contract and its effects

Learning activity 4.3

Review study session 2 on conditions, warranties and innominate terms, and consider the effects of a breach of these terms.

Feedback on page 72

Breach of contract may occur where either contracting party fails to fulfil their contractual obligation in whole or in part. The remedy for the innocent or aggrieved party is then to claim damages and in certain circumstances the possibility of bringing the contract to an end. The normal remedy for breach is damages and in certain circumstances the courts will order specific performance.

It is important to know the difference between the different terms of the contract, whether condition or warranty, as the effect of the breach depends on the type of term breached. Remember that in the case of an innominate term the court ultimately has the power to decide on an appropriate remedy.

A clear example of use of terms is found in the Sale of Goods Act 1979 where the various implied terms as to title, quality and description are specifically labelled as either conditions or warranties. In other contracts it is more difficult to decide which category the terms fall into. Sale of goods is discussed later on in section 4.5 below.

In the case of *Hong Kong Fir Shipping C Ltd* v *Kawaski Kisen Kaisha* [1962] it was suggested that a condition was a clause that would deprive the other party of substantially the whole benefit of the contract. However, in the case of *Bunge Corp* v *Tradax Export SA* [1981] it was stated that time clauses in mercantile contracts should usually be treated as conditions. The test to be applied was whether the term was central to the contract. So in the absence of guidance from the usual custom, the courts have to decide the importance of the term. Where the parties have stated in the contract that a particular term is a condition and if breached the contract will be terminated, then the courts will give effect to that intention.

In the past, a claim for breach of condition for minor matters allowed a party to escape from a contract. See the case of *Arcos Ltd* v *Ronaasen & Son* [1933]. This case involved a contract for the supply of barrel staves half an inch thick. The staves were about 9/16 of an inch thick when delivered. The House of Lords held that the purchaser (who could by then have got the staves more cheaply elsewhere) was entitled to reject the consignment even though the extra sixteenth would make no difference to the usefulness of the staves. Under s13 Sale of Goods Act 1979, compliance with description is a condition of sale of goods. However, this position has now altered under s15A Sale and Supply of Goods Act 1994, which reduces the right to rescind a contract for minor breaches of ss13 and 14 in non-consumer contracts.

Breach of contract can occur at any time during the lifetime of the contract. Anticipatory breach relates to a breach before the date for performance has been reached. Remember that what is important is that for an action of anticipatory breach to succeed it must be clear that the repudiating party had decided irrevocably not to perform their contractual obligations.

The usual remedy for breach of contract is damages. You are now going to consider equitable remedies. Injunctions and specific performance have been discussed already in study session 3. You should revisit it and refresh your memory.

Equitable remedies

Injunctions

These are granted to prevent a breach that is anticipated or to prevent a person acting on breach. Specific types of injunction include interlocutory, full and Mareva injunctions.

- Interlocutory injunctions: granted during legal proceedings to ensure the maintenance of status quo pending a full hearing of a court case.
- Full injunctions: granted at the end of the court case and lasting as long as decided by the courts.
- Mareva injunctions: these prevent the disposal of assets or the subject matter of the dispute or the removal of the assets out of the jurisdiction of the court pending a full hearing of the case. This type of injunction can freeze assets in a bank account in the UK

Specific performance

This is another type of equitable remedy and is an order available to the courts where a contract has not been properly formed or there is a defect such that one party has clearly benefited to the detriment of the other. The court will order specific performance where:

- damages are an inadequate remedy;
- the party seeking this remedy must not have brought the problem on themselves;
- supervision of the order must be possible.

Self-assessment question 4.3

The Sale and Supply of Goods Act 1994 introduced a change of law in relation to breach of warranty. Discuss what this change was.

Feedback on page 74

4.4 Assessment of unliquidated damages

As it is important to distinguish between liquidated and unliquidated damages, you should revisit and reflect on study session 2, which discussed

4

the distinction between penalties and liquidated damages. A reminder of the difference is set out below.

Liquidated damages is where the parties insert a clause into the contract which states an agreed sum which is payable in the event of a breach of contract. Such a clause for an agreed sum will be held enforceable by the courts provided the court is satisfied that it is a genuine pre-estimate of loss and not a penalty clause.

Unliquidated damages is where there is no agreed figure for damages payable in the event of a breach. The aggrieved party will sue for unliquidated damages and it is left up to the courts, or arbiter in the case of arbitration, to decide on a sum they consider appropriate to compensate the injured party for the loss suffered as a result of the breach.

Learning activity 4.4

Look at the case of *Hadley* v *Baxendale* [1854] and identify the purposes of an award of damages.

Feedback on page 74

The normal remedy for breach is damages. The topic of damages has already been discussed in study session 3. You may wish to revisit and refresh your memory on this topic.

Where a party wins a case for breach of contract then they are entitled to damages and costs. As you have seen from the above the parties can decide on an agreed sum, liquidated damages, or the courts decide on the sum due when an action for unliquidated damages is raised. So how does the court go about assessing unliquidated damages?

If there is no loss sustained as a result of the breach of contract, the courts will award nominal damages in order to acknowledge that the breach took place.

Assessment

The function of awarding contractual damages is to compensate the victim or aggrieved party for their loss. This was confirmed by the Court of Appeal in the case of *Surrey County Council* v *Bredero Homes Ltd* [1993]. In this case the developer purchased land from the Council and covenanted to develop it in a certain way. In breach of the covenant he did not do so, but obtained planning permission to develop in a different way. The council sued for the amount they might have received for agreed modifications to the covenant. The starting point or the conventional rule was that the remedy for breach of contract was an award of damages and damages at common law were intended to compensate the victim for his loss, not to transfer to the victim, if he had suffered no loss, the benefit which the wrongdoer had gained by his breach of contract. The council had suffered no loss and therefore was only awarded nominal damages. As you have seen in the case of *Hadley* v *Baxendale* [1854], the damages must relate to loss that is foreseeable at the time the contract is made. In short, recoverable damages are those which arise in the usual course of events from the breach and which may be reasonably foreseeable by the contracting parties at the time they made the contract.

The intention of damages is to put the aggrieved party in the same position they could have been in had the contract been performed.

Type of loss recoverable

Damages can include compensation for financial loss, personal injury and damage to property. They can also include compensation for mental distress, disappointment and vexation. See the case of *Jarvis* v *Swans Tours* [1973]. In this case there was a disastrous failure by a tour company to match the expectations arising from its brochure. Swan promised the claimant a 'houseparty' holiday in Switzerland. Some other promises included a welcome party, afternoon tea and cake, Swiss dinner by candlelight, fondue party, yodeler evening and farewell party. Swan also claimed that the hotel owner spoke English. The claimant complained that the hotel owner did not speak English and this meant he had no-one to talk to despite there being 13 people present in the first week of the holiday. The other promises did not come up to expectation and the court held that the claimant was entitled to damages in this case, the damages awarded being for disappointment, inconvenience and loss of enjoyment. Damages for disappointment, inconvenience and loss of enjoyment are only awarded in contracts for the provision of pleasure, such as holidays. Such damages may be foreseeable in other types of contract but are not awarded as a matter of public policy.

Speculative loss is not recoverable. See the case of *Victoria Laundry (Windsor) Ltd* v *Newman Industries Ltd* [1949]. Contrast this with the case of *Blackpool and Fylde Aero Club* v *Blackpool Borough Council* [1990], where the courts did allow damages to be paid for a lost opportunity to tender. This case is discussed in Level 4, Developing Contracts, study session 17 and also in study session 12 on the tendering process.

Remoteness

As you can imagine, the consequences of a breach of contract could be far-reaching so a line must be drawn somewhere. This is called remoteness of damage. The law regarding remoteness is based on the case of *Hadley* v *Baxendale* [1854], which you have already looked at. Remoteness was further explained in the case of *The Heron II* (*Koufos* v *Czanikow*) [1967]. These cases are the authority on remoteness. In summary, damages will be too remote unless they arise naturally in the usual course of things, or if they do not arise naturally they are such that a reasonable man ought to have contemplated them as likely to result from a breach.

Mitigation of loss

There is a duty on the injured party to minimise their loss. In assessing damages the court will take into account the steps taken by the injured or

4

aggrieved party. The injured party has a duty to take all reasonable steps to reduce their loss. See the case of *Brace* v *Calder* [1895]. In this case the defendants were a partnership consisting of four members. They agreed to employ the claimant as manager of a branch of their business for two years. Five months later the partnership was dissolved because of retirement of two members. The business was transferred to the remaining two. They offered to employ the claimant on the same terms as before, but he refused. He raised an action for breach of contract seeking to recover the salary that he would have received had he served the whole period of two years. The dissolution of the partnership constituted a wrongful dismissal. However, the court held that he was only entitled to nominal damages as it was unreasonable to have rejected the offer of continued employment.

Self-assessment question 4.4

In an action for unliquidated damages, what criteria will the court consider when assessing damages? Discuss with reference to case law.

Feedback on page 74

4.5 Remedies for breach of a sale of goods contract

A sale of goods contract is discharged and brought to an end like any other contract: that is, by complete and unconditional performance of the contract by the parties. In study session 3 you have considered remedies for breach of contract. Now you are going to look at the remedies available to the buyer and those available to the seller in the event of a breach of contract for the sale of goods.

Traditionally the sale of goods was regulated by the maxim caveat emptor, meaning let the buyer beware. However, this was not always satisfactory for the consumer and legislation was introduced by Sale of Goods Act 1893 eventually modernised under the Sale of Goods Act 1979 (SGA). Other legislation and topics, such as passing of property, title and risk relating to sale of goods is discussed in study sessions 6, 8 and 9.

Both buyer and seller have statutory remedies available to them in respect of breaches of contract for failure to pay for the goods or failure to deliver the goods.

Buyer's remedies where seller is in breach of contract

Under s27 Sale of Goods Act 1979 the seller's basic duty is to deliver goods in accordance with the terms of the contract. If the seller does not do this then they are in breach of contract. Where the seller is in breach of contract the buyer's remedies include:

- a right to reject the goods;
- a action for damages;
- an action for specific performance.

Right to reject the goods: the buyer may repudiate the contract and reject the goods where the seller is in breach of a condition. This means the buyer can refuse to pay the price, or recover it if he has already paid it, or sue for damages on the basis that the seller has failed to deliver the goods in accordance with the contract. Under s11(4) Sale of Goods Act 1979 this right is lost if the property in the goods has passed to the buyer and if the goods have been accepted by the buyer following a reasonable opportunity to examine the goods. The Sale and Supply of Goods Act 1994 introduced a new provision, which states that where a breach is trivial or minor it will be treated as a breach of warranty and the buyer cannot reject the goods. In such a situation the buyer is entitled to damages only.

Claim for damages: the buyer can claim damages for non-delivery where the seller has neglected or refused to deliver the goods to the buyer. The buyer will recover the difference if any between the market price for the goods and the contract price. If the buyer can buy similar goods at a cheaper price then damages will be nominal.

Specific performance: as you know from your previous studies, this remedy is at the discretion of the court, where an order for specific performance may be granted where the court deems an award of damages inadequate. However, in the case of contracts for the sale of goods, the courts will only grant specific performance where the goods are of a unique nature. See the case of *Behnke* v *Bede Shipping Co* [1927]. In this case a ship owner agreed to buy a ship called *The City* which he required immediately and which satisfied all relevant shipping regulations in terms of equipment. There was only one other ship available at the time. *The City* proved to be unsatisfactory. The court made an order for specific performance since damages would not have been an adequate remedy in this case.

Seller's remedies where buyer in breach of contract

Where a buyer fails to pay for the goods, the unpaid seller has the following remedies:

- remedies against the goods sold: lien, stoppage in transit, resale;
- personal remedies against the buyer: action for the price, action for damages.

Remedies against the goods sold

Lien: under s41 Sale of Goods Act 1979 where the property has passed to the buyer but the seller still possesses the goods, the seller can retain possession until the buyer pays for the goods.

Stoppage in transit: under s44 Sale of Goods Act 1979 where the seller has delivered the goods to a carrier and the buyer becomes insolvent the seller may demand return of the goods as long as the goods have not reached the buyer. You may recall that the seller can avoid this situation if they insert a retention of title clause. You can revisit and reflect on study session 2. The matter of 'transit' only ends on fully delivery of goods, not partial delivery.

Resale: under s48 Sale of Goods Act 1979 an unpaid seller can resell goods and give good title to a new buyer.

4

Personal remedies against the buyer

Under s49 Sale of Goods Act 1979 the seller can sue for the price of the goods where the property has passed to the buyer and the buyer has accepted the goods.

Under s50 Sale of Goods Act 1979 the seller can sue for damages for non-acceptance of the goods by the buyer where the property in the goods has not passed to the buyer and the buyer has not accepted the goods.

If the property has passed to the buyer but the buyer will not accept the goods then the seller can sue for the price or for damages.

The topics of passing of property, title and risk are discussed later on in this study guide under study sessions 8 and 9. At this stage it is sufficient to know about remedies available to buyer and seller where there is a breach of contract for sale of goods.

Learning activity 4.5

List and provide a brief explanation of the statutory remedies available to both the buyer and the seller where there is a breach of contract for the sale of goods.

Feedback on page 74

Do not worry about some of the phrases referring to passing of property, title and risk. These are discussed in later sessions. At this stage what is important is that you can identify the remedies available in the event of a breach of contract by either buyer or seller.

Self-assessment question 4.5

Analyse this short case study and advise Gogh as to what remedies are available to him.

Jennings buys a painting for £1,000 from Gogh, his local art dealer. Jennings puts down a deposit of £200 and Gogh allows Jennings to take the painting away. Jennings is now refusing to pay the balance.

Feedback on page 75

Revision question

Now try the revision question for this session on page 312.

Summary

On completing this session on termination of contracts and the remedies available on breach of contract, including breach of a contract for the sale of goods you have now studied the contractual process from formation to termination. Later you will learn more about sale of goods contracts, implied terms under the various Acts and transfer of property, title and risk. We recommend that you revisit and reflect on the previous sessions to gain a full understanding of the contractual process.

You will now study the alternative methods of resolving commercial disputes.

Suggested further reading

Griffiths and Griffiths (2002). You should read the chapter on contract formation, part I, chapter 5.

Smith and Keenan (2003), chapters 6 and 13.

Feedback on learning activities and self-assessment questions

Feedback on learning activity 4.1

Having revisited Level 4, Developing Contracts, study session 13 and read the above information you should now be able to do this learning activity. Your answer should take the form of a short essay divided into short paragraphs detailing each of the ways in which a contract can be terminated. Your paragraph on performance must include that the performance must be complete and unconditional. Your explanation about terminating a contract by agreement could include a situation where the parties agree that the contract ends automatically on the expiry of a fixed period, for example in a fixed term lease. When explaining frustration you could refer to the case of *Couturier* v *Hastie*, which you studied in study session 3 under common mistake, or cases where the subject matter of the contract is destroyed such as in the case of *Taylor* v *Caldwell*. In this case the plaintiff agreed to hire the defendants music hall for a series of concerts on certain dates. However, before the dates arrived the hall was destroyed by fire without negligence by any party. The claimant sued for wasted advertising expenses. The court held that there was an implied term of the contract that it would be discharged by the destruction of the hall and the plaintiff could not recover damages. The contract was impossible to perform and the defendant was not liable. When you are explaining about breach you can refer to the information learned under the session on contractual terms, conditions and warranties.

Feedback on self-assessment question 4.1

You should include in your answer the different types of performance, including full performance and partial performance and whether the partial performance is of a minor matter or substantial. Describe what happens in instalment contracts.

When describing how the parties can agree to terminate the contract you should include the ways in which they can do this. They may include it as an express term of the contract or the contract may be for a fixed period or come to an end when a particular event takes place. Explain the difficulties that arise when the agreement to terminate is after the commencement of the contract but before all obligations are completed. Distinguish between bilateral and unilateral agreements. The agreement to terminate must satisfy the requirements of the binding contract. The essential element is that consideration must be present.

Feedback on learning activity 4.2

You should start by providing a brief explanation of what is meant by frustration of a contract. Frustration occurs when the contract is rendered impossible to perform because of subsequent change in circumstances. Reflect on the previous studies and cases relating to frustration: for example, the case of *Taylor* v *Caldwell* [1863]; or the coronation case of *Krell* v *Henry* [1903] contrasted with the decision in the case of *Herne Bay Steamship* v *Hutton* [1903]. In *Krell* v *Henry* [1903] the plaintiff agreed to let a room to the defendant in Pall Mall for Coronation Day. Both parties knew that the defendant intended to use it with friends to watch the coronation procession. The coronation was postponed at short notice owing to the King's illness. The plaintiff sought to recover the agreed hiring fee. The Court of Appeal rejected the claim and said that the contract had been frustrated. The sole foundation of the contract, that is, the viewing of the coronation procession, had been destroyed.

Herne Bay Steamship v *Hutton* [1903] involved the contract for the hire of a steamboat for viewing the King's naval review and for a cruise round the fleet. The review was cancelled. The Court of Appeal held that the contract was not frustrated by the cancellation of the review as the review was not the sole foundation of the agreement and the cruise around the fleet could still have gone ahead.

Compare with the case of *Couturier* v *Hastie* [1856] where the contract was void ab initio, meaning from the start.

Feedback on self-assessment question 4.2

The first scenario relates to the case of *Taylor* v *Caldwell*. You should mention that monies were not recoverable in that case but the inflexibility of this has been changed by future cases and the Law Reform (Frustrated Contracts) Act 1943.

The second scenario relates to the coronation cases *Krell* and *Herne Bay*. You should mention that there would be a difference in outcome if the hire related to the 'start' of the race and not just viewing the 'yachts'.

The third scenario relates to the case of government intervention and outbreak of war.

Feedback on learning activity 4.3

You should start with a definition of each of the terms and then specifically detail the effect in the event of such terms being breached. This will require reflection of previous studies on the difference between each of the terms as this has a bearing on what happens to the contract.

If the term is a condition, the breach of this term has the effect of destroying the contract and the innocent party will have a right to repudiate the contract and seek damages. You will recall from previous studies and should mention in your answer that the innocent party can take alternative action. They can elect to continue with the contract and seek damages by way of compensation. If this option is taken then they continue to be bound by the terms of the contract and therefore liable for breach of contract if they did not fulfil their contractual obligations properly.

Where a party breaches a warranty, they can only claim damages. They have no right to repudiate the contract.

The more difficult situation concerns breach of innominate terms. Once again, you should have revisited and reflected on this in previous session. You will recall that the term innominate is a fairly recent introduction first discussed in the case of *Hong Kong Fir Shipping Co Ltd* v *Kawasaki Kisen Kaisha Ltd* [1962]. In this case the defendants chartered a ship which was to be fitted out for ordinary cargo service but in fact it was in a poor state of repair and incompetently crewed. The defendants sought to terminate the contract but the Court of Appeal said this was a warranty rather than a condition and the proper remedy was an award of damages. In such cases the seriousness of the consequences of a breach of contract should determine whether repudiation or damages was the more appropriate remedy. The innominate term falls between the above two terms and the court determines which is the most appropriate remedy, whether the contract should end or damages awarded. It will depend on whether the injured party has been denied the benefit of the contract. For the courts to be certain of the decision they prefer to stipulate a term as a condition or warranty. See the cases of *The Mihalis Angelos* [1971] and *Bunge Corporate* v *Tradax Export SA* [1981]. In the former case the owners of a ship let it to charterers, undertaking that the ship would be expected ready to load about 1 July, would proceed to a certain port for the loading of cargo, and that the charterer would have the option of cancelling the charter if the ship was not ready to load by July 20. The charterer was unable to get a cargo by July 17 and cancelled the charter, alleging that it was frustrated. The ship itself was not ready until July 23. In court it was argued that the charterer was entitled to avoid the contract on July 17 because of a breach of contract by the shipowner, that is, he had impliedly promised that he had reasonable grounds for believing that the ship would be ready to load on July 1, and that there were no such grounds. The Court of Appeal held that the term was a condition and that the charterer had properly avoided the contract even though he had done so on the ground that the contract was frustrated when this was not the case.

The latter case involved a contract for the sale of soya bean meal. The contract provided for a delivery to be made in June, the buyers giving fifteen days' notice of their readiness to collect it. They gave such notice and the sellers claimed the right to repudiate the contract because of breach of an essential term. The House of Lords held that although s41 Law of Property Act 1925 states that a stipulation as to time of performance is not to be

4

regarded as being of the essence of the contract there were three exceptions, these being, where the contract expressly stipulates that time conditions must be strictly complied with, or where the nature of the subject matter or surrounding circumstances show clearly that time should be of the essence, or where a party who has been subjected to unreasonable delay gives notice to the party in default.

Innominate terms are discussed in more detail in the session on Supply of Goods and Services Act 1982 ss13–15 inclusive study session 7.

Anticipatory breach as the term suggests happens before the agreed date of performance. The innocent or aggrieved party has the right to claim damages immediately. An innocent party will only be successful in an action for damages if it was clear that the party who is repudiating the contract had decided irrevocably not to perform their contractual obligations. The innocent party does not need to give formal notice of acceptance of the anticipatory breach, their conduct is sufficient. All that matters is that the repudiating party knows the innocent party has accepted the repudiation.

Feedback on self-assessment question 4.3

You should discuss that under the Sale of Goods Act 1979 the sections relating to title, quality and description refer to the fact that compliance with these sections are to be taken as conditions. This could mean that a party could escape from the contract for minor defects. The Sale and Supply of Goods Act 1994 affected this by the addition in s15A of reducing the right to rescind for minor breaches of ss13 and 14 Sale of Goods Act in non-consumer contracts.

Feedback on learning activity 4.4

You should explain that the basic principle for the award of damages was set out in the case of *Hadley* v *Baxendale* where the court held that special damages only arise where there are special or knock-on circumstances which lead to an unusual or special loss. A party in breach is not liable for such special damages unless they know of the special circumstances at the time the contract was formed. In the Hadley case, no special damages were awarded as the special circumstances had not been properly explained when the contract was formed.

Feedback on self-assessment question 4.4

You should provide a brief explanation of unliquidated damages and then explain the intention of the award of damages, the types of damage that can be recovered, remoteness of damage, foreseeability and the duty of mitigation of loss. Cases referred to should include Hadley, Victoria Laundry, *The Heron II* and Blackpool Fylde.

Feedback on learning activity 4.5

Your list should include the rights of the buyer, namely, to reject the goods, action of damages and specific performance. You should then do the same for the seller, with your list including rights against the goods sold, namely, lien, stoppage in transit and resale and personal remedies against the buyer, to recover the price and damages. Your explanations for each should include in what situations these rights are available.

Feedback on self-assessment question 4.5

You should identify that this is a breach of contract by the buyer Jennings and that the remedies available in this case with Gogh is the personal remedies against the buyer. The rights against the goods are not applicable in this situation. You should mention that s49 Sale of Goods Act 1979 is applicable here as the buyer has taken the painting away and on the face of it accepted the goods. The seller can therefore sue for the price or the balance in this case. If this is a situation where the buyer is no longer accepting the goods then the seller can sue for damages under s50 Sale of Goods Act 1979.

4

Commercial dispute resolution

5

Introduction

This session requires no prior learning. You will be studying all aspects of commercial dispute resolution. You have already seen the words 'sue' and 'claim for damages' used in previous sessions. These are used in relation to a person, a claimant, taking court action against another person, a defendant, for example for breach of contract. This is also known as litigation proceedings. In this session you will be looking at litigation and the alternative methods of resolving a dispute.

Session learning objectives

After completing this session you should be able to:

5.1 Identify and evaluate litigation as a method of commercial dispute resolution.
5.2 Distinguish between mediation and conciliation.
5.3 Define adjudication.
5.4 Explain the arbitration process.

Unit content coverage

This study session covers the following topics from the official CIPS unit content document:

Learning objective

1.5 Critically evaluate the alternative methods of resolving commercial disputes.
   • Litigation
   • Arbitration
   • Mediation
   • Conciliation
   • Adjudication
   • International arbitration

Timing

You should set aside about 5 hours to read and complete this session, including learning activities, self-assessment questions, the suggested further reading (if any) and the revision question.

5

5.1   Litigation as a method of resolving commercial disputes

Litigation as a method of resolving disputes has several drawbacks. In addition to the drawbacks it often does not lead to the best result. Some of the disadvantages include:

*   it is expensive and slow;
*   it can give advantage to a wealthier party;
*   it is not suited to disputes involving technical issues;
*   it is adversarial;
*   it can destroy harmony between the parties, personal and business relationships while the case is in progress and afterwards.

When considering litigation you must look at the court system and the rules of judicial precedent. Litigation is expensive and time consuming because of the court system and the hierarchy of the courts in decision making. A wealthy party can string things out as they have the money to do so, sometimes even until their money runs out. The ordinary judge will not be familiar with technical issues and therefore court cases may not be suited to litigation. Being adversarial means that each side is trying to gain as much and give away as little as possible without regard often to what would be a fair solution. The very adversarial nature of court proceedings often means a breakdown in relationships between the parties, both personal and business. This has knock-on effects if the parties are involved in current or future business with each other.

Litigation should be used where an injunction is required or where there is no dispute as such but a debt owed. The creditor should issue a claim form or consider insolvency proceedings in the event of the unlikelihood of the debt being paid. Where the law is unclear, litigation should be used where a ruling by the court is required.

Learning activity 5.1

Has your organisation been involved in court proceedings in relation to a commercial dispute? Review the situation and consider the advantages and disadvantages of litigation. Consider the parties. Was your organisation the claimant or defendant? If you are unable to source any material within your organisation then look to some of the cases on contract that you have read in the previous sessions. Identify which party is the claimant, which is the defendant and so on. You will recall in some cases that the court made a decision, in other cases it was the Court of Appeal, and in some it was the House of Lords that made a decision. Imagine the time it took for a case to come to court and proceed as far as the House of Lords. Briefly explain the advantages and disadvantages of litigation as a method of commercial dispute resolution.

Feedback on page 87

To fully understand the litigation route you must have an understanding of the court system. You will be considering the English court system here as the courts outside England and Wales differ in name and content. The European Union (EU) dimension will be discussed later in this session.

In the previous sessions you have been looking at contract law. The relevance to this session is that contract law was established many years ago and is based on 18th and 19th century cases. The legal principles are established by judges in court cases and followed according to **judicial precedent**. This is the doctrine by which the lower courts follow the decisions of the higher courts in the court hierarchy. You should revisit section 5.1 above where the hierarchy of the courts is explained in detail. The system of dispute resolution will also take into account the European dimension. The parties to litigation in England and Wales are known as the plaintiff or claimant: that is, the person raising the action; the defendant is the person against whom the action is taken. In an appeal the parties become appellant and respondent.

The courts in England and Wales

The emphasis here will be on the county court as this is the court most likely to deal with business, at least small business issues. Before going into more detail on the county court, it is worth mentioning the magistrates court which deals mainly with criminal law. They have some civil jurisdiction and this relates to council tax and rates enforcement, licensing of pubs and restaurants, casinos and betting shops.

County Court

These courts were created by the County Courts Act 1846 and they deal exclusively with civil cases. Originally they dealt with debt recovery but over the years they deal with a large number of cases. For further information you should read Smith and Keenan, *Law for Business*, chapter 2, which explains and details the court system, fast track procedures and monetary levels for claims. Briefly the county court deals with cases involving breaches of contract and torts such as injury caused by negligence. The monetary value for cases to be heard in these courts is less than £15,000 in the case of claims for debt or unascertained damages. This excludes claims for death or personal injury. For personal injury claims the monetary value is less than £50,000. These figures are current at time of writing this guide. Claimants can choose to go to the High Court where they feel that the case is complex or of public importance. The county court also deals with small claims. Read more about this in Smith and Keenan *Law for Business*.

High Court and Court of Appeal

This consists of the Queens Bench Division, Chancery Division and Family division. The appeal from the High Court is to the Court of Appeal and from there to the House of Lords.

Business courts

These are the courts that are more relevant to businesses. Since 1964 the High Court operates as a commercial court. Complex technical issues are heard by the Technology and Construction Court.

House of Lords

In civil cases the House of Lords hears appeals from the Court of Appeal among others in the UK. The House of Lords is important in developing UK law on human rights.

5

Self-assessment question 5.1

Explain the meaning of litigation and provide a brief description of the parties and their role.

Feedback on page 87

5.2 Mediation and conciliation

You have been looking at court proceedings and the advantages and disadvantages. You are now going to consider two alternatives to raising a civil court case. The other alternatives of adjudication and arbitration are discussed later in this session.

Mediation

This is used widely in domestic disputes, for example, divorce and custody cases. It does operate in other fields as well as it is often much quicker than litigation. Judges often encourage the parties to try mediation before going to court as a last resort. A third party acts as mediator. The mediator does not impose any decision but encourages the parties to discuss their differences and to reach their own agreed solution. Mediation has the advantage of allowing the parties to vent their non-legal grievances, free from the constraints of court requirements such as relevant evidence. Even a commercial dispute of some £500,000 might take just one or two days as opposed to months, even years, in court.

Mediation procedures

These vary but usually there is an initial meeting at which each party puts forward their position. This is followed by a private meeting between the mediator and each party. There is then a second meeting with all parties at which the mediator helps parties to negotiate face to face. All proceedings are confidential. Lawyers may be present but there are rarely any outside witnesses giving evidence. The mediator should not disclose to one side the contents of any discussion with the other side except by consent. The mediator is the facilitator and the intention is to determine each side's 'bottom line'. The ultimate decision is the responsibility of the parties. Once reached, the decision may be enforceable as an ordinary contract.

Conciliation

This is similar to mediation and some people use the word when they mean mediation and vice versa. The difference with conciliation is that the conciliator takes a more pro-active role than a mediator. The conciliator gives their own opinion from time to time and in the event that no decision is reached by the parties, the conciliator will indicate how a court might decide. One conciliation service that you have probably heard of is ACAS (the Advisory, Conciliation and Arbitration Service), which operates a conciliation scheme in cases of unfair dismissal.

Learning activity 5.2

Has your organisation been involved in mediation or conciliation or both relating to resolution of a commercial dispute? If you have no information within your organisation on which to draw, read the notes above carefully then compare and contrast the mediation and conciliation service.

Feedback on page 88

When using alternative dispute resolution routes such as mediation and conciliation the processes may and often do vary according to the style and manner of the mediator and conciliator. Even after choosing such routes there may not be a decision and the parties end up embroiled in a court action. In theory the alternatives to court proceedings were introduced as quicker less expensive routes to resolving disputes. However, in practice some parties in commercial disputes are still appointing lawyers to be present. You will find that this is the case when you are looking at adjudication, which is discussed below.

Self-assessment question 5.2

Define the terms 'mediation' and 'conciliation' and explain the difference.

Feedback on page 88

5.3 Adjudication

Adjudication was introduced by the Housing Grants, Construction and Regeneration Act 1996 as a faster and significantly cheaper method of resolving disputes than litigation or arbitration. Adjudication is now firmly established in the construction industry as the preferred method of formal dispute resolution.

Since its introduction it has been widely used in commerce and industry. However, the procedure, which was introduced as an alternative to court proceedings, may be quicker but as more and more parties to commercial disputes are employing lawyers to advise on the process, attend meetings and represent them at the adjudication hearing it is doubtful whether this method of resolution is in practice less expensive.

Adjudication process

There are several nominating bodies within the UK, all of which provide adjudicators for a wide range of construction professionals, and all of which have different criteria for the initial selection of individuals on to the adjudicator's panel.

The decision as to which nominating body to approach for selection of an adjudicator will depend on the nature of the dispute, that is, an architect or an engineer would perhaps be more qualified to decide on a dispute relating to workmanship or design whereas a quantity surveyor may be better suited to deciding on matters of measurement, quantum or costs.

The competency of adjudicators is taken seriously by awarding bodies and individuals are required to be fully conversant with current practice, law and adjudication procedures. Appropriate training is undertaken to achieve continuing professional development.

It is also possible for the parties to a dispute to make a private appointment of an adjudicator without seeking selection from a nominating body. However, as the parties are already locked into a dispute that cannot be resolved it is highly unlikely that they will reach consensus on the appointment of an adjudicator.

Initial nomination and selection of an adjudicator

It is important to establish the availability of an individual for selection. The selected individual then receives the names of the referring party and responding party along with a summary of the nature of the dispute. The selected individual must consider whether the subject matter of the dispute falls within their sphere of professional expertise. They must also be able to adhere to the strict timescales associated with the adjudication process. S108 Housing Grants, Construction and Regeneration Act 1996 stipulates that an adjudicator must reach a decision within 28 days of the referral notice. This period can be extended by 14 days with the consent of the referring party and longer with the consent of both parties.

The selected individual must ensure that there is no conflict of interest between them and either of the parties or between the selected individual's organisation and either of the parties.

To summarise: if the selected person is confident that they have the expertise, that they can adhere to the tight timescales and that there is no conflict of interest then they should advise the nominating body of their availability. A formal letter of appointment is sent to the adjudicator. Under s108 of the 1996 Act the time between submission of the application by the referring party and the appointment of the adjudicator must be no more than 7 days and in practice is usually between 24 and 48 hours.

Adjudicator's next steps

The adjudicator:

- confirms there is no conflict of interest;
- advises that the referral notice must be issued within 7 days of the original notice of intention to refer to adjudication;

- seeks clarification as to who the representatives of the parties are (if any);
- directs that there will be no telephone communication from either party to the adjudicator;
- advises both parties of the terms of appointment and encloses an adjudication agreement for signing by both parties.

The receipt of the referral notice by the adjudicator starts the 28 day process.

Jurisdiction

The jurisdiction of an adjudicator is governed by the Housing Grants, Construction and Regeneration Act 1996 and the associated Scheme for Construction Contracts and or the adjudication provisions within the building contract.

With increasing regularity, in practice the responding party immediately suggests that the adjudicator does not have jurisdiction to deal with the alleged dispute and requests that the adjudicator resigns. The adjudicator must take this seriously even though in some cases it may be a delaying tactic.

Jurisdictional challenges may be made for many reasons, some of which include:

- the construction contract is not in writing;
- the contract is not a 'construction contract' as defined by the 1996 Act;
- the selection of the adjudicator has not complied with the adjudication clause in the contract;
- there is no dispute in the first place.

Referral notice, response and other submissions

Paragraph 7(a) of the Scheme for Construction Contracts stipulates that the referring party must issue a referral notice no later than 7 days from the date of notice of adjudication. On receipt of the referral notice, the adjudicator writes to the parties acknowledging it and requesting the response to be submitted by a certain date, normally within 7 days. There can be another response by the referring party and a further final reply from the respondents. The adjudicator controls the proceedings and the dates of receipt of these responses. The adjudicator can propose a meeting which is fairly informal even although it is called a hearing by some. The adjudicator sets out the procedural matters, the need for a site visit and confirms the date for reaching the decision.

Meeting and independent advisors

The meeting is held to establish the facts and not to argue the law. The adjudicator may want to clarify jurisdictional issues, appointment of advisers and whether the parties want reasons to be issued with the decision. Where the adjudicator seeks independent advice then he or she must notify the parties of this intention and parties must be given the opportunity of

5

commenting on it. See the case of *Balfour Beatty Construction* v *London Borough of Lambeth* [2002]. In this case Balfour Beatty were seeking to enforce the decision of the adjudicator and applied for summary judgment. Lambeth had deducted approximately £356,000 in liquidated damages and Balfour Beatty disputed their entitlement to do so. This dispute was referred to an adjudicator who decided that Balfour Beatty were entitled to an extension of time and that therefore Lambeth should pay to Balfour Beatty the sum of approximately £284,000 plus interest. He also decided that Lambeth would be liable for his fees.

Decision

The object of adjudication is to reach a decision, however temporary or binding it may be. The adjudicator establishes what facts are agreed or not, on whom the burden of proof lies and if it is sufficient on the balance of probabilities or if the opposing evidence is sufficient to rebut it. The adjudicator looks for corroboration. They can draw on their own experience where appropriate. The adjudicator will then consider what law governs the dispute, whether contract law or statute, find out what law is agreed or not, and if case law has been referred to the adjudicator will ask for the case details. Finally the adjudicator will apply the law to the facts and write the decision.

The decision must be written with clarity and set out the obligations and liabilities of the 'losing party' and include reasons if they have been requested by the parties.

Learning activity 5.3

Read the above carefully before doing this activity. It may be that your organisation has been involved in an adjudication process. If so, you may wish to draw on this experience. Now describe the adjudication process briefly and identify any advantages and disadvantages.

Feedback on page 88

More and more cases that commenced as an adjudication process are proceeding to the court for decisions on jurisdictional matters and the role of the adjudicator. See the case of *London & Amsterdam Properties* v *Waterman Partnership* [2004]. This action arose out of a claim for professional negligence. L & AP argued that Waterman (a firm of structural engineers) had caused them to incur additional costs of approximately £1.9m due to the late release of steelwork design information. This led to a substantial period of exchanges of arguments and information between the representatives of the parties although this focused on liability. The case went to adjudication and the adjudicator decided that Waterman should pay L & AP the sum of £659,346. Waterman then applied to the court to have the decision declared not binding on the grounds that the adjudicator did not have jurisdiction. The court held that the adjudicator had acted in breach of the rules of natural justice and therefore his decision was unenforceable. The court held that the adjudicator did not appear to have appreciated that in accordance with the rules of natural justice he should either have excluded late additional information or should have given the other party reasonable opportunity of responding to it. A more decisive approach would have avoided this.

Self-assessment question 5.3

Read the following sentences and decide whether true or false.

1   An adjudicator can only be appointed by a nominating or awarding body.
2   An adjudicator must not breach the rules of natural justice.
3   An adjudicator must reach a decision within 28 days of being appointed.
4   The 28-day period can be extended beyond 14 days.
5   The Referring Party must issue a referral notice no later than 7 days from the date of notice of adjudication.
6   Evidence is heard at a formal hearing set by the adjudicator.
7   The adjudicator must give reasons for the decision.

Feedback on page 88

5.4   Arbitration

Arbitration is another alternative method to raising court proceedings or litigation. It is quite usual in commercial contracts for the parties to agree to submit disputes arising out of the contract to an arbitrator. The arbitrator may be a lawyer but not necessarily so. The arbitrator is usually someone with specialist knowledge of the subject matter of the contract, for example, a surveyor in a construction dispute.

Arbitration proceedings are different from court proceedings in two ways:

*   arbitration proceedings are held in private;
*   arbitrator will have special experience of the particular business or trade.

However, arbitration is not cheap. An arbitrator who is a specialist in the subject matter of the dispute may charge high daily rates for their services. The parties also employ lawyers to appear on their behalf at the arbitration and the lawyers charge the same fees as they would if appearing in a court case.

The arbitration process is not quick as it may take several months for parties to agree on an arbitrator with the appropriate expertise. It will also depend on the availability of the arbitrator.

The parties can make provision for arbitration within the contract. With regard to such clauses, the Unfair Terms in Consumer Contracts

5

Regulations 1999 applies to abuse of clauses that businesses put in their consumer contracts. The Arbitration Act 1996 applies the provisions of the regulations to arbitration clauses. An unfair clause cannot be enforced against a consumer who can take court action where there is a breach of contract by a supplier depending on the amount involved.

Arbitration can also occur under codes of practice of trade associations with the assistance of the Office of Fair Trading.

You will recall from section 5.1 above that since 1964 the High Court has operated as a commercial court. Under the Arbitration Act 1996 a judge of the commercial court can take arbitration with the approval of the Lord Chief Justice.

Learning activity 5.4

Do you know if your organisation has been involved in the arbitration process? If so, try to identify whether this was UK or international arbitration. If you cannot obtain any information from your organisation, then carefully read the information on arbitration above and explain what type of process it is and the advantages if any as an alternative to court proceedings.

Feedback on page 89

It is worthwhile remembering that often commercial disputes are unavoidable. However, their impact can be out of all proportion to their substance. Commercial disputes at best can distract the companies and at worst destroy their business relationships and even their businesses. That is why it is important to know about alternative ways of resolving disputes. You now know from this study session that disputes can be managed and resolved. Proactive dispute resolution techniques can deliver the desired commercial result.

It is also important in business to take early action to resolve disputes to avoid becoming entrenched in the breakdown of relationships and even the business.

To become involved in litigation requires commitment, tenacity and experience. It is often very lengthy and extremely costly. The alternatives to litigation were developed to resolve disputes as quickly, economically and advantageously as possible. The first step should be negotiation. The alternatives are summed up briefly here:

- Mediation: confidential, consensual, quick, relatively cheap, and helps preserve trading relationships.
- Adjudication: leads to an enforceable expert's decision and is used often in building disputes.
- Arbitration: is useful for its confidentiality, flexibility and speed.

Self-assessment question 5.4

Define arbitration and discuss its advantages - why would you want to
include it in a contract?

Feedback on page 89

5

Revision question

Now try the revision question for this session on page 312.

Summary

In this study session you firstly looked litigation and its drawbacks as a
way of resolving disputes. You then looked at the alternatives: commercial
dispute resolutions such as arbitration, mediation, conciliation and
adjudication and their advantages.

Suggested further reading

Waring (2006), all chapters.

Mills (2005), all chapters.

Smith and Keenan (2003), chapters 2 and 5 on dispute resolution and the
lawmaking process.

Feedback on learning activities and self-assessment questions

Feedback on learning activity 5.1

This exercise should be in the form of a short essay with brief paragraphs
on the advantages and disadvantages of going to court in the event of a
dispute arising. The advantages may be that it was a debt owing or the
dispute required a ruling by the court. Maybe your organisation needed
an injunction and had to use the court route. You should provide a short
explanation on the disadvantages, including expense, adversarial, breakdown
in relationships for current or future business. Difficulties could arise where
the issue was particularly technical, something a judge would not be familiar
with.

Feedback on self-assessment question 5.1

Your answer should include the explanation that litigation is the raising
of an action in court and that it is an adversarial system. The court case is
raised by a claimant against the defendant. Business cases are heard in the

County Court, which is presided over by a circuit judge. There are levels of monetary value that dictate in which court the case is heard, with small business issues being dealt with in the county court. A short description of each of the courts should be given.

Feedback on learning activity 5.2

Your answer should include a brief description of mediation and conciliation and the process of each. Then provide a paragraph on the similarities and one on the differences. If you have personal experience you may wish to recall your own experience or that of your organisation and make a note of the advantages and disadvantages.

Feedback on self-assessment question 5.2

Mediation is where an impartial third party acts as mediator to encourage the parties to a dispute to reach their own agreed solution. The mediator does not impose their opinions or decisions on the parties. An ultimate decision agreed between the parties can be enforced as an ordinary contract.

Conciliation is similar to mediation but the conciliator takes a more proactive role. The conciliator offers their own opinion and if no agreement is reached between the parties then the conciliator will indicate how the court will decide.

The difference is mainly in the role of the third party. Other than that, they are fairly similar and are often confused by lay people. In both circumstances the parties can still end up taking court action.

Feedback on learning activity 5.3

Your answer should include an outline of the adjudication process: the selection and nomination process; importance of there being no conflict of interest; timescales of referral and responses, jurisdictional matters, meetings and decision with reasons. The advantages are that it is quicker and supposedly less expensive although more and more parties are involving lawyers whose charges are the same as in court proceedings. Another disadvantage may be that the parties may still end up in court.

Feedback on self-assessment question 5.3

1   False: the parties can make a private appointment of an adjudicator of their own choice without having to seek selection from a nominating body. Although as they are in dispute over a matter, it is unlikely that they would reach consensus on appointment of an adjudicator.
2   True: the adjudicator can avoid breaching natural justice by notifying the parties at all times of his intentions for example to seek independent advice and if the advice is taken to disclose it to the parties. See the case of *BAL (1996) Ltd* v *Taylor Woodrow Construction* [2004]. In this adjudication BAL were a subcontractor to Taylor Woodrow. Disputes in relation to payments arose. BAL referred the matter to adjudication. The adjudicator decided in favour of BAL. Proceedings

were brought by summary judgment to enforce the adjudicator's decision. Taylor Woodrow defended the application for summary judgment on the grounds that the adjudicator had acted in breach of the principles of natural justice. The court held that in this case there was no acquiescence to the procedure adopted by the adjudicator and that there was a strong argument that there had been a breach of the principles of natural justice. The court accordingly refused the application for summary judgment.

3   False: the 28-day period starts from the date of receipt of the referral notice.

4   True: timescales are tight and should be adhered to, although the period can be extended for up to 14 days with the consent of the referring party and longer with the consent of both parties.

5   True: this is governed by paragraph 7(a) of the Scheme for Construction Contracts.

6   False: the adjudicator can call a meeting that is informal, although parties now tend to be represented by lawyers. The purpose of the meeting is for establishing the facts and for clarification. No legal debate is undertaken.

7   False: the adjudicator need not give reasons for the decision unless requested to do so by either of or both parties.

Feedback on learning activity 5.4

Your answer should include that arbitration can be introduced by the parties in their contract, by court or statute. Advantages include that it is informal as opposed to the court formalities. It is also confidential and held in private. However, it is not inexpensive owing to the time it takes for the parties to agree on the arbitrator and the availability of the arbitrator. Disadvantage is that the right of appeal is limited. The parties should assume that the arbitrator's decision is final. Unlike court cases where the parties have to disclose information to each other, the parties in an arbitration do not need to do so and this can make it difficult to prepare a case if the necessary information is in the exclusive hands or control of the opposition.

Feedback on self-assessment question 5.4

Your definition could be something along the lines that arbitration is an alternative to litigation in the resolution of a commercial dispute. The advantages are that it is confidential and held in confidence. It is also advantageous where there are complex technical issues as the arbitrator will be a person with expertise in the subject matter of the dispute and in that trade or profession. Including a clause referring a dispute to arbitration will avoid any doubt as to the method of dispute resolution.

5

Study session 6
Distinguish between Sale of Goods and Supply of Goods and Services acts

Caviar emptor –
beware of the fish?!
Anon

Introduction

In study sessions 1 – 3 you studied the general principles relating to contracts, various terms and clauses and what factors can affect contracts. You should ensure that you are familiar with these principles. In study sessions 6 – 10 you are going to look at special categories of contracts that are regulated by both case law and statute.

We recommend that you read this session very carefully as it is of special relevance to purchasing and supply personnel. Students also find it difficult to distinguish between contracts for the sale of goods and contracts for the supply of goods and services, especially in the examination arena. In this study session you will look at these particular contracts, that is, those under the Sale of Goods Act 1979 (SGA) (as amended) and those under the Supply of Goods and Services Act 1982 (SOGAS).

Session learning objectives

After completing this session you should be able to:

6.1 Describe the Sale of Goods Act 1979 (SGA) (as amended) on contract law.
6.2 Describe the Supply of Goods and Services Act 1982 (SOGAS) on contract law.
6.3 Distinguish between the SGA and SOGAS statutes.

Unit content coverage

This study session covers the following topics from the official CIPS unit content document:

Learning outcome

Distinguish between the statutes relating to sale of goods and the supply of goods and services in specific circumstances and apply those rules to given practical situations.

Learning objective

2.1 Distinguish between the statutes relating to the sale of goods and the supply of goods and services to specific circumstances and apply those rules to given practical situations.
  • Sale of Goods Act 1979 (as amended)
  • Supply of Goods and Services Act 1982

- Contracts for the sale of goods
- Contracts for work and materials

Timing

You should set aside about 5 hours to read and complete this session, including learning activities, self-assessment questions, the suggested further reading (if any) and the revision question.

6.1 Sale of Goods Act 1979 (as amended)

6

Learning activity 6.1

Read the phrases below and answer which would fall within the Sale of Goods Act 1979.

- cleaning materials;
- energy supplies;
- animals;
- office cleaning services.

Feedback on page 98

Traditionally the sale of goods was regulated by the old maxim of caveat emptor, let the buyer beware. As this was not very satisfactory for the consumer, legislation was introduced to modernise the law. This resulted in the Sale of Goods Act 1979 (SGA). Later on in this session you look at the important difference between the sale of goods and the supply of goods and services.

In this part you will only be considering the Sale of Goods and the contracts regulated by this Act. The SGA consolidated the law relating to the sale of goods and replaced the Sale of Goods Act 1893. You will see that some case law that is cited is dated before 1979 so it is important to know that the provisions of the 1893 Act were carried over into the 1979 Act. We start with a definition.

Definition of a contract for sale of goods

Under s2(1) 1979 Act a contract for the sale of goods is a contract where the seller transfers or agrees to transfer the property in the goods to the buyer for a money consideration called the price. This definition includes an agreement to sell. This is where the transfer of property in the goods is to take place at a future time or subject to some condition that is to be fulfilled later.

The SGA relates only to contracts of sale of goods so it does not cover:

- gifts;
- free offers to promote a product;

- exchange of goods for work done or for rent, lodging, board;
- exchange of vouchers, tokens (regarded as barter);
- hire purchase agreements.

Some of the above are governed by other legislation and you will look at the Supply of Goods and Services Act 1982 later on in this session.

If you go back to the above definition of a contract for the sale of goods important words are 'goods' and 'transfer of property'. These are discussed in more detail in study sessions 8 and 9. In study session 7 you consider implied terms. So let us look at the essential elements of a contract for the sale of goods.

Essential elements

These are the same as any other contract. So you should revisit study session 1 to refresh your memory on these essentials.

The parties to a contract of sale are usually known as the buyer and the seller. The consideration is the price that must be paid in money at the time the contract is made or promised later.

In your learning activity above you were asked to identify to which category the words belonged, whether goods or not goods. Categories of goods that apply to a sale of goods contract are governed by s5 SGA. There are five categories of goods:

- existing goods;
- future goods;
- specific goods;
- unascertained goods (subdivided into generic, goods still to be manufactured, part of a bulk);
- ascertained goods.

Existing goods

S5(1): goods that are owned or possessed by the seller at the time of the contract of sale.

Future goods

S5(1): goods to be manufactured or acquired by the seller after the contract of sale has been made, for example, timber to be cut or fruit to be harvested.

Specific goods

S6(1): goods that are identified at the time the contract is made. For example, where the fruit has been harvested and selected at the time the contract is made.

Unascertained goods

- generic: goods of a particular kind, such as, 50 tons of sugar;
- goods not in existence: goods yet to be manufactured or produced by the seller;

- part of a bulk: the part is not identified but the bulk is specified, for example, you identify a bulk of 200 tons of sugar stored in warehouse B, you want 50 tons of it.

Ascertained goods

These are goods originally not ascertained at the time the contract is made but have been identified according to the parties' agreement after the contract of sale. An example would be where the sugar has now been weighed.

6

Self-assessment question 6.1

Read the following sentences and answer whether true/false.

1 Contracts for the sale of goods are regulated by the Sale of Goods Act 1979.
2 When Annie gave her friend Jean a new tea set, she was bound by the rules of the 1979 Act.
3 Bill agreed to buy a horse owned by his friend John. He was not sure of the horse's name. The horse is classed as unascertained goods.
4 Agnes, who had a sewing business, was interested in some silk that she had seen in a magazine. She contacted the factory and agreed to buy two rolls of the silk, which was in the process of being made. The rolls of silk are classed as future goods.
5 James purchased petrol at his local station and received six free glasses. This falls within the SGA.

Feedback on page 98

6.2 Supply of Goods and Services Act 1982 (SOGAS)

Learning activity 6.2

Read the phrases below and answer which would fall within the Supply of Goods and Services Act 1982.

- cleaning materials;
- energy supplies;
- animals;
- office cleaning services.

Feedback on page 98

The SOGAS Part I applies to contracts for the supply of goods (or materials) such as work and materials, for example car repairs. Part II of the 1982 Act applies to contracts for the supply of services.

The 1982 Act was amended by the Sale and Supply of Goods Act 1994. In study session 7 you will look at implied terms. In general, many of the implied terms applied to the contracts of sale under the SGA apply also to contracts under the SOGAS. You will consider each of the Parts of SOGAS in turn, starting with Part I.

Part 1 of SOGAS governs the following types of contract:

- contracts for work and materials, that is, the supply of goods (or materials);
- contracts for exchange or barter, hire, rental or leasing.

It is important to remember that contracts for the transfer of property in goods are excluded, for example, contracts for sale of goods and hire-purchase contracts.

As with other contracts, under the 1982 Act there must be a contract between the parties. If there is no contract then the statutory implied terms cannot be relied upon. You will be looking at the implied terms later in study session 7.

Contracts for work and materials

You must remember the distinction between these contracts and the contracts of sale of goods. It is not possible to provide an exhaustive list of contracts for work and materials but some examples include maintenance contracts, construction contracts and contracts for installation or improvement.

Contracts for exchange or barter, hire, rental or leasing

This covers the situation where goods are exchanged for other goods. The most likely contracts are those where there is an exchange of goods for coupons or vouchers, for example, in promotional schemes. Where a retailer supplies goods under a contract of this kind the retailer is liable if the goods are not of satisfactory quality. This is an implied term of the Act and is discussed later on in study session 7. The Act also regulates situations where you acquire goods by way of a gift.

Contracts for the hire of goods fall within Part I. Under s6(1) 1982 Act a contract for the hire of goods means a contract where one person bails or agrees to bail goods to another person by way of hire. There must be a contract. Some main areas of hiring, renting or leasing include, office equipment, building plant and equipment and consumer hiring of goods such as televisions, videos, cars, etc.

Part II of SOGAS governs the following:

Contracts for the supply of services where a person agrees to carry out a service. The 1982 Act does not provide a definition of what is meant by service. However, services provided by professionals such as lawyers, accountants and architects are included in the Act. Employment contracts and apprenticeships are not included.

Once again it is important to know that there must be a contract. Where there is no contract then the implied terms of the Act do not apply. These

6

implied terms are discussed later in study session 7. This means that where you work for a friend this will not be covered by the Act. Where injury is caused by a supplier to someone who is not in a contractual relationship with that supplier, action may be taken under the tort of negligence. This is discussed later in study session 10.

Self-assessment question 6.2

Read the following sentences and answer true/false.

1   Demco Ltd leases office equipment from Xero plc. The equipment is faulty. They know they have rights under the SOGAS.
2   Pat hires her washing machine from Rentex Ltd. This is governed by the Sale of Goods Act 1979.
3   Bill's cat Persia has caused so much damage to his wallpaper that he has called in local decorators to paper and paint his home. The decorating of the house falls within the SOGAS Part II.
4   Joan needs a lawyer for her divorce action. This falls within SOGAS Act 1982 Part II.
5   The local DIY store supplies security fencing to GMC Construction Ltd on a regular basis for their building sites. This falls within 1982 Act Part I.

Feedback on page 99

6.3   The difference between the Sale of Goods Act (SGA) and the Supply of Goods and Services Act 1979 (SOGAS)

Learning activity 6.3

Review the previous sections on both statutes. Can you identify any contracts that you have entered into which might fall within the SGA and those that would be considered to fall within the SOGAS? You could also look at your organisation and see if you can identify contracts that would fall within either of these Acts.

Feedback on page 99

You are going to recap now on both statutes, the SGA and SOGAS.

Sale of Goods Act 1979 definition

Under s2(1) 1979 Act a contract for the sale of goods is a contract where the seller transfers or agrees to transfer the property in the goods to the buyer for a money consideration called the price. This definition includes an agreement to sell. This is where the transfer of property in the goods is to take place at a future time or subject to some condition which is to be fulfilled later.

Supply of Goods and Services Act 1982 Part I contracts

- Contracts for work and materials, that is, the supply of goods (or materials).
- Contracts for exchange or barter, hire, rental or leasing.

Supply of Goods and Services Act 1982 Part II contracts

Contracts for the supply of services where a person agrees to perform a service. The 1982 Act does not provide a definition of what is meant by service. However, services provided by professionals such as lawyers, accountants and architects are included in the Act. Employment contracts and apprenticeships are not included.

In the next session you will be looking at the similarities between the Acts with regard to implied terms.

6

Self-assessment question 6.3

Read the following two short scenarios and explain which Act will apply and why.

James needed a car. He saw an advertisement by CarFU Ltd in his local newspaper giving details of a second-hand car they had for sale. James visited CarFU to purchase the second-hand car but was told by CarFU that it had just been sold. They showed him a small Victor Micro (VM) but said that it still had some work to be done on it but that he could have it for £800 and pick it up later that month. James paid £800. Before leaving the showroom, CarFU said that he could have one of their hire cars at a discount price. They said he could return the hire car when he came to pick up his VM. Explain which Act governs the two contractual situations in this scenario.

Anne is employed by Dialtone Ltd. Her role within her contract of employment is that of purchasing manager. She is being pressurised at work to find the best price for new office equipment. In the past her organisation has always purchased their office equipment but she has just returned from a seminar on the benefits of leasing. She decides to go ahead with leasing new equipment from Modcube Ltd. This still leaves the problem of what to do with the old office furniture. She remembers that the local charity shops are looking for desks and chairs. She decides to take the old office furniture to the charity shop. Explain which Act governs the contractual situations in this scenario.

Feedback on page 99

Revision question

Now try the revision question for this session on page 312.

Summary

Having completed this study session you should be aware of the differences between contracts for the sale of goods and those for the supply of goods and services. You have also studied these contracts as regulated by case law and statute, and in particular the Sale of Goods Act 1979 (as amended) and the Supply of Goods and Services Act 1982.

Before moving on, we recommend that you read this session very carefully as it is of special relevance to purchasing and supply personnel. Also, in the examination arena, knowing the difference between contracts for the sale of goods and those for the supply of goods and services is often an area that students find challenging and confusing.

Suggested further reading

Griffiths and Griffiths (2002). You should read the chapters on sale of goods and supply of goods and services (part II, chapters 7 and 8).

Smith and Keenan (2003), part 3, chapters 15–18.

Feedback on learning activities and self-assessment questions

Feedback on learning activity 6.1

You should identify that they are the following:

- cleaning materials: goods;
- energy supplies: not goods;
- animals: goods;
- office cleaning services: not goods.

Feedback on self-assessment question 6.1

1   True.
2   False: Annie gave a gift to her friend Jean. There was no valuable consideration given. It is not governed by the SGA rules.
3   False: the horse is in the category existing goods – the horse was owned by the seller at the time the contract was made.
4   True: the silk is still to be manufactured by the seller after the contract was made. This contract also operates as an agreement to sell under s5(3). The contract becomes a contract of sale when the silk is made.
5   False: the glasses are considered free offers and for promotion purposes. This is not governed by the SGA 1979.

Feedback on learning activity 6.2

- Cleaning materials: these are goods and do not fall within the 1982 Act.
- Energy supplies: these would fall within the 1982 Act.
- Animals: these are goods and do not fall within the 1982 Act.
- Office cleaning services: these fall within the 1982 Act.

6

You will note from the previous part of this session that where the above are 'goods' they fall within the SGA.

Feedback on self-assessment question 6.2

1   True: this falls within Part I 1982 SOGAS as being a contract for the supply of goods.
2   False: this is a hire contract and falls within Part I 1982 Act.
3   True: the materials will fall within the 1982 Act Part I but the decorating does fall within Part II.
4   True: this is a hire of services of a lawyer and falls within Part II of 1982 Act.
5   True: where the fencing is supplied as a service. If the fencing is actually sold to the construction company then it will fall within the SGA 1979.

Feedback on learning activity 6.3

Your answer should include contracts such as buying a newspaper, your bus ticket, which would fall within SGA, and if you have had painters decorate your home or taken the advice of a lawyer, or had an architect design your new kitchen: these would fall within SOGAS. Did you manage to make a list of any contracts that your organisation has entered into? These could be the lease of office equipment such as the photocopy machine, the fax machine, computers, which fall within the SOGAS. Perhaps the machinery has a service agreement for regular service. This would fall within the SOGAS too. Maybe your organisation has just purchased new desks for the office. This would fall within the SGA.

The intention of this learning activity is to ensure that you are clear about the difference between the types of contracts. If you are having any difficulty, revisit and refresh your memory on the definition of the types of contract under each of the statutes.

Feedback on self-assessment question 6.3

In the first scenario, James enters into a contract for the purchase of the VM car. This is a contract for the sale of goods by CarFU to James and will therefore fall within the Sale of Goods Act 1979. On the other hand, the contract of hire falls within the 1982 Supply of Goods and Services Act 1982. It will be governed by Part I of this Act as a contract for hire.

In the second scenario the first contract which is mentioned is the contract of employment. From the studies of this section you should know that such a contract does not fall within either the SGA or SOGAS. The leasing of the new office equipment from Modcube falls within the SOGAS as a leasing contract. Finally, taking the old furniture to the charity shop does not fall within either of the Acts as it is not a contract for the sale of goods, nor is it for supply; it is similar to a gift for no consideration.

6

6

Implied terms under SGA and SOGAS statutes

Introduction

In study session 6 you were looking at the difference between the Sale of Goods Act 1979 (SGA) and the Supply of Goods and Services Act 1982 (SOGAS). In study session 2 you studied pre-contractual representations and contractual statements, such as conditions, warranties and innominate terms. You should revisit that session to refresh your memory because in this session you will be looking at implied terms that apply in contracts for the sale of goods under the SGA and contracts for the supply of goods and services under the SOGAS.

> 'A store's best advertisement is the service its goods give, for upon such service rest the future and the goodwill of the store.'
> **James Cash Penney**

7

Session learning objectives

After completing this session you should be able to:

7.1 Describe the implied terms under the SGA 1979 (as amended).
7.2 Explain the effect of Part One of the SOGAS Act 1982.
7.3 Describe the category of transaction covered by Part II of SOGAS 1982.

Unit content coverage

This study session covers the following topics from the official CIPS unit content document:

Learning outcome

Distinguish between the statutes relating to sale of goods and the supply of goods and services in specific circumstances and apply those rules to given practical situations.

Learning objective

2.2 Recognise the protection provided by implied conditions and warranties contained in the Sale of Goods Act 1979 (as amended) and the Supply of Goods and Services Act 1982.
   • S12 – S15 Sale of Goods Act
   • Part one and Part two Supply of Goods and Services Act

Prior knowledge

Level 4, Developing Contracts, study session 14, or equivalent material, and also, within this course book, study sessions 1 – 6.

7

Timing

You should set aside about 5 hours to read and complete this session, including learning activities, self-assessment questions, the suggested further reading (if any) and the revision question.

7.1 Implied terms under the Sale of Goods Act 1979 and the Supply of Goods and Services Act 1982

Learning activity 7.1

Review study session 2 and refresh your memory on express and implied terms. Describe the difference between express and implied terms. As the remedy available in the event of a breach of contract depends on the type of term, describe the legal meaning of each of the terms 'conditions' and 'warranties'.

Feedback on page 110

Remember in study session 2 you looked at statements made in the course of negotiating an agreement. You will recall that these statements may be:

- pre-contractual, that is, representation; or
- contractual, that is, terms of the contract which in turn may be conditions or warranties.

It is important to remember the difference between conditions and warranties, as the remedy available depends on the type of term.

Now you are going to look at terms implied into contracts for the sale of goods by the Sale of Goods Act 1979 (as amended). The 1979 Act does not define a condition, but in line with your previous study of conditions it is a contractual term of major importance. A breach of a condition gives rise to a rejection of the goods and to treat the contract as repudiated.

Section 61 of the 1979 Act defines a warranty as a term within a contract which is minor. A breach of warranty gives rise to a claim for damages.

The 1979 Act does not distinguish between conditions and warranties and sometimes parties to a contract will use the term 'warranty' when it is a condition. The words used by the parties are important but if there is any doubt the court will look at the contract and all circumstances to decide the intentions of the parties. The court will also decide the effect of the breach on the parties. From previous study in study session 2 you will recall that this is the concept of innominate terms.

Terms implied by the Sale of Goods Act 1979

In some contracts for the sale of goods the parties attempt to cover every situation and eventuality. However, many parties in contracts for the sale of goods deal only with the subject matter and the price. The provisions of the 1979 Act are designed to fill the gaps by implied terms and other rules. The rules relating to the passing of property and damages is covered in the next study session. The question of time and delivery is discussed in study session 8. We are now going to look at implied terms under ss12–15 of the 1979 Act. You must remember that the 1979 Act applies only to contracts for the sale of goods. Also ss12, 13 and 15 apply to both contracts 'in the course of business' and private sales. However, s14 applies only to contracts 'in the course of business'.

Section 12 (1): implied condition as to title or right to sell

Unless the circumstances indicate a different intention, s12(1) provides that there is an implied condition that in a contract of sale the seller has a right to sell the goods and in an agreement to sell the seller will have a right to sell the goods at the time when the property is to pass to the buyer. This right is interpreted as the seller having freedom to sell the goods. See the case of *Niblett Ltd* v *Confectioners' Materials Co* [1921] where the defendants sold tins of 'Nissly Brand' condensed milk to the plaintiff. Nestle obtained an injunction preventing the resale of the tins as they infringed Nestle's copyright. The Court of Appeal held that the defendants had breached s12 as they did not have the freedom to sell the product.

Section 13 (1): implied condition – sale by description

This section provides that where there is a contract for the sale of goods by description, there is an implied condition that the goods will correspond with the description.

Definition of sale by description

- Where a buyer has never seen the goods and buys from a description, such as a mail order purchase.
- Where a buyer purchases goods over the counter in a shop or self service store, that is, where the goods are seen, even examined, because the goods are described on the package.

See the case of *Beale* v *Taylor* [1967] where the defendant advertised a car for sale as being a 1961 Triumph Herald 1200. The defendant believed the description. The claimant read the ad and visited the defendant to examine the car. During the inspection the claimant noticed a disc stating 1200. The claimant purchased the car. Later he discovered the car was made up of the rear of a 1200 car welded to the front of an older model. The welding was unsatisfactory and the car unroadworthy. The Court of Appeal held that there was a breach of implied condition s13.

It is necessary for the buyer to show that it was the intention of the parties that the buyer relied on the description. See the case of *Harlingdon Ltd* v *Christopher Hull Fine Art Ltd* [1990] where Hull was asked to sell two oil paintings described as being by Munter, a German expressionist. Hull did not know of this expressionist school. He contacted Harlingdon who were specialists in that field. Harlingdon sent an expert to examine the paintings. Hull made it clear he was not an expert. After the inspection Harlingdon bought one of the paintings which turned out to be a forgery. Harlingdon sued under s13 but the Court of Appeal held his claim failed as he had not relied on the description but bought it after expert examination. See

7

also the case of *Ojjeh* v *Galerie Moderne Ltd* [1998]. In this case Ojjeh was a collector and purchased purple Lalique glass mascots from the Galerie Moderne. Waller was the manager of the Galerie and an expert and dealer in Lalique glass. He confirmed that the purple colouring had been carried out by the manufacturers. Ojjeh relied on this and bought the glass. It turned out later that the statement was not true. Ojjeh raised an action against the Galerie. The court held that the Galerie were in breach of s13 Sale of Goods Act 1979 and held them liable as Waller had used his personal reputation in making the statement and Ojjeh had relied on it.

S13 is strictly applied. This means that buyers can reject the goods even on trivial grounds because it is considered a breach of condition. However, under s15A 1997 Act (inserted by the Sale and Supply of Goods Act 1994) the consumer buyer retains the right of rejection where the breach is only slight but the business buyer loses this right and has to sue for loss if any.

Under s13, description means statements that identify the goods. See the case of *Reardon Smith Line* v *Yngvar Hansen-Tangen* [1976]. In this case the buyer ordered a ship which was described in the contract as No 354 from Osaka Zosen shipyard. Although the ship conformed to the buyer's specification it was in fact built in another shipyard. The buyer tried to reject the ship but the Privy Council held that the buyer could not reject the ship as the statements about the number and shipyard were not part of the description of the ship. This is different from statements such as misrepresentations that induce the buyer to buy. You can revisit study session 3 on vitiating factors, which includes misrepresentation. S13 is closely linked with the next, s14.

Section 14: implied conditions of satisfactory quality and fitness for purpose – do not apply to private sales, only to sales 'in the course of business'

S14 is often regarded as the central core of 1979 Act and possibly the most well known. The two implied conditions of satisfactory quality (s14(2)) and fitness for purpose (s14(3)) are the standard by which most purchasers assess the value for money.

Before the Sale and Supply of Goods Act 1994 the phrase used in s14(2) was 'merchantable quality', the reason being that it related to merchant contracts as opposed to consumer contracts. However, the 1994 Act introduced an objective test for quality with the new phrase used in s14(2) now being 'satisfactory quality'. Please remember that this is now the term to use. This terminology is often confused by students, particularly in an examination setting.

Section 14(2) Satisfactory quality

Goods are of satisfactory quality if they meet the standard that a reasonable person would regard as satisfactory, taking account of any description, price and other relevant circumstances.

Although the actual wording of s14(2) refers to satisfactory quality as being an implied term, s14(6) renders it an implied condition. For more on the history of the development of this implied condition we recommend you read *Law for Purchasing and Supply* by Margaret Griffiths and Ivor Griffiths, particularly chapter 7 on implied conditions in sale of goods. Older cases on this subject area are used to assist in interpretation of the new implied condition of satisfactory quality.

'In the course of business'

The importance of s14 lies in the difference between a business sale and a private sale. You might think this distinction is easy but this is not so. The Trade Descriptions Act 1968, which provides for criminal liability, did try to draw boundaries between core and periphery sales. However, in the case of *Stevenson* v *Rogers* [1999] the distinction is no longer relevant in civil law and the Court of Appeal held that all sales by a business are considered 'in the course of business'. In this case Rogers who was an experienced fisherman sold a merchant fishing vessel to Stevenson. This case involved the issue about whether there was an implied condition as to the satisfactory quality of the vessel which in itself depended on whether the sale was in the course of business. The Court of Appeal held that 'in the course of business' should be interpreted widely and at face value as the intention of the legislation was to protect consumers. Therefore any sale by a business would be in the course of business. They held that in this case there had been an implied condition as to the satisfactory quality of the vessel. There is a difficulty with people who are involved in hobbies as in the case of *Blakemore* v *Bellamy* [1982]. In this case a postman's hobby was to refurbish cars. He would then sell the cars. The issue here was whether a hobby could be deemed a business. If so it would mean that all sales would fall within s14 Sale of Goods Act 1979. The question is whether the activity is a hobby or a business. It will depend on the facts of each case.

Liability under s14 is strict and even where the traders are not directly responsible for making the goods or their satisfactory quality, they are held liable for the quality and direct consequential losses. Of course remember that retailers can pass liability back up the distribution chain by including a valid exclusion clause (see study session 2 on exclusion clauses). The business seller should also consider insurance against the risk of liability for defective goods that could cause injury.

Section 14 does not apply:

- where whatever is making the quality unsatisfactory is drawn to the attention of the buyer before the contract is made;
- where the buyer examines the goods before the contract is made and the examination ought to have revealed the unsatisfactory quality;
- in sale by sample which would have been apparent on reasonable examination of the sample.

Section 14(3) Fitness for purpose

This overlaps with the above section on satisfactory quality. Remember that s14 applies only to contracts for sale of goods 'in the course of business'. S14(3) provides that where the buyer makes known expressly or impliedly to the seller any particular purpose for which the goods are being bought, there is an implied condition that the goods supplied under the contract are reasonably fit for that purpose whether or not that is the purpose for

7

which they are commonly supplied. This section will not apply where the circumstances show that the buyer does not rely on or it would be unreasonable for him to rely on the skill or judgment of the seller. We recommend that you read more on this in *Law of Purchasing and Supply* by Margaret Griffiths and Ivor Griffiths in chapter 7 on implied conditions in sale of goods.

Sale of Goods to Consumers Regulations 2002

These regulations implement EU Directive 1999/44/EC. They have made substantial amendments to the 1979 Act: for example, they have set out additional rights for consumers who purchase goods that turn out to be defective. S14 is amended by requiring that the seller delivers goods that conform to the contract of sale. In consumer contracts statements made by the seller, the producer or their representative such as in advertising or labelling about the goods include public statements. This will not apply if the seller shows that at the time the contract was made they were not or could not reasonably have been aware of the statement; before the contract was made the statement had been withdrawn or the buyer's decision to buy was not influenced by the statement.

The 2002 regulations also states that 'producer' means manufacturer of goods, the importer of goods into the European Economic Area or any person purporting to be a producer by placing their name, trade mark or distinctive mark on the goods. S20 of the 2002 regulations amends the rules on passing of risk and acceptance of goods in consumer contracts. This is discussed later in this session.

Section 15: sample

This section of the 1979 Act governs both business and private sales. The purpose of a sample was defined in the case of *Drummond* v *Van Ingen* [1887]. This case defined the purpose of a sample. The definition is 'to present to the eye the real meaning and intention of the parties as regards the subject matter of the contract...the sample speaks for itself. Once a contract by sample is established then s15 provides for two implied conditions:

- the bulk will correspond with the sample in quality;
- the goods will be free from any defect which would be apparent on examination of the sample.

It is in the buyer's interest to inspect goods thoroughly before accepting them.

Self-assessment question 7.1

Read the following scenarios and identify which section of the SGA would apply.

1   James owns a 1998 second-hand car which he advertises for sale in the local newspaper, stating the car is as good as new. Bill purchases the car

(continued on next page)

Self-assessment question 7.1 *(continued)*

from James. Bill takes the car to a local garage who advises that the car is not roadworthy.

2   Anne has a small carpet manufacturing business. One of her major clients chooses a carpet for their new superstore from her book of samples. When the carpet is laid the colour bears no resemblance to the sample.

3   George buys training shoes from his local sports shop. He tells the shop assistant that he is a professional cross-country runner and will be using the trainers in the next cross-country event. After a couple of weeks training in the fields, the stitching comes loose and the shoes start to let water in.

4   Jenny buys a painting from Sofia for £5,000. Unknown to Jenny the painting had been stolen.

Feedback on page 110

7.2   Part I of the Supply of Goods and Services Act 1982 implied terms

In the last section you looked at the implied terms of the SGA 1979 which applies only to contracts for the sale of goods. There are many more situations where goods change hands either temporarily or permanently without a sale taking place, such as hire goods. You might also receive a gift from a manufacturer. Or you may also receive ownership of goods that are part of a separate contract for services, such as service of your central heating. You may need a new pump for your heating system. You acquire title to the pump but as an effect of the contract for services.

The above situations are governed by the Supply of Goods and Services Act 1982. You are now going to consider the implied terms under the 1982 Act, Part I, which governs the following types of contract:

* contracts for work and materials, the supply of goods or the materials used;
* contracts for exchange or barter, hire, rental or leasing.

Part II of the 1982 Act is considered in the next part of this session. Please note that it is important for you to know the difference between contracts under the Sale of Goods Act 1979 and contracts for work and materials under the Supply of Goods and Services Act 1982. We recommend that you revisit study session 6 and refresh your memory on the different types of contract covered under the 1982 Act, for example:

* maintenance contracts;
* building and construction contracts;
* installation and improvement contracts.

The implied terms in the SOGAS are similar to those in the SGA but the sections that apply in the 1982 Act are:

* s2: title;
* s3: description;

- s4: quality and fitness;
- s5: sample.

Section 2: implied condition relating to title

Under s2(1) there is an implied condition that the supplier has a right to transfer the property in the goods to the customer. Cases involving title are less common than those that arise in contracts for the sale of goods under the 1979 Act. Under s2(2) there are two warranties which are implied and these are that:

the goods are free from any charge or incumbrance that has not been disclosed to the customer;

the customer will enjoy quiet possession except where the owner or person who has a charge over the goods has been disclosed. Of course, the customer can take action if he suffers loss as a result of the true owner reclaiming the goods.

Section 3: implied condition relating to description

There is an implied condition that where a seller transfers property in goods by description, the goods will correspond to the description. S3 will apply where a house extension is to be built and the customer agrees with the contractor the detailed specification on the materials.

Section 4 (1): satisfactory quality and fitness for purpose

Where the materials used are dangerous, do not work properly or are unsafe then the supplier is in breach of this condition.

Learning activity 7.2

Revisit the above part on implied terms found in the SGA and then provide a brief description of the similar implied terms found in the 1982 Act. Identify the contracts that are governed by the 1982 Act.

Feedback on page 111

Now complete the following self-assessment question.

Self-assessment question 7.2

Reflect on the above information and consider some contracts within your own organisation. Can you distinguish between contracts of sale and contracts for the supply of services? You should be able to identify which Act governs which type of contract. Can you also recognise any implied terms and conditions?

Feedback on page 111

7.3 Part II of Supply of Goods and Services Act 1982 implied terms

You have studied the 1982 Act Part I and implied terms in the above part of this session. You will now look specifically at the implied terms in Part II of the 1982 Act.

You will recall that Part II governs contracts for supply of services whether or not any transfer of goods is involved.

Learning activity 7.3

Consider your organisation and the various contracts entered into. Can you list some of the contracts for supply of services? Was the contract formed and completed according to the intention of the parties or was there a breach of any of the implied terms and if so, which ones?

Feedback on page 111

Remember that this part of the Act covers contracts for the supplies of services, whether or not there is any transfer of goods is involved. The terms implied into such contracts include:

- care and skill (section 13): this is about the quality of service to be provided in a contract for services. The work must be done with reasonable skill and care. You would expect a higher service from someone with expertise such as a doctor or lawyer;
- time for performance (section 14): where no time is specified then the supplier must complete the work within a reasonable time;
- consideration (section 15): where there is no agreement about price, the customer will pay a reasonable price for the services provided.

Part II does not make it clear whether these implied terms are conditions or warranties. It depends on whether breach of the terms goes to the root of the contract.

Self-assessment question 7.3

Read the following scenario and identify which Part of the 1982 Act will apply and which term, if any, has been breached.

JBG Ltd entered into a contract with Compu Ltd to service the 10 computers in their offices. Compu Ltd performed the service but within two weeks of the service all 10 computers broke down. Compu Ltd refused to come out to rectify the problem saying that the failure was due to the computer operators. Meanwhile Elos builders were 6 months behind with the erection of the extension to JBG's store. JBG also noticed that Elos had used flooring that was not according to the agreed specification.

Feedback on page 112

Revision question

Now try the revision question for this session on page 313.

Summary

Having completed this study session, you should now be able to distinguish between the 1979 SGA and SOGAS 1982 and know the different types of contract governed by which acts. You should be able to identify the different implied terms and whether they are conditions or warranties and which are appropriate in any given situation.

Suggested further reading

Griffiths and Griffiths (2002), part II, chapters 7 and 8.

Smith and Keenan (2003), part 3, chapters 15 and 18.

Feedback on learning activities and self-assessment questions

Feedback on learning activity 7.1

Express terms are terms that are inserted into the contract by the contracting parties. Express terms can take two forms. They can be formally written into the contract such as in standard forms or they can be those verbally agreed between the parties. It is important to know the type of express term as this reflects the remedy available on breach of contract.

Implied terms are those that are never written into the contract but are implied by law. Such terms can be implied by the courts or implied by statute as under the SGA and SOGAS.

The term 'conditions' is used in a contract to describe an important term. This means that if there is a breach of such a term, the injured party can discharge themselves from the contract and sue for damages.

The term 'warranties' in a contract is of lesser importance. It such a term is breached then the injured party has the right to claim damages but not to discharge themselves from the contract.

Whether the term is a condition or warranty depends on the intention of the parties.

Feedback on self-assessment question 7.1

1   This scenario falls within s13 implied condition of description. It is similar to the case of *Beale* v *Taylor* [1967] where it was held that there was a breach of the implied condition. You may wish to contrast this with the case of Harlingdon above where the examination of the goods took place before the contract and was carried out by an expert. The court held that there was no breach of the implied condition. However,

in this present case the examination was after the contract was made. This implied condition applies to business and consumer contracts.

2   This falls within s15 sale by sample. According to s15 the bulk must correspond with the sample. So in this case there has been a breach of an implied condition. This implied condition applies to business and consumer contracts.

3   This scenario falls within s14: satisfactory quality and fitness for purpose. The buyer George told the shop assistant what he needed the shoes for. In this case there has been a breach of both implied conditions. You should mention that s14 does apply as the contract is 'in the course of business'. Remember that s14 only applies to business contracts and not private contracts. Also the retailer can pass the liability up the supply chain to the manufacturer.

4   This scenario concerns a breach of s12 implied condition relating to title. In this situation Sofia had no title to sell but Jenny as an innocent buyer has an action for breach of condition.

In each of the scenarios you should include that breach of a condition the customer/buyer can treat the contract as repudiated. In the case of breach of a warranty the buyer only has the right to sue for damages.

Feedback on learning activity 7.2

Once you have revisited the part on the implied terms in 1979 Act you will be able to carry out this activity. You should provide a brief description of the sections of the 1982 Act and the applicable terms. This will include s2 title, s3 description, s4 quality and fitness, and s5 sample. You should state the contracts governed by the 1982 Act that fall within Part I are: contracts for work and materials, the supply of goods or the materials used and contracts for exchange or barter, hire, rental or leasing. Contracts within Part II are contracts for the supply of services.

Feedback on self-assessment question 7.2

Some contracts that you might list will be purchase of office furniture where the SGA applies; contract for cleaning services where SOGAS applies. Your organisation may also be involved in contracts for computer repairs or refurbishment of office premises. These fall within the 1982 Act. Your list will not be exhaustive as long as you are able to categorise the different types of contract.

After this, look at some of the situations before and during the contracts. Take the refurbishment contract, did your organisation and the contractor reach agreement on the detailed specification? Was the work carried out satisfactorily? Did any problems arise about quality? Recognise that this would fall within s4 of the 1982 Act.

Feedback on learning activity 7.3

Your list could include:

*   contract for supply of cleaning materials;
*   contract for cleaning services;

- contract for lease of office equipment;
- contract for the extension to office premises.

Feedback on self-assessment question 7.3

You should identify that the servicing of the computers is a contract for the supply of services and falls within Part II of the 1982 Act. There has been a breach of s13 relating to skill and care. Explain that the service should be done with reasonable skill and care and that the level of care and skill should be appropriate to a person in that profession. Regarding the erection of the extension, this is also a contract for services and may have breached s14 relating to time for performance. The question will be whether 6 months is too long or whether there were other circumstances. However, where there is no agreement about time for performance, then the contract must be completed within a reasonable time. Finally, for the flooring, this falls within Part I of the Act, being a contract for the supply of goods and services, the goods being the flooring and being a side effect of the contract for services. Where the specification has been agreed as in this case, there has been a breach of s4 satisfactory quality.

7

Transfer of property, risk and title

'I buy when other people are selling.'
J Paul Getty

Introduction

In study sessions 6 and 7 you studied the Sale of Goods Act 1979 (SGA) and Supply of Goods and Services Act 1982 (SOGAS) and what types of contract they govern. Throughout these sessions you have heard the words property, title, risk, transfer of property and goods.

In this session you are going to examine the passage of title to goods. This is governed by ss16–19 SGA. However, to be able to interpret and apply these rules you must be able to distinguish between the different types of goods. You have already looked at the different categories of goods in study session 6 and we recommend that you revisit that session and refresh your memory.

8

Session learning objectives

After completing this session you should be able to:

8.1 Distinguish between the different categories of goods.
8.2 Describe sections 16–20 of the SGA 1979.
8.3 Distinguish between delivery and payment.
8.4 Describe the effects of acceptance of goods on remedies for breach.

Unit content coverage

This study session covers the following topics from the official CIPS unit content document:

Learning outcome

Distinguish between the statutes relating to sale of goods and the supply of goods and services in specific circumstances and apply those rules to given practical situations.

Learning objective

2.3 Differentiate between ownership, risk, delivery and acceptance of goods and examine when each passes under the Sale of Goods Act 1979.
  • S16 – S20 Sale of Goods Act
  • S30 Delivery
  • S31 Instalment deliveries
  • S34 – S35 Acceptance of goods

Prior knowledge

Study sessions 1 – 7.

Timing

You should set aside about 5 hours to read and complete this session, including learning activities, self-assessment questions, the suggested further reading (if any) and the revision question.

8.1 Different categories of goods

8

Learning activity 8.1

The rules governing passing of property depend primarily on the type of goods in the contract. For this exercise we ask you to make a list of goods and the category to which they belong. You should also think of your organisation and what types of goods are involved in the different types of contract of sale or supply of services.

Feedback on page 126

The common law rules as to whether the ownership or property in goods has passed to the buyer from the seller under a contract of sale have been incorporated into ss16–19 SGA.

You need to be able to distinguish between specific, unascertained and ascertained goods to interpret and apply ss16–19 SGA. At the time a contract for the sale of goods is made the goods are either specific or unascertained.

Specific goods

Under s61 SGA the definition of specific goods is goods identified and agreed on at the time the contract of sale is made – for example, when you pick loose potatoes at the supermarket, bag them and take them to the checkout desk. These are specific goods because they are identified and agreed on at the time the contract is made, that is, at the checkout desk.

Unascertained goods

You now know what specific goods are. Therefore it follows that any goods that are not specific and cannot be identified at the time the sale is made are classed as unascertained goods. For example, if you are a builder and you buy 10 tons of gravel from a pile of 100 tons stored at the builder's merchant, the precise 10 tons in the pile of gravel cannot be exactly identified so the 10 tons of gravel are unascertained. As soon as it is separated and weighed it becomes ascertained. There is a difference between specific goods and ascertained goods. Remember that specific goods are identified at the time the contract is made. Ascertained goods start out as unascertained at the time the contract is made: they never fall within the class of specific goods and once identified they become ascertained.

Self-assessment question 8.1

Read the following short scenarios and explain what category the goods fall into.

Jane has been invited to a dinner party and decides to purchase a new dress for the occasion. She goes to her local designer shop and tries on a variety of styles. She is uncertain which one to choose. After a while she decides on the red dress. She takes it to the cash desk and pays for the dress.

John is a local vet and needs straw for bedding for some of the animals. He visits his local farmer, Fred, who has already harvested his crop but it has not yet been separated into straw bales. John tells Fred that he needs six bales of straw. Fred tells John that six bales will cost £60. John pays £60 and Fred agrees to deliver six bales to the vet's surgery later that week.

Feedback on page 127

8

8.2 Sections 16–20 of the Sale of Goods Act 1979

In section 8.1 above you have again looked at the different categories of goods.

In this session you are going to look at two important issues in relation to sale of goods contracts. The first relates to the time at which property passes to the buyer. The use of different words can cause confusion to students. Where possible we have made reference to the different words used to mean the same thing. For example: title, property, legal ownership. The second issue relates to risk and risk avoidance.

Title or property in goods: meaning legal ownership

Property in the goods or legal ownership does not necessarily mean that the buyer has actual possession of the goods, or even paid for them. In some circumstances the buyer may have possession and have paid for the goods but does not have property or ownership of the goods. This happens in hire purchase agreements where you have possession of the hired goods but you do not own or have property in the goods until you pay the final instalment. So until the final instalment is paid you have no right to sell the goods.

Why is it so important to know when property passes?

This is important because it is all about risk and who will be liable or who will bear the loss in the event of something going wrong: for example, when the goods are destroyed or damaged.

Under s16 SGA no property or ownership passes until the goods are ascertained. Ss17 and 18 are discussed in more detail below.

115

S19 provides that where there is a contract for the sale of specific goods or the goods are subsequently appropriated the seller may reserve the right of disposal of the goods until the condition is fulfilled. This means even where the goods are delivered to the buyer; the property in the goods does not pass until the conditions are fulfilled. S19 allows for retention of title clauses or a Romalpa clause, which were discussed in study session 2 and are referred to below.

S20(1) SGA provides that unless otherwise agreed the goods remain at the seller's risk until the property in them passes to the buyer. When property passes to the buyer, the buyer takes on the risk whether delivery of the goods has been made or not.

Rules have been introduced by the SGA to assist in understanding when property passes.

Section 17 general rule under the SGA

This general rule relates to specific goods. You already know that s61 SGA defines specific goods as goods identified and agreed on at the time the contract of sale is made. So according to s17 the property in specific goods passes to the buyer when the parties intend it to pass. In the example of purchasing goods from the supermarket, the time of passing of ownership in the goods is clear. The ownership of the goods passes to the buyer when the goods are paid for at the counter.

However, there may be no express agreement as to when ownership passes or the intention of the parties regarding ownership or property passing is often silent or unclear. To cover such situations the SGA introduced rules under s18.

Section 18: the five rules

Where it is difficult to prove the intention of the parties s18 provides some guidelines. There are five s18 rules and they are mutually exclusive. Rules 1–4 relate to specific goods and rule 5 to unascertained goods.

Rule 1: specific goods in a deliverable state

This relates to specific goods as defined by s61(1) SGA, which are goods specific and in a deliverable state. Rule 1 means that there must be an unconditional contract, that is, with no conditions still to be fulfilled by the buyer before title or property or ownership will pass.

See the case of *Kursell* v *Timber Operators & Contractors Ltd* [1927] where the plaintiffs sold to the defendants trees growing on an estate, which conformed to certain measurement requirements. The buyers were to cut and remove such trees when they reached the required measurements, but this must be within 15 years. The court held that the property had not passed to the defendants as the goods were not sufficiently identified by the contract to enable them to be ascertained at the time the contract was made. They were not specific goods and did not fall within rule 1 of s18 SGA.

Where goods are not in a deliverable state, the buyer can reject them, for example, where they have a defect.

'Deliverable state' means that the seller should not need to do anything to the goods before the buyer is obliged to take them. For example, if something is attached to the land then it will not be in a deliverable state until it is severed from the land. See the case of *Underwood Ltd* v *Burgh Castle Brick & Cement Syndicate* [1922] where a machine was bolted to the floor and the contract required that the seller remove it from the building and deliver it on to the train. The machine was damaged in the removal process. It was held that the goods were not in a deliverable state at the time of the contract so rule 1 did not apply.

The parties can override rule 1 by agreeing to the time that ownership passes. See the case of *Ward* v *Bignall* [1967], where it was agreed between the parties that ownership could not pass until the price was paid in full. Later, you will see that s19 allows for this.

Rule 2: specific goods but not in a deliverable state

For rule 2 to apply, notice must be given to the buyer that the goods have been put in a deliverable state by the seller. Notice means knowledge and it need not come from the seller, it can be from a third party.

Rule 3: specific goods in a deliverable state but still to be weighed

This is where the seller is still bound to weigh, measure or test the goods in order for the seller to ascertain or calculate the price. Testing does not mean for quality. Property in the goods will not pass to the buyer until the weighing, measuring or testing is carried out by the seller. The buyer must have notice of this having been done. Rule 3 does not apply where the buyer is to ascertain the price. See the case of *Nanka-Bruce* v *Commonwealth Trust* [1925] where the buyer agreed to weigh the cocoa to establish the price of the original contract. It was held that rule 3 did not apply. The parties of course can override this rule by expressly stating when title is to pass.

Rule 4: specific goods 'on approval' or 'sale or return' basis

Goods 'on approval'

This means that the buyer is concerned with the quality of the goods and whether they will be suitable for their particular purpose before buying. Property will pass to the buyer if they:

- indicate their approval or acceptance of the goods; or
- act as if they are adopting the contract, for example, where they resell the goods to a third party;
- use the goods for longer than necessary to assess suitability. See the case of *Ferrier* [1944] where in a fixed-term contract the buyer could not return the goods because they were seized by sheriff officers along with the buyer's property and kept for 4 weeks. Also, in a fixed-term contract, property will pass to the buyer if they retain goods without rejecting them beyond the contract fixed period: see the case of *Poole* v *Smith Car Sales Ltd* [1962]. Where it is not a fixed-term contract, property will also pass where the buyer keeps the goods beyond a reasonable time.

8

Goods on 'sale or return'

This is where the buyer is not committed to the purchase until they sell on to a sub-buyer.

In both the above situations the goods are delivered in response to the buyer's request. The seller must sell if the buyer indicates acceptance but the buyer is under no obligation to accept the offer. Of course, if the buyer did not request the goods then they can be treated as a gift as they are unsolicited goods.

As with the other rules, the parties can override this rule by expressly agreeing to the time when property passes.

Rule 5: unascertained goods

This rule applies in a contract for the sale of the following type of goods:

- goods wholly unascertained;
- unascertained goods from an identified source;
- future goods by description.

This rule is subject to s16 SGA, which has been discussed previously and states that no property passes until the goods are ascertained.

Rule 5 applies where the goods are unconditionally appropriated to the contract. This is where the seller earmarks the goods for the contract and it is unconditional. This means the seller must not have exercised a right to retain ownership under s19. The buyer must also assent to the appropriation, which is usually by accepting delivery of the goods.

Learning activity 8.2

Describe the meaning of 'property' and consider a situation where someone may have possession and or paid but not have property of the goods. Briefly explain each of rules in s18.

Feedback on page 127

New rules relating to unascertained goods were introduced by the Sale of Goods (Amendment) Act 1995 s20A. This provides that where the purchaser buys a specific quantity of goods from an identified bulk source and has paid for some or all of it, the buyer becomes co-owner of the bulk. The buyer is therefore protected if the seller becomes insolvent.

You have now seen that where it is unclear as to when property passes, the s18 rules provide guidelines for the various categories of goods. You know that the importance of establishing when property passes is to know where the risk lies or who bears the loss in the event of goods being destroyed or defective.

However, you also know that the parties can override the rules by expressly providing for the time when ownership passes. S19 allows the parties to insert retention of title clause, also known as a Romalpa clause. We suggest that you revisit study session 2 on retention of title to refresh your memory.

Risk avoidance

A point already mentioned above is about the importance of knowing when property passes. This is because knowing when ownership passes helps in establishing where the risk lies or who bears the loss where something goes wrong with the contract, for example, where the goods are lost, destroyed or defective.

In general when title passes, risk passes. When entering into a contract the seller will want to ensure that the risk is avoided or limited. Where the risk cannot be avoided then it would be best to consider insuring against the risk.

You should revisit study session 2 on exclusion and indemnity clauses and the Unfair Contract Terms Act 1977 to refresh your memory.

Exclusion and limitation clauses

You will recall from previous studies that it is possible in a commercial contract to exclude or limit liability. You cannot exclude liability for death or personal injury. It is not always possible to exclude or limit liability in consumer contracts. Also, the contractual clause must be reasonable in all the circumstances. See the case of *George Mitchell (Chesterfield) Ltd* v *Finney Lock Seeds Ltd* [1983]. This was a landmark case. It was the last case heard by Lord Denning. George ordered cabbage seed from Finney. The seed was defective as the cabbages had no heart and the leaves turned in. Although the seed only cost £192 the actual loss was £61,000, being one year's production from the 63 acres planted. George Mitchell did not have any insurance. George sued Finney, who defended the claim on the basis of an exclusion clause which limited their liability to the cost of the seed or its replacement. The court held that Finney was liable. In reaching this decision the court looked at the test of reasonableness and whether the exclusion clause was fair and reasonable and it was held that it was not fair and reasonable to allow the seed merchants to rely on the clause to limit their liability.

It is possible to insert an indemnity clause that ensures that any supplier of goods or services that are defective or ineffective can pass the liability down the supply chain, for example, to the manufacturer. This clause applies whether the liability is in contract, tort or under Consumer Protection Act 1987 which relates to product liability. This is discussed later on.

Force majeure clause

This was discussed in study session 2. We recommend that you revisit this study session to refresh your memory. Remember, this is the mechanism whereby the parties to a contract may provide for a specific remedy in the event that the contract cannot be performed or becomes too onerous.

Separating risk and title

You know from previous studies that a contract can consist of implied and express terms. In relation to the passing of title the parties to a contract can insert an express term which overrides the s18 rules. This means that the parties can expressly provide for the time at which title and risk pass. These can be at different times.

For example, the parties to a contract can expressly state that title does not pass until the goods are paid for but that the risk does pass to the buyer whether payments are made or not. This means that the risk is on the buyer and they should insure against any risk. The buyer is not the owner in this situation but the bailee. Bailment and agency are discussed in study session 11. The separation of title and risk can work the other way with the risk remaining with the seller. Whether it is the buyer or the seller who is bailee, they must take reasonable care of the goods.

8

Self-assessment question 8.2

Read the following short questions/statements and provide a brief answer.

1   Why is it important to establish when property passes?
2   Discuss two ways in which the parties to a contract can override the s18 SGA rules.
3   A sells his second-hand car to B. A agrees to change the tyres before delivering the car to B. Discuss when the property passes.
4   Alum Ltd agreed to sell the heavy duty cutting machine to Newfound Ltd. At the time of the contract the machine was bolted to the floor at Alum's factory. Alum agreed to remove the machine and have it delivered to Newfound. The machine was damaged on removal. Alum state that the property had passed to Newfound at the time of the contract and they have to accept the machine. Is Alum correct? Discuss when property passes in this situation.

Feedback on page 128

8.3   The difference between delivery and payment

Learning activity 8.3

Review the concepts of transfer of possession and the passage of title or property. Describe two situations where the buyer may have possession but not title. Can you identify a situation such as this within your organisation?

Feedback on page 128

Before moving on to consider the difference between delivery and payment you should ensure that you understand the concept of transfer of possession and passing of title or property or legal ownership. You know from the above information that having possession is not the same as having title and indeed you may have possession of goods but not the ownership.

Possession means the physical control of the goods. So in the hire purchase agreement you have possession or the physical control of the goods from the start but will not own the goods until the last payment is made. In this situation the finance company do not have possession but they still own the goods until you make the last payment.

What about the situation where the contract is one for repairs? Take the situation where you put your car into the garage for repairs or a service. You no longer have possession of your car, the garage has. However, you still own the car. You are now going to be looking at delivery, which is concerned with the transfer of possession.

Delivery

S61 SGA defines the meaning of delivery as ' the voluntary transfer of possession from one person to another'. Delivery is very important in commercial contracts because normally when the goods are delivered by the seller to the buyer, the seller has a right to payment from the buyer.

Under s29 SGA the delivery of the goods and the payment of the price are concurrent conditions. However, as you know from the above study, the parties can expressly agree to the contrary.

Delivery need not be carried out only by the seller. The goods can be delivered by a carrier. Under s32 SGA delivery to the carrier is prima facie delivery to the buyer. Where goods are being delivered by sea the seller is under an obligation to tell the buyer so that the buyer can arrange insurance. The question of carriage of goods by sea is discussed later in study session 19.

Place of delivery

The place of delivery can be expressly or impliedly agreed by the parties. The parties can decide on whether the buyer will collect the goods or the seller will deliver. Where there is no agreement, delivery is deemed to be the seller's place of business or if none, the seller's residence. If the contract is for the sale of specific goods that are held at another place, the delivery is deemed to be at that place. Where the goods at the time of the contract are in the possession of a third party, there is no delivery until the third party acknowledges to the buyer that the goods are now held on behalf of the buyer.

Time of delivery

In previous study sessions you have already heard the phrase 'time is of the essence'. Time is particularly important in commercial transactions. In commerce the buyer may be buying in order to sell on to another buyer under another contract for example wholesale, retail or contract in the production process. So in commercial transactions it is usually assumed that 'time is of the essence'. The parties can expressly agree a delivery date and if the seller fails to meet the delivery date then the buyer is entitled to reject the goods. See the case of *Rickards* v *Oppenheim* [1950] where the seller agreed to build a car for the buyer with delivery due on 20 March. The car was not ready on time but the buyer allowed the seller to continue with the project. At the end of June the buyer told the seller that if the car was not ready in four weeks he would repudiate the contract. The car was not ready.

Where there is no agreement as to delivery date it is the seller's responsibility to deliver the goods to the buyer within a reasonable period. The question of reasonable is one of fact and depends on the circumstances in each case.

Delivery of the incorrect quantity

There is an obligation on the seller to deliver the correct quantity ordered. Minor differences are tolerated. See the case *Shipton, Anderson & Co* v *Weil Bros & Co* [1912] where the contract was for the seller to deliver 4,950 tons of wheat. The seller actually delivered in excess of that ordered, namely, 55 lb too much. The excess was worth 20p in a contract worth £40,000. The court held that the excess was of no effect as too slight.

Consumer buyer

S30 SGA regulates the delivery of an incorrect amount where the buyer is a consumer, for example:

* where less than the contracted amount, the buyer can reject them but if accepted then the contract price must be paid for them;
* where larger than the contracted amount, the buyer can accept the contracted goods and reject the rest or reject the lot.

Commercial buyer

The parties in commercial transaction often include a clause stipulating an acceptable difference or tolerance level in the amount delivered. A commercial buyer cannot reject the goods, no matter whether the seller delivers more or less than the contracted amount if it is so slight that it would be unreasonable to do so. This distinction was introduced by the Sale and Supply of Goods Act 1994.

Instalment delivery

This is governed by s31 SGA and unless otherwise stated the buyer is not bound to accept delivery of goods by instalment.

Where the contracting parties agree that the goods are to be delivered by instalments that are paid separately and the seller delivers defective goods in relation to one or more instalments whether there is a breach depends on the circumstances of each case.

Payment

As you learned earlier under s29 SGA, the delivery of the goods and the payment of the price are concurrent conditions. However, you also know that the parties can expressly agree to the contrary.

Under s10 SGA time is not of the essence for payment unless there is an intention to the contrary in the contract. So, although payment becomes due when the goods are delivered or when the parties agree that it is due, a failure by the buyer to make payment is not a breach that entitles the seller to repudiate the contract but the seller would have a right to sue for damages for non-payment.

Remedies are discussed in more detail below.

Self-assessment question 8.3

Read the following short case study and answer the questions.

Budget Builders is a construction company. They are building a block of 12 flats in the city centre. Gilpa Merchants agree to sell to Budget Builders bathroom suites at a cost of £400 each. The suites are to be delivered in four instalments of three suites per instalment. More than half of the bathroom suites were damaged. Gilpa Merchants also agreed to deliver 100 tons of sand and cement at 10 tons per week. The sand and cement was to be in the ratio of one part sand to three parts cement. The last instalment was found to be three parts sand to one part cement. Budget Builders are now refusing to pay Gilpa for the bathroom suites or the sand and cement.

1 Advise Budget Builders whether they have a right to repudiate the contract for the bathroom suites.
2 Advise Budget Builders on whether they have a right to repudiate the sand and cement contract.

Feedback on page 128

8

8.4 The effects of acceptance of goods on remedies for breach

Now that you have looked at delivery and payment you are going to learn about the rights of the buyer to examine the goods and when acceptance takes place. Remedies available to buyer and seller depend on when the goods are accepted.

Examination

Section 34 SGA provides the buyer with a statutory right to examine the goods. The buyer must be given a reasonable time in which to examine the goods, unless there is an agreement to the contrary between the parties. Under s29 SGA the delivery of the goods and the payment of the price are concurrent conditions. However, as you know from the above study, the parties can expressly agree to the contrary.

Examination is only to see if the goods conform to the contract and if sale by sample to compare the bulk with the sample.

Acceptance

Under s35 the buyer is deemed to have accepted the goods:

- when they have intimated to the seller that they have accepted them; or
- when the goods have been delivered to the buyer and they act in such a way which is inconsistent with the seller's ownership of the goods;
- where the buyer retains the goods beyond a reasonable time without telling the seller;
- only after they have had a reasonable opportunity of examining the goods where they are delivered to them but they have not previously been examined by them.

The buyer cannot make a claim under the SGA:

- if they had examined the goods before buying and the defect was obvious; or
- the defect was pointed out to them; or
- they were told the goods did not meet the description on the packaging; or
- they were told the goods were not fit for the purpose for which they were buying them.

A consumer buyer has responsibilities and if they have accepted the goods they cannot claim a refund. However, the buyer still has a right to compensation if the goods are faulty.

The buyer has a 'reasonable' time to return the goods if they are faulty. So the buyer should try out the goods as soon as possible after purchase.

If the buyer merely changes their mind about the goods after they have purchased them then they have no rights under the SGA. However, in practice, some shops do give exchanges or credit notes, but they have no obligation to do so.

Under s35 the buyer is not deemed to have accepted the goods merely because they have asked for them to be repaired or delivered to another person under a sub-sale.

Learning activity 8.4

Consider the main provisions of ss34 and 35 SGA relating to examination and acceptance. Think of the situation where goods purchased are found to be faulty. Describe in what circumstances you would be entitled to reject them.

Feedback on page 129

The seller may try to get the buyer to waive his right to examine. Where the goods are delivered to the buyer's home they buyer may be asked to sign a document that states 'received in good condition'. Even although the buyer signs such a document they still have rights under the SGA as amended by the Sale and Supply of Goods Act 1994. In practice if you are ever in such a situation you can sign 'received but not examined'.

Where a non-consumer or commercial buyer signs such a document then they may be waiving their rights under the Act so they should be careful about signing such a document.

Remedies of the buyer

You now consider the remedies available to the buyer where the seller is in breach of contract. The buyer can:

- reject the goods, that is, a right to repudiate the contract and reject the goods;
- claim damages for non delivery;
- raise an action for specific performance: this is at discretion of the courts.

The circumstances in which the buyer can reject the goods are discussed above. Damages and specific performance have been discussed in study session 2. We suggest that you revisit that session and refresh your memory.

Remedies of the seller

These include:

- Action for damages where the seller has not been paid.
- Lien on the goods – the unpaid seller has a statutory power to sell.
- Stoppage in transit – this action can only be taken where the seller is unpaid, the goods are not in the seller's possession and the goods are in transit. This action does not rescind the contract or give the title in the goods back to the seller. See the case of *Booth SS Co Ltd* v *Cargo Fleet Iron Co Ltd* [1916].

The seller can take personal action against the buyer for the price or for damage for non-acceptance of the goods by the buyer. The passing of property and the conduct of the buyer will determine what action the seller can take.

8

Self-assessment question 8.4

Read the following sentences and answer true/false.

1   If you have accepted the goods you cannot claim a refund.
2   You must return the goods immediately if they are faulty.
3   If you buy goods at an auction and there is a notice stating that the SGA does not apply, then this means that the SGA does not apply.
4   You have bought a tea set at the local car boot sale. When you get home you notice that some of the cups are damaged. You can reject them under the SGA.
5   You bought a bag of fruit from the local supermarket. On getting home you notice the fruit is rotten and not able to be eaten. You only manage

(continued on next page)

Revision question

Now try the revision question for this session on page 313.

Summary

This study session has covered all the important issues surrounding transfer of property, risk and title, which includes the different categories of goods, the definitions of the words used; the effects that the passage of title has on a contract and the effects on remedies available in the event of breach of contract. Having studied this session and in particular study session 6 you will now be able to apply this knowledge to practical situations.

Suggested further reading

Griffiths and Griffiths (2002), part II, chapter 10.

Smith and Keenan (2003), part 3, chapter 16.

Feedback on learning activities and self-assessment questions

Feedback on learning activity 8.1

In this exercise you should first of all list the types of category into which goods fall. This includes existing goods, future goods, specific goods, unascertained goods and ascertained goods. Once you have made a list of these you should give a brief explanation of the meaning of the category and try to name goods that would fall into that particular category.

- Existing goods: office furniture owned by your organisation which is being sold.
- Future goods: a farmer selling hay to his local stables evenb though he still has to harvest his crop.
- Specific goods: goods that are identified and agreed on at the time the contract is made. For example where the farmer has already harvested his crop and the stable owner picks out the bales of hay for purchase. The stable owner has selected the particular bales of hay he wants to buy.
- Unascertained goods: generic goods such as one kilogram of coffee from a large bag of loose coffee; or goods still to be manufactured by the seller.

8

- Ascertained goods: goods identified after the contract has been made, for example, where the coffee has now been weighed and taken to the checkout desk.

Goods include: clothes, furniture, food, electrical items, animals.

Services include: dry cleaners, travel agents, garages, hairdressers, builders, nurseries, childcare.

The above lists are not exhaustive. Many more could be included.

Feedback on self-assessment question 8.1

In the first scenario you should identify that the red dress falls within the category 'specific' goods as it is selected in the shop and identified at the cash desk when the contract is made.

In the second scenario you should immediately identify that the 'straw' is unascertained goods. John is not able to identify which bales of straw he will be getting. So at the time the contract is made the goods are unascertained. Once the straw is put into six bales they are identified and therefore become ascertained.

Feedback on learning activity 8.2

Your answer should include that property means legal ownership but does not necessarily mean that the buyer has possession of the goods. You can also identify that the buyer may have possession but not ownership as in the case of hire purchase. For example, a person may enter a hire purchase agreement for the purchase of a car. Although they possess the car they do not own it until the last instalment is paid.

The explanation of the five rules are that rules 1–4 relate to specific goods and rule 5 to unascertained goods. The rules are guidelines when the intention of the parties is unclear or not expressly provided for in the contract. Then provide a brief summary of each such as the following.

Rule 1: there must be an unconditional contract for sale of specific goods.

Rule 2: although relating to specific goods it is where they are not in a deliverable state and the buyer must have notice that they have been put in a deliverable state, which notice can be by seller or a third party.

Rule 3: where the specific goods are in a deliverable state but still need to be weighed, tested or measured. This is for cost only and not to test the quality.

Rule 4: this relates to goods on approval or sale or return. Property will pass if the buyer holds on to the goods for longer than the period where there is a fixed term contract or beyond a reasonable time where it is not a fixed period contract.

Rule 5: relates to unascertained goods, whether in whole or part of an identified bulk or future goods described. Describe how s16 provides that no property passes until goods are ascertained.

You should also mention that the parties can override the rules by expressly providing for the point at which property passes.

Feedback on self-assessment question 8.2

1 It is important to establish when property passes as this determines when the risk passes, in other words who bears the risk or who bears the loss. Where the intention is unclear or not expressly stated, the s18 rules are there to guide.
2 The parties can override the s18 rules by expressly providing for the point at which property passes or retaining the goods beyond the fixed term period of the contract without rejecting them or beyond a reasonable time where there is no fixed period.
3 Property passes in this situation when A has changed the tyres and B knows that this has been done, whether notified by A or a third party.
4 The facts of this case are similar to the case of *Underwood Ltd* v *Burgh Castle Brick & Cement* [1922]. Under rule 1 s18 the machine is a specific good and it is not in a deliverable state as it still has to be removed from the floor. Until the machine is removed and the other party notified, the risk stays with Alum.

Feedback on learning activity 8.3

Your answer should include the definition of the meaning of property and that the buyer may have possession of goods but not necessarily ownership. This occurs where you purchase a car under a hire purchase agreement. Your organisation may have purchased goods under a hire purchase agreement. If so, then the goods will be within the organisation but they will not own them until they have paid the final instalment under the hire purchase agreement. In such situations the buyer has no right to sell the goods.

Another situation may be where an individual or organisation may have the goods on the premises, that is, have possession, but they do not and will never own them. This is the situation where you rent a television or photocopy machines.

Feedback on self-assessment question 8.3

The first question relates not only to instalment delivery but to the question of defective goods in one instalment. In this case the parties agreed to instalment delivery. Each of the instalments can be separated and this indicates that the instalments are severable and carry with each a right to payment. Budget Builders must pay for the instalments. However, the issue here is the question of damaged goods being delivered. We are not told whether it is one damaged suite per instalment or all bathroom suites in one instalment. It will be depend very much on the circumstances, but if the damage is all in one delivery Budget Builders can reject the whole consignment. See the case of *Jackson* v *Rotax Motors* [1910]. In this case the claimants supplied motor horns to the defendants and one consignment was rejected by the defendants who alleged they were unmerchantable (this is now known as unsatisfactory). One half of the goods were scratched and dented due to bad packing. The Court of Appeal held that the buyers were entitled to reject the consignment. Of course under the 1979 Sale of Goods Act this case would have fallen within s15 of the 1979 Act, and s15 would have allowed rejection.

In the second question it is a matter of whether the instalments are severable or not. In this instance only the final instalment is defective, being of the incorrect ratio. This is similar to the case of *Maple Flock Co Ltd* v *Universal Furniture Products (Wembley) Ltd* [1934]. In this case the claimants agreed to sell 100 tons of black linsey flock to the defendants. The claimants guaranteed that the flock would not contain more than 30 parts of chlorine to 100,000 parts of flock. The sixteenth delivery contained 250 parts of chlorine to 100,000 parts of flock. The buyers repudiated the contract and refused to take further deliveries. The sellers sued for breach of contract. The court held that the buyers were not entitled to repudiate the contract and were in breach of contract as only one delivery had been defective. They could have recovered damages in respect of the defective delivery but they did not claim any because the delivery had already been used in the manufacture of bedding and furniture before the sample was tested and found defective.

Feedback on learning activity 8.4

Your answer should be in the form of a short essay detailing the main provisions of ss34 and 35 SGA. In particular you should refer to the buyer's right to examine the goods and whether any fault would have been obvious; or whether the fault was pointed out to the buyer. You should also mention that where the goods were part of a larger lot the buyer can accept the goods which are not defective or damaged and reject those which are. You could cite the case of *Maple Flock Co Ltd* v *Universal Furniture Products (Wembley) Ltd* [1934].

Feedback on self-assessment question 8.4

1   True. However, you can still claim compensation if the goods are faulty.
2   False. You must return the goods within a reasonable time. The matter of what is reasonable is a question of fact in all the circumstances.
3   True. The SGA does not apply where there is a notice or if this has been pointed out to you by the auctioneer.
4   False. The car boot sale is treated like a private sale and the SGA does not apply.
5   True. As the goods are perishable you should return them immediately. Reasonable time to return goods depends on the type of goods. (For the sake of a good relationship with customers you may find that some shops do give you a replacement, credit note or money, but this is not your right under the SGA.)
6   False. Changing your mind does not entitle you to claim your money back. However, you may find that for good customer relations, some shops will give you money back or a credit note, but this is not your right under the SGA.

8

Passing of title – exceptions to the rules

No-one can give as good a title as they have themselves.

Introduction

This session is a natural follow-on from study session 8 relating to transfer of property, risk and title. As you now know, the question of transfer of property in goods is important because risk generally passes with the property. Remember that property means ownership of goods or title in the goods so you are now going to learn about the passing of title. In short, the basic rule is that a person cannot pass to another property they do not own.

Session learning objectives

After completing this session you should be able to:

9.1 Describe Nemo dat rule and the exceptions.
9.2 Describe more exceptions to the Nemo dat rule.
9.3 Describe even more exceptions to the Nemo dat rule.

9

Unit content coverage

This study session covers the following topics from the official CIPS unit content document:

Learning outcome

Distinguish between the statutes relating to sale of goods and the supply of goods and services in specific circumstances and apply those rules to given practical situations.

Learning objective

2.4 Analyse the rules relating to the passing of title by a non-owner under legislation and the exceptions to these rules.
   • The Nemo dat rule
   • Romalpa clauses
   • Estoppel
   • Sale by a mercantile agent
   • Sale under a voidable title
   • Sale by a seller in possession
   • Sale by a buyer in possession
   • Sale of a motor vehicle on hire purchase
   • Sale under a court order

Prior knowledge

Study sessions 1 – 8.

Timing

You should set aside about 6 hours to read and complete this session, including learning activities, self-assessment questions, the suggested further reading (if any) and the revision question.

9.1 The Nemo dat rule and exceptions

Learning activity 9.1

Read the short scenario and advise if G can sue for non-delivery.

X agrees to sell 100 bags of cement to G. X arranges for a carrier to deliver them to G. However, on the way to G the carrier's lorry breaks down and the bags of cement are stolen and sold to Y. G is now suing X for non-delivery.

Feedback on page 138

9

In previous study sessions you have learned about common law of contract. Over the years, commercial law developed, much of it by the traders themselves. You also know that a significant amount of this 'man made' law is embedded in statute law through statutes such as the Sale of Goods Act, which applies to all contracts where the seller transfers or agrees to transfer property in goods to the buyer for a money consideration called the price.

The Sale of Goods Act 1979 (as amended by Sale and Supply of Goods Act 1994) provides consumers with options that are not open to them under common law or case law of contract. The Act is intended to make clear the rights and obligations of both parties and to avoid the need for formal legal action such as going to court.

When studying sale of goods you must understand the meaning of the important words such as property, types of goods, implied conditions and warranties and transfer of property and possession. To ensure that you do, we recommend that you revisit study sessions 7 and 8 to refresh your memory.

S20 provides that unless otherwise agreed the goods remain at the seller's risk until the property is transferred to the buyer but when the property is transferred to the buyer, the goods are at the buyer's risk whether delivery has been made or not. See the case of *Pignataro* v *Gilroy & Son* [1919], where the buyer acquired bags of rice but failed to uplift them from the seller's premises. When the bags were stolen from those premises the buyer had to bear the loss. Consequently, as a matter of practice, it is wise in any contract to clarify when risk passes, who will have the benefit of any insurance over the goods and who is paying the insurance premiums.

Under s20(2) where delivery is delayed through the fault of the seller or the buyer, the goods will be at the risk of the party at fault. Under the general rule of Nemo dat the seller cannot transfer any better rights than they themselves have. If it turns out that the seller's title is defective or even non-existent, then the same will apply to the buyer's title even where the buyer is the innocent party and has acted in good faith.

There are occasions where the seller might not even own the goods, for example, where the goods have been stolen as in the learning activity example. The seller may even believe that they own the goods where they have been misled by a previous seller. The law seeks to protect bona fide owners and honest buyers who pay a fair price.

Section 21 – Nemo dat rule

The basic rule is known as Nemo dat quod non habet. This means that a person cannot pass to another property they do not own. It can also be stated as no-one can give a better title that they have. S21 states that where a buyer has no title to the goods then they must be returned on demand to the true owner or face action for tort. Tort is discussed later in study session 10. The buyer of course can recover damages from the seller for breach of s12 (relating to title). In practice this is often difficult as the seller may or will have absconded, run off. This would be harsh on an innocent buyer. It is because of this harshness that there are exceptions to the Nemo dat (s21) rule.

The essence of the Nemo dat rule for students is to be able to identify the exceptions to the Nemo dat rule. In this part you are going to be looking at two of the exceptions. The others are explained later on.

Section 21(1) – Estoppel

This is where the true owner of the goods is by their conduct precluded from denying the seller's authority to sell. This happens when the owner deliberately gives someone else the appearance of having a right to deal with the goods. See the case of *Eastern Distributors Ltd* v *Goldring* [1957] where a car owner gave a dealer documents which made the dealer appear to be the owner as part of a scheme to enable the car owner to borrow money without adequate security. The scheme failed but the dealer went ahead and sold the car to a finance company. The court held that the finance company obtained a good title because, although the dealer had no right to sell, the owner's conduct estopped, that is, prevented him from relying on this.

S21 is to protect the innocent buyer. Where goods are sold by someone who is not the owner and does not have the authority or consent of the owner, the buyer acquires no better title than the seller had, unless the owner of the goods acts in such a way as to preclude him from denying the sellers authority to sell. So an innocent party will obtain title if:

- the owner by conduct or words made representations that the seller has authority to sell;
- the buyer acted on the representation in good faith;
- the representation is made intentionally or recklessly.

Section 22 – Market overt abolished by Sale of Goods (Amendment) Act 1994

This rule related to properly constituted markets overt established by royal charter or statute or long usage. Where a bona fide buyer purchased goods at the market they obtained a good title provided the goods were on display to the public at the market according to normal usage. The reason for abolishing this was that it would be an easy way for stolen goods to be disposed of. Since the 1994 Act innocent buyers are not protected where they buy goods from a market trader who does not have a right to sell. This means the innocent buyer will have to surrender the goods to the true owner and try to recover the price from the market trader. Watch out for EU Directives which may come into force to protect the rights of an innocent buyer.

Section 23 – Sale under a voidable title

You must know the meaning of the words 'voidable title'. You can revisit study session 2 to refresh your memory. However, a recap here is that a valid title is one that has full legal effect. A void title is one that has no legal effect. Voidable title is one that is valid until it is avoided. Avoidance can occur in several ways and it is recommended you revisit study session 3 on vitiating factors. See the case of *Lewis* v *Averay* [1971] where Lewis sold his car to a fraudster who claimed to be Richard Greene, an actor and star of television. When paying by cheque the fraudster for proof of identity produced what appeared to be a pass from Pinewood Studios. He then sold the car to Averay. The court held that the contract was not void for mistake but voidable for fraudulent misrepresentation. The court held that the fraudster's identify was not important to the seller at the time the contract was made. As the fraudster had sold the car to Averay before Lewis avoided the contract, Averay obtained a good title to the car. See also the cases of *Cundy* v *Lindsay* [1878] and *Phillips* v *Brooks* [1919] (see study session 3 for details of these cases).

Self-assessment question 9.1

Explain the Latin maxim 'Nemo dat quod non habet' and two exceptions to the rule.

Feedback on page 139

9.2   More exceptions to the Nemo dat rule

Learning activity 9.2

Using case law, can you describe a situation where the seller has retained possession after the sale and a situation where the buyer acquires possession before acquiring property or title in the goods?

Feedback on page 139

9

You have studied some of the exceptions to the Nemo dat rule above. Now you are going to consider more exceptions.

At all times go back to the basic rule: a seller cannot transfer any better rights than they themselves have.

Section 24 – sale by seller in possession

This is where a person allows the seller of the goods to remain in control and possession of the goods after the sale has taken place. There are situations where this can occur, such as the goods being too big for the buyer to move them at the time the contract is made. This section allows the seller to appear to still be the owner and he resells the goods to an innocent third party. The innocent third party will obtain a good title because it is based on the idea that the original buyer has not acted with due diligence. All that is needed for this exception to apply is for the seller to have physical possession of the goods and a subsequent purchase in good faith by a new buyer. It does not matter if the second contract is deliberate of negligent on the part of the seller. However, there must be delivery or transfer of the goods to the third party. See the case of *Nicholson v Harper* [1895]. This case related to the issue of a seller in possession. In this case the seller of the goods left the goods in the possession of a warehouseman who stored them. When he pledged them for a second time to the warehouseman the court held that there had been no physical delivery. However, see the case of *Michael Gerson (Leasing) Ltd* v *Wilkinson* [2001] where the owner of goods sold them to a finance company under a sale and lease agreement which stated that the seller would retain possession of the goods under a hire agreement from a finance company. The seller then sold part of the goods to a second finance company under a similar agreement. The question for the court to decide was whether there had been physical delivery. The Court of Appeal held that although the second finance company did not get physical possession, the sale and lease agreement constituted a voluntary transfer of possession which gives the second finance company a good title.

S24 does not affect the right of the unpaid seller to resell the goods under s48 SGA and if a resale takes place, the second buyer obtains a good title as against the original buyer. The seller is not in breach of contract in such a situation.

Section 25 – Buyer in possession

This section applies where the buyer is allowed to have possession of the goods even though the title or ownership has been reserved to the seller. You are already aware of such a situation where there is a Romalpa clause. You should revisit study session 3 on vitiating factors to refresh your memory. In retention of title cases where the original buyer sells to a second buyer who is buying in good faith and without knowledge of the restriction on the title, the second buyer obtains a good title.

Obviously, in these cases, there is an innocent party and in both s24 and 25 above there is still a right to sue for breach of contract or under the tort of conversion. Damages would be based on the amount needed to put the innocent party back in the position they would have been but for the breach.

Self-assessment question 9.2

Read the following short case study and advise.

Anne went in to Diamonte Jewellers of London and asked to see some jewellery. She selected some emerald and diamond chains to the value of £2,000 and paid for them. She asked Diamonte to set them aside for her to uplift later as she was concerned about carrying the jewellery around with her while she shopped. Later that day one of the shop assistants sold the jewellery to Jean. Anne returns to find her jewellery had been sold to Jean. Advise Anne what action she can take, if any, against Diamonte or Jean.

Feedback on page 139

9

9.3 Even more exceptions to the Nemo dat rule!

By this time you should be aware of the Nemo dat rule and some of the exceptions. Well there are still more to come! You are now going to be looking at the remaining exceptions to the Nemo dat rule.

Hire Purchase: Act 1964 – disposals by hirer

Part III of this Act provides one exception with regard to hire purchase agreements. You have already seen that under a hire purchase agreement although purchasers have possession of the goods they do not obtain ownership until the last instalment is paid. This means that the hirer cannot dispose of the goods. In the event that a hirer does dispose of the goods the finance company who still own them has the right to recover them.

The exception relates to disposal of motor vehicles. S27 provides that where the hirer of a motor vehicle under a hire purchase agreement disposes of the vehicle before title has passed to them, the first purchaser to acquire the vehicle in good faith obtains a good title and can pass such a good title on to subsequent purchasers.

The Act only applies to hire purchase or conditional sale contracts and to private purchasers. It does not apply to leases or where the car is a company car.

Learning activity 9.3

Examining the Hire Purchase Act 1964 explain the provisions of the act in respect of hire-purchase agreements and identify who benefits from this provision. Can you give any restrictions to this provision.

Feedback on page 140

Other exceptions to the Nemo dat rule include the following.

Sale by bailee

You are going to be looking at agency and bailment in study session 11. It is sufficient at this point to say that s62(2) SGA provides that the rules relating to the law of agency, that is where there is a principal and an agent, are preserved.

This means that a purchaser obtains a good title where an agent sells without the actual authority of the principal but with ostensible or usual authority. This is discussed in more detail in study session 11.

Sale by court order

S21(2)(b) SGA provides that the Act does not affect the validity of any contract of sale under any special common law or statutory power of sale or under the order of a court with competent jurisdiction. This covers situations such as:

- Pawnbroker: they have the right to sell goods which have been pledged to them if the loan is not repaid. The purchase obtains a good title.
- Bailiffs: they have power by statute to sell goods taken by them from premises where a person has not paid their debt under the court order.
- Innkeepers: under the Innkeepers Act 1878 an innkeeper has a lien over the guests goods for payment due. This lien may be converted into a power of sale and the purchaser obtains a good title.

Mercantile agent

This is a person who is independent of the seller and acts in the course of a business on behalf of one or more principals. They can buy or sell goods, raise money on security of goods. S2 Factors Act 1889 provides special protection to bona fide purchasers who buy from mercantile agents. The purchaser will obtain good title if the following criteria are satisfied:

- the purchaser is acting in good faith;
- mercantile agent must be acting in the course of business as such an agent;
- the purchaser has possession of the goods (actual goods or title documents) with the consent of the owner.

See the cases of *Stadium Finance Ltd* v *Robbins* [1962] and *Colwyn Bay Motorcycles* v *Poole* [2000]. In the former case the owner of a car gave it to a trader to get offers for it prior to sale. The owner left the registration document in the car but he kept the keys. The trader then got a spare key and sold the car to an innocent third party. The court held that this was not a sale in the ordinary course of business of a mercantile agent and title did not pass to the innocent third party. In the latter case Colwyn Bay Motorcycles sold a motorcycle to a fraudster who paid by telephone with a fraudulent credit card. He then took possession of the motorcycle. Later the plaintiff found out about the fraud and avoided the transaction. He informed the police and tried to contact the fraudster. Meanwhile the fraudster sold the motorcycle to a dealer who sold it to a consumer. The

9

court held that as the seller had avoided the contract prior to the fraudster re-selling the motorcycle the dealer did not get a good title and therefore could not pass title to the consumer.

Self-assessment question 9.3

Read the following statements and answer true/false.

1   A hirer under a hire purchase agreement can dispose of the goods at any time.
2   A purchaser obtains a good title when buying from a mercantile agent who is acting in the course of business as such an agent.
3   Bailiffs have a right to sell the goods they have taken from the premises of someone who owes debt under a court order.
4   A purchaser obtains a good title when buying from an agent who has ostensible authority.

Feedback on page 140

Revision question

Now try the revision question for this session on page 313.

Summary

By studying this and study sessions 6 – 8, you should have a full understanding of passage of title. This session was a natural follow-on from the previous sessions as it discusses what right is passed from seller to buyer. Under the Nemo dat rule the seller cannot pass to the buyer property they do not own. However, you have also learned that it is not as simple as this. In certain situations this would be harsh on an innocent buyer. By studying this session you will now know the important of being able to identify the exceptions to the Nemo dat rule.

Suggested further reading

Griffiths and Griffiths (2002), part II, chapter 10.

Smith and Keenan (2003), part 3, chapter 16.

Feedback on learning activities and self-assessment questions

Feedback on learning activity 9.1

This case is concerned with the passing of property and what remedies are available for non-delivery. You should explain that for property to pass the goods must be ascertained. In relation to specific or ascertained goods property passes when it is intended to pass (s17). However, if there is no express provision as to when property passes, then the s18 rules will apply. There is no mention of any express agreement in the above short case. S18 will apply and it is almost certain in this case that the goods are unascertained. This means that the relevant rule is rule 5. The rule states that property in the goods will pass when they are unconditionally appropriated to the contract. You should also explain that part 2 of rule 5 states that delivery to the carrier is considered as unconditional appropriation. So if X has delivered all 100 bags to the carrier then the property has passed to G. G will have to sort out the issue with Y. So the answer is that G cannot sue X for non-delivery.

Feedback on self-assessment question 9.1

You should include in your answer the translation of the Latin into words such as 'no-one can give any better title than they have' or 'a person cannot pass to another property they do not own'. You may also wish to explain the meaning of property and bring into your answer information learned in study sessions 7 and 8 such as that property means ownership or title. You should then go on to explain estoppel, where the true owner of the goods is by their conduct precluded from denying the seller's authority to sell. This happens when the owner deliberately gives someone else the appearance of having a right to deal with the goods. See the case of *Eastern Distributors Ltd* v *Goldring* [1957]. S21 is to protect the innocent buyer.

Then go on to explain the market overt abolition and that an innocent party under the Sale of Goods (Amendment) Act 1994 is no longer protected if they buy from a market trader or you might choose to talk about a sale under a voidable title. You will have to explain that 'voidable' is where a contract is valid up until the point it is avoided. If title is passed at the time the contract is valid then the buyer will obtain a good title.

Feedback on learning activity 9.2

For the first part of this learning exercise you should describe retention of title or Romalpa clause situation. You might want to revisit study session 2 on retention of title. One such case where there was a rolling Romalpa clause is the case of *Armour and Carron Ltd* v *Thyssen Edelstahlwerke AC* [1990]. In this case the House of Lords took the approach that a retention of title clause is effective even if it is an 'all monies' clause where the seller seeks to retain title to any of his goods still in the buyer's possession until the buyer has settled all the debts that he owes to the seller. This is a wide approach which permits goods from one contract to be used as security for debts owing to the seller from other contracts. It also means that the seller does not need to identify which batch of goods was delivered in relation to each contract. In the second part of this activity you should describe a situation such as hire purchase transactions where the buyer has possession of the goods but does not obtain title until the last instalment of the hire purchase agreement is paid.

Feedback on self-assessment question 9.2

In this case the seller has retained possession of the jewellery until the buyer returns. You should explain that normally payment is made before the seller will transfer property in the goods to the buyer. In this case Anne has paid for the jewellery and therefore property has transferred to her. In effect Anne owns the jewellery but does not have possession of it. S24 SGA covers this very situation, where there is the possibility of the seller reselling to an innocent second buyer. So the question is which of the two innocent buyers, Anne or Jean, should be able to claim ownership? This scenario satisfies the provisions of s24 and the second buyer, Jean, obtains a good title. This leaves Anne to sue the seller for compensation.

Feedback on learning activity 9.3

You should outline Part III provisions of the 1964 Act and that a hirer does not obtain title to goods until the last instalment is paid. The ownership of the goods lies with the finance company. The hirer has no right to dispose of the goods. However, there are occasions where the hirer does this. If this occurs the finance company can recover the goods. S27 introduces an exception to this rule and it refers to motor vehicles. Where a hirer who does not have title disposes of the car to an innocent first buyer, they obtain a good title which they can pass to subsequent purchasers. This only applies to private purchasers and only to hire purchase or conditional sale agreements. It does not apply to leases or company cars.

Feedback on self-assessment question 9.3

1   False: a hirer can only dispose of the goods once he has paid the final instalment as this is when the title in the goods will pass to him. Where he does dispose of the goods the finance company can recover the goods except where the goods are a motor vehicle – this is the one exception under the Hire Purchase Act 1964.

2   True: as long as the mercantile agent is acting in the course of business, has possession of the goods with the consent of the owner and the purchaser is acting in good faith.

3   True: bailiffs have the power by statute to order the sale of goods taken by the them from premises of someone who has failed to pay the debt under a court order

4   True: as long as the agent has actual or ostensible and usual authority of his principal, the purchaser obtains a good title.

9

Privity of contract and potential problems

Introduction

In this study session you will be learning about the doctrine of privity and how to get round the problems it creates. This will include looking at collateral contracts and warranties as well as legislation such as Unfair Contract Terms Act 1977 and Consumer Protection act 1987. You will find out how parties who are not party to a contract may still be able to enforce their rights under contract, in negligence and product liability. Before continuing with this study session we recommend that you revisit study sessions 1, 2 and 4 on contract law and contractual terms to refresh your memory.

'It would be monstrous to say that a person was a party to a contract for the purpose of suing upon it for his own advantage, and not a party to it for the purpose of being sued.'
Judge Crompton, 1871

Session learning objectives

After completing this session you should be able to:

10.1 Explain the doctrine of privity.
10.2 Explain liability in tort.
10.3 Describe Consumer Protection Act 1987 (Part 1) and Contracts (Rights of 3rd Parties) Act 1999.
10.4 Explain the mitigating factors to the privity rule.

10

Unit content coverage

This study session covers the following topics from the official CIPS unit content document:

Learning outcome

Judge when it would be appropriate for legal action to be taken against a third party.

Learning objective

2.5 Evaluate the various methods for circumventing the problems created by privity of contract.
   • Collateral contracts and warranties
   • Negligence
   • Indemnity clauses
   • Agency arrangements
   • Consumer Protection Act 1987 part one
   • Contract (Rights of Third Parties) Act 1999
   • Assignment and novation of rights and obligations to a third party

Prior knowledge

Study sessions 1 – 9.

Timing

You should set aside about 6 hours to read and complete this session, including learning activities, self-assessment questions, the suggested further reading (if any) and the revision question.

10.1 Doctrine of privity

Learning activity 10.1

Review previous studies and sections on formation of contract and ensure you understand the essential elements to a contract. You should recognise that in practice only an actual buyer of a defective product may sue and this is limited to claiming against the person from whom they bought the item, for example the retailer. Think of something you did not personally buy. Imagine how you would feel if you could not do anything about this. Now look at how the law has developed to take this into account. Re-examine the situation and describe what action is open to you.

Feedback on page 157

10

Doctrine of privity of contract – the general rule

As you have seen from the learning activity, under common law of England only the parties to a contract can acquire rights under it and be bound by it. This means that third parties cannot acquire any rights in a contract between two other parties and, of course, these two parties cannot impose obligations on a third party who is not a party to the contract.

So, for example, if X and Y enter into a contract, can Z enforce it in the event of breach of contract by X or Y? According to the doctrine of privity, the answer is no. The reason only the parties to a contract have rights or obligations under it is because they will have provided consideration. The matter of consideration was discussed in previous study session 1. You might want to go back and revisit that study session to refresh your memory on consideration.

See the case of *Dunlop Pneumatic Tyre Co Ltd* v *Selfridge & Co Ltd* [1915]. In this case the House of Lords held that in the law of England certain principles are fundamental. These principles were stated by Judge Viscount Haldane as:

- that only a person who is a party to a contract can sue on it;
- if a person with whom a contract has not been made is to be able to enforce it consideration must have been given by him to the promisor or to another at the promisor's request;
- a principal not named in the contract may sue upon it if the promisee really contracted as his agent but in order to sue he must have given consideration.

In the Dunlop case, the contract was between Selfridge and Dew. Selfridge promised Dew that they would not sell Dunlop tyres below the listed price. They promised Dew that if they sold Dunlop tyres below the listed price they would pay Dunlop £5 for each tyre sold. Selfridge sold two tyres below the listed price and Dunlop brought an action for damages and an injunction. Dunlop was clearly a third party to the contract and could not succeed. Also Dunlop did not give consideration to Selfridge to buy its promise. The House of Lords held that Dunlop could not enforce the contract as they were not privy to the contract.

Statutory exceptions where third parties are allowed to acquire rights

As you can imagine this is an obstacle in certain situations. There are statutory exceptions where third parties are allowed to acquire rights. These are in:

- Insurance contracts: where you insure your life for the benefit of your partner/children the life insurance contract is between the insurance company and you, but your partner/children who are third parties to the contract can sue the insurance company on your death in the event of non-payment by the insurance company.
- Road Traffic Act 1988: where you drive your car you are legally obliged to take out third party insurance. So where you knock someone down while driving your car that person has a direct action against the insurance company.

In the above situations the third party does not have to prove that they have given consideration to buy the promisor's promise. It is sufficient that the promisee has given consideration to the promisor.

Later on you will be considering the Contracts (Rights of Third Parties) Act 1999. This is not discussed under statutory exceptions as the purpose of the 1999 Act is to give a third party a right to enforce a contractual term which is designed for the benefit of the third party. For example, see the case of *Tweddle* v *Atkinson* [1861] in which a prospective bridegroom could not enforce a contract entered into by his father and prospective father-in-law despite the fact that the bridegroom was an intended beneficiary of the contract. The court held he was not party to the contract and could not enforce it. If this case had been after the 1999 Act then the bridegroom would have succeeded, as the 1999 Act would confer a right on the bridegroom to enforce the contractual term against the promisor.

Common law exceptions where third parties are allowed to acquire rights

Other common law exceptions include:

- Agency, which is discussed in more detail in study session 11.
- Joint parties: see the case of *Lockett* v *Charles* [1938] where a husband and wife had food and paid for a meal in a restaurant. The wife suffered food poisoning and when she sued the restaurant the restaurant pleaded that she was a third party. The court held that she was a joint party as the restaurant would have looked to her for payment if the husband had forgotten his wallet.

10

- Contracting on behalf of a group: see the case of *Jackson* v *Horizon Holidays Ltd* [1975] where Mr Jackson booked a holiday for himself, his wife and children. The holiday provided was not as advertised and Mr Jackson sued for damages for distress on behalf of his wife and children. The issue was whether Mr Jackson, a contracting party, could claim damages for his wife and children, who were considered third parties. The court held that Mr Jackson was entitled to obtain damages on behalf of his wife and children. However, this is restricted to situations where there is a clear presumption that the plaintiff was acting on behalf of the group as a whole. In a later similar case of *Woodar Investment Development Ltd* v *Wimpey Construction UK Ltd* [1980] the court held that Jackson decision did not apply in commercial situations. The court stated that the Jackson case must be confined to family situations. This was a commercial construction contract. Under the contract Wimpey had agreed to pay £150,000 to a third party, Transworld, on completion of the contract with Woodar. The question that the court had to decided was whether Woodar in an action against Wimpey for breach of contract could recover the £150,000 promised to Transworld. The House of Lords held that Woodar could not recover the money promised to Transworld.
- Assignment: where a contracting party assigns the right to a third party. If the assignment is valid the assignee has the right to enforce the contractual rights which have been assigned.
- Collateral contracts: this is discussed in more detail below.

Collateral contracts

These occur where a separate contract related to the main contract exists between a third party and one of the main contracting parties. See the case of *Shanklin Pier Ltd* v *Detel Products Ltd* [1951] where the claimant, Shanklin Pier, wanted the pier painted. It contracted with a firm of painters to do the job. Detel approached Shanklin to tell them about a special paint assuring Shanklin that the paint would last for seven years. Shanklin then asked the paint firm to use the Detel paint. The paint only lasted three months. Shanklin sued Detel, the defendants Detel argued that the contract to sell the paint was with the painter and that Shanklin was a third party with no right to sue. The court agreed with this but also stated that there was a collateral contract between Shanklin and Detel which allowed Shanklin to sue Detel.

Self-assessment question 10.1

Three cases A, B and C are stated below with options provided for choosing the correct answer or answers. Choose the appropriate options where asked.

A. In *Tweddle* v *Atkinson* [1861] why did the claimant fail in his breach of contract action against his father-in-law's estate? Circle the three options that are the correct answers

1   The parties did not intend to create legal obligations.
2   The father-in-law died and the cause of the action died with him.
3   It was inequitable to permit the claimant to sue.

(continued on next page)

Self-assessment question 10.1 (continued)

4 The claimant did not provide consideration to buy his father-in-law's promise.
5 The claimant was not a party to the contract between his father and father-in-law.

B. In *Dunlop Pneumatic Tyre Co Ltd* v *Selfridge & Co Ltd* [1915], what was the decision of the court? Circle one option that is the correct answer.

1 The court held that Dunlop could sue under the contract.
2 The court held that Dunlop was not privy to the contract and therefore had no right to enforce it.
3 The court held Dew acted as agent of Dunlop when it contracted with Selfridge.
4 The court held that Dunlop could sue as he had given consideration to Selfridge.

C. In *Jackson* v *Horizon Holidays Ltd* [1975] what reason was given by the court for concluding that Mr Jackson could sue for damages on his own behalf and on behalf of his wife and children? Circle one option which is the correct answer.

1 Mr Jackson sued as trustee on behalf of his family.
2 Mr Jackson was acting as agent for his family.
3 All members of the family were joint parties to the contract.
4 Mrs Jackson and the children assigned their contractual rights to Mr Jackson.
5 Mr Jackson made a contract for the benefit of himself, his wife and children as a group and was entitled to sue on their behalf.

Feedback on page 158

Manufacturer's guarantees and warranties, and Unfair Contract Terms Act 1977

Under the Unfair Contract Terms Act 1977, manufacturers are prevented from excluding or restricting their liability to a consumer provided three criteria are met, namely:

- the goods are of a type ordinarily supplied for private use or consumption;
- the goods have provided defective in consumer use;
- the manufacturer or distributor did not sell the goods directly to the consumer.

Under the 1977 Act a trader cannot by the use of an exclusion clause in the contract exclude his liability for death or personal injury resulting from negligence.

And where a clause in the contract restricts liability for other loss or damage resulting from negligence it can only be used if the exclusion satisfies the test of reasonableness.

The 1977 Act was discussed in study session 2 and we recommend that you revisit this study session to refresh your memory.

Guarantees

A guarantee is most often issued by the manufacturer of goods or by a company that has provided services. It is normally provided free of charge at the time the goods or services are purchased. A guarantee is considered in law to be an agreement to provide some benefit for a set period in the event of the goods or services being defective. Manufacturers are not legally obliged to provide a guarantee but if they do it must be in plain English and clearly explain how to make a claim.

Warranties

A warranty provides similar cover to that of a guarantee but you often have to pay extra for it. These kinds of warranties are insurance policies issued by and underwritten by insurance companies. They are often very confusing as they are sometimes known as 'extended guarantees' or 'extended warranties'.

Tort of negligence

This is considered in more detail in the next part of this session but briefly the principles of the tort of negligence were laid down in the classic case of *Donoghue* v *Stevenson* [1932]. This case decided that three things need to be proved to establish a claim. The three things are:

1 That a duty of care exists between the parties.
2 That the duty has been breached.
3 That loss or damage has resulted from that breach.

Fair Trading Act 1973/Enterprise Act 2002

Much of the 1973 Act has been reformed by the Enterprise Act 2002, which has extended protection for consumers. The Enterprise Act 2002 is discussed in detail in the last part of study session 16.

The next section provides more detail on the tort of negligence. You will learn that the privity of contract rule can be avoided by suing under tort.

10.2 Liability in tort

You have learned the meaning of privity of contract and some of the statutory and common law exceptions. You are now going to look at how privity of contract can be avoided by suing in tort. As you have seen in the previous study sessions on contract law, because of the doctrine of privity, the law of contract only benefits the parties to the contract. So in the case of sales contracts the only people who have rights and obligations are the buyer and seller. As you can imagine from the learning activity that you did in the above part of this session, this can cause problems to those who are perhaps injured by a product that they personally did not purchase. It can also cause problems in the sales environment where the purchaser of a product would only have rights against the immediate seller.

Of course, from the previous section in this study session you also know that manufacturers can be held liable in contract where there is a collateral contract. See the case of *Shanklin Pier Ltd* v *Detel Products Ltd* [1951].

However, there are still problems in other situations because of the privity rule. These problems are resolved by the law of tort, which is now discussed in detail. We will be particularly concerned with the tort of negligence.

Definition of tort

A tort is a civil injury or civil wrong. There are other types of civil wrong such as breach of contract and breach of trust. The definition below is an attempt to distinguish tort from other civil wrongs:

Liability in tort arises from the breach of a duty primarily fixed by law; this duty is towards people generally and redress for breach is an action for unliquidated damages.

General characteristics of liability in tort

The general characteristics of liability in tort include:

- Liability for a wrongful act or wrongful omission: where one person is liable for the wrongful act or wrongful omission by another. One situation is the case of the employer–employee relationship. The law imposes liability on the employer when the employee commits a tort during the course of his employment. In these situations the employee will be personally liable and the employer is vicariously liable
- Liability is based on 'fault' of the defendant. Fault means that the claimant must prove that the defendant committed the act or omitted to perform the act either intentionally or negligently. (Although some tortious liability is 'strict': see the case of *Rylands* v *Fletcher* [1868] where the plaintiff owned a colliery with mine shafts that reached under the land of the defendant. The defendant built on his land a water reservoir, with its position located over the mine shafts. Many of the mine shafts were old and disused. The soil between the mine shafts and the base of the reservoir was unable to support the pressure of the water and subsequently collapsed causing the water to flood the mine. The plaintiff sought damages from the defendants in the Court of Exchequer Chamber in February 1866. Judgement was given to the plaintiff and the defendants appealed. The appeal was dismissed as the Court of Appeal held that, if a person brings or keeps anything on his land that should later escape and is a cause of damage to neighbouring properties, the owner is responsible for its effects no matter how careful he has been to retain that item. So in this case the owner of the burst reservoir was judged as being responsible for the damages so their appeal was dismissed.)
- Damage not too remote: the claimant must prove that they suffered damage as a result of the wrongful act or omission and such damage must not be too remote a consequence of the wrongful act or omission.

One tort is that of negligence, which will be considered now.

Negligence

The modern law of negligence is founded on the famous case of *Donoghue* v *Stevenson* [1932]. In this case Mrs Donoghue went to a café with a friend.

10

The friend purchased a bottle of ginger beer for Mrs Donoghue to drink. The drink was in an opaque bottle. After drinking half of it, Mrs Donoghue poured the remainder into a glass when the remains of a decomposed snail floated out. Mrs Donoghue suffered from shock and gastroenteritis as a result of this experience. She wanted to sue for compensation but was not able to do so under contract law as she had not purchased the drink and therefore was not party to the contract, which was between her friend and the café. She then tried to sue the manufacturer for her injuries but she had no contract with them either. The case went to the House of Lords to decide whether as a matter of law the manufacturer of a product owed any duty of care to the ultimate user or consumer of his product. The House of Lords held that such a duty does exist.

Manufacturer's duty of care

The Donoghue case above spelt out the duty of care on a manufacturer to the ultimate user or consumer as well as laying the foundations for a wider concept of duty of care. In the Donoghue case Lord Atkin stated:

'that a manufacturer of products which he sells in such a form to show that he intends them to reach the ultimate consumer or user in the form in which they left the manufacturer with no reasonable possibility of intermediate examination and knowing that absence of reasonable care in the manufacture of the products will result in injury to the consumer owes a duty to that consumer to take reasonable care'.

Remember that to establish a claim for negligence you must prove three things.

Learning activity 10.2

Consider a situation where there is a legal duty that is not part of a contract. Explain what tort is and describe the three things you have to prove to establish a claim for negligence

Feedback on page 158

Donoghue v *Stevenson*

It is important to consider in more detail the three essential elements that must be proved to establish a claim for negligence as laid down in the classic case of *Donoghue* v *Stevenson* [1932]. To establish a claim three things must be proved:

- that a duty of care exists between the parties (standard of care will be considered below);
- that the duty has been breached;
- that loss or damage has resulted from that breach (foreseeability is discussed below).

We will now look at these in turn.

Duty of care

A duty of care is owed to all neighbours. A neighbour is someone who is so closely affected by what you do or fail to do that you ought reasonably to have them in mind when considering what you do or do not do. See the case of *Wilson & Clyde Coal Co* v *English* [1934]. In this case an employer was held to owe a duty of care to employees to provide reasonably safe premises, machinery, systems of work and colleagues. Of course, if a similar case were to be raised today the employer would also be governed by health and safety legislation.

Clearly, however, the duty of care goes beyond a manufacturer's liability to consumers. It applies to employees, visitors, local community and the environment as a whole.

Standard of care

This is also important. The basic requirement is that the defendant must exercise the same standard of care as would be exercised by an ordinary reasonable man. A recent example of this approach can be seen in the case of *Mansfield* v *Weetabix Ltd* [1998]. This case arose out of a road traffic accident. A lorry driver crashed his vehicle into shop premises after his ability to drive was impaired by a medical condition of which he did not know. Evidence showed that had he known he would not have continued to drive. The Court of Appeal held that he was not liable as he should be judged against the standard expected of a reasonably competent driver who was unaware of a medical condition.

See also the case of *Nettleship* v *Weston* [1971] where the court held that a learner driver would be expected to display the same level of skill as a qualified driver.

As regards people in professional positions who profess some expertise, then the higher the level of expertise, the higher the standard of care demanded.

Breach of duty of care

This is the second essential element that must be proved to establish a claim for negligence. However, although the duty must be broken, it is not an absolute duty. It is a duty to take reasonable care.

The victim in a claim for negligence must show that the duty was breached and this can often be difficult as the victim may not be in a position to have the facts to prove this. This problem has been resolved to some extent by the introduction of product liability laws. You will be looking at the Consumer Protection Act 1987 below.

Loss or damage resulting from the breach

For a claim for negligence to succeed loss or damage must occur which can be attributable directly to the breach. See the case of *Barnett* v *Chelsea and Kensington Hospital Management Committee* [1969]. In this case a night watchman died of arsenic poisoning. He had been accidentally poisoned at work but the junior hospital doctor failed to diagnose it. His widow sued the hospital but as the loss was not attributable to the hospital's breach of duty she failed in her action. Medical evidence showed that the dose of arsenic would have been fatal even had the doctor diagnosed it properly.

Recoverable damage – foreseeability

Even where loss or damage occurs because of the breach, it is important to consider what damages are recoverable in the event of a breach. Damages must be foreseeable.

The leading authority on this point is the case of *Overseas Tankship (UK) Ltd* v *Morts Dock and Engineering Co Ltd, The Wagon Mound No 1* [1961] where it was decided that the test of remoteness in negligence should be one of 'reasonable foreseeability'. In this case the defendants caused an oil slick when they spilt some oil in the water at the harbour. The oil slick spread to a nearby jetty belonging to the plaintiffs. Welding work on two ships at the jetty was underway at the time. Believing that the oil posed a fire risk, the plaintiffs stopped work. When the work was re-started, an expert confirmed that there had been no fire risk from the oil. Subsequently the two ships and the jetty were damaged when the oil caught fire. The Privy Council held that the defendants were not liable for the damage caused by the fire as damage by fire was unforeseeable. If it had been damage due to oil pollution then that would have been foreseeable.

Once foreseeability is established the defendant is liable for all the damage suffered by the plaintiff even though the extent may be greater than expected. This is known as the 'eggshell skull' rule. It means you take the person as you find them whether think skull or weak heart.

Damages are recoverable for:

- death and personal injury;
- property damage: both personal and business property;
- nervous shock;
- economic loss.

The areas that are less clear cut are those of nervous shock and economic loss.

Nervous shock

This occurs where someone witnesses an accident and as a result suffers from shock. So, for example, you might see a car accident from a window and suffer shock. However, this does not automatically entitle you to damages. If it were then you can imagine that the defendant in such an action might be liable to many people.

A definition of nervous shock was given by Lord Denning in the case of *Hinz* v *Berry* [1970]. He stated that in English law no damages are awarded for grief or sorrow caused by a person's death...'.

In the case of *Hay or Bourhill* v *Young* [1942] the position of bystander was considered. In this case decision of the House of Lords held that a driver of

10

a car, even though careless, is entitled to assume that passers by in the street will have enough fortitude to endure such incidents. This means the law expects a bystander to an accident to be courageous and remain cool when witnessing an accident or its aftermath. A bystander who suffers nervous shock will not be awarded compensation.

However, would it make a difference where the incident was particularly horrific? This was considered by the House of Lords in the case of *White and Others* v *Chief Constable of South Yorkshire* [1998]. This case arose out of the Hillsborough disaster. Some of the judges expressed the view that if the accident is particularly horrific then a bystander who witnesses the incident and suffers nervous shock may be entitled to compensation. However, the court decided that the extent to which a plaintiff may be able to claim damages for nervous shock depends on:

- whether they were physically injured in the incident;
- whether they were put in physical danger (but actually suffered only psychiatric injury) (known as a primary victim);
- whether they were not at physical risk but suffered psychiatric injury as a result of the aftermath (known as secondary victims);
- whether they were just a bystander.

There are many court cases on this subject and each will be decided on the facts of each case. See also the case of *Alcock* v *Chief Constable of South Yorkshire* [1991]. This was another case arising out of the Hillsborough disaster. In this case the House of Lords stressed the need for a relationship of proximity between the claimant and the defendant. This means that the claimant must be closely and directly affected by the defendant's actions.

It is also worthwhile considering under the nervous shock heading the matter of stress claims against employers. The employers have a common law duty and a statutory duty under section 2 of the Health and Safety at Work Act 1974 to ensure the welfare, physical and mental, of their employees. More recently, the Health and Safety Executive Management Standards on stress were introduced in 2003, which emphasise the employer's duty to look after the mental well-being of employees. See the case of *Walker* v *Northumberland County Council* [1995] where it was held that a social worker was entitled to damages for a second nervous breakdown caused by stress at work. The case was decided on well-established general principles of negligence.

As you can see from the above, the area of nervous shock is a vast one and there are many cases on this issue. It is sufficient for your studies and examination to be aware of the criteria in the case of *White and Others* v *Chief Constable of South Yorkshire* [1998].

Economic loss

The matter of recovery of damages for economic loss is of importance to commercial situations because it refers to the limited opportunity to recover monetary loss such as profit. The law takes a restricted approach to this and this approach is confirmed in case law.

10

It is important to know the difference between:

- financial loss resulting from physical injury or property damage; and
- pure economic loss that is not connected to other damage.

The difference is: the former is recoverable, whereas in most situations the latter is not. See the case of *Spartan Steel & Alloys* v *Martin & Co (Contractors) Ltd* [1973]. In this case the defendants cut through a power cable to the plaintiff's factory, resulting in interruption to their electricity supply. The plaintiffs claimed damage to the metal in the furnace at the time of the power cut and for lost profit on that metal. They claimed also for the lost profit on another four melts that had been planned but could not go ahead because of the power cut. The courts held that the plaintiffs could not recover for lost profit on the four melts as it was considered pure economic loss and not attributable to any physical damage. They only recovered damages for the first metal damage and lost profit on that metal.

Pure economic loss is rarely recoverable. It falls into three categories:

- economic loss suffered because of an inherent defect in the quality of products or services;
- loss of profit or caused by the defendant's negligent; and
- suffered through relying on negligent advice.

Hedley Byrne & Co Ltd v Heller & Partners Ltd

You may recall that this case was considered under negligent misrepresentation in study session 3. You may wish to revisit that study session to refresh your memory.

This case is considered here again because before 1963 the law of tort did not recognise any liability for negligent misstatements, only for fraud-based tort of deceit. The House of Lords in the case of *Hedley Byrne* decided upon a new liability. This liability would arise in respect of a statement made by a defendant to someone with whom he had a special relationship if he had not validly disclaimed his liability. You may recall that in this case Hedley were retained as advertising agents for Easipower Ltd. They wanted to know if Easipower were creditworthy and asked their bankers to enquire about this. Heller were Easipower's bankers and the confirmed in a statement to Hedley that Easipower were good for normal business commitments. Heller had put the words 'without responsibility' on their statement. Hedley relied on Heller's statement and did business with Easipower. They lost money when Easipower went into liquidation. The House of Lords held that Heller did owe a duty to Hedley in this situation and they would have been liable for the negligent misstatement, only escaping liability because of the exclusion clause.

On the matter of statements it is worthwhile mentioning the case of *Spring* v *Guardian Assurance plc* [1995] where an employer provided a reference for an employee. The court held that the employer owes a duty of care to the employee and will be liable to him in damages for any economic loss suffered as a result of a reference being prepared negligently. Of course, this duty exists in tort but also a duty arises as a result of an implied term within the contract of employment.

10

Self-assessment question 10.2

Read the following questions and statements. Circle one statement option only for the correct answer.

A. What is the standard of care that has to be attained by a doctor? Circle one answer only.

1   The standard of care of all other doctors.
2   The standard of care of the average reasonable person.
3   The standard of care of some other doctors.
4   The standard of care of a judge of the court.
5   The standard of care of the doctor who is the defendant in the case.

B. What is the standard of care that has to be attained by a 'do it yourself' joiner? Circle one answer only.

1   The standard of the defendant joiner.
2   The standard of a professional joiner working for reward.
3   The standard of the judge.
4   The standard of the claimant.
5   The standard of a reasonably competent joiner.

C. What is the standard of care that has to be attained by a learner driver? Circle one answer only.

1   The standard of other learner drivers.
2   The standard of the defendant learner driver.
3   The standard of a competent and experienced driver.
4   The driving standard of the judge.

D. Who bears the burden of proof that the defendant did not comply with the requisite standard of care? Circle one answer only.

1   The claimant.
2   The defendant.
3   The court presumes that the defendant was negligent.

E. What is a tort? Circle one answer only.

1   All civil wrongs.
2   All civil wrongs other than a breach of contract.
3   All wrongs other than a criminal wrong.
4   A type of civil wrong.

F. To whom do we owe a duty in tort? Circle one answer only.

1   To the whole world.
2   To our neighbour.
3   To persons generally.

(continued on next page)

10.3 Consumer Protection Act 1987 Part I and Contracts (Rights of Third Parties) Act 1999

Consumer Protection Act 1987 Part I

This Act came into force in 1988 and although it is divided into three distinct parts. The only part that concerns you in this study session is Part I.

Part I gave effect to the European Union (EU) Directive on Product Liability and introduced what is known as strict liability on producers of defective products for any injuries that such products can cause. The claim includes for personal injury and damage to personal property valued at £275 or more.

Strict liability means that the liability is placed on the actual manufacturer;

- anyone importing product into the EU from a country outside the EU;
- anyone else who holds themselves out as being the producer of the product, for example, the own-brand products, that is, retail stores with their own brands, such as Sainsbury, Asda and many other high-street stores and supermarkets.

Where a product is proven defective, any of the above may then be liable for any death, personal injury or property damage caused, subject to a minimum claim.

The 1987 Consumer Protection Act as to product liability only protects consumers and not commercial undertakings. For commercial undertakings, the liability of subcontractors is discussed below.

Contracts (Rights of Third Parties) Act 1999

The purpose of this Act is to give a third party a right to enforce a contractual term which is designed for the benefit of the third party. As you saw earlier in the case of *Tweddle* v *Atkinson* [1861], the bridegroom could not succeed in his action against his father-in-law's estate as he was not party to the contract between his father and father-in-law. However, it was clear that the contract was for the bridegroom's benefit and the contract expressly conferred a right of action on the bridegroom. This being so, if a similar case arose today, then under the 1999 Act the bridegroom would succeed. Similarly, if a case such as *Dunlop Pneumatic Tyre Co Ltd* v *Selfridge & Co Ltd* [1915] were to arise today, then the 1999 Act would allow Dunlop to sue.

The 1999 Act represents significant changes in the law, namely:

- third parties now have the right to bring a direct action without having to rely on the promise to sue on the third parties behalf;
- the 1999 Act gives a right of action to a third party without the need for consideration to have been made.

Subcontractor liability

The 1999 Act also attempted to deal with the problem of privity of contract in relation to subcontractors. The 1999 Act provides for a mechanism whereby third party rights may be created in the principal contract. It may not always be possible for the purchaser to hold a contractor liable for the defects of the subcontractor in contract in which case there is a similar problem to that of the manufacturer-consumer relationship. The liability will have to be framed either as:

- a collateral contract under the principles of *Shanklin Pier* v *Detel* case, which is discussed earlier on;
- in negligence.

Subcontractor liability in negligence

This can be summed up as follows, a subcontractor:

- owes a duty of care to a purchaser in relation to any physical loss, that is, damage to property or injury to persons and even a duty of care for the reputation of the purchaser if the reputation is affected by the acts or omissions of the subcontractor;
- owes no duty of care to purchasers in relation to pure economic loss. This means that if the only loss is inability to earn profit then there is no duty on the subcontractor and if there is no contract the subcontractor has no liability at all;
- owes a duty of care if the subcontractor has been nominated by the purchaser. This is often the case in construction contracts where the purchaser specifies a particular subcontractor. The relationship is then closer and the subcontractor has a duty of care and this includes liability for economic loss. In most cases a subcontractor connected closely with a purchaser would be able to be sued in contract through the main contractor.

10

Self-assessment question 10.3

Analyse the position in the following short case study referring to current legislation and case law.

Bridgeman Engineers employ Quikbuild to renovate their offices. They will be the main contractors but they will have to engage subcontractors to install the heating and ventilation. Bridgeman suggest Ventilo Ltd, with whom they have had previous successful dealings, perform the heating and ventilation work. Quikbuild engage Ventilo to install the heating and ventilation. Ventilo perform the work so negligently that someone is injured when the property is finished. Advise Bridgeman on what action they can take.

Feedback on page 158

10.4 Mitigating factors to the privity rule

In addition to the 1999 Contracts (Rights of Third Parties) Act 1999, there are a few situations where the harshness of the privity rule may be mitigated by other factors. These mitigating factors have already been discussed in section 10.1 above.

Learning activity 10.4

Look back at the part of the study session to ensure you understand the meaning of privity of contract.

Feedback on page 159

You should revisit the first part of this study session and refresh your memory on the mitigating factors. They are detailed under the heading 'common law exceptions where third parties are allowed to acquire rights'.

The exceptions are summed up again below as:

- agency (see the next study session 11);
- joint parties: see the case of *Lockett* v *Charles* [1938];
- contracting on behalf of a group: see the case of *Jackson* v *Horizon Holidays Ltd* [1975];
- assignment: where a contracting party assigns the right to a third party;
- collateral contracts: which are discussed in the section 10.1 above.

Self-assessment question 10.4

Two short scenarios are presented below. You are required to identify the mitigating situation and the case to which they relate.

(continued on next page)

Self-assessment question 10.4 *(continued)*

Scenario one: John books a holiday through Sunhols for his wife Jean and two children. The holiday proves to be unsatisfactory and not as advertised. John's wife and the children are distressed by the whole experience and John wants to sue for damages for his wife and children. Advise John of the action he can take.

Scenario two: Gericho Builders need the walls of their building painted with long-lasting anti-graffiti paint. They contract with Decopainters to perform the work. Grafi, painting specialists, approach Gericho and tell them about their special anti-graffiti paint. They assure Gericho it will do the job and last for 10 years. Gericho ask Decopainters to use Grafi's special paint. Contrary to expectations, the paint starts to peel off the walls after only one month and the local children have sprayed graffiti all over it. Advise Gericho on the action they can take and against whom.

Feedback on page 159

Revision question

Now try the revision question for this session on page 313.

Summary

In this study session you have learned about privity of contract and how the problems it raises can be circumvented by common law exceptions. Having completed this study session you are now aware that liability for defective products is not limited to contractual actions by the purchaser against the seller. You can identify the various other possibilities where the person injured by the product can enforce their legal rights under contract law, collateral contract, warranties, negligence or product liability. These rights can be enforced against the manufacturer and supplier of goods irrespective of privity of contract.

Suggested further reading

Griffiths and Griffiths (2002). You should read the chapters on contract formation, negligence and product liability: part I, chapter 1.11 and part II, chapters 11 and 12.

Feedback on learning activities and self-assessment questions

Feedback on learning activity 10.1

This activity is intended to get you to think about who the parties are to a contract and who can sue under it if something goes wrong. You may have thought of something you have bought as a present for a friend. Then your friend finds the present damaged or they may even be injured by the present. Under common law of England only the parties to a contract can acquire rights and be bound by duties. In the case of your present, your friend was not party to the contract and therefore according to common law they have no rights. You know from experience or from past studies on the law of contract and the doctrine of privity that this of course is not the case and that they can do something about it.

Feedback on self-assessment question 10.1

Case A: the correct answers are 3, 4 and 5.

Case B: the correct answer is 2.

Case C: the correct answer is 5.

Feedback on learning activity 10.2

Provide the definition as: liability in tort arises from the breach of a duty primarily fixed by law; this duty is towards people generally and redress for breach is an action for unliquidated damages.

Go on to describe the principles laid down in the classic case of *Donoghue* v *Stevenson* [1932] and that three things must be proved to establish a claim for negligence. These are: that a duty of care exists between the parties; the duty has been breached; and loss or damage has resulted from that breach.

Feedback on self-assessment question 10.2

A: the correct answer is (a).

B: the correct answer is (e).

C: the correct answer is (c).

D: the correct answer is (a).

E: the correct answer is (d).

F: the correct answer is (d).

Feedback on learning activity 10.3

You should identify that Jean is an end user of the new fast action hair dryer. Jean is also not a party to the contract with the manufacturer. The contract is between Jim and the supermarket. However, you should identify that under the Consumer Protection Act 1987 as an end user Jean can use the manufacturer of the finished product . She can claim for personal injury and damage to personal property if any valued at £275 or more.

Feedback on self-assessment question 10.3

This case is about subcontractor's liability. You should explain when a subcontractor owes a duty of care, referring to the three situations referred to in the study session. You should identify that this is a construction

10

contract, and in this case Ventilo was nominated by Bridgeman. The relationship is a close one and Ventilo as subcontractor has a duty of care, which includes liability for economic loss as well as injury or damage caused. Also in such situations, the subcontractor connected closely as in this case would be able to be sued in contract through the main contractor

Feedback on learning activity 10.4

Your answer is to explain that privity of contract means that only the actual purchaser of a defective product may sue and the right to sue is limited to claiming against the person from whom they bought the item, which is normally the retailer.

Feedback on self-assessment question 10.4

Scenario one. This is the case of *Jackson* v *Horizon Holidays Ltd* [1975] where Mr Jackson booked a holiday for himself, his wife and children. The holiday provided was not as advertised and Mr Jackson sued for damages for distress on behalf of his wife and children. The issue was whether Mr Jackson, a contracting party, could claim damages for his wife and children who were considered third parties. The court held that Mr Jackson was entitled to obtain damages on behalf of his wife and children. So in this situation, as long as it is clear that John was acting on behalf of the group as a whole, then he can obtain damages from Sunhols for his wife and children.

Scenario two. This is the case of *Shanklin Pier Ltd* v *Detel Products Ltd* [1951] where the claimant Shanklin Pier wanted the pier painted. It contracted with a firm of painters to do the job. Detel approached Shanklin to tell them about a special paint assuring Shanklin that the paint would last for seven years. Shanklin then asked the paint firm to use the Detel paint. The paint only lasted three months. Shanklin sued Detel; the defendants Detel argued that the contract to sell the paint was with the painter and that Shanklin was a third party with no right to sue. The court agreed with this but also stated that there was a collateral contract between Shanklin and Detel which allowed Shanklin to sue Detel. So in this situation Gericho can sue Grafi as the court would hold that there was a collateral contract between them.

10

10

Study session 11
Agency and bailment

Introduction

In this study session you will be looking at the law of agency. This is where a person, called an agent, has power to make a binding contract between two others, known as the principal and the third party. As contract law is applicable to this study session you must ensure that you are well versed in study sessions 1 – 10. In this study session you will also look at: how agency is created; the different types of agent; the duties and responsibilities of the parties; and how the agency can be terminated. In the last section of this session you will look at the responsibilities arising from bailment, which is the act of placing property in the custody and control of another, usually by agreement in which the holder is responsible for their safe keeping and return of the property.

Agency is a tri-partite relationship where one person (the agent) is allowed to stand in for another individual to fulfil their wishes.

Session learning objectives

After completing this session you should be able to:

11.1 Create of agency agreement.
11.2 Describe the rights and duties of an agent.
11.3 Describe the relationship between principal/agent and third parties.
11.4 Explain the responsibilities arising from bailment.

Unit content coverage

This study session covers the following topics from the official CIPS unit content document:

Learning objective

2.6 Test the legal principles that apply to agency and bailment in a given situation
  • Creation of agency
  • Rights and duties of agents and principals
  • Relationship of principal/agent with third parties
  • Responsibilities that arise from a bailment relationship.

Prior knowledge

Study sessions 1 – 10.

Timing

You should set aside about 4 hours to read and complete this session, including learning activities, self-assessment questions, the suggested further reading (if any) and the revision question.

11.1 How agency is created

First of all, what is an agent? An agent is a person who has the power to make a binding contract between two others who are known as the principal and the third party without incurring any personal liability. The agent will be instructed by the principal to enter into negotiations with a third party for the purpose of creating a contractual relationship between that third party and the principal. So you can see that there is a relationship between the principal and the agent which can be created in different ways (see below). The agent negotiates with the third party. You will find out later on that in certain circumstances the agent may become personally liable. Finally, the end result is a contractual relationship between the third party and the principal.

Learning activity 11.1

The purpose of this learning activity is for you to think about situations where someone else has formed a contract between others yet not been a party to the contract itself. Consider pre-contractual negotiations: can you think of a situation where another person was used to negotiate the terms of a contract, for example, an agent of some kind? Think also of yourself as an employee of your organisation: do you negotiate contracts for your employer where the result is a contract between your employer and the third party? Briefly describe some situations where agents are used.

Feedback on page 173

Creation of agency

You have already looked at one definition of an agent. Another is that an agent is a person who has the power to represent another legal party (principal) in order to create a legal relationship with a third party.

So agency is a relationship existing between two parties called the principal (P) and the agent (A) which is for creating a contractual relationship between the principal (P) and a third party (T). Figure 11.1 gives an overview of the relationship between the parties.

Figure 11.1: The relationship between the principal (P), agent (A) and third party (T)

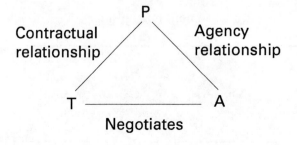

There are five ways in which an agency relationship can be created. These are by:

- express agreement in writing or orally;
- implication where the agency agreement is implied from the conduct of the parties: see the case of *Spiro* v *Lintern* [1973], which is described below;
- estoppel: see also the case of *Spiro* v *Lintern* [1973];
- necessity: there it must be an emergency; it must be impossible for the agent to obtain instructions from the principal; and the agent acted in good faith: see the case of *Great Northern Railway* v *Swaffield* [1874], which is also described below;
- ratification which arises when the agent exceeds his authority as an agent but the principal adopts, that is, ratifies (at a later date) the contract made by the agent.

By express agreement

This is where the agency agreement is created by a formal agreement, that is, either a written contract or orally. However, the most common way in which agency is created is by implication from the conduct of the parties.

By implication

As stated above this is where the agency is created from the conduct of the parties. One example would be where you (the principal) instruct an estate agent (the agent) to sell your property for the purpose of concluding a successful contract between you the principal and the third party (the buyer). By implication the agent is expected to act on your behalf in their usual capacity as estate agents. No written contract is required, although in practice you may be required to sign an agreement confirming your instructions. See the case of *Spiro* v *Lintern* [1973], which is also referred to below.

Some other examples of agency relationships include: insurance agent where the agent acts in order to form a binding contract between his client (the principal) and the insurance company (the third party); employment procurement such as modelling agencies; contract negotiation as in publishing; show business agents. In some cases independent contractors may be considered as agents of the builder or principal contractor but this very much depends on how the relationships are formed and proceed.

Estoppel

Estoppel is defined in English law as a principle of justice and equity. It means that when someone by their word or conduct leads another to believe in a particular state of affairs, then they will not be allowed to go back on their word or conduct when it would be unjust or inequitable for them to do so.

This is demonstrated in the case of *Spiro* v *Lintern* [1973] where the defendant instructed his wife to arrange for the sale of their house even although she did not have authority to enter into a binding contract. The estate agents acted on her instruction and sold the house to the

11

plaintiffs. The defendant knew about the sale and allowed the plaintiffs to make arrangements for alterations to the house. The defendant then refused to complete the contract of sale relying on the fact that his wife had no authority to enter into a binding contract. The court held that the defendant was bound by the contract as he had affirmed the contract by his conduct, that is, by allowing the plaintiffs to arrange the alterations.

So if a principal creates the impression that an agent is authorised but there is no actual authority, third parties are protected so long as they have acted reasonably. This is called agency by estoppel or the doctrine of holding out where the principal will be estopped from denying the grant of authority if third parties have relied on the representations made.

By necessity

As you have seen from the above, agency of necessity arises when three criteria are fulfilled:

- where an emergency requires the agent to act, and
- it was impossible for him to obtain instructions from the principal, and
- the agent acted in good faith and in the interest of all parties. See the case of *Great Northern Railway* v *Swaffield* [1874] where a railway company had carried a horse to its destination but there being no-one to receive it, had placed the horse with a stable keeper. The company paid the charges. The court held that although the company had no express or implied authority to incur such charges, it had acted in an emergency as an agent of necessity and was therefore entitled to claim an indemnity from the owner of the horse.

Contrast the case of *Springer* v *Great Western Railway* [1921] with the Swaffield case. In the Springer case a consignment of tomatoes arrived late at the port of destination. There was a further delay in unloading. The consignment was bad due to the delays. The railway company sold the tomatoes locally. The railway company failed to establish an agency of necessity because they had not contacted the principal before acting. The railway company were held liable to the owner for wrongly selling the goods.

By ratification

This occurs when an agent acts beyond their authority or with no authority but the principal then adopts or ratifies the contract which resulted from the agents actions. Once adopted or ratified the agent gets retrospective actual authority and is deemed to have been acting within his authority from the outset. The principal is bound by the contract from the outset (ab initio).

Self-assessment question 11.1

Describe the five ways in which an agency relationship can be created.

Feedback on page 173

11

11.2 The duties, authority and rights of an agent

You have already looked at the different ways in which agency can be created. You also know that the purpose of agency is for a contract to be formed between the principal and the third party without the agent incurring personal liability. However, this does not mean that the agent has no rights and duties.

The role of the agent is extremely important as is agency in the area of commercial law. It deals with a three-sided set of relationships when an agent acts on behalf of another called the principal to create a legal relationship with a third party. To fully understand the law of agency you need to know about the different relationships between:

- agents and principals;
- agents and the third parties with whom they deal on behalf of the principal;
- principals and third parties with whom the agent deals on behalf of the principal.

The relationships are dealt with in section 11.3 below. In this part you will look at the authority of an agent and their rights and duties.

Learning activity 11.2

Having studied the above part of this study session, see if you can now identify an agency situation. Once you have identified an agency situation, describe in what way it was created.

Feedback on page 173

11

Agent's duties to the principal

As you now know from the above information, the function of an agent is to bring about a valid, legally binding contract between his principal and a third party. You can see from the learning activity and previous information that the agent is really acting as a negotiator as there is no intention for him to be personally liable by the contract.

The agency relationship is a fiduciary one. This means that an agent is in a position of trust and confidence. They must be loyal to the principal. An agent must follow instructions. They must exercise care and skill and carry out instructions personally. They must keep an account of money owed and not allow any conflict of interest to arise. They must not make any secret profit and must not take bribes.

To sum all this up, the agent acts on authority from the principal. There are various types of authority, which are discussed below.

Agent's authority

The authority of an agent dictates the level of power to act on behalf of the principal.

Actual authority

This arises where the principal's words or conduct reasonably cause the agent to believe that they have been authorised to act. Actual authority can be:

- express authority; or
- implied actual authority.

Express authority

Where the agency has been created by a written agency contract, then the extent of the express authority will be determined from the interpretation and terms of the contract. Where the agency has been created orally then the extent of the authority will depend on what the parties agreed the agent would be authorised to do.

Implied actual authority

This is more complex than express authority as it must be determined by all the surrounding circumstances. Agency may be implied because what is said or done make it reasonable for the person to assume the powers of an agent. Where there is no contract of agency but the principal's words or conduct reasonably led the third party to believe that the agent was authorised to act then the principal will be bound.

The scope of implied authority was considered by the Court of Appeal in the case of *Hely Hutchinson* v *Brayhead Ltd* [1968]. In this case the chairman had not been formally appointed as managing director of the defendant company but acted as managing director with the acquiescence of the other directors. He issued letters of guarantee to the plaintiffs, which they subsequently sought to enforce. The defendants denied liability on the grounds of lack of authority. The court held that the managing director had implied actual authority as he had acted with the agreement of the defendants.

Usual authority

This can be considered under implied actual authority as it is the authority that an agent has as a result of his profession or trade. It is limited to situations where the agent has an identifiable profession or job. See the case of *Panorama Developments (Guildford) Ltd* v *Fidelis Furnishing Fabrics Ltd* [1971]. The court held that a company secretary has implied authority to enter contracts that deal with the administrative affairs of the company. The secretary would be in a position to hire cars, arrange flights for directors, buy office equipment, etc. This authority could therefore be extremely wide and therefore it is appropriate that the principals are able to limit the extent of such an agent's powers.

Apparent or ostensible authority

This arises if the principal's words or conduct would lead a reasonable person in the third party's position to believe that the Agent was authorised to act. The matter of agency by estoppel has been discussed earlier on.

11

Remember this is where a principal creates the impression that an agent is authorised but there is no actual authority.

Authority by virtue of position held

This occurs, for example, in partner relationships where partners have apparent or ostensible authority to bind the other partners in the firm. The liability of partners is joint and several. In a company situation all executives and senior employees with decision-making authority by virtue of their position have apparent authority to bind the corporation.

Authority by ratification

This has already been discussed earlier. Where an agent acts without authority the principal may ratify or adopt the transaction and accept liability on the transactions as negotiated. The ratification or adoption may be express or implied from the principal's conduct.

Rights of an agent

An agent has the following rights:

- to be indemnified for expenses incurred for work done;
- to be remunerated according to the express terms of the agreement or implied from the nature of the agent's services;
- to retain the goods as security for payment of a debt. This is called a lien over the goods. An agent can only claim a lien if they have lawful possession of the property concerned.

These rights have been enhanced where the Commercial Agents (Council Directives) Regulations 1993 apply. In the absence of express agreement on the amount of remuneration to be paid to an agent, then the agent is entitled to receive such an amount as is customarily paid to a commercial agent dealing in the type of goods to which the agreement relates. See more detail on the 1993 Regulations below.

11

Self-assessment question 11.2

Read the short case study and explain whether an agency agreement has been created between the parties.

Greenshaws purchased and paid for a consignment of flowers from Jacksons who were wholesale florists. Jacksons agreed to store the flowers overnight until Greenshaws collected them the following morning. Greenshaws failed to uplift the flowers. Jacksons worried that the flowers would wilt and die so they sold them on behalf of Greenshaws to Florantines, another customer.

Has an agency agreement been created between Greenshaws and Jacksons?

Feedback on page 174

Before moving on to the next part of this study session, which deals with the relationships, we will look at the Commercial Agents (Council Directives)

Regulations [1993]. These regulations re-state the agent's common law duties in broad terms. Regulation 4 provides that an Agent must:

- look after the interests of the principal and act in good faith;
- make proper efforts to negotiate and conclude transactions that the principal instructs him to carry out;
- communicate to the principal all necessary and available information;
- comply with all reasonable instructions given by the principal.

Where the agent breaches any of the above duties the remedies available to the principal include:

- sue the agent for damages for breach of contract;
- where the agent refuses to return the principal's property, the principal can sue for the tort of conversion;
- sue the agent to recover a bribe, secret profit or any money received by the agent on behalf of the principal;
- sue for an account if the agent fails to keep proper accounts of the agency transactions;
- dismiss the agent without compensation.

11.3 The relationship between principal/agent and third parties

In section 11.2 above you learnt about the duties of an agent and the type of authority he is given by the principal. You are now going to look at the relationship between the principal and the agent, and the third party and the principal. Then you are going to look at how an agency agreement can be terminated.

Learning activity 11.3

To ensure an understanding of the agency relationship, draw a diagram showing the three-sided relationship. Then describe the duties of an agent.

Feedback on page 174

To understand more fully the three-sided relationship you are going to look at the following:

- liability of the agent to the principal;
- the liability of the principal to the agent;
- the liability of the third party to the principal;
- the liability of the agent to the third party.

Liability of agent to principal

If the agent has acted without authority, but has apparent or ostensible authority then the principal is bound by the contract. The agent, however, is liable to indemnify the principal for any resulting loss or damage. The duties and authority of an agent have been discussed in detail in section 11.2 above.

Liability of principal to agent

If an agent acts within actual authority, the principal must indemnify the agent for payments made during the course of the agency relationship, whether the expenses were expressly authorised or were a necessity in promoting the principal's business. In addition to this duty to reimburse the agent expenses, under common law the principal must also pay the agent his fee or commission when it is due.

Liability of third party to principal

Where an agency relationship exists, the third party is liable to the principal on the terms of the agreement made with the agent unless the principal was undisclosed.

Where the agent has acted within his actual authority or where the principal has ratified the agent's actions, the principal and third party will be bound in a normal contractual relationship with the ability to sue and be sued on the contract.

Agency relationships are common in many professional areas. Some examples have already been given earlier on in this session. For example in show business and entertainment the negotiation of entertainment deals is done by an agent, such as an agent for actors, models and athletes. In publishing an agent acts for an author to sell their manuscripts. Often in the publishing world, publishers pay more attention to manuscripts that are submitted by an agent than directly by the author.

Liability of agent to third party

There should be no liability of an agent to the third party, as you have already seen from the information in section 11.2 above that the intention of the agency relationship is for the agent to have no liability to the third party. However, there are some situations where personal liability on the agent will arise. For example, in the case of an undisclosed principal or where the principal does not exist, the agent is personally liable. Another example is where the agent, unknown to the third party, acts beyond his authority.

Termination of agency

This can occur in several ways:

- by agreement between the parties;
- by the principal revoking the agent's authority;
- by the agent renouncing his authority;
- by completing of the duties and obligations of the agreement;
- by lapse of time where the agency has been created for a specified period of time;
- by the death of either the principal or the agent;
- where the principal becomes bankrupt;
- where the agent becomes bankrupt to such an extent that it prevents them from carrying out their duties;

11

- by frustration: see the case of *Marshall* v *Glanville* [1917]. In this case a representative for a firm of drapers joined the Royal Flying Corps. He would have been conscripted four days after that. The court held that the contract of service had been terminated and not merely suspended as it had become unlawful for the representative to fulfill his part of the contract by serving his former master;
- by the insanity of the principal or the agent.

It must be noted that not all the consequences of the agency relationship cease on termination of the agency relationship. For example, if at the time of the termination of the agency agreement, the agent has a right to commission or indemnity then these rights do not cease. Also, where an agent is in breach of his duties, the principal can dismiss the agent but the principal can still sue the agent for breach of agency even although the agency agreement is terminated.

Self-assessment question 11.3

Read the following statements and answer true or false.

1 Where a principal adopts the actions of an agent the agency is said to be created by ratification.
2 An agent does not need to perform his duties personally.
3 An agent is personally liable if he signs a deed in his own name.
4 An agent is not personally liable when the principal is non-existent.
5 An agency relationship is a fiduciary one.
6 In an emergency where an agent can contact his principal but fails to do so, an agency of necessity can be created.

Feedback on page 174

11.4 Responsibilities arising from bailment

The definition of bailment is the act of placing property in the custody and control of another, usually by agreement in which the holder (bailee) is responsible for their safekeeping and return of the property.

Contracts of bailment cover a wide range of transactions. Bailment occurs when goods are delivered to a person (the bailee), on condition that they will ultimately return to the bailor. Such situations include when you take your car to the garage for repairs, when you take a coat to the cleaners to be cleaned, hand your coat in to the cloakroom, or put your car in the car park and so on.

For purchasing professionals it is an important area as bailment can arise when goods are loaned or delivered on terms that will ultimately require the goods to be returned; for example, special patterns or tools or designs.

Bailment can also arise where goods are delivered and then rejected. If the purchaser requires the supplier to uplift the rejected goods from the purchaser's premises, then the purchaser is the bailee of the goods until they are uplifted by the supplier.

Learning activity 11.4

Can you think of a situation where you were bailee? Think of your personal situation and then that of your organisation.

Feedback on page 175

Contracts of bailment can arise under contract of bailment or by operation of the law. In the learning activity you have looked at contracts of bailment. We will now look at bailment that arises by operation of the law.

Bailment by operation of the law

Gratuitous loan for use might be considered bailment. However, because it is gratuitous, there is no contract and the bailee must return the goods on demand or in accordance with the agreement. However, the bailee is not liable for wear and tear.

Hotels and innkeepers

Under the Hotel Proprietors Act 1956, a common innkeeper is a bailee of the guests' property which is brought on to the premises. See the case of *Olley* v *Marlborough Court Hotel* [1949]. This case concerned the plaintiffs, who had furs stolen from their hotel bedroom. The plaintiffs were Mr and Mrs Olley, who booked into a hotel for the first time. The concluded contract for the stay was left at the reception desk. On their bedroom wall was a notice that read that the proprietors would not hold themselves responsible for articles lost or stolen unless handed to the manageress for safe custody. When the furs were stolen, the plaintiffs took action against the hotel as bailees of the plaintiffs' furs. The hotel tried to deny liability by relying on their exclusion clause. However, the Court of Appeal held that the exclusion clause had not been validly incorporated as it was not included at the time the contract was made and had only come to the notice of the plaintiffs later. The hotel could not rely on the exclusion clause and were held liable for the loss of the furs.

The defence to the bailee in the hotel situation is to show that the loss is due to the guest's negligence, Acts of God or enemies of the Crown!

Also, the bailee in the hotel situation has a lien over the property of the guest (the bailor) to secure payment of the hotel account. Under the Innkeepers Act 1878 the bailee has a right to sell the goods deposited with them in lieu of payment.

Involuntary bailment

This occurs where goods are placed with a person without the bailee's consent. The bailee will not be liable in negligence but must not wilfully damage or sell the goods. They also have no obligation to return the goods.

11

The position of the bailee

A bailee is liable for the loss occurring to the bailor where the bailee wrongfully refuses or is unable to restore the goods to the bailor under the terms of the contract of bailment.

If the goods are damaged by a third party while in the possession of the bailee then the bailee may sue the third party direct and hold the money in trust for the bailor.

A bailee may also insure the goods as there is an insurable interest in the goods but again the bailee holds the sums recovered under an insurance policy as trustee for the bailor.

Bailee's duty

The bailee has a duty to take care of the goods bailed. They must not be negligent. However, the duty of care is subject to reasonable exclusion and limitation clauses under the Unfair Contract Terms Act 1977. Such clauses have already been discussed in study session 2. You should revisit that study session to refresh your memory.

Bailee's right to sell

Under common law the bailee has no right to sell the goods in his care even though expenses may have been incurred. However, under the Torts (Interference with Goods) Act 1977 an unpaid bailee has the right to sell the goods on giving reasonable notice to the bailor and then to keep expenses from the proceeds of sale. The balance must be held in trust for the bailor.

11

Self-assessment question 11.4

Alison takes her car to the garage owned by Bill to be repaired. When Alison returns to collect her car the garage owner Bill tells her that the garage was broken into and the CD player in her car was stolen. Bill informs Alison that there is no burglar alarm at the garage as they never had problems of theft in the past. Advise Alison of her rights against Bill.

Feedback on page 175

Revision question

Now try the revision question for this session on page 314.

Summary

In this study session you have studied the ways in which an agency agreement can be created, such as expressly , by implication, by ratification, by necessity and estoppel. You have also looked at the rights and duties of an agent as well as the three-sided relationship which exists in agency between the agent and the principal, the agent and third party, and the principal and third party. You know that the intention of an agency agreement is to have a valid binding contract formed between the principal and the third party with no personal liability falling on the agent. You have learnt that there are situations where an agent will be liable. Finally, you looked at the contract of bailment and the rights and duties arising out of this on the bailee, both under common law and statute.

Suggested further reading

Griffiths and Griffiths (2002), part I, chapter 6.

Feedback on learning activities and self-assessment questions

Feedback on learning activity 11.1

Your answer could include estate agents, who negotiate the purchase and sale of property with a view to a successful contract being formed between the purchaser and seller. You might think of a situation where you acted as an agent: one example might be as a sales agent for a company such as Virgin Cosmetics or the well-known 'Avon lady'. Examples of being an employee might include negotiating as a procurement professional. You will not be a party to the contract between your company and the successful supplier but you have acted as an agent in the negotiations.

Feedback on self-assessment question 11.1

Your answer should include the following.

Agency can be created by express agreement in writing or orally. However, the most common form is by implication where the agency agreement is implied from the conduct of the parties. Examples are estate agents, insurance agents. A person may be stopped or estopped from backing out of the contract by their conduct as in the case of *Spiro* v *Lintern* [1973] where the husband had allowed his wife to instruct the estate agent for the sale of their house even though she had no authority to enter a binding contract. When the house was sold, the husband allowed the buyers to make arrangements to alter the property. However, he then refused to complete the contract of sale, relying on the fact his wife had no authority. The courts held that by his actions he was stopped from backing out of the contract.

There are emergency situations where a party can act as agent when they are unable to contact the principal to obtain instructions. However, they must act in good faith and in the interests of all parties. You could refer to the two cases of *Great Northern Railway* v *Swaffield* [1874] and *Springer* v *Great Western Railway* [1921].

Finally, you should mention that agency can be created by ratification or adoption at a later date by the principal of the agent's actions. This then provides the agent with actual authority.

Feedback on learning activity 11.2

Your answer can include estate agents, insurance agents, perhaps your role as employee where you are an agent for your employer in dealing with transactions such as procurement of say stationery and other supplies. In these situations the agency will probably have been created by implication. You may have signed an agreement and in this situation it will be created expressly.

Feedback on self-assessment question 11.2

You must refer to the criteria required for an agency of necessity to be created. This will include that there must be an emergency; it must be impossible for the agent (Jacksons) to obtain instructions from the principal (Greenshaws). Jacksons as agents must have acted in good faith and in the interests of all the parties. If an agency of necessity has been created then Jacksons will be entitled to reimbursement of any incurred expenses.

Feedback on learning activity 11.3

You should draw the triangular diagram showing the Principal, Agent and Third Party – (see figure 11.2)

Figure 11.2

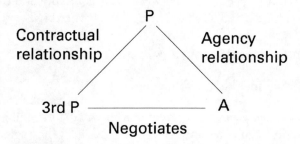

The lines connecting them should be the agency relationships between the principal and the agent, the negotiations between the agent and the third party and finally the function of the agent, the line showing the contractual relationship formed between the principal and the third party as a result of the agent's actions.

You should explain that the function of an agent is to bring about a valid, legally binding contract between his principal and a third party. The agency relationship is a fiduciary one. This means that an agent is in a position of trust and confidence. They must be loyal to the principal. The duties of an agent include that he must follow the principal's instructions. They must exercise care and skill and carry out instructions personally. They must keep an account of money owed and not allow any conflict of interest to arise. They must not make any secret profit and must not take bribes. The agent acts on authority from his principal. He obtains authority in different ways, which include actual, implied, apparent and through ratification.

Feedback on self-assessment question 11.3

1   True: at a later date, a principal can adopt or ratify the actions of the agent and then becomes bound in the contract with the third party.
2   False: an agent must personally carry out his duties.

11

3   True: an agent will be personally liable if he executes a deed in his own name.

4   False: an agent is personally liable if the principal does not exist or if the principal is undisclosed.

5   True: the agent is in a position of trust and must be loyal to his principal.

6   False: where an agent is in a position of obtaining instructions from his principal but does not do so, no agency of necessity can be created. An agency of necessity is only created where it is impossible for the agent to obtain instructions.

Feedback on learning activity 11.4

You could provide a situation where you have left your coat in the cloakroom at a hotel or disco. The position of the receptionist is that of bailee and they must look after your coat. A situation within your organisation might be where you have purchased goods but they are not what you ordered and you reject them. You phone for the supplier to come and uplift them. You are then in the position of the bailee until the supplier picks the goods up.

Feedback on self-assessment question 11.4

You should identify that this situation is one of bailment and that Bill is the bailee of Alison's car. Bill therefore has a duty to take reasonable care of the car bailed to him and he must show that he had taken such care. The next question to ask is did Bill take reasonable care: would it have been reasonable to expect him to have an alarm system to deter burglars?

Of course, Bill can insure the goods while in his possession as bailee and it is probably normal business practice to have such insurance. If this is the case then a claim can be made against Bill's insurance rather than Alison's insurance. However, Bill does not have a duty to insure the goods and if they have no insurance then Alison would have to claim on her insurance.

11

11

Tendering and e-tendering procedures

Introduction

In this section you will be learning about tenders and the tendering process. You will also learn about the different types of tender and the collateral obligations that arise from the tendering process. You will be looking at the ongoing development and use by organisations of e-tendering and considering the key benefits of e-tendering. Finally you will look at how to avoid the battle of the forms.

Session learning objectives

After completing this session you should be able to:

12.1 Explain the tendering process.
12.2 Describe the types of tenders and the collateral obligations that arise from the tendering process.
12.3 Explain pre- and post-award obligations.
12.4 How to avoid the battle of the forms.

Unit content coverage

This study session covers the following topics from the official CIPS unit content document:

Learning outcome

Examine the impact of e-trading on traditional contract law.

Learning objective

3.1 Determine the collateral legal obligations that arise from a tendering process (including e-tendering) and distinguish between those obligations that arise before the tender is awarded and those that arise after the tender is awarded.
  • Legal status of the tender bid
  • Open and closed tenders
  • Duty to consider all compliant tenders
  • Equal and timely access to information
  • Fair treatment and good faith
  • Post award negotiations
  • Letters of intent
  • Avoidance of the battle of the forms

12

Prior knowledge

Study sessions 1 – 11.

Timing

You should set aside about 6 hours to read and complete this session, including learning activities, self-assessment questions, the suggested further reading (if any) and the revision question.

12.1 The tendering process

Learning activity 12.1

Before looking at the tendering process, go back to study sessions 1 and 4 to ensure you know how a contract is formed and concluded. Look at the offer, counter-offer, qualified acceptance and acceptance. Look at some of the contracts within your organisation. How do you contract with your suppliers? Do you use standard forms and can you identify some of them? Are you so familiar with the terms of the contract that you rarely refer to them? Is this a good thing?

Feedback on page 188

12

Standard form contracts

In previous sessions you have looked at and learned about how a contract is formed. In the above learning activity you should have looked at some of the standard forms used by your organisation in the contract process. Having identified some of the forms used in contract formation, you will realise that each of these different forms can and do contain terms and conditions. This applies to your organisation and that of the supplier organisation. Each organisation will want the best terms and conditions for them and therefore may and will often alter the terms and conditions in these standard forms to suit what is best for them. This is why you must carefully manage a contract, looking at all the terms and conditions in each of the documents making up the contract until it is concluded between the parties. All these forms and differences amount to a 'battle' and that is why forming a contract in such a way is called a 'battle of the forms'. This is looked at again in the last part of this session. The so-called battle can be avoided by the tendering process.

Tendering process

Using a tendering process will avoid the battle of the forms. This is because the offer or standing offer is made on the buyer's terms supplied with the invitation to tender. Any contract must be carefully managed to ensure clarity and to avoid difficulties arising in the future in the event of a dispute.

You need to know whether the tender is an offer or an invitation to treat. Some words used in the tendering process can be confusing. For example, purchasers may talk of accepting a tender and you need to be sure whether this is an acceptance or not.

The law makes a distinction between tenders in which the invitation states that the buyer will buy the goods that are the subject of the tender and those where the buyer indicates that they may buy the goods at the price quoted.

Tenders may be used to establish two different types of contract; briefly we can look at them as:

1   offer and acceptance which successfully creates a binding contract; or
2   standing offers.

In (1) this is an invitation to tender for the supply of a quantity of specific goods or services in accordance with the terms and conditions of the tender documents and attached schedule, etc.; an acceptance will result in a legally binding contract. The contract will be concluded as soon as the offer is unconditionally accepted.

However, in (2) the tender invites a quotation for the supply of certain goods from a prospective supplier from time to time. The supplier in this case creates a standing offer and each call-off order creates a separate contract between the parties on the terms set out in the tender documents. The standing offer can be revoked at any time but all orders placed before any are revoked must be honoured. See the case of *Great Northern Railway Co* v *Witham* [1873]. In this case the tender submitted by the defendant was a standing offer to supply for 12 months such quantities of specified goods as the company may order from time to time. There was no guarantee that an order would actually be placed by the company. However, if and when an order was placed there would be a contractual obligation on the defendant to satisfy such an order. The defendant did satisfy some orders but then refused to honour an order made by the company. They were sued for breach of contract. The court held that the defendant was in breach of contract as the tender was a standing offer which was converted into a series of contracts as and when the company made an order. So although the defendant might revoke his offer for the remainder of the tender period, the defendant must supply the goods already ordered by the company.

Later, you will see that the acceptance of the tender is not necessarily the end of the tender negotiation as there can be post-tender negotiations where matters are thrashed out in more depth between the contracting parties.

Tendering procedure

The actual procedure to be followed in the tendering process involves various steps, which can be summarised as follows:

- establish a list of people/organisations to be invited to bid;
- check if contract is covered by procurement directives (see study session 13);
- prepare the tender documents;

12

- decide on type of tender (see next part of this session);
- review the submitted tenders;
- letter of intent or letter of comfort may be issued to the chosen supplier;
- award tender;
- formal agreement drawn up between the parties.

So who and how do you invite to tender? You need to establish who you are going to invite to bid for the work. You can do this either by direct contact with potential bidders or you can advertise your intention to run a tender in a newspaper or trade journal. You will see in study session 13 that it is necessary to advertise if the contract is covered by the procurement directives.

Prepare the tender documents and what is included. The tender documentation will usually consist of:

- the specification: this is the precise description of the work required;
- the contract terms and conditions: these are the detailed terms of the proposed contract;
- the instructions to tenderers: there will be blanks as to the cost in the tender documents, which the tenderers will be required to complete. Other instructions will include details of the submission, such as to a specified person by a specified time.

Tenderer's bid

The tenderer should carefully look at the tender documentation and the instructions. The tenderer will require to include the completion of the blanks as to cost, a written statement as to the price they will charge for the work and if they want to make any changes or exceptions then they must include a list of these changes and exceptions.

Where all bidders are happy with the terms and conditions of the tender documentation, then the contract will be awarded and normally to the lowest bidder.

Letters of intent and letters of comfort

Tenders are commonly used for the provision of services and in construction contracts. The types of tender are discussed in the next part of this session.

Once the tenders have been submitted by the prospective suppliers, the prospective purchaser may choose to issue a letter of intent to the chosen supplier indicating their intention to enter into a contract with them. Just as the prospective purchaser can do this, the prospective supplier may decide to issue letters of intent to prospective sub-contractors in the event that they are successful. There is no intention to be bound contractually at this stage yet work can commence on the issue of a letter of intent. See the case of *British Steel Corpn* v *Cleveland Bridge and Engineering Co Ltd* [1984]. In this case the defendants negotiated with the plaintiffs for the plaintiffs to manufacture specialist steel parts to be used in constructing a bridge. The defendants sent a letter of intent to the plaintiffs proposing that any contract would be on the defendant's standard terms. Work commenced.

The plaintiffs were not prepared to contract on the defendant's standard terms. When work was completed the plaintiffs sued for the price and the defendants sued for damages for late delivery. The court held that there was no contract, only a letter of intent, the final terms not having been agreed. However, the plaintiffs were entitled to claim **quantum meruit** for the goods supplied.

Letters of comfort

These are not necessarily legally enforceable and whether they are or not will depend on the facts of each individual case. When issuing a letter of comfort it is essential to make your intentions clear and that you want it to be legally binding. See the case of *Kleinwort Benson Ltd* v *Malaysian Mining Corporation Bhd* [1989]. In this case the person issuing the letter of comfort did not intend to create a legally binding contract. The plaintiff bank agreed to provide a loan to the defendants' wholly owned subsidiary, MMC Metals Ltd. The defendants refused to provide a guarantee for the loan but did provide 'two letters of comfort' in which they stated 'It is our policy to ensure that the business of MMC Metals Ltd is at all times in a position to meet its liabilities to you under the arrangements (loan facility)'. MMC went into liquidation due to the collapse in the tin market. They still owed the plaintiffs the whole of the loan. The plaintiffs sued the defendants on the strength of the letters of comfort. The Court of Appeal held that the defendants had shown no intention of creating a legally binding contract as they had refused to guarantee the loan. The court held they were not liable as the letters of comfort were merely statements of fact about the defendant's present intentions. They were not contractual promises about future conduct.

Collateral obligations

It is important to understand the meaning of collateral obligations. In short, these are obligations that are distinct from but run alongside the main contract; that is, collateral to it.

Collateral obligations include:

- to award to lowest bidder
- no withdrawal of bid within the specified time;
- consider all tenders that comply with requirements (*Blackpool and Fylde Aero Club* v *Blackpool Borough Council* [1990]);
- all tender bids treated equally (*R* v *Lottery Commission (ex parte Camelot plc)* [2000]);
- to conduct the tender process in good faith.

Award to lowest bidder: For example where the person or organisation issuing the tender documents states that the tender will be awarded to the lowest bidder then the lowest bidder will enforce this obligation. This is rarely done; in fact, the tender documents usually state that there is no requirement to award the contract to the lowest bidder.

No withdrawal of bid within specified time: another example of a collateral obligation is an implied obligation that the bid will not be withdrawn within the time specified in the tender documents. As you know from study session 1, an offer can be withdrawn at any time up to the formal acceptance. However, in the tender process the tender price is open for acceptance for a specified period. This allows the person running the tender process to assess the various tenders submitted. It is therefore an implied collateral obligation that the bid will not be capable of withdrawal within that specified period. The period can be anything for example 90 days. It should be enough time to consider the tenders.

Consider all bids that comply: An example of this is seen in the case of *Blackpool and Fylde Aero Club* v *Blackpool Borough Council* [1990]. In this case the Council were under an implied obligation to consider all tenders that complied with their requirements regardless of whether the tender had physically reached the appropriate council offices in time. The Council required that sealed bids be delivered to the town hall by 12.00 noon on a specified date. The plaintiffs complied well before 12.00 noon on the specified date. However, although the tender was delivered on time it did not reach the person running the tender until much later than 12.00 noon, by which time the contract had been awarded to another bidder. The council did not state that the tenders had to be submitted to a particular council official, just to the town hall. The plaintiffs had complied and the court held that they were entitled to damages for breach of this collateral obligation.

All tender bids treated equally: This point was considered in the case of *R* v *The National Lottery Commission (ex parte Camelot plc)* [2000]. In this case a tendering process was run by a government agency to run the United Kingdom national lottery. Only two bids were received, one from the existing contractor, Camelot plc, and the other from a consortium known as the Peoples Lottery. There followed extensive negotiations and discussions after which the government agency decided to reject both bids. After rejecting both bids they began negotiations with Peoples Lottery with a view to awarding them the contract if they could show that they could fulfil certain requirements. No such negotiations were allowed or took place with Camelot. Camelot sought a judicial review to challenge the decision of the government agency. The court ruled that the tender process was unfair and unjust. The agency should have treated all bidders the same. The direct outcome of this decision applies to public bodies but it may be seen as a collateral obligation in all tender situations in the future.

Conduct tender process in good faith: There is an implied obligation that the tender process will be conducted in good faith. Where one bidder is treated more fairly than another then it can and may give rise to legal action.

Collateral obligations can arise in the course of any contractual negotiations. In the real world of commercial contracts it is unlikely for bidders to find all the terms and conditions of the tender documentation acceptable. This means that there will be considerable changes and exceptions listed. In turn it is unlikely that the prospective purchaser will find the bidder's changes and exceptions acceptable in their entirety. In reality, instead of just awarding the contract to the lowest bidder, negotiations will take place between the prospective purchaser and the lowest bidder in order to finalise the terms and conditions of the contract.

12

The last part of the tendering process, after the award and negotiations to finalise the contract terms and conditions, is the signing of a formal agreement which sets out and records the terms of the contract between the parties. Remember, however, in the tendering process that the main contract comes into existence when the successful bidder is notified that their bid has been successful. So it does not really matter whether a formal agreement is subsequently agreed.

What has been discussed above is the tender negotiation that takes place before the contract is awarded. This differs from post-tender negotiations, which are discussed later in this session.

Self-assessment question 12.1

Briefly describe two situations in which a collateral obligation may arise in a tender process and refer to appropriate legal cases.

Feedback on page 189

12.2 Types of tender and collateral obligation

Learning activity 12.2

Consider the tendering process within your own organisation. Can you identify the various steps in the tender process?

Feedback on page 189

12

Types of tender procedure under EU Public Procurement Directives

Types of tender procedure are stipulated by the EU Public Procurement Directives, which is examined again in study session 13.

The Directives allow three types of tender procedure:

- open;
- restricted;
- negotiated.

Open procedure: This allows all interested suppliers to tender for the contract.

Restricted procedure: This is limited to suppliers who are invited to submit a tender by the prospective purchaser.

Negotiated procedure: This procedure is more limited even than the restricted procedure. In the negotiated procedure the prospective purchaser identifies a prospective supplier or suppliers and negotiates the terms of the contract directly with them.

The Directives stipulate the way the tenders are handled including the relevant notices to be published by way of the *Official Journal of the European Communities* (OJEC) and Tenders Electronic Daily (TED) database, the strict timetable for the various stages in the process. The process and deadlines are different for each of the types of procedure. However, the aim is the same: to gain the best value for money in the award of public contracts.

More detail on the three procedures is provided in study session 13. The aim of any type of tendering procedure is to gain the best value. In addition to this, the tender process must be fair and equitable.

EU tender thresholds

Tenders under the EU Public Procurement Directives are required to comply where the intended purchase is of ICT equipment, services or projects above a certain threshold.

The thresholds were revised in January 2006 and the current thresholds can be found on the Office of Government Commerce (OGC) website. It is important that you check the current threshold values before choosing your procurement route. If your planned purchase is above the threshold then you will need to use the EU tender route. This is discussed in more detail in study session 13.

E-tendering

More and more organisations are turning to e-commerce and e-procurement, which leads us to look at e-tendering.

There are websites offering assistance on e-tendering and e-procurement. They also provide details on some case studies on public bodies using e-procurement. You can find the websites by typing 'e-tendering' into one of the search engines such as Google: http://www.google.com.

The elements of e-procurement adopted by some organisations include:

- e-sourcing;
- e-transactions;
- e-contents;
- e-payments;
- management information online.

Many organisations have or are currently redefining procurement. Some, if not most, organisations are mature users of web technology and most will have or are moving towards having a PC (personal computer) and web browser on nearly every employee's desk. Computer and web technology bring many opportunities, such as raising awareness of e-procurement. It also challenges existing thinking and practice. It enables broader information to be obtained. Supply management and supplier relationships can be improved.

When considering e-procurement or ongoing improvement of e-procurement it is important to consider what the key drivers are, the key benefits and the key lessons learned.

Some key drivers include:

- business efficiency;
- meeting government targets;
- improved supplier relationships and communication;
- savings;
- consistency;
- improved expenditure control;
- best value.

Organisations that have moved into using e-procurement have found key benefits to include:

- improved information management on purchasing matters;
- improved purchasing practices because of standardisation and streamlining;
- 'hands-on' control on budgets;
- improved timely payment of supplier bills;
- reduction in paperwork and duplication of records;
- improved customer service;
- ability to analyse and measure expenditure and performance;
- managing contracts centrally;
- reduced processing of orders, invoices and cheques.

12

The above lists are not intended to be exhaustive but are a guideline. If your organisation has already developed an e-procurement strategy you can consider the benefits. If your organisation is not yet using e-procurement in all or most aspects then consider the benefits and why they are not developing it further.

Lessons have been learned by organisations that use e-procurement and they include the necessity to have a plan for communicating the process across the whole organisation. It is essential to have clear aims and objectives and to be disciplined in contract management. Also, remember that when introducing something new it takes time for people in the organisation to digest the change and the new system, both physically and emotionally!

You can search the Google website for the National e-Procurement Project's case studies, which represent real-life experience of a range of authorities detailing the barriers they face and decisions they have made to implement e-procurement solutions. These authorities were early adopters of e-procurement and provide valuable learning for all authorities who are implementing e-procurement.

Useful web links are OGC: http://www.ogc.gov.uk, which provide a guide to the changes introduced by the new Public Procurement Directives, and

I&DeA: http://www.idea-knowledge.gov.uk, which outlines government targets for English law authorities and discusses the significant benefits that can be obtained through adopting e-procurement. Look again at some of the benefits listed above.

You must remember that the various steps in the tendering process still exist even where the tendering process is e-tendering.

Self-assessment question 12.2

Summarise what you know of each of the tendering procedures: open, restricted and negotiated.

Feedback on page 189

12.3 Pre- and post-award obligations

Learning activity 12.3

Looking at tendering within your own organisation, explain how you ensure fair and equal treatment for all.

Feedback on page 190

12

Pre-tender obligations

As you have seen from the previous part of this session, and in particular the case of *R* v *Lottery Commission (ex parte Camelot plc)* [2000], it is important that all tenderers receive equal treatment. If negotiations are entered into with one tenderer before the contract has been awarded then all other tenderers must be offered the same opportunity. This differs from post-tender negotiations, which are discussed below. The pre-tender obligations include those discussed above and are detailed again below:

- to award to lowest bidder
- the tender price to remain open within the specified time;
- to consider all tenders that comply with requirements (*Blackpool and Fylde Aero Club* v *Blackpool Borough Council* [1990];
- to treat all tender bids equally (*R* v *Lottery Commission (ex parte Camelot plc)* [2000];
- to conduct the tender process in good faith.

Post-tender obligations

This differs from pre-tender obligations in that once the contract is awarded in the tendering process, negotiations can and usually do continue. These negotiations are to thrash out the details of the terms and conditions until there is agreement between the parties. The Peoples Lottery would not have had a case if in the case of *R* v *Lottery Commission* the contract had been awarded to Camelot and then further negotiations had taken place. So it is all about timing of the negotiations.

As you have already seen from earlier information, once post-tender negotiations have been finalised and an agreement has been reached, a formal agreement is or may be entered into.

Self-assessment question 12.3

Read the following short case study and answer the questions which follow:

Churbiton Council required cleaning services for their offices. They issued tender documents within which there was a requirement that the tenders be submitted to Room 101 on the second floor of their head office at Churbiton Council. There was no requirement that Churbiton accept the lowest tender. Tenders were to be submitted before 12.00 noon on the 30 May. Mangle Cleaning Services submitted their tender at 10.00 a.m. on 30 May, leaving the tender at the reception area. Churbiton accepted the tender of Thuraclean. Cleanquick challenged the award to Thuraclean on the grounds that Cleanquick were the lowest tenderer. Mangle Cleaning raised an action for damages on the grounds that their tender was not considered.

1   Advise Cleanquick on the success or otherwise of their action against Churbiton. Support your answer with case law.
2   Advise Mangle Cleaning on the success or otherwise of their action against Churbiton. Support your answer with case law.

Feedback on page 190

12

12.4 How to avoid the battle of the forms

See section 1.4.

Learning activity 12.4

Consider the previous information read in this session and your organisation. When entering into a contract, can you identify some of the documents that are used which will contain the terms and conditions of your organisation?

Feedback on page 190

Avoiding the battle of the forms

You have already learned how to avoid the battle of the forms, and that this is by using the tendering process. There are various steps in the process.

Where an organisation is a public authority then they must comply with the EU Public Procurement Directives, which are discussed in study session 13.

Self-assessment question 12.4

Explain the various steps in the tendering process.

Feedback on page 190

Revision question

Now try the revision question for this session on page 314.

Summary

In this session you looked at some of the forms used in contract formation, and that they often cause a 'battle' as to whose terms apply in the contract. You learned how to avoid the battle of the forms by using the tendering process. You looked at the various steps in the tendering procedure and collateral obligations. You also learned about the different types of tender for public authorities. You looked at how e-tendering is being used and developed and finally looked again at how tendering avoids the battle of the forms.

Suggested further reading

Griffiths and Griffiths (2002), part I, chapter 1, and part V, chapter 17.5.

Feedback on learning activities and self-assessment questions

Feedback on learning activity 12.1

This learning activity is to ensure that you understand the contract formation process and your understanding of the difference between an offer and an invitation to treat. You should recall that an offer indicates a willingness to enter into a legal obligation. Remember that to conclude a valid contract there must be clear and unqualified acceptance of the terms of the offer. You should also recall that if there are any qualifications then these become a counter-offer which terms must then be accepted in order to conclude the contract.

You also had to look at your organisation and the kinds of contract used. Did you recognise any of the documents used? Did they include order forms, enquiry forms, acknowledgements, despatch notes, delivery notes, invoices, confirmation of orders etc? Each of these documents may or will contain the terms and conditions of the organisation originating them. Where the buyer makes an offer on an order form it may be responded to by an acknowledgment slip which may contain different terms than the order form. In view of this you must not be complacent about all the different forms used. You should look at each one to ensure that you know what terms and conditions they contain. If there are differing terms then these require to be dealt with and accepted or otherwise. You must be able to recognise that there are a wide variety of possible scenarios which might arise when standard documents are used. They need to be managed carefully.

Feedback on self-assessment question 12.1

Your answer should include:

- to award to lowest bidder;
- no withdrawal of bid within the specified time;
- to consider all tenders that comply with requirements (*Blackpool and Fylde Aero Club* v *Blackpool Borough Council* [1990];
- all tender bids treated equally (*R* v *Lottery Commission (ex parte Camelot plc)* [2000];
- to conduct the tender process in good faith.

Feedback on learning activity 12.2

For this learning activity you should have looked at the tender process in your organisation. You should be able to identify the various steps, which include:

- establishing a list of people/organisations to be invited to bid;
- checking if contract is covered by procurement directives (see study session 13);
- preparing the tender documents;
- deciding on type of tender (see next part in this section);
- reviewing the submitted tenders;
- perhaps issuing letters of intent or letters of comfort to the chosen supplier;
- awarding the tender;
- formal agreement between the parties

Maybe you also identified the lengthy negotiations before the contract was awarded. Was there a formal agreement drawn up with the chosen bidder?

Feedback on self-assessment question 12.2

Your answer should provide a short paragraph on each of the procedures such as the following:

Open procedure: this allows all interested suppliers to tender for the contract.

Restricted procedure: this is limited to suppliers who are invited to submit a tender by the prospective purchaser.

Negotiated procedure: this procedure is more limited even than the restricted procedure. In the negotiated procedure the prospective purchaser

12

identifies a prospective supplier or suppliers and negotiates the terms of the contract directly with them.

Feedback on learning activity 12.3

For this learning activity you should refer to collateral obligations. If you understand these and write about these then you will ensure fair and equal treatment for all tender submissions. You should mention that the collateral obligations are distinct from but run alongside the main contract. Describe in brief paragraphs that usually it is stated that the contract will not necessarily be awarded to the lowest bidder; the tender must remain open for the specified time; all compliant tenders must be considered: you should refer to the *Blackpool and Fylde Aero Club* v *Blackpool Borough Council* [1990]. Mention also that all tender bids must be treated equally. You should refer to the case of *R* v *Lottery Commission (ex parte Camelot plc)* [2000]. And of course the process in tendering must be in good faith or it may or will give rise to legal action.

Feedback on self-assessment question 12.3

1   As far as Cleanquick is concerned, they have no grounds for action as Churbiton did not state in the tender documents that they were required to accept the lowest bid. Only if Churbiton had expressly required that they accept the lowest bid would Cleanquick have a case on the ground of breach of a collateral obligation.
2   For Mangle Cleaning, this relates to the collateral obligation of a requirement on Churbiton to consider all tenders. However, you must consider whether Mangle submitted their tender on time and at the specified place. Mangle did not comply with the requirements of the tender document, which stated that the tender had to be submitted to Room 101. In this case Mangle will not be successful. You can refer to the *Blackpool and Fylde Aero Club* case.

Feedback on learning activity 12.4

This learning activity requires you to consider contracts entered into by your organisation for the supply of goods and services. You should identify forms such as order forms, enquiry forms, acknowledgement slips, despatch notes, delivery notes, invoices, order confirmations. You should also mention that each of these documents may and will contain the terms and conditions of your organisation. Likewise, when a supplier responds, they may or will have terms and conditions on their acknowledgement slips and offers, etc. It is because of all the differing forms containing terms and conditions that a 'battle' can arise as to whose terms and conditions apply in the contract.

Feedback on self-assessment question 12.4

The various steps that you will set out include:

*   establishing a list of people/organisations to be invited to bid;
*   checking if contract is covered by procurement directives (see study session 13);

- preparing the tender documents;
- deciding on type of tender;
- reviewing the submitted tenders;
- perhaps issuing letters of intent or letters of comfort to the chosen supplier;
- awarding the tender;
- formal agreement between the parties.

You should also mention that there may be, and often are, lengthy negotiations before the contract is awarded. Once the contract is awarded you can also draw up a formal agreement.

12

12

Implications of EU Public Sector Directives

'Ensuring value for money and encouraging strong competition go hand in hand.'
Pre-Budget Report 2002

Introduction

In this session you will be looking at the impact of the European Union (EU) Public Sector Directives, framework agreements, the different types of tendering procedure and in particular competitive tendering. You will also learn about e-procurement, its increasing use and the function of centralised purchasing bodies.

Session learning objectives

After completing this session you should be able to:

13.1 Examine the impact of the EU Public Sector Directives.
13.2 Describe framework agreements.
13.3 Identify and describe the open, restricted, negotiated and competitive tendering procedure.
13.4 Assess the use of e-procurement mechanisms and central purchasing bodies.

Unit content coverage

This study session covers the following topics from the official CIPS unit content document:

Learning outcome

Diagnose the impact of specific UK and EU regulations on the purchasing and supply function.

Learning objective

3.2 Critically assess the responsibilities of public procurement staff resulting from the EU Public Sector Directive 2004/18/EC (including the Utilities Directive).
  • Thresholds, time limits, advertising
  • Award criteria
  • Right to feedback
  • Framework agreements
  • Open, restricted, negotiated and competitive dialogue procedure
  • E-procurement mechanisms
  • Central purchasing bodies
  • Social and environmental considerations

13

Prior knowledge

Study sessions 1 – 12, particularly study sessions 1 and 12.

Timing

You should set aside about 6 hours to read and complete this session, including learning activities, self-assessment questions, the suggested further reading (if any) and the revision question.

13.1 EU Public Procurement Directives

In study session 12 you looked at the use of tendering in commercial buying. Tendering procedures can apply to private and public sectors. However, the major difference is that public sector bodies are subject to the European Union (EU) Directives on Public Procurement. You will look at these Directives in this session. The Directives are legal rules that only apply to public sector bodies in the European Community. The legal rules stipulate how public sector bodies should approach the award of high-value contracts for the supply of goods and services. What is meant by high-value is dictated by the threshold levels, which are discussed later in this session.

Total public expenditure in the EU, of goods, services and public works by governments and public utilities, was estimated at about €1500 billion in 2002. Public procurement varies significantly between member states and the opening of public procurement within the internal market has increased cross-border competition and improved prices by public authorities.

The European Commission adopted a package of amendments to simplify and modernise the public procurement Directives. Directive 2004/18/EC coordinates the procedures for the award of public works contract, public supply contracts and public service contracts.

EU key objective

The key objective of the EU was and is the establishment of a free market without trade barriers between member states. It follows that the aims of the EU Public Procurement Directives are intended to guarantee fair and non-discriminatory international competition in bidding for goods, services and works above specified threshold values. The threshold values are reviewed on a regular basis, normally every two years. It is recommended that as a procurement professional you should regularly check the levels of the thresholds. The current levels of thresholds can be viewed on the internet at government websites. These levels are also shown in table 13.1 in learning activity 13.1 below, and on the government website OGC: http://www.ogc.gov.uk.

13

Learning activity 13.1

Search the website OGC: http://www.ogc.gov.uk to find the current thresholds for procurements. List or draw in table form the current levels

(continued on next page)

Learning activity 13.1 *(continued)*

applicable to the Supplies Directive, Services Directive and the Works Directive.

Feedback on page 208

Background to EU Public Procurement Directives

In many countries the public sector accounts for much of the economic activity in the economy. The Treaty of Rome (Article 86) establishing the European Community aimed to establish freedom of movement of goods, persons, services and capital by the existence of a single market in which there are no internal borders, which could be barriers to free trade and competition within the external boundaries of the European Union. There were a series of Directives introduced to implement the provisions of the Treaty of Rome.

There are six Directives constituting the Public Procurement Directives that are applicable to contractor authorities. The contracting authorities are:

- the state;
- regional authorities;
- local authorities;
- bodies governed by public law;
- associations formed by one or more bodies governed by public law.

The first two Directives (Council Directive 89/665/EEC – December 1989 and 92/13/EEC – February 1992) provide for remedies in the event of non-compliance with the set procedures laid down in the other four Directives. These four Directives lay down the procedures to be followed in tendering and award of relevant contracts. The regulations were amended by the Public Contracts (Works, Services and Supply) (Amendment) Act 2000.

Just as the thresholds differ between sectors so does the effect of the EU procurement directives. For the full extent of the effect of the directives we recommend the further reading suggested at the end of this session. In brief, the Directives have opened up supply markets in areas where competition had been restricted.

The policy of the EU is to open up public procurement and encourage member states to take tenders from firms throughout the community and to award contracts to the best contender, which may or may not be in their own country.

EU Public Sector Directives

These include:

- Public Works Directive;
- Public Supplies Directive;
- Public Services Directive;
- Utilities Directive;

13

- Compliance Directive - Public Purchasing Remedies Directive 1989 amended by the Services Directive 1992.

There are features that are common to all Directives and are discussed in more detail below. The main provisions of the EU Directives include:

- thresholds (supplies, services, works);
- advertisements and prior indicative notices (PIN);
- technical standards and specifications;
- timescales;
- framework arrangements which are discussed in the next section below;
- procedures (open, restricted, negotiated), which are discussed in the last section of this session;
- evaluation criteria.

Thresholds (supplies, services, works)

The Directives apply to procurements above specified threshold values. By following learning activity 13.1 above, you should already be familiar with the levels. Also, from the information at the beginning of this session, you know that they are reviewed on a regular basis, normally every two years.

Despite the levels of threshold, all Directives allow certain exceptions. For the EU services exceptions table, you can go to the internet and find out through the government website.

Advertisements and prior indicative notices (PINs)

One of the main provisions of the Directives is that contracts are published EU-wide to give firms across the EU Community the opportunity to participate in the submission of a tender.

The individual public sector bodies, that is, the contracting authorities, must publish a notice giving brief details of prospective contracts that are likely to be let in the following 12 months. This includes contracts within each category which individually or in aggregate are expected to exceed the threshold level. Where such a prior indicative notice (PIN) is given, then the open and restricted procedures may be shortened. These types of procedure are discussed in study session 12 and later in this session.

Technical standards and specifications

All Directives provide that specifications for contracts subject to the Directives must refer to a British Standard that implements a European Standard where possible. The words used after British Standard within a tender are 'or equivalent' to indicate if a European Standard is not used. Exceptions can be made where the use of a European Standard is not possible owing to national binding rules, such as health and safety, or the European Standard being incompatible, too costly, technical difficulties arising, etc. In such cases reasons must be given in the contract.

Specifications should not refer to proprietary brands but if this is not possible then the appropriate words 'or equivalent' should be inserted after the brand name.

13

Timescales

There are minimum timescales laid down by the Directives. These are aimed at providing prospective suppliers with sufficient time to respond to notices. Timescales can be reduced for urgent requirements under restricted and negotiated procedures. The reason for the urgency must be stated in the notice. Reducing the timescale is done through an accelerated procedure which can be challenged by the Commission.

Timescales must be built into projections for contract awards. After a notice has been sent to the *Official Journal of the European Communities* (OJEC), the Department of Trade and Industry (DTI) can alert companies who have shown an interest in tendering. These companies should be sent a copy of the notice. No additional information should be given to these companies.

Under Directive (2001/78/EC), the European Commission has made the use of standard forms for notices to be published mandatory. As the standard forms are complex and time-consuming, it is DTI policy that a web-based software package is used to generate OJEC notices and to transmit them to the OJEC in Luxembourg. Information on this can be obtained through the government internet site.

Framework arrangements and tender procedures are discussed later in this session.

Evaluation criteria

The main criterion is to award the contract to the economically most advantageous bid. Detailed evaluation must be provided within the invitation to tender; this includes quality, experience and resources.

Good practice information

It is worthwhile noting some good practice points. To improve the procurement process, development of suppliers and future competitiveness, the purchasing organisation should debrief all suppliers so that those who were unsuccessful will understand why they were not selected and failed to win the contract. Debriefing should be done by experienced professionals and it must be accurate.

We will now look at each of the Directives in turn.

Public Works Directive

This Directive consolidates previous directives on public works contracts. The Directive redefines public words to include those with 50% public funding. The contract value threshold refers to contracts valued at more than specific amounts of European Currency Units (ECUs; now renamed Euros). The threshold is re-assessed every two years.

Two important changes were made relating to the requirement of purchasers. These were:

- to give more notice of construction projects; and
- to provide reasons for refusing a contractor's application or bid.

Public Supplies Directive

As with the Public Works Directive, this consolidated all previous directives and set out procedures to be followed where a public body wanted to enter into a contract for the rental, lease, purchase or hire purchase of goods worth more than the specific amount of ECUs. The threshold levels differ depending on whether the contract relates to matters covered by the General Agreement on Tariffs and Trade (GATT) or World Trade Organization (WTO) agreements on government procurement. In this Directive, three types of tender procedure were set out. These tender procedures are, briefly:

- open tender procedure: a procedure when anyone can apply. This procedure is used when the main criteria is lowest price;
- restricted tender procedure: where applications have been pre-vetted. This procedure is used where only suppliers who are pre-qualified are invited to make a bid. This is the procedure used for most tenders;
- negotiated tender procedure: where contractors are chosen. This procedure is used in certain circumstances only, such as an emergency or in the case of a supplier who must be used again because they have retained some design or intellectual property right.

These tender procedures have been discussed in study session 12. We recommend that you return to that session to ensure you understand the different tender procedures.

The Public Supplies Directive included details of the following:

- when each type of tender procedure should be used;
- advertising requirements;
- time limits;
- publication of results;
- the use of European standards and technical specifications;
- strict award criteria.

Member states are required to report annually on contracts awarded by public bodies in their territory.

Public Services Directive

This covers most contracts that are not classified as public works or supplies. It applies where contracts have a bid value of over a specified number of ECUs. This Directive divides contracts into 'priority' and 'residual' categories with different procedures applying in each case. The Directive is also concerned with contracts relating to:

- advertising services;
- computer and maintenance services;
- financial services;
- transport (except rail);
- some telecommunications;
- refuse disposal and sewage;
- design contests to award contracts;

13

- defence services unless they fall within national security provisions.

Utilities Directive and Utilities Regulations 2006

The Public Supply Directive does not include public utilities. They were governed by the Excluded Sector Directive 1990, also referred to as the Utilities Directive, which has since been further developed by a new Directive 2004/17/EC. This new Directive came into force on 30 April 2004 and was implemented on 31 January 2006. The Utilities Contracts Regulations 2006 coordinates the procurement of utilities such as energy, water, transport and postal services sectors.

The Utilities Directive is a vast subject area. In developing its policy for the new Directive, the OGC consulted widely including utilities, the Chartered Institute of Purchasing and Supply, Confederation of British Industry, Department for Environment, Food and Rural Affairs, Northern Ireland Office, Heads of Procurement in other government departments, Office of the Deputy Prime Minister, Small Business Service and Trades Union Congress. The full text of the new Utilities Directive (2004/17/EC) is available at EU: http://www.europa.eu.int.

In addition to implementing the new Directive (2004/17/EC), the European Court of Justice (ECJ) ruled in *Alcatel Austria* v *Bundesministerium für Wissenshaft und Verkehr* [C-81/98], known as the 'Alcatel case [1998]', that for procurements caught by the EU Procurement Directives a contract award decision must in all cases be open to review before contract conclusion to enable the award decision to be set aside by a court where an aggrieved bidder has been prejudiced by a breach of the rules, notwithstanding the possibility of damages being awarded after contract conclusion. To comply with this judgment the UK government agreed on a 10-day mandatory standstill period to be introduced in the UK between the communication of award decision and contract conclusion for procurements subject to the EU Directives.

Impact of the new Directive on public sector bodies

The Directive does not impose any burdens on business generally as in the main it clarified, simplified and modernised existing legislation. It was also anticipated that the savings from increased competition and structured procurement would outweigh the costs of compliance. There should be no disproportionate effect on any particular business sectors and public sector bodies in other EU member states as they will all be subject to the rules in the same way.

Compliance Directive (as amended by Services Directive 1992)

This Directive governs compliance with public procurement procedures for public works and supply contracts. It set up a national appeals procedure for infringements. It provided for damages for victims.

The study of EU Directives is challenging as it is not only a vast subject area but always evolving and developing. It is recommended that as a procurement professional you should continue to seek out information from the appropriate government websites.

13

13.2 Framework agreements

Framework agreements are usually public sector agreements as they are used for the specific needs of a group of organisations. Such groups include, for example, local enterprise agencies, colleges and regional buying consortia, etc. The agreements can be set up for any type of goods or services. To set up a framework agreement you need to go through the tendering process and select consultants who will be able to offer the services required under the agreement.

Framework agreements are designed to provide better value for money than an organisation would find elsewhere. Such agreements foster shared innovative and quality products and services across government and its partners. This enables joined-up, effective service delivery and improved communication. Efficiency savings are achieved through this collaborative procurement process and cost-effectiveness of shared resources.

Framework agreements are set up for several, say 3–5, years and provide a list of consultants and contractors to provide services within certain categories. You may have a list of 20 or more consultants in a framework agreement who can offer services varying from procurement and finance, to management and recruitment, and so on. When a framework agreement is in place and you identify a specific need, you then identify who, listed in the agreement, is available and ask them to provide a specific price.

Where a framework agreement is being considered it is important to ensure that its scope enables the organisation, buying consortia, etc to use it. If the purchase exceeds the EU threshold then it is important to ensure that the framework agreement is compliant with the EU Directives and the EU tendering process. If the framework agreement does not comply then neither will any subsequent individual contract.

Framework agreements generally provide a list of approved suppliers from whom to choose to buy the goods or services. One of the advantages of a framework agreement is that it consolidates all information. This results in better price, better quality for the price paid and added-value benefits. Organisations that use the framework agreement know that approved prospective suppliers have been checked for reliability and capability.

The framework agreements should contain the fundamental terms and conditions under which the contracts are entered into and any contracting organisations should ensure that framework agreements do establish such fundamental terms as price, on which subsequent contracts will be awarded.

Where the framework agreements contain the fundamental terms and conditions of the contract then subsequent individual contracts under such an agreement can be awarded without a further need to call for competition.

Where framework agreements containing the fundamental terms and conditions are extended to several suppliers the basis for awarding the framework agreements and deciding between the suppliers is the criteria allowed under the EU Directives, which is the lowest price or the most economically advantageous tender.

An organisation must also ensure that if the intended purchase falls above the EU thresholds then the framework agreement must comply; that is, the framework agreement must be set up by the EU tendering process.

Self-assessment question 13.2

Read the following short statements and answer true or false to each.

1 A framework agreement is used by a group who have specific needs for the purchase of goods or services to obtain better value for money.
2 Where a framework agreement has not followed the EU tendering process you can still use the framework agreement to purchase your goods where the value is above the EU thresholds.
3 Where the framework agreement contains the fundamental terms and conditions of the contract, subsequent individual contracts under the agreement can be awarded with any further competition process.
4 The terms established in the framework agreement are open to renegotiation even after the contract is awarded.

Feedback on page 209

13

13.3 Open, restricted, negotiated and competitive tendering procedures

The tendering procedures of open, restricted and negotiated have been discussed in study session 12. We recommend that you revisit that session to ensure your understanding of these processes and refresh your memory.

In this part, we are going to briefly consider these procedures again, but the focus will be on the competitive tendering procedure.

Learning activity 13.3

Having already considered the tendering process, describe the types of tender learned.

Feedback on page 210

Tendering procedures

By revisiting study session 12 and doing learning activity 13.3 above, you should have knowledge of the different types of tendering procedure. The difference between the open and restricted tendering as opposed to the negotiated process is that in the open and restricted procedure the tendering process is competitive. It is this competitive process that we are interested in discussing in this part of the session.

In the competitive tendering process, prospective suppliers are invited to submit their prices for a particular contract. The procedure starts by the buyer issuing an invitation to tender either through an advertisement or directly to selected vendors. You know from study session 12 that the buyer will list details of their requirements, provide adequate specification, their statement of the terms and conditions of the contract and the date by which the offers should be submitted to the buyer.

The tendering process can apply to private and public sectors. However, the major difference in tendering is that the public sector bodies are subject to the EU Directives on Public Procurement. You learned about these in the previous part of this session.

You are now going look at when competitive tendering is appropriate and the compulsory competitive tendering to which certain public bodies are subject.

Competitive tendering

The use of tendering and competitive bidding to find prospective suppliers and award contracts may not be the most appropriate way of buying. Whether you use the method of competitive tendering will depend on certain conditions. These include looking at various aspects and asking questions such as:

- Does the value of the purchase justify the time and effort of the tendering process?
- Are the specifications clear to all parties?
- Are there enough suppliers?
- Do the suppliers have the technical competency and expertise?
- Do the suppliers actually want the contract?
- Is there enough time to carry out the tendering process?

In addition to these questions, the buyers should have knowledge of the prices for the goods and services they want to buy, they should not be

13

performing a tendering exercise just to test the market, and they should have a good reputation and be trusted by suppliers.

Now you are going to look at competitive tendering within public sector bodies.

Compulsory competitive tendering (CCT)

Compulsory competitive tendering (CCT) was introduced in the UK in the 1980s to bring greater efficiency to local government and health services by competition. At the time it was recognised that strong incentives were needed to stimulate reform, but the aspect of it being compulsory was one of the reasons for resistance by local authorities and health trusts.

The main aim of CCT was to ensure that value for money was achieved for the services that are used directly by the public sector body. The Local Government Act 1992 introduced 'best value authorities' which included local authorities, police authorities, fire authorities and more.

Best value authorities

'Best value authorities' have a duty to ensure continuous improvement of all their functions by taking cognisance of three main factors, namely:

- efficiency;
- effectiveness;
- economy.

To fulfil their obligation in these areas the best value authorities must consult with various groups such as tax payers, rate payers, those using the services and all interested parties. The authorities must also be subject to performance indicators and standards against which they can assess their performance. They must review their ongoing performance and prepare best value performance plans each financial year.

The plans are made available to the electorate before voting, which for local authorities takes place in May of each year. The Secretary of State for Trade and Industry dictates what factors must be included in the plans and how they are published. Such factors include what are the objectives of the authority, the timetable for implementation of its plans, its performance progress and assessment. The performance plan of the authority is subject to audit by the authority's auditor, who can make recommendations and amendments in order for the plan to comply with legislation. The auditor can forward the plan to the Secretary of State who can also require further amendments for compliance with the 1999 Act. The Secretary of State can require the authorities to follow specified procedures for their performance plans.

Ongoing improvement in the public sector

The subject of 'best value authorities' is a vast one and much information can be obtained from the internet by looking at government websites, the website of the Audit Commission, and by typing in the words 'compulsory competitive tendering' into one of the search engines such as Google. Much

13

research is also being undertaken by universities, and the positions for 'best value' vary throughout the UK.

Some councils responded well to best value and use it to deliver improved services. The Audit Commission report *Changing Gear* of December 2005 identified some critical factors underlying performance of the best councils. These factors included:

- support and commitment from authority members and staff;
- effective performance management systems;
- integration with other planning systems such as budgeting.

The Audit Commission made recommendations in their report which included finding better ways of communicating the audit findings to local people, and that councils should critically evaluate their progress in best value.

Self-assessment question 13.3

Answer the following questions.

1 What questions should you ask before embarking on competitive tendering?
2 What should the buyer be aware of before carrying out a tendering exercise?
3 What three factors should best value authorities take into account in order to ensure continuous improvement of all their functions?

Feedback on page 210

13.4 E-procurement mechanisms and central purchasing bodies

E-procurement can be defined as the use of the internet or IT for the purchase of goods and services. The 'e' stands for electronic and therefore it includes the use of email and other forms of electronic exchange between parties.

Changes in business throughout the world make the procurement function of an organisation an increasingly vital one. With the increased global scope of operations, e-procurement and electronic exchanges are become more necessary.

Learning activity 13.4

Consider your own organisation and find out if your organisation uses the internet for e-procurement or uses electronic exchanges in the procurement process. If it does, describe some of the benefits and some

(continued on next page)

Learning activity 13.4 *(continued)*

of the disadvantages. You will learn more about these in this session. The purpose of this exercise is to find out the practical use of e-procurement.

Feedback on page 211

E-procurement

As you know from the brief introduction above, e-procurement is the term used to describe the use of electronic methods at every stage of the purchasing process from identifying the requirement to purchase goods and services through to electronic payment for the goods and services. In addition to the actual procurement process, electronic methods can be used to manage the contract.

Benefits of e-procurement

The benefits of procurement through electronic methods include:

* improved efficiency in the way people work;
* improved commercial relationships with suppliers;
* improved supply chain management.

In addition to the above benefits, e-procurement also modernises the procurement process, and where suppliers are dealing with government bodies it reduces costs.

Private and public sector organisations are recognising the improved efficiency and reduced costs that e-procurement can bring. Central government, local government and strategic private partners are introducing and developing e-commerce systems for public sector purchasing.

A new team has been set up with the Office of Government Commerce (OGC), called the Cross Sector eProcurement Team (CSePT), to promote efficiency gains across the public sector by highlighting the opportunities provided by electronic procurement. The main aim of this team is to assist the public sector to realise the benefits of e-procurement.

Targets for adoption of e-procurement by local authorities were set up by the government, with deadlines by December 2005. Information on the targets and best value indicators can be found in the paper 'e-Procurement Government Targets for English Authorities' (2004), which is accessible with other information and links on OGC: http://www.ogc.gov.uk.

National e-procurement was studied across various local authorities (see OGC: http://www.ogc.gov.uk) and several key drivers, benefits and lessons were identified. There are too many to list here but some are shown below.

Key drivers of e-procurement

The following list is not exhaustive and is intended as a guideline only:

* best value;
* business efficiency;
* improved and more accurate supplier management and communication;
* consistent terms with suppliers;

13

- savings and reduced processing costs;
- reduced manual and paper based work;
- centralised and controlled purchasing.

Not all the above were considered key drivers by all the authorities participating in the study. The key driver for most of the local authorities was business efficiency.

Key benefits of e-procurement

The list of key benefits identified below is not exhaustive but is intended as a guide only. Also, the key benefits identified varied across the local authorities participating in the project:

- improved management information across all areas of purchasing;
- standardisation of purchasing practices;
- better use of corporate contacts;
- budget holders have 'hands-on' control;
- reduced paper work;
- improved customer service;
- supplier bills paid on time.

The major benefit identified by most of the authorities involved in the case study was improved management information across all areas of purchasing.

Key lessons learned from e-procurement

The lessons learned varied across the different local authorities but some included:

- authority-wide communication plan;
- need to know level of resources required to implement and maintain the system;
- necessary to involve all levels of the organisation from chief executive to base level;
- prepare for the unexpected;
- clear vision of aims and objectives.

The two major lessons learned by most of the authorities were the need for an authority-wide communication plan and not to underestimate the level of resources needed.

Future of e-procurement

Many councils are redefining their procurement processes. It is good practice to have an e-procurement policy, strategy and investment plan.

Some of the elements of e-procurement include the following electronic elements:

- e-sourcing;
- e-transactions;
- e-content;
- e-payments;
- e-management information.

13

Centralised purchasing bodies

A specific provision on central purchasing bodies was included in the new public procurement Directives, which required the UK to implement them by 31 January 2006.

A centralised purchasing body (CPB) is defined in the public contracts regulations as a contracting authority that:

- acquires goods or services for one or more contracting authorities;
- awards public contracts for one or more contracting authorities;
- concludes framework agreements for work, goods or services intended for one or more contracting authorities.

Where works, goods or services are acquired by a contracting authority through a CPB, then it will be deemed to have complied with the regulations provided the CPB has complied with them in the original acquisition or award. If the CPB does not comply then the contracting authority will not comply either.

Self-assessment question 13.4

Define e-procurement and why organisations are using it more. List some of the benefits of e-procurement.

Feedback on page 211

A suggested procedure for a public authority

As you have been looking at the tendering processes in this session and in study session 12, it is worthwhile to include a suggested procedure that can be followed by a public authority embarking on the tendering process. It is not exhaustive and is intended as a guideline only.

When considering the procurement process you will recall from the above sessions that the value of the contract has to be looked at in light of the threshold levels set by the EU Public Procurement Directives.

The basic principles of these Directives are to prevent discrimination against companies from any member state and to remove restrictions on free movement of goods and services. These Directives also set out clear standards and procedures to be followed by public authorities in choosing tenderers and awarding contracts. The standards are based on fairness, openness, non-discrimination and competition.

The types of contract must also be considered: from one-off purchases of a specific product or service by a specific date; or purchase of goods or services over a period of time; or a framework agreement over a specific period.

There must then be decisions on advertising the contract, the requirements and advice for tenderers such as deadlines, any pre-qualification stages and any evaluation information to be included in the invitation to tender.

13

When it comes to awarding the contract the aim is usually to award to the supplier who offers the most economically advantageous tender based on the combination of price and quality.

Other matters to consider are the payment of invoices and payment certificates. Health and safety issues may need to be considered where the contract requires that contractors are certified under the appropriate health and safety scheme.

As you will see from this session and study session 12, the tendering process is a vast subject area and more information can be read in the suggested further reading below.

Revision question

Now try the revision question for this session on page 314.

Summary

In this session you have looked at the impact of the EU Public Sector Directives and framework agreements. Although you looked at different types of tender in study session 12, you learned more about them in this session as well as studying competitive tendering.

Because of changes in global business, you learned about e-procurement, its increasing use and the function of centralised purchasing bodies.

Suggested further reading

Griffiths and Griffiths (2002), part V, chapter 17.4.

OGC: http://www.ogc.gov.uk and related websites.

Feedback on learning activities and self-assessment questions

Feedback on learning activity 13.1

This learning activity is firstly to get you used to looking outside your organisation for threshold information and not just relying on internal information. This is necessary as the threshold levels are reviewed regularly. You should then show the levels as you have identified them to be in each of the following areas: the current levels as at 31 January 2006 are shown in table 13.1.

Table 13.1

	Supplies	Services	Works
Central government bodies subject to the World Trade Organization (WTO) and Government Procurement Agreement (GPA)	£93,738 or €137,000	£93,738[1] or €137,000	£3,611,319[2] or €5,278,000

(continued on next page)

Table 13.1 *(continued)*

	Supplies	Services	Works
Other public sector contracting authorities	£144,371 or €211,000	£144,371 or €211,000	£3,611,319[2] or €5,278,000
Indicative notices	£513,166 or €750,000	£513,166 or €750,000	£3,611,319[2] or €5,278,000
Small lots	£54,738 or €80,000	£54,738 or €80,000	£684,211 or €1,000,000

[1]With the exception of the following services that have a threshold of £144,371 (€211,000):

- Part B (residual) services.
- Research and Development Services – category 8.
- Telecommunications services – category 5, that is, TV and Radio, interconnection, integrated telecommunications.
- Subsidised services contracts under regulation 34.

[2]Includes subsidised services contracts under regulation 34.

Utilities is not included in this learning activity, but information on thresholds is available on the government website.

Feedback on self-assessment question 13.1

You should provide a short paragraph on each of the main provisions as described in the text of this part of the session. This will include short description of each of the following:

- thresholds (supplies, services, works);
- advertisements and prior indicative notices (PIN);
- technical standards and specifications;
- timescales;
- framework arrangements (which are discussed in section 13.2);
- procedures (open, restricted, negotiated) (which are discussed in the section 13.4);
- evaluation criteria.

Feedback on learning activity 13.2

Your activity should involve thinking about groups of organisations that might use a framework agreement. This could be schools or colleges, or your local enterprise agency and so on. The advantages that you should describe include the pulling together of resources and therefore achieving cost-efficiency, innovation and improved communication.

Feedback on self-assessment question 13.2

1 True: this is the purpose of framework agreements, to consolidate information for better price, quality, value.
2 False: if the intended purchase is above the EU threshold, then the framework agreement must follow the EU tendering process.
3 True: this is one of the advantages of the framework agreement. Where it contains all the fundamental terms and conditions then

13

subsequent individual contracts can be awarded without going through the competitive process again. This saves on costs.

4   False: once the contract is awarded, the framework agreement is not open to renegotiation upwards or downwards. When a contract is awarded based on a framework agreement then the parties may not make amendments to the terms laid down in the framework agreement. When you identify the need under a framework agreement you then identify the consultant who can provide the required service and ask them to give you a specific price. In the framework agreement they may have given an hourly rate.

Feedback on learning activity 13.3

This learning activity is to ensure your understanding of the different types of tender. You should write a paragraph on each of the types of open, restricted and negotiated tender. This information should be something along the lines of the following.

Open procedure allows all interested suppliers to tender for the contract.

Restricted procedure is limited to suppliers who are invited to submit a tender by the prospective purchaser.

Negotiated procedure is even more limited than the restricted type as the prospective purchaser identifies the prospective supplier and negotiates the terms of the contract directly with them.

Feedback on self-assessment question 13.3

Question 1

- Does the value of the purchase justify the time and effort of the tendering process?
- Are the specifications clear to all parties?
- Are there enough suppliers?
- Do the suppliers have the technical competency and expertise?
- Do the suppliers actually want the contract?
- Is there enough time to carry out the tendering process?

Question 2

Buyers should have knowledge of the prices for the goods and services they want to buy, they should not be performing a tendering exercise just to test the market, and they should have a good reputation and be trusted by suppliers.

Question 3

'Best value authorities' have a duty to ensure continuous improvement of all their functions by taking cognisance of three main factors, namely:

- efficiency;
- effectiveness;
- economy.

13

Feedback on learning activity 13.4

In this learning activity you should have discovered whether your organisation is using the internet for procurement purposes. If so, did you discover if they have an e-procurement framework that lists some of the main procurement areas such as the purchasing tasks, the internal and external tasks. Your organisation may not yet be using, or using to its best effect, the e-procurement route. You may have discovered that this is because of a lack of understanding of the use of the process or because it is thought to be too complex and therefore perceived as more expensive.

Even if your organisation does not use the internet it will, like most, use email and other electronic exchanges. This will certainly be internal. Does it use such exchanges for external matters? If not, did you find out why and did that include a lack of knowledge of the use of emails externally or was there a perceived worry about the confidentiality?

Feedback on self-assessment question 13.4

You should define e-procurement as the use of the internet or information technology (IT) for the purchase of goods and services. The 'e' stands for electronic; therefore it also includes the use of email and other forms of electronic exchanges between parties.

The reason for its increased use is global changes in business making the procurement function of an organisation an increasingly vital one.

Your list of benefits can include:

- improved management information across all areas of purchasing;
- standardisation of purchasing practices;
- better use of corporate contacts;
- budget holders have 'hands-on' control;
- reduced paper work;
- improved customer service;
- supplier bills paid on time.

Of the above, in some case studies the major benefit identified by most of the authorities involved was improved management information.

13

Legal impact of Freedom of Information Act 2000

Introduction

In this study session you are going to learn about the Freedom of Information Act 2000 and its impact on procurement. You will also learn that under the Freedom of Information Act 2000 there is a right to request information. However, you will also be looking at certain exemptions that fall into two categories: one where all information of certain types cannot be disclosed; the other where information may be exempt subject to a 'prejudice' test.

'...It is inevitable...that a government is going to have some defensive reaction and say, "We are not going to tell you anything more than we can about what is going to discredit us".'

Maurice Frankel, Director of Freedom of Information Campaign, 2004

Session learning objectives

After completing this session you should be able to:

14.1 Evaluate the impact of the Freedom of Information Act 2000 on procurement.
14.2 Explain disclosure.
14.3 Describe and explain the exemptions.

Unit content coverage

This study session covers the following topics from the official CIPS unit content document:

Learning objective

3.3 Critically evaluate the impact of the Freedom of Information Act 2000 on the procurement function
  • Right to request information
  • Absolute exemptions
  • Qualified exemptions
  • Partial disclosure

Prior knowledge

Study sessions 12 and 13.

Timing

You should set aside about 4 hours to read and complete this session, including learning activities, self-assessment questions, the suggested further reading (if any) and the revision question.

14

14.1 Impact of the Freedom of Information Act 2000 on procurement

What is freedom of information?

It could be said that commitment to freedom of information is a political principle which asserts that members of the public have a right to know what the state is doing and what it knows about them.

In practice, freedom of information usually means a statutory right on the part of the public to see certain types of recorded information held by public authorities. This right to know has existed in other countries for many years; for example, it has existed in Sweden since the 18th century. In the UK freedom of information was given statutory force by the Freedom of Information Act 2000.

Background

Before the Freedom of Information Act 2000 the British state had a long tradition of secrecy and unwillingness to publish information about its workings. Under the Official Secrets Act 1911 it was a criminal offence for any civil servant or public contractor to reveal any information that they had learned in the course of their work. Prosecutions under the 1911 Act continued into the 1980s despite recommendations from the Frank Committee that reform was needed.

Progress was made through the 1970s, with the Labour Party including a Freedom of Information Act in its 1974 manifesto. Support was given to a private member's bill introduced in 1978 by Liberal MP Clement Freud.

The introduction of the Data Protection Act 1984 gave members of the public a right to see computerised records about themselves. The Local Government (Access to Information) Act 1985 required meetings of local authorities and associated documentation to be open to the public. The Personal Files Act 1987 gave the public access to manually held social work and housing records. This was extended to medical records under the Medical Reports Act 1988. Access to health records followed in the Access of Health Records Act 1990. However, it took some time before the Freedom of Information Act 2000 was finally passed, and it only fully came into force in January 2005.

Public Records Act 1958

The 2000 Act amends the Public Records Act 1958, which placed a duty on the Keeper of Public Records to provide reasonable facilities for inspecting and obtaining copies of records. Under the 2000 Act the powers of the Information Commissioner extend to the information contained in these records.

Data Protection Act 1998

The 2000 Act makes some minor amendments to the 1998 Act but more particularly extends the provisions of the Data Protection Act 1998 about access to personal information held by public authorities to include relevant personal information processed by or on behalf of both Houses of Parliament.

14

Freedom of Information Act 2000

The Act is an important area for procurement professionals, particularly in the public sector, as it requires public bodies to adopt publication schemes that state what, when and how the public bodies make certain types of information available. The 2000 Act also sets the fees that are required to be paid for access to such information.

Although the 2000 Act came into force in November 2000, one of the new rights under the Act came into force in January 2005. This new right provided that any person making a request in writing to a public authority for information must be told whether the authority holds the information and if they do hold the information the person must be provided with the information unless it falls within the exempt categories which are discussed later on.

Publication scheme

A publication scheme is a public commitment to make certain information available to the public and it is a guide to how the information can be obtained by the public.

Summary of the 2000 Act

The main provisions of the Act are that it:

- provides a general right of access to all types of recorded information held by public authorities;
- imposes an obligation on public authorities to produce and maintain a publication scheme approved by the independent Information Commissioner;
- exempts certain information from disclosure (see later on in this session);
- establishes the process for enforcement and appeal.

The impact of the 2000 Act is the obligation it places on public bodies to provide access to the public to recorded information. The Act has further impact because of the wide interpretation on what is meant by 'public authority'. This is discussed further later on.

Of course, certain conditions require to be fulfilled before a public authority is obliged to comply with a request from a member of the public. The public body can also charge fees, which are set by the Secretary of State for Constitutional Affairs.

14

Learning activity 14.1

Read through the above information and describe what impact the Freedom of Information Act 2000 has had on public bodies.

Feedback on page 221

The Freedom of Information Act 2000 is divided into eight parts. These are summarised as follows.

Part I relates to access to information held by public authorities.

Part II concerns exempt information which is discussed later on.

Part III details the general functions of the Secretary of State, Lord Chancellor and Information Commissioner.

Part IV provides information on the enforcement process.

Part V details the appeals procedure for a public authority and a member of the public.

Part VI relates to historical records and Public Record Office records.

Part VII contains the amendments to the Data Protection Act 1998.

Part VIII contains various miscellaneous provisions.

For this study session you are concerned mainly with Parts I and II as these relate to the right of access to information and what information can be disclosed and what is exempt. The meaning of disclosure and exemptions are discussed later on.

Who can request information?

A request for information can be made by any individual or body. They are known as the applicant. The application need not be a UK national or resident. The applicant requires to identify themselves for the purposes of the application but the identity of the applicant is otherwise of no concern to the authority except in the case of repeated or vexatious requests and where the applicant is seeking personal information. Where the applicant is the subject of the personal information then the provisions of the Data Protection Act 1998 will apply. Under the 2000 Act a response to a request must be made within 20 working days.

Access to information

S1 of the Freedom of Information Act 2000 confers a general right of access to information held by public authorities. Where a member of the public requests information about themselves then that individual has a right to be told what information is held by the authority. The public authority must inform the person whether they hold the information requested or not. If they do hold the requested information then the public authority must release the information to the individual.

The public authority can ask for further information to enable them to identify and locate the whereabouts of the information requested. The person requesting the information must describe it in sufficient detail to enable the public authority to identify and locate it. This does not mean that the person requesting the information must have an exact record number or particular record detail.

14

Once the public authority has communicated the information to the person requesting it, the public authority will be deemed to have complied with the 2000 Act.

Public authority

As this has a wide meaning under the 2000 Act it is not possible to list all the authorities within the Act. However, the meaning 'public authority' covers the public sector at national, regional and local levels. The Act covers the bodies, the persons or office holders specified in Schedule 1 of the Act and publicly owned companies (see below). The Act also includes powers to specify further public authorities where appropriate.

Public authorities are required to provide advice and assistance to applicants, that is, persons requesting information. Where a public authority refuses such a request then they must inform the applicant for their reason for refusal. As discussed above the public authority must adopt and maintain a publication scheme and publish information accordingly.

Publicly owned companies

The Act defines a publicly owned company as one that is wholly owned by the Crown or by any public authority listed within the Act (Schedule 1).

Public sector contracts

Before the Freedom of Information Act 2000, information about commercial contracts and relationships would be considered as confidential. Indeed many contracts would contain a confidentiality clause. Public authorities and private sector companies remain concerned about the validity of such confidentiality clauses in existing contracts and how information will be protected in the future.

The 2000 Act recognised these concerns and that there are valid reasons for withholding some information in response to a request. Disclosure and exemptions are discussed later.

14

Self-assessment question 14.1

Provide a brief summary of what public authorities must do to comply with the 2000 Act.

Feedback on page 221

14.2 The meaning of disclosure

Learning activity 14.2

Consider the overview of the Act provided in section 14.1 above. Can you identify some public authorities that will have to comply with the 2000 Act?

Feedback on page 221

Disclosure

So what must be or can be disclosed? Part II of the Freedom of Information Act 2000 deals with exemptions.

The Act recognises that there are grounds for not disclosing information, that is, for withholding information. The Act therefore provides for certain exemptions. The Act draws a distinction between absolute exemptions and those that are subject to a public interest test.

In section 14.1 above you read about the concerns of public authorities and private sector companies about how confidential information is and will be protected in light of the 2000 Act. The Act recognised these concerns and provided for exemptions.

Reasons for non-disclosure

The two most relevant exemptions about a relationship between a public authority and a contractor are sections 41 (confidential information) and 43 (public interest).

Section 41: This relates to information that has been provided in confidence. In these circumstances, such information could be withheld, but it is important that contractors and public authorities know what information may be available and that access to such information may change over time. Guidelines are published by the Information Commissioner to raise awareness of this issue.

To determine what is confidential under the 2000 Act the courts will look to case law as the law of confidence is a common-law concept.

Section 43: This relates to the release of information that is likely to prejudice someone's commercial interest. In these circumstances, such information could be exempt from access, but again it is important that contractors and public authorities know what information may be available and also that access to it may change over time. The guidelines published by the Information Commissioner cover such circumstances.

The commercial interest referred to in section 43 above is subject to a public interest test.

Public interest test

Public authorities can only withhold information that is commercially sensitive where withholding the information in the public interest outweighs the public interest in disclosing it.

You have already learned a little about the impact that the 2000 Act has on public authorities. It has a further impact in that public authorities can face difficulty in deciding whether to disclose information or not which might affect the commercial interest of a third party. Of course, it is important for contractors to understand that some requests for information may fall within an exemption and therefore not be disclosed.

14

Public authorities can raise awareness of the Act by informing contractors about the Freedom of Information Act 2000. This can be done by including reference to this within the contract itself. However, the public authority may decide that it is not practical to identify all commercially sensitive information at the outset and merely advise that any such information will be protected subject to the public interest test. In this latter case, were a request to be made later for information, the public authority may have extra work to do to identify the commercially sensitive information. So you can see that public authorities face challenges under the Act.

The Information Commissioner recognises that there is a place for confidentiality clauses where their purpose is to identify information that may be exempt. This is not an automatic exemption, and if a request were made for disclosure, the information would be reviewed taking account of all the circumstances at the time the request was received. Care should be taken by public authorities when negotiating confidentiality clauses.

Fees: what does it cost to make a request?

Section 9 of the 2000 Act provides for authorities to notify applicants that a fee is payable and the authority are not obliged to disclose information until the fee has been paid. The applicant has three months from the date of notification to pay the fee before their request lapses. The Secretary of State for Constitutional Affairs is responsible for regulating the fees that authorities charge. The Secretary of State can prohibit a fee for certain types of request or set an upper limit on the amount of the fee.

If you are requesting information contained in an authority's publication scheme, the scheme will also give details of whether and how much the authority will charge for providing the information.

If you are requesting information not contained within the publication scheme, the authority may charge you a fee as laid down in regulations which currently provide that requests which will cost less than £450 to answer (or £600 where requests are made to central government) will be free of charge. However, public authorities may charge for the cost of photocopying and postage and such sundries.

If your request will cost more than this to answer, the public authority can refuse to answer your request, answer it for free, or charge up to and including the full cost of answering.

If you refuse to pay the fee, the public authority can refuse to supply the information.

14

Self-assessment question 14.2

List the two main reasons for not disclosing information.

Feedback on page 221

14.3 Exemptions under the 2000 Act

In sections 14.1 and 14.2 above you have learned about the Freedom of Information Act 2000 and its impact on public authorities. Some reference has been made to the exemptions under the Act and the public interest test. When a request is made for access to information, some information may be disclosed and some not disclosed. You have learned about ss41 and 43 of the 2000 Act, which are of particular importance to procurement professionals.

Learning activity 14.3

In section 14.2 above you learned about how a public authority may decide to include a confidentiality clause within the contract or they may decide that it is not appropriate to disclose commercially sensitive information from the outset. Can you identify information that you would consider as commercially sensitive? We recommend that you surf the internet for information on disclosure or partial disclosure.

Feedback on page 222

You should revisit the previous parts of this session to look at exemptions, or non-disclosure and public interest test again before answering self-assessment question 14.3 below.

Self-assessment question 14.3

Read the short scenario below and explain whether the Home Office should disclose the information requested. Provide reasons for your answer.

A request is made to the Home Office for information on the National Identity Cards Programme and the name of the Marketing Director for the programme. The cost of supplying the information is going to be £1,500.

Feedback on page 222

Revision question

Now try the revision question for this session on page 314.

Summary

In this study session you have been looking at the Freedom of Information Act 2000, the background to its development and its impact on procurement, which is of particular importance to purchasing professionals. You have also learned about disclosure of information, who can request information, and what it costs to request information. You also know

14

that not all information needs be disclosed, as there are exemptions under the 2000 Act.

Suggested further reading

Freedom of Information Act 2000.

Feedback on learning activities and self-assessment questions

Feedback on learning activity 14.1

You should explain that public bodies are required to publish certain information through a publication scheme. The Act provides a right of access to recorded information albeit there are exemptions, which at this stage you need not write about as they are discussed later. You should also explain that if information is not exempt and the public body holds such information then they must provide it to the member of the public. They can of course charge a fee for this, the fee being set by the Secretary of State for Constitutional Affairs.

Feedback on self-assessment question 14.1

Your answer should take the form of a short essay. You should start with the obligation on a public authority to provide information to an applicant who requests information. They have an obligation to tell the applicant whether they hold such information or not. If they do have the information then they must communicate this to the applicant provided it is not exempt. The public authority must adopt and maintain a publication scheme. The authority must offer advice and assistance to an applicant who is requesting access to information.

Feedback on learning activity 14.2

Your activity might include central government departments or agencies. You might mention local government. Others are the police, the NHS, state schools, state colleges and universities. You could have also included publicly owned companies, for example, companies owned by enterprise bodies, such as Scottish Enterprise, the Ministry of Defence and others. You may want to surf the internet to look for more.

Feedback on self-assessment question 14.2

You should refer to sections 41 and 43 of the Freedom of Information Act 2000 and describe each briefly. Section 41 relates to confidential information. You should go on to explain that the law of confidentiality is a common law concept and that the courts will look to case law for direction. Section 43 refers to commercially sensitive information and you should describe how this is dealt with between public authorities and contractors such as including a clause in the contract and raising awareness of the 2000 Act with contractors. You should also refer to the public interest test and

14

that the information will only be exempt if withholding it outweighs the public interest in disclosing it.

Feedback on learning activity 14.3

This is a subjective learning activity and will vary from person to person. However, the purpose is to get a feel for the 2000 Act and what information you think might be considered commercially sensitive. This can include information relating to national security.

Commercially sensitive information will differ from sector to sector depending on the maturity of the market. What may be commercially sensitive in one context may not be in another. Also, sensitivity may decline over a period of time.

Types of commercial interest include information that constitutes a trade secret and whether the release of the information would likely prejudice commercial interests such as in some types of contract. Payment processes may need to be treated as commercially sensitive whereas in another context contractors may claim that competitors would obtain commercial advantage if they received information on legal ownership issues, funding, borrowing and pricing structures. Also, disclosure of a company's share price may cause them to drop; this may not be sufficient to establish prejudice to commercial interests. Each case will be different and will need careful consideration.

Feedback on self-assessment question 14.3

You should identify the public interest consideration, namely that the Home Office needs to balance the public interest in withholding the information against the public interest in disclosing it. The public interest here includes the protection of the policy-making process. The disclosure of the name of the civil servant might harm future advice from civil servants if they feel that their discussions might become public.

In addition, you should identify that the cost of supplying the information exceeds the current limit of £600, so the Home Office can refuse to disclose the information.

This is an actual example, where a request was made to the Home Office for information on the Identity Cards Programme. The Home Office responded by claiming exemption on grounds of public interest as it related to the formulation and development of government policy. They would not disclose the name of Head of Marketing for the Identity Cards Programme as it might have harmed future advice from civil servants. They also claimed exemption as the cost of supplying the information would exceed £600.

14

Legal implications of outsourcing

Introduction

In this session you will look at the impact of Transfer of Undertakings (Protection of Employment) (TUPE) regulations on organisations as well as redundancy law and its alternatives.

Session learning objectives

After completing this session you should be able to:

15.1 Explain the implications of TUPE.
15.2 Describe redundancy law.
15.3 Describe the alternatives to redundancy.

Unit content coverage

This study session covers the following topics from the official CIPS unit content document:

Learning objective

3.4 Predict whether outsourcing a service or operation is compliant with legal requirements
- TUPE
- Consultation
- Redundancy law
- Alternatives to redundancy

Prior knowledge

Study sessions 1 – 14.

Timing

You should set aside about 5 hours to read and complete this session, including learning activities, self-assessment questions, the suggested further reading (if any) and the revision question.

15.1 The implications of TUPE

When deciding to outsource a facility or service, an employer will be require to consider several legal issues which will have a significant impact on

'Everybody should know where they stand...so that employers can plan effectively in a climate of fair competition and affected employees are protected as a matter of course – unfortunately the reality seems to be far from the case.'
Reynolds Porter Chamberlain 2006

15

223

the price of the service or the ability to deliver the service. It is becoming increasingly common for organisations to outsource some of the functions of the organisation to make savings. Savings of course will only be made if the outsourcing is properly managed and the organisation takes proper cognisance of the Transfer of Undertakings (Protection of Employment) (TUPE) Regulations relating to employees and contracts of employment.

Outsourcing can also occur where there is compulsory competitive tendering within the public sector. Where the public sector provider loses the tender to provide services, then the service is outsourced and the public authority becomes the manager of the contract with the new service provider.

Outsourcing with or without existing staff?

Where an organisation is considering outsourcing they must decide whether the service is to be outsourced with or without the existing staff. If it is with existing staff then the organisation must comply with the TUPE Regulations, which are discussed below. Where the decision is to outsource without existing staff then the organisation must comply with the law of redundancy, which is discussed in section 15.2 below.

General background:

As the TUPE Regulations discussed in this session relate to employment rights, it is worthwhile remembering what you learned from study sessions 1 and 2 on contract law, as the ordinary principles of contract law apply to the contract of employment. In a contract of employment there must be an offer and acceptance, which is in effect the agreement. There must be an intention to create legal relations, consideration and capacity. There must be proper consent, which means no mistake, misrepresentation, duress or undue influence. All these topics have been discussed in the previous sessions. We recommend that you revisit these sessions to refresh your memory.

History of TUPE Regulations

A transfer of undertaking occurs when a business is transferred from one legal ownership to another as a going concern. It can apply where there is only transfer of a part but the part must be sufficient to be a viable business in its own right.

This is a complex area of the law and to understand the subject in depth it is recommended that further reading is undertaken from the suggestions at the end of this session. Further information can also be obtained from the website DTI: http://www.dti.gov.uk.

The Transfer of Undertakings (Protection of Employment) Regulations 1981 were introduced in the UK to comply with relevant EC Directives about transfers of undertakings. These Directives included the Acquired Rights Directive EC 77/1981, 98/50/EC and Acquired Rights Amendment Directive 2001/23/EC.

15

There was a major overhaul and revision of the Regulations and the main legislation now governing transfers of undertakings is the Transfer of Undertakings (Protection of Employment) Regulations 2006, referred to from now on in this session as TUPE 2006.

Overview of TUPE 2006

TUPE 2006 came into force on 6 April 2006. In general these regulations left the TUPE Regulations 1981 unaltered, but TUPE 2006 was reworded in places to reduce or eliminate confusion and to increase user-friendliness in this area of the law.

TUPE 2006 ensures:

- comprehensive application for 'service provision changes' whether they are outsourced, assigned to a new contractor or brought back 'in-house';
- the transferee is aware of employees' rights, obligations and liabilities on transfer;
- clarification of when ETO (economic, technical, organisational) reasons can be applied to the change in terms and conditions of employment;
- clarification of when employers can lawfully make transfer-related dismissals;
- special provisions for insolvent businesses to be transferred to new employers;
- provisions for failure to comply with the 'employee liability information' and consultation requirements.

In brief the Regulations apply to 'relevant transfers:', which can be categorised as:

- when a business or undertaking, or part of one, is transferred to a new employer; or
- when a service provision change takes place, such as where a contractor takes on a contract to provide a service for a client of another contractor.

Learning activity 15.1

Consider the scenario where a business is being transferred to a new employer. First, describe the legal principles applicable to a contract of employment. Secondly, describe 'relevant transfers', which are the circumstances when the TUPE regulations would apply.

Feedback on page 235

TUPE Regulations

As you may have gathered from reading the above information TUPE Regulations are intended to preserve the continuity of employment and the terms and conditions of employees who are transferred to a new employer when the 'relevant transfer' takes place. You are now going to consider in more detail the following:

- relevant transfers;
- changes to terms and conditions of contract of employment;
- ETO (economic, technical and organisational) reasons for dismissal;
- consultation rights.

Relevant: transfers

As you have read above, the TUPE Regulations apply to 'relevant transfers'. These were categorised as:

- when a business or undertaking, or part of one, is transferred to a new employer; or
- when a service provision change takes place, such as, where a contractor takes on a contract to provide a service for a client of another contractor.

These two categories are not mutually exclusive and it is possible and likely that some transfers will qualify under both business transfer and service provision change. One such example is the outsourcing of a service.

Business transfer: to qualify as a business transfer the identity of the employer must change. The business transfer must involve the transfer of an economic entity that retains its identity. An economic entity is the organised grouping of resources whose objectives are to pursue an economic activity. What is a business transfer depends on the facts of each case. Where it is uncertain whether there has been a business transfer, the decision will be one for a tribunal or court to decide.

Service provision change: to qualify as a relevant transfer under the TUPE Regulations a service provision change can take place in three main ways:

1   where a service is in-house and is then awarded to a contract out-house, known as outsourcing;
2   where a contract is assigned to a new contractor on re-tendering;
3   where the contract returns to the organisation, that is, comes back 'in-house'.

For a relevant transfer to take place under the category of service provision change, there must be an identifiable group of employees performing the work.

The TUPE Regulations do not apply where a client buys in services from a contractor on a 'one off' basis, which must be of 'short-term' duration.

Public Administration transfers: the reorganisation of a public administration or the transfer of functions between public administrations is not covered by the Regulations and are not deemed as relevant transfers. However, the treatment of employees is the same as under TUPE Regulations under the Cabinet Office's Statement of Practice, '*Staff Transfers in the Public Sector*'. Also, transfer of employees from public sector to private sector is covered by the TUPE Regulations.

15

226

Where employees work outside the UK, the Regulations apply where the undertaking is situated in the UK immediately before the transfer. In a change of service provision, whether the Regulations apply depends on whether there is an organised grouping of employees in the UK immediately before the service provision change.

Changes to terms and conditions of contract of employment

Under the TUPE Regulationsm, when employees are transferred they must not be placed on inferior terms and conditions. This means that their pre-existing terms and conditions under the old employer are transferred across to the new employer on day one. The TUPE Regulations also impose limitations on the old employer (transferor), the new employer (transferee) and the employee to vary the terms and conditions after the transfer. In other words, the terms and conditions cannot be varied except for economic, technical and organisational (ETO) reasons, which are discussed below.

ETO reasons

As you have learned from the above there must be no variations to terms and conditions of the employment contract unless for ETO reasons. ETO means economic, technical and organisational. There are no statutory definitions of these terms. However, they can be interpreted as follows.

Economic reason: this reason relates to the profitability or market performance of the transferee's (new employer's) business.

Technical reason: this reason relates to the equipment or production processes of the transferee (new employer).

Organisational reason: this reason relates to the management or organisational structure of the transferee's (new employer's) business.

Information and consultation rights

Under the TUPE 2006, the employer is required to provide information and undertake consultation, namely:

* provision of information: the transferor (old employer) to provide information, before the transfer takes place, to the transferee (new employer) about the employees who are being transferred; and
* consultation: both transferor (old employer) and transferee (new employer) to consult, before the transfer takes place, the representatives of all affected employees.

15

Self-assessment question 15.1

Read the following short scenario and answer the question.

Sprigotts Ltd are proposing to outsource their cleaning facilities at their factory. The cleaning facility is now to be provided on Sprigott's factory

(continued on next page)

Self-assessment question 15.1 (continued)

site by Cleankwik Ltd who specialise in providing cleaning services. The cleaning function is to be transferred in its entirety.

What legal requirements will Sprigotts and Cleankwik have to comply with on the transfer of the cleaning services?

Feedback on page 235

15.2 Redundancy law

In section 15.1 above you looked at the TUPE Regulations and where transfer of undertakings are being carried out with existing staff.

However, where the organisation wants to outsource without using existing staff, then it must consider and comply with the laws of redundancy. The existing employer will need to ensure that the cost of redeployment or redundancy of staff is built into the contract price.

Redundancy under the Employment Rights Act 1996

In redundancy law there is a difference between voluntary and compulsory redundancy.

Voluntary redundancy: It would really be better to call this voluntary severance. This occurs where an employee leaves by agreement; but they are agreeing to be dismissed, they are not agreeing to resign. It is not technically redundancy either, as there is no need for the employer to prove that the job has gone.

Under voluntary redundancy the employer can put someone else into the post of the person who has left voluntarily. Voluntary severance does not have to comply with the Employment Rights Act 1996. The employer does not need to:

* Prove that the needs of the organisation are diminished by the employee leaving.
* Consult with representatives of the employees either on the scale of redundancy or methods of redundancy.
* Justify its actions before a tribunal because voluntary redundancy is where the employee agrees to be dismissed. However, if the dismissal amounts to constructive dismissal then the organisation will need to explain its actions in front of a tribunal.

Compulsory redundancy: This is covered by the Employment Rights Act 1996. Under this Act dismissal of an employee is taken to be dismissal on grounds of redundancy if it is wholly or partly for the following reasons:

* the employer has ceased or intends to cease to carry on the business for the purpose of which the employee was employed or ceases to carry on the business in the place where the employee was employed;
* the requirements of the business have ceased, either the particular kind of business carried out by the employee or the place where the employee worked.

Handling procedures

Compulsory redundancies have given rise to a considerable amount of litigation. Employers therefore should follow certain procedures in dismissals and redundancies. They should act in accordance with the Dispute Resolution Regulations, which came into force on 1 October 2004. Further information on these can be read in the DTI publication *Resolving Disputes at Work: New Procedures for Discipline and Grievance* and by viewing the website DTI: http://www.dti.gov.uk. In addition to these Dispute Resolution Regulations, the TUPE Regulations provide additional protections, which limit the ability of employers to dismiss employees when transfers arise.

You have already looked at the ETO reasons. Where there are ETO reasons then the dismissal of an employee will be deemed to be fair. If there are no ETO reasons, the dismissal will be treated as unfair. The onus is on the employer to show that the dismissal falls within the ETO reasons.

If the dismissal occurred for reason of redundancy then the usual redundancy arrangements will apply and the dismissed employee could be entitled to a redundancy payment.

As well as complying with the ETO reasons, the employer must comply with other employment legislation, such as ensuring:

- fair selection for redundancy;
- entitlement to redundancy payments if the employee has been with the organisation two years or more;
- consultation and the required period of notice is allowed.

These are discussed in more detail later on in this part.

Learning activity 15.2

What is the difference between voluntary and compulsory redundancy?

Feedback on page 236

Fair selection for redundancy

The selection process must be fair, reasonable and consistent. It must also be objective. Where the jobs have gone the employer must select from the persons affected by the loss of those jobs.

The easiest way to select is last in, first out (LIFO). This is not used very often nowadays. Employers tend to use an objective system of points where the points are awarded to vulnerable staff affected by the possible redundancies. The points will take account of length of service, skills, appraisals and performance reviews. Points will be taken off for poor performance and reviews, etc.

Employers may decide to open the jobs up to application by employees. This is where employees re-apply for the reduced number of jobs. In such situations the job description provided will be more detailed and comprehensive. In the case of *Safeway plc* v *Burrell* [1997], which involved an overall reduction in managers but not a reduction in the total amount of work, the Employment Appeal Tribunal (EAT) decided that the correct approach for determining what is a dismissal by reason of redundancy in terms of s139(1)(b) Employment Rights Act 1996 involves a three-stage process. To decide whether an employee's job is redundant the process begins by asking three questions:

1 Was the employee dismissed?
2 Has the work of the kind carried out by the employee ceased or diminished?
3 Was the dismissal to cease or diminish the work of the kind carried out by the employee?

By using these three questions the employer can take an overall view of the organisation when deciding on redundancies.

Several grounds are considered automatically unfair. An employer cannot select someone on the following grounds:

- pregnancy, childbirth, maternity leave;
- health and safety reasons;
- employee representatives;
- protected shop workers;
- trustees of an occupational pension scheme.

Redundancy payments

Redundancy payments are whatever can be agreed with the employer, and they can be generous. However, to allow for some reasonable levels of payment where companies are not generous in their payouts, there are statutory minimum payment levels.

There is no automatic right to a redundancy payment. Your employer must give you a lump sum payment if:

- your are made redundant;
- you have at least two years' continuous service since the age of 18 years; and
- you meet the other conditions set out in redundancy legislation.

An employee can lose their entitlement to redundancy if they unreasonably refuse an offer of reasonable alternative employment. What is reasonable depends on the facts of each case and will be judged on the basis of the employee's job role, position, responsibilities, mobility and sometimes personal circumstances.

Calculating redundancy payment

Redundancy payments are calculated as follows.

- For each complete service year between 18 and 21 years of age: half a week's pay.

15

- For each complete service year between 22 and 40 years of age: one week's pay.
- For each complete service year between 41 and 65 years of age: one and a half weeks' pay.

The calculation is based continuous service and on a maximum weekly entitlement, which at 1 February 2006 was £290. This amount is reviewed annually. An employee may only take a maximum of 20 years' service into account when calculating the amount of redundancy due. No account is taken of work carried out before 18 years of age. No payment is made if the employee is over retirement age and in the year before retirement the amount due is reduced by one-twelfth for each complete month of that year.

Consultation with representatives

The procedures for handling redundancies originate in EC law, Directive 75/129. The procedures were enacted into UK law by the Trades Union and Labour Relations (Consolidation) Act 1992 (TULRA). These have been amended by the 1995 Regulations.

The employer who is considering compulsory redundancies must consult with representatives of the affected employees, whether that is the recognised trade unions, or elected representatives. The employer must provide for a minimum consultation periods and the aim of the consultation must be to reach agreement. However, consultation does not mean negotiation, and the unions have no rights to insist on negotiation over the scale of employees to be made redundant or the selection process. Meaningful consultation should take place with a view to either avoiding the redundancies or mitigating the effect of the redundancies.

Notice of redundancy

The number of employees and periods of notice required where an organisation is intending to make employees redundant are as follows:

- 100 or more employees to be made redundant: the period of notice must be 90 days;
- 20 or more employees to be made redundant: the period of notice must be 30 days.

The period of notice must start as soon as possible and consultation must take place within the period. Notices of redundancies can still be issued during the period of notice. The period runs from the date on which notice is given to the Department of Trade and Industry (DTI) until the effective date of dismissal.

In the cases of redundancy covered by the Employment Rights Act 1996, the employer has a duty to disclose certain information to the affected employee.

If notice is not given to the affected employee or employees, then in addition to any compensation awarded by a tribunal for possible unfair dismissal, the employee is entitled to a protective award representing the notice they should have been given.

15

Feedback on page 236

Self-assessment question 15.2

Read the following short case study and answer the question.

DIY Buildit Ltd have decided to outsource their security services at their factories across UK. They have reached an agreement with Securit Limited to provide security at all of their UK sites. Securit Limited do not want to take on DIY Buildit's 30 security staff.

What must DIY Buildit do to comply with the law in terms of dismissing their security staff on grounds of redundancy?

Feedback on page 236

15.3 Alternatives to redundancy

Learning activity 15.3

What questions relating to redundancy laws would you need to ask if your organisation was experiencing a drastic downturn in business?

Feedback on page 236

As you will recall from section 15.2 above, the employer must consult with the affected employees. The objective of such a consultation is to reach agreement and try to avoid redundancy or mitigate its effects.

A redundancy programme is only one solution to business problems. It is often not the complete solution or necessarily the answer. There needs to be planning. An organisation needs to ensure that it has considered all avenues and approaches.

Failing to address workforce issues and pushing the company into bankruptcy where all jobs are lost does not really make sense.

Alternative to redundancy

There are advantages and disadvantages to all alternatives: what is suitable for one organisation may not be suitable for another.

Alternative strategies include:

Stopping overtime where it has become part of the normal working practice: the disadvantage is that there may be difficulties in meeting deadlines and the impact will differ on the various work groups.

Early retirement measures: This may be welcomed by some but the downside is that you may or will lose some of your most experienced employees.

Terminating temporary contracts: This is a strategy that is quick to implement. The downside is that it can cause insecurity for some employees. You may also cause concern for suppliers who might lose confidence in your organisation. You may also incur contractual penalties.

Retraining and redeployment: This is probably the most cost-effective alternative to redundancy. It is well worth exploring this possibility in depth. This strategy is less expensive than paying compensation, then recruiting new people and the resulting induction costs.

Offering alternative work: instead of making an employee redundant, the employer may consider offering the employee other work. The employee of course can choose to accept it or not. You already know from previous information above that if the employee unreasonably refuses the offer then the employer may avoid paying that employee redundancy. The refusal by an employee is looked at from the employee's point of view. The job offered can be identical to the current job or be one with similar skills. The job must have similar pay, conditions and skill requirements.

The alternative job must be offered before the current job ends and the start date must be within four weeks of the end of the old job. The first four weeks in the new job is on a trial basis and the employee can still leave and claim dismissal on grounds of redundancy and redundancy pay. If retraining is required then the trial period can be extended by written agreement to consider the retraining requirements.

Relocation: This may also be an alternative but again it depends on the employee's viewpoint. The employee does not need to take an alternative job if it means further to travel, new location, etc.

So far, you have been learning about the rights and duties of employers and employees. We are going to look briefly at constructive dismissal before moving on to the role of employment tribunals.

Constructive dismissal

Constructive dismissal occurs where an employee leaves their job because of the employer's behaviour. This behaviour of course can be carried out by another employee. One example is where the employee's working life has been made very difficult because of the employer and the employee feels that they can no longer remain in their job.

Where the employee decides to resign because of the difficult situation then the resignation will be treated as actual dismissal by the employer and the employee can claim unfair dismissal. The employer's actions in such situation must be such that they have breached the contract of employment. There are many situations that would be considered constructive dismissal. Some include:

- victimisation;
- harassment;
- excessive disciplining;
- changing job content and role without consultation;
- significant change in job location.

15

The above list is not exhaustive and is intended as a guideline only.

This is a complex area of employment law as even where an employee is considered constructively dismissed, it only proves that they were dismissed, not that it was unfair. They have to go on to prove that the dismissal was unfair. The employee may claim that constructive dismissal was due to the employer's behaviour but the employer may counter-claim by saying that the dismissal was due to reorganisation of the business. Employment tribunals do not like to interfere with the management of businesses, so the employer may be given the benefit of the doubt. However, it would be easier to prove the dismissal was unfair if the employee had been treated too harshly over a disciplinary matter.

You are now going to look at the role of the employment tribunal and what remedies are available to an employee who considers that their contractual rights have been infringed.

Employment tribunals

An employee can make a claim to an employment tribunal under certain circumstances, which are discussed below. The claim must be within three months of the date when their employment ended. The tribunal can extend the three months if it considers that it was not reasonably practicable for the complaint to be made within the three month time limit. The time limits also vary, for example, where an employee wishes to claim a redundancy payment the application should be made within six months of the dismissal.

The circumstances when an employee can make a claim include where the employee:

- has been dismissed; or
- has resigned in circumstances where they considered they had to resign because of the consequences of transfer or anticipated consequences of a transfer;
- is a trade union representative or elected representative and the employer has not complied with the information or consultation requirements;
- is a representative who has been unreasonably refused time off by an employer or the employer has refused to make appropriate payment for time off.

This area of the law is complex and for comprehensive understanding and more information you should undertake further reading in the suggested books at the end of this session. You can also find more information on government web sites such as DTI: http://www.dti.gov.uk.

15

Self-assessment question 15.3

Describe at least two alternatives to redundancy.

Feedback on page 237

Revision question

Now try the revision question for this session on page 314.

Summary

In this session you have learnt about the impact of the TUPE Regulations on organisations, as well as redundancy law and its alternatives. You should now realise the complexity of this area of the law but also know that the ordinary principles of contract law apply to the contract of employment. Ensure you understand these by revisiting study session 1 and extend your knowledge of TUPE by undertaking further reading of the suggested book below and visiting the DTI website.

Suggested further reading

Griffiths and Griffiths (2002), part V, chapter 17.

DTI website DTI: http://www.dti.gov.uk – see the DTI publication *Resolving Disputes at Work: New Procedures for Discipline and Grievance*.

Feedback on learning activities and self-assessment questions

Feedback on learning activity 15.1

This learning activity is to ensure your understanding of the basic principles of contract law because they apply to contracts of employment. You should have described that there must be an offer and acceptance which is the agreement. There must be an intention to create legal relations, consideration and capacity. There must be proper consent, which means no mistake, misrepresentation, duress or undue influence.

You should then go on to describe when the TUPE Regulations apply which is:

- when a business or undertaking, or part of one, is transferred to a new employer; or
- when a service provision change takes place, such as, where a contractor takes on a contract to provide a service for a client of another contractor.

Feedback on self-assessment question 15.1

Under the TUPE 2006 Regulations both old and new employer will require to inform all affected employees of the transfer. They must consult with the representatives of the affected employees. Cleankwik will have to give all the transferred employees new contracts of employment but these contracts will be required to contain the same terms and conditions as those in their previous contracts with Sprigotts.

15

Cleankwik will not be able to make any changes to the new contracts of employment unless they can show that variations are needed because of economical, technical or organisational reasons.

Feedback on learning activity 15.2

For this activity you should describe each of the different types of redundancy in turn. For example, in the case of voluntary redundancy you can state that this is not technically redundancy as the employee is agreeing to be dismissed, not agreeing to resign. The employer does not have to prove that the job is gone. The employer can also put someone else in job. Where the employee leaves under these circumstances the Employment Rights Act 1996 does not apply. You can go on to state that the employer does not need to prove that the needs of the organisation are diminished by the employee leaving and they do not need to consult with any representatives of the employee. As long as it is not constructive dismissal then the employer will not have to justify its actions to anyone.

However, in the case of compulsory redundancy, this is covered by the Employment Rights Act 1996 and the employee will be taken to be dismissed on the grounds of redundancy if the employer has ceased or intends to cease to carry on the business for the purpose of which the employee was employed or cease to carry on the business in the place where the employee was employed or the requirements of the business have ceased, either the particular kind of business carried out by the employee or the place where the employee worked.

Feedback on self-assessment question 15.2

Your answer should describe the procedures to be followed by DIY Buildit and include the selection process, the entitlement and calculation of redundancy payments, consultation and notice. DIY Buildit should calculate the number of staff to be made redundant, serve notice on DTI and any employee representatives, including trade unions if appropriate. They must give the required notice and in this case as there are 30 employees then the notice is 30 days. You should also mention that the selection of employees must be fair. They can also look at any possible other jobs within their company to avoid dismissal. Finally you should describe how the redundancy payments will be calculated.

Feedback on learning activity 15.3

This learning activity is intended to get you thinking about what needs to be considered when making people redundant when an organisation can no longer sustain the level of employment due to decreased business.

You should mention voluntary and compulsory redundancy. It may be that employees voluntarily agree to dismissal. However, the main point relates to ETO and in particular the economic ground for dismissing employees. Remember that the onus is on the employer to show that the dismissal falls within the ETO reasons.

15

As well as complying with the ETO reasons, the employer must comply with other employment legislation, such as ensuring:

- fair selection for redundancy;
- entitlement to redundancy payments if the employee has been with the organisation two years or more;
- consultation and the required period of notice is allowed.

Feedback on self-assessment question 15.3

You have a wide choice of alternatives from the reading the above text. However, you may also have experience of this within your organisation. If so you can describe what happened. From this session you can choose to describe any two of the following:

Stopping overtime where it has become part of the normal working practice: the disadvantage is that there may be difficulties in meeting deadlines and the impact will differ on the various work groups.

Early retirement measures: this may be welcomed by some but the downside is that you may or will lose some of your most experienced employees.

Terminating temporary contracts: this is a strategy that is quick to implement. The downside is that it can cause insecurity for some employees. You may also cause concern for suppliers who might lose confidence in your organisation. You may also incur contractual penalties.

Retraining and redeployment: this is probably the most cost-effective alternative to redundancy. It is well worth exploring this possibility in-depth. This strategy is less expensive than paying compensation, then recruiting new people and the resulting induction costs.

Offering alternative work: instead of making an employee redundant, the employer may consider offering the employee other work. The employee of course can choose to accept it or not. You already know from previous information above that if the employee unreasonably refuses the offer then the employer may avoid paying that employee redundancy. The refusal by an employee is looked at from the employee's point of view. The job offered can be identical to the current job or be one with similar skills. The job must have similar pay, conditions and skill requirements.

The alternative job must be offered before the current job ends and the start date must be within four weeks of the end of the old job. The first four weeks in the new job is on a trial basis and the employee can still leave and claim dismissal on grounds of redundancy and redundancy pay. If re-training is required then the trial period can be extended by written agreement to consider the re-training requirements.

Relocation: this may also be an alternative but again it depends on the employee's viewpoint. The employee does not need to take an alternative job if it means further to travel, new location, etc.

15

15

Study session 16
Competition law

Introduction

In this study session you will be looking at competition law and the legislation governing it. This includes the Competition Act 1998 through to the Enterprise Act 2002. Competition has an impact on international trade, which is discussed in study sessions 19 and 20.

With increased globalisation of markets and companies, focus should be on effectiveness of national competition policies...

Session learning objectives

After completing this session you should be able to:

16.1 Describe the Competition Act 1998.
16.2 Explain Article 81 EC Treaty.
16.3 Explain Article 82 EC Treaty.
16.4 Describe Enterprise Act 2002.

Unit content coverage

This study session covers the following topics from the official CIPS unit content document:

Learning outcome

Diagnose the impact of specific UK and EU regulations on the purchasing and supply function.

Learning objective

3.5 Examine the laws that regulate anti-competitive behaviour and abuse of a dominant market position in both the UK and the EU.

- Competition Act 1998
- Article 81 EC Treaty
- Article 82 EC Treaty
- Enterprise Act 2002

16

Timing

You should set aside about 5 hours to read and complete this session, including learning activities, self-assessment questions, the suggested further reading (if any) and the revision question.

16.1 Competition Act 1998

The UK government is committed to improving cooperation between UK competition authorities and their counterparts abroad to further international efforts to fight anti-competitive practices, especially international cartels. There are ongoing active efforts by the Department of Trade and Industry (DTI) to build a framework for improved cooperation between competition authorities.

Competition Act 1998

This Act came into force on 1 March 2001. It changed the picture in relation to UK law and regulation. This Act replaced existing law in relation to monopolies and mergers, restrictive trade practices (under Restrictive Trade Practices Act 1976) and resale price maintenance (under Resale Prices Act 1976).

The Fair Trading Act 1973 remains in force but amendments are made to it by the 1998 Act. The Fair Trading Act 1973 contains complex monopoly powers which fill the gap between the two prohibitions detailed below. These powers include investigation of markets where there is parallel behaviour by companies but no actual agreement.

The Competition Act 1998 was created to simplify the law in relation to European Community (EC) legal and business environments. We are concerned in this study session with the two main types of prohibition created by the Act. These prohibitions are in Chapters 1 and 2 of the Act and are as follows:

- Chapter 1 prohibitions cover most forms of anti-competitive practices, based closely on Article 81 of the EC Treaty which is discussed later in this study session.
- Chapter 2 prohibitions cover the abuse of monopoly situations in a given market, based closely on Article 82 of the EC Treaty which is discussed later in this study session.

The Competition Commission replaces the previous Monopolies and Merger Commission. Under the 1998 Act the Director General of Fair Trading still had powers to investigate prohibitions under Chapter 2. However, these powers have been transferred to the Office of Fair Trading (OFT) under the Enterprise Act 2002, which is discussed in the last section of this study session.

Chapter 1 prohibitions

This chapter replaces the provisions of the Resale Prices Act and the Restrictive Trade Practices Acts. Chapter 1 prohibits anticompetitive agreements. It prohibits any agreements between undertakings, decision by associations of undertakings or concerted practices which have as their object or aim the prevention, restriction or distortion of competition in the UK (or any part thereof) and which may affect trade in the UK (or part of it).

16

Types of agreement include those that:

- directly or indirectly fix purchase or selling prices or any other trading conditions;
- limit or control production, markets, technical developments or investment;
- share markets or sources of supply;
- apply dissimilar conditions to equivalent transactions with other trading parties thus placing them at a competitive disadvantage;
- make the conclusion of contracts subject to acceptance by the other parties of supplementary obligations which have no connection with the subject matter of such contracts.

The agreement must have considerable effect on competition. As you have learned from the above (and later on in section 16.4 below) it is the OFT which investigates such agreements. The OFT will normally take the view that there is considerable effect on competition where a shared market exceeds 25%.

Where it can be shown that the agreement will contribute to improvements in production, distribution or promotion of technical or economic progress an individual exemption may be granted. The OFT can only grant exemptions once the agreement has been notified. There is no obligation to notify the OFT but if you wish to claim exemption then the OFT must be notified.

There are occasions where block exemptions may be granted to cover certain categories of agreement.

Chapter 2 prohibitions

This chapter covers abuse of a dominant position in a market in the UK (or any part of it) which may affect trade in the UK. Some examples of such conduct include:

- directly or indirectly imposing unfair trading conditions or unfair purchase or selling prices;
- limiting production, markets or technical development to the prejudice of consumers;
- applying dissimilar conditions to equivalent transactions with other trading parties thus placing them at a competitive disadvantage;
- making the conclusion of contracts subject to acceptance by the other parties of supplementary obligations which have no connection with the subject matter of such contracts.

Definition of dominant market

Dominant market is when an undertaking can behave to an appreciable extent independently of its competitors and customers and ultimately of consumers when making commercial decisions. See the case of *United Brands Company & United Brands Continentaal BV* v *Commission of the European Communities* [1976]. In this case the court stated that it is a 'position of economic strength enjoyed by an undertaking which enables it

16

to prevent effective competition being maintained on the relevant market by giving it the power to behave to an appreciable extent independently of its competitors, customers and ultimately of its consumers'. Significant exclusions include:

- agreements which are already regulated by other legislation;
- agreements already complying with the current restrictive trade practices legislation;
- agreements exempted by the EC;
- agricultural products.

The 1998 Act brings the UK law into line with European competition laws and covers agreements in the UK that are both vertical and horizontal.

Vertical agreements

These are agreements between supplier and dealer.

Horizontal agreements

These are agreements between two or more competitors operating at the same level.

Learning activity 16.1

Compare and contrast Chapter 1 and Chapter 2 of the Competition Act 1998.

Feedback on page 249

As you have learned from the above information, the powers of the Director General of Fair Trading (DGFT) has been transferred to the OFT under the Enterprise Act 2002 and this is discussed in more detail in the last section of this study session.

The key points of the Competition Act 1998 can be summed up as follows:

- anti-competitive agreements, cartels and abuse of dominant position are unlawful;
- businesses which infringe the prohibitions are liability to financial penalties of up to 10% of UK turnover for up to 3 years;
- competitors and customers are entitled to damages;
- the OFT (previously has powers to step in at the outset to stop anti-competitive behaviour;
- investigators can enter premises with reasonable force and launch dawn raids.

The intention of the Competition Act 1998 was to create regulatory framework that is hard on those trying to impair competition but allows an opportunity to thrive for those who compete fairly.

16

Regulation 1/2003

European competition law was radically reformed by Regulation 1/2003 (replacing Regulation 17/62). This regulation has four main effects on European competition:

- it abolishes notifications;
- it sets minimum standards of competition enforcement;
- it requires member states to cooperate closely in enforcing competition law and provides for exchange of information and investigations on each other's behalf;
- it clarifies the Competition Commission's powers of investigation, widens the range of available remedies and provides harsher sanctions for procedural infringements.

In radically reforming EC competition law Regulation 1/2003 created a difference between the UK and EC competition law. However, in 2004 the UK government implemented Regulation 1/2003, thus re-aligning the Competition Act 1998 with the new modernised EC regime. This removes the burden on businesses of having to comply with two different competition systems.

Self-assessment question 16.1

In relation to competition policy what do you understand by the following expressions?

- dominant market position
- relevant market
- concerted practice.

Feedback on page 249

16.2 Article 81 EC Treaty

It can be said that competition is a basic mechanism of the market economy and is a simple and efficient means of guaranteeing consumers a level of excellence in terms of quality and price of products and services. For competition to be effective, it assumes that the market is made up of suppliers who are independent of each other and subject to competitive from others.

Learning activity 16.2

You are going to learn about Article 81 in this part of the study session and that it relates closely to Chapter 1, which you learnt about in section 16.1

(continued on next page)

16

Learning activity 16.2 *(continued)*

above. Consider what kind of agreements under Chapter 1 will affect trade between member states and will prevent, restrict or distort competition.

Feedback on page 250

Article 81 EC Treaty

As you read in the above section, Article 81 is closely related to Chapter 1 of the Competition Act 1998. Article 81 prohibits anti-competitive agreements that may have an appreciable effect on trade between member states and which prevent, restrict or distort competition in the single market.

Types of agreement include those that:

- directly or indirectly fix purchase or selling prices or any other trading conditions;
- limit or control production, markets, technical developments or investment;
- share markets or sources of supply;
- apply dissimilar conditions to equivalent transactions with other trading parties thus placing them at a competitive disadvantage;
- make the conclusion of contracts subject to acceptance by the other parties of supplementary obligations which have no connection with the subject matter of such contracts.

The European Commission can grant individual or group exemptions from this prohibition if there are overriding benefits such as an improvement in efficiency or the promotion of research and development.

Article 81 is broad, covering horizontal and vertical agreements. It is concerned with the effect of the offending agreements. This highlights two aspects.

First the agreement must have as its object or effect the prevention, restriction or distortion of competition within the **Common Market**. (Common Market is the informal name for the European Community (EC).) This allows the EC to be proactive in the enforcement of Article 81 by considering the effect of the agreement rather than waiting until the distortion occurs. Second, the agreement must affect trade between member states.

General exceptions

Article 81 applies only where there is an appreciable impact on intra-community trade. The current relevant minimum thresholds where Article 81 will not apply are where:

- the products covered by the agreement do not constitute more than 5% for horizontal agreements and 10% for vertical agreements available in the area of the Common Market affected by the agreement;
- the total annual turnover of the undertaking participating in the agreement does not exceed EUR (euros) 200 million.

16

Hard-core restrictions

If the above thresholds are not met at any of the relevant markets, the infringement of competition law will not be sanctioned by the Commission. However, there are what are known as hard-core restrictions for which infringement will always be sanctioned. These restrictions are:

- in horizontal agreements restrictions that:
  - fix prices;
  - limit production;
  - share markets;
  - share sources of supply.
- in vertical agreements restrictions that:
  - fix resale prices;
  - confer territorial protection.

In addition to exceeding the minimum thresholds, the agreement still requires an appreciable effect on trade between the member states.

Self-assessment question 16.2

What are the levels of agreement not affected by Article 81?

Feedback on page 250

16.3 Article 82 EC Treaty

Competition between companies, governments and states within and across the global trading market has become a vital part of the trading world where there are fewer political and economic boundaries. Competition law therefore must regulate the market powers of those who participate in the global exchange of goods and services. It has substantial impact on the outline of agreements.

You have studied Article 81 above. You are now going to study Article 82. With Articles 81 and 82 of the EC Treaty, European jurisprudence and the legislative bodies of the member states have a basis to work on a topic of immense importance.

16

Learning activity 16.3

You have studied Chapter 2 of the Competition Act 1982 and know that it relates closely to Article 82. Now define dominant position and list the types of conduct considered abuse of a dominant market under Article 82.

Feedback on page 250

Article 82

This is the EC's monopolies and merger control. It seeks to prevent abuses of a dominant position which may distort trade between member states. The abuses covered by Article 82 include:

- directly or indirectly imposing unfair trading conditions or unfair purchase or selling prices;
- limiting production, markets or technical development to the prejudice of consumers;
- applying dissimilar conditions to equivalent transactions with other trading parties thus placing them at a competitive disadvantage;
- making the conclusion of contracts subject to acceptance by the other parties of supplementary obligations which have no connection with the subject matter of such contracts;

If an undertaking can transact its business and act on its own decisions without the need to take account of the actions of its competitors or the views of consumers, then it is in a dominant position. This will not necessarily equate with the same market share in all situations and therefore this is a more flexible approach and more accurately reflects the true situation.

Self-assessment question 16.3

Read the following sentences and answer true or false.

1   Rules relating to abuse of a monopoly position are contained in Chapter 1 of the Competition Act 1998.
2   The role of DGFT is now undertaken by the OFT.
3   The conduct of limiting production to the prejudice of consumers is an abuse under Article 82.
4   The minimum threshold for the application of Article 81 is 40% of the product market in vertical agreements.
5   Competition is not of itself unlawful.
6   Chapter 2 of the Competition Act 1998 is related closely to Article 81 EC Treaty.

Feedback on page 251

16.4 Enterprise Act 2002

The Enterprise Act 2002 contains measures that reform competition law, strengthen consumer protection and modernises the insolvency regime.

The Enterprise Act 2002 created the Office of Fair Trading (OFT), which has taken over the role previously undertaken by the DGFT. It also created the Competition Appeal Tribunal (CAT) to which there is a right of appeal. It created the Competition Service, which is an independent body that makes the decisions on mergers and markets.

16

Consumers have a greater voice on competition matters and can complain to the OFT, which is required to respond within 90 days. Individuals can more easily bring claims for damages for loss suffered due to anti-competitive behaviour. The Act also extended consumer protection from traders who do not meet their legal obligations. This applies to infringements of a wide range of consumer protection legislation, for example failing to carry out a service such as building work or home maintenance to a reasonable standard.

The Act introduced criminal sanctions for cartels: that is, those who operate agreements to fix prices, share markets, limit production and rig bids. The maximum penalty is 5 years in prison.

OFT functions

The main functions of the OFT are:

- as the lead enforcement body for taking action in the UK;
- to be responsible for education and training required under Part 8 of Enterprise Act 2002;
- to provide advice and case support and manage the Consumer Regulations Website;
- to ensure that the OFT and its enforcement partners take consistent and cohesive action;
- to be the body which enforcers must notify before taking action;
- to have a coordinating role to ensure that action is taken by the most appropriate enforcer.

There are three types of enforcer, which are:

- general enforcer: the OFT, trading standards departments, and the Department of Enterprise, Trade and Investment in Northern Ireland have powers to enforce the Act against all types of infringement;
- community enforcer: an EU-based enforcer of consumer protection laws;
- designated enforcer: the Secretary of State can designate certain regulators and consumer protection bodies to enforce the Act against all or a limited range of infringements. Some bodies include: Civil Aviation Authority; Director General of Electricity Supply for Northern Ireland; Director General of Gas for Northern Ireland; Director General of Telecommunications; Information Commissioner.

If more than one UK enforcement body is involved, the OFT will decide which body should take action.

Where a business is based in another EU country and that business harms the collective interests of UK consumers, the OFT will usually ask the relevant community enforcer to take enforcement action. Where there is no such enforcer in an EU member state then the OFT is able to take action.

Where a UK-based business is harming the collective interests of consumers in other EU countries, a community enforcer, in consultation with the OFT, may either take action in the UK courts or ask the OFT to act on its behalf.

16

Part 8 – Enterprise Act 2002

Part 8 deals with provisions for enforcement of consumer protection legislation. Under Part 8, the OFT can apply for an Enforcement Order (also known as a Stop Now Order) to stop a business from breaching certain legislation where the breach harms the collective interests of the consumers. These can be domestic infringements or community infringements.

The OFT share power with the Trading Standards service in prosecuting infringements. Action is taken in the High Court or County Court.

The OFT is committed to transparency and usually puts the information on completed Part 8 cases in the public domain. The information must be accurate, balanced and fair. They will take into account certain factors such as legal restrictions on disclosure of information; public accountability; deterring other businesses from such conduct; increasing consumer awareness of their rights; facilitating complaints on further breaches and educating the market.

Learning activity 16.4

Read through the notes on the 2002 Act and then describe a situation where the OFT is required to make the public aware of information. Use the internet to search for current news on the Act (see OPSI: http://www.opsi.gov.uk).

Feedback on page 251

The 2002 Act takes the politics out of competition decision making with the creation of the independent body of the OFT. It has also increased protection for consumers by extending the enforcement order or stop now order to protect consumers from traders who do not meet their legal obligations.

Self-assessment question 16.4

What are the main functions of the Enterprise Act 2002?

Feedback on page 251

Revision question

Now try the revision question for this session on page 315.

Summary

As the attention grabber of this study session stated, with increased globalisation of markets and companies focus should be on effectiveness of national competition policies. This study session has shown you how this is being fulfilled through the aligning of competition law under the Competition Act 1998 and Articles 81 and 82 of EC Treaty. There are also ongoing efforts to continue to improve cooperation between competition authorities.

You will realise that competition law is a vast subject area of the law. However, you have learned the key provisions of Chapters 1 and 2 of the Competition Act 1998 applicable to the UK and the closely related Articles 81 and 82 which are applicable to the EU. You also learned about the substantive competition and consumer provisions of the Enterprise Act 2002.

Remember that competition law impacts on international trade, which is discussed in study sessions 19 and 20.

Suggested further reading

Griffiths and Griffiths (2002), part V, chapter 18.

OPSI: http://www.opsi.gov.uk

Feedback on learning activities and self-assessment questions

Feedback on learning activity 16.1

Chapter 1 replaces the provisions of the Resale Prices Act and the Restrictive Trade Practices Acts. It prohibits anticompetitive agreements and also any agreements between undertakings, decisions by associations of undertakings or concerted practices which have as their object or aim the prevention, restriction or distortion of competition in the UK (or any part thereof) and which may affect trade in the UK (or part of it).

Chapter 2 on, the other hand, covers abuse of a dominant position in a market in the UK (or any part of it) which may affect trade in the UK.

Feedback on self-assessment question 16.1

The dominant market position is not defined by percentage share. It depends on the position of economic strength enjoyed by an undertaking which enables it to prevent effective competition in a relevant market by giving it power to behave to an appreciable extent independently of its competitors, customer and consumers.

Relevant market can mean a market for a particular product or a group of products or for a single product or generic group of products as long as that single product is capable of being a market in itself (as the bananas in the United Brands case). In the case of *United Brands* they had a dominant position in relation to bananas but not in relation to other fresh fruit as a whole. The relevant market may also be a market in relation to a product over which the supplier has total control.

16

Concerted practice is something less than an agreement or undertaking between organisations. It is a simple understanding as evidenced by the behaviour of the organisations.

Feedback on learning activity 16.2

This learning activity relates to Chapter 1 of the Competition Act 1998. You should explain that the chapter replaces the provisions of the Resale Prices Act and the Restrictive Trade Practices Acts. It prohibits agreements between undertakings, decision by associations of undertakings or concerted practices which have as their object or aim the prevention, restriction or distortion of competition in the UK (or any part thereof) and which may affect trade in the UK (or part of it). Go on to describe that the types of agreements included are those agreements that:

- directly or indirectly fix purchase or selling prices or any other trading conditions;
- limit or control production, markets, technical developments or investment;
- share markets or sources of supply;
- apply dissimilar conditions to equivalent transactions with other trading parties thus placing them at a competitive disadvantage;
- make the conclusion of contracts subject to acceptance by the other parties of supplementary obligations which have no connection with the subject matter of such contracts.

The agreement must have considerable effect on competition. As you have learned from the above (and later on in the Enterprise Act section) it is the OFT that investigates such agreements. The OFT will normally take the view that there is considerable effect on competition where a shared market exceeds 25%.

Feedback on self-assessment question 16.2

This question requires you to know the minimum thresholds, which are: where the products are not more than 5% in horizontal agreements and 10% in vertical agreements available in the area of the Common Market affected by the agreement.

Article 81 does not apply where the total annual turnover of the undertaking participating in the agreement does not exceed EUR 200 million.

Feedback on learning activity 16.3

You should define dominant market as when an undertaking behaves to an appreciable extent independently of its competitors and customers and ultimately of consumers when making commercial decisions.

Then list the following conduct:

- directly or indirectly imposing unfair trading conditions or unfair purchase or selling prices;

16

- limiting production, markets or technical development to the prejudice of consumers;
- applying dissimilar conditions to equivalent transactions with other trading parties thus placing them at a competitive disadvantage;
- making the conclusion of contracts subject to acceptance by the other parties of supplementary obligations which have no connection with the subject matter of such contracts.

Feedback on self-assessment question 16.3

1 False.
2 True.
3 True.
4 False.
5 True.
6 False.

Feedback on learning activity 16.4

You should explain the various factors that the OFT will take into account when publishing information in the public domain. These factors include any legal restrictions on disclosure of information; public accountability; deterring other businesses from such conduct; increasing consumer awareness of their rights; facilitating complaints on further breaches and educating the market. You should also mention that the published information must be accurate, balanced and fair.

Feedback on self-assessment question 16.4

The Enterprise Act 2002 introduced reform of competition law as well as increased consumer protection.

It also created the body of Office of Fair Trading (OFT), which has taken over the role previously undertaken by the Director General of Fair Trading (DGFT). It also created the Competition Appeal Tribunal (CAT) to which there is a right of appeal. It created the Competition Service, which is an independent body that makes the decisions on mergers and markets.

On increasing consumer protection consumers also have a greater voice on competition matters and can complain to the OFT. The OFT is required to respond within 90 days.

The Act introduced criminal sanctions for cartels, that is, those who operate agreements to fix prices, share markets, limit production and rig bids. The maximum penalty is 5 years in prison.

16

Intellectual property rights

Introduction

Intellectual property rights (IPRs) is the term used to describe the various rights that give protection to innovative and creative endeavours whether in words or goods. In this session you are going to be looking at the various types of intellectual property rights including patents, trademarks, design rights and copyrights. You will also look at the difference between registerable and unregisterable rights.

Session learning objectives

After completing this session you should be able to:

17.1 Explain patents.
17.2 Explain trademarks.
17.3 Explain design rights and copyright.
17.4 Distinguish between registerable and non registerable intellectual property rights.

Unit content coverage

This study session covers the following topics from the official CIPS unit content document:

Learning outcome

Examine those intellectual property rights that are registerable and those that are un-registerable.

Learning objective

4.1 Distinguish between those intellectual property rights that are registerable and those that are unregisterable
   • Patents
   • Trade marks
   • Design rights
   • Copyright
   • IPR protection through contractual clauses

17

Timing

You should set aside about 5 hours to read and complete this session, including learning activities, self-assessment questions, the suggested further reading (if any) and the revision question.

17.1 Patents

Patent overview

You are now going to be looking at patents. Details of each of the main points is discussed later but, in short, patent rights are territorial rights which means that a UK patent does not give rights outside the UK. In general they last for up to 20 years in the UK. Patents are negative rights, which means they stop anyone else from making, using or selling an invention. In the business world patents have value to the inventor as they can be sold, mortgaged or licensed to others.

Patents Act 1977

This Act governs patents. They are statutory property rights that give the owner of the patent the exclusive or monopoly right to use certain inventions. Inventions can be products, components or processes. Patents are about the functional and technical aspects of products and processes.

Before someone can apply for a patent the invention must fulfil specific conditions which are:

- the invention must be novel (see explanation of Novelty test below);
- it must be able to be applied to industry (see below for more information); and
- capable of an inventive step (see below for more information on what this means).

In the business world a patent means that an inventor can prevent competitors from using the invention.

Application procedure for a patent

As a patent is a territorial right, the inventor or person who has created the invention applies to the Patent Office in the jurisdiction for which they want protection. For example, the inventor might want protection in the UK and therefore will apply to the UK Patent Office. If the protection is for Europe then an application for each of the European Union (EU) member states submitted to the European Patent Office (EPO). There is currently no single European patent.

Duration of a patent

As you know from the above overview, a patent lasts for up to 20 years. Some patents for medicinal products may be eligible for protection for a further 5 years.

The Novelty test

This is an objective test. S2(1) Patent Act 1977 provides that the invention must not have formed part of what is called 'state of the art'. Under s2(2), state of the art is everything that has been made available to the public before the date of the patent application. The word 'anticipation' is used alongside the word novelty. An invention is said to be anticipated where the prior art contains either enabling disclosure for product patents or clear and unmistakable directions to do what has been invented. The decision on novelty is decided by the Patent Office through searches and examinations.

Industrial application

This condition means that the invention can be made or used in any kind of industry. This seems easy to understand as nearly all inventions meet this requirement. However, difficulties do arise in the exceptions such as methods of treating humans or animals. Surgery, therapy or diagnosis are deemed not capable of industrial application.

Inventive step: the Windsurfer test

This means something that is not obvious to a skilled person in that area of technology. Another word used for this is non-obviousness. The statutory test to assess obviousness is called the Windsurfer test, which provided for a series of questions to be asked to assess obviousness. See the case of *Windsurfing International Inc.* v *Tabur Marine (Great Britain) Limited* [1985] (modified later in *PLG Research Ltd* v *Ardon International Ltd* [1995]). In the former case a patent was challenged where the windsurfboard had been shown as a primitive prototype to have been built and used in public by a 12-year-old boy. The court set out the four steps required to be taken when ascertaining the validity of a patent: 'The first is to identify the inventive concept embodied in the patent in suit. Thereafter, the court has to assume the mantle of the normally skilled but unimaginative addressee in the art at the priority date and to impute to him what was, at that date, common general knowledge in the art in question. The third step is to identify what, if any, differences exist between the matter cited as being "known or used" and the alleged invention. Finally, the court has to ask itself whether, viewed without any knowledge of the alleged invention, those differences constitute steps which would have been obvious to the skilled man or whether they require any degree of invention.' Questions now to be asked include 'what is the inventive step involved in the patent?'; 'how does that step differ from that available in the public domain (state of the art)?'; 'at the date of the first application of the patent, what was the state of the art in relation to that inventive step?'; 'would taking that inventive step be obvious to a skilled person in that art?'

What is not capable of being patented?

The Patents Act 1977 does not provide a definition of invention. S1(2) lists some things that are not considered inventions. These include things that are abstract, not technical, aesthetic, for example scientific discoveries, literary and dramatic works, musical and artistic works and the like. So you may be thinking it is quite easy to identify what would be capable of being patented. The difficulties arise in things such as computer programs; mental acts, playing games or business methods; or presenting new information; inventions contrary to public policy or morality. Let us look at a few of these.

Computer programs

Under s1(2)(c) Patents Act 1977 list, computer programs are *not* regarded as inventions. However, patents are granted for some software inventions where substantial technical contribution is made to the making of the software. See the case of *Vicom's Application* [1987] which was a European Patent Office (EPO) decision. The EPO approach was changed in case of *IBM's Application* [1999] where it was accepted that if programs run on a computer to produce a technical effect then they are patentable.

In 2005 a draft EU Directive was being discussed in an attempt to clarify this situation. The pro-patent lobby deem that the directive would maintain the status quo, whereas the anti-patent lobby feel that it is like trying to patent music or maths. It is a waiting game at the moment; we can only suggest you watch out for the issue of an EU Directive on patents. As at 6 July 2005, the EU Parliament voted by a massive majority to reject the software patents directive, formally known as the Directive on the Patentability of Computer Implemented Inventions. The vote to scrap the bill was passed by a margin of 648 votes to 14, with 18 abstentions. The Foundation for a Free Information Infrastructure (FFII) says the rejection is a logical response to the Commission and Council's refusal to take parliament's will into consideration. You should look out for news on the world wide web.

Mental acts, playing games or business methods

These are deemed not capable of being patented. See the case of *Raytheon* [1993] where a new process was used to identify ships by digital comparison of the silhouette of the unknown ship with the silhouette of known ships held on the computer memory. It was held that this was an automated method performed by individuals, hence mental acts.

The rules for playing games are not patentable unless they provide a substantial technical contribution to the game, which is difficult to see.

For business methods, the invention must make a substantial technical contribution. The UK courts have taken a strict approach that advances in the field of business are not technical. See the case of *Merrill Lynch's Application* [1989]. However, the EPO approach moves towards a more relaxed approach. See the case of *PBS Partnership/Pension Benefits System* [2000] where in practice many modern business methods involve the use of computer programs, and therefore if there is substantial technical contribution then it may be patentable.

Presenting information

This is not regarded as inventions that are patentable.

Inventions contrary to public policy or morality

This is where the commercial exploitation of an invention would be contrary to public policy or morality and would not be granted. See the EPO case of *Harvard/Onco-Mouse* [1991] where the patent office was to consider the application for patenting of a mouse or other non-human mammal genetically engineered to develop cancer. It was held that the suffering of the mouse and environmental risks were outweighed by the use of the invention for the benefit of humans and the mouse was held not to be immoral. Further guidance on this is provided by Directive 98/44/EC.

17

There is no need in this study guide to provide more information on this topic.

Who is granted the patent?

The basic rule is that patents are granted to:

- the inventor or joint inventors: these are the people who actually devise the invention;
- the inventors successors in ownership; or
- the employer of an employee who invents something (while in the course of employment): compensation may be available to the employee provided the patent is of outstanding benefit to the employer; the invention satisfies the patent criteria and it is fair and just that compensation be awarded.

Cases on compensation are usually settled out of court so there are no reported cases.

Infringement of a patent

What counts as an actionable infringement is governed by s61(1) Patents Act 1977. An infringement occurs where a person does certain things when the patent is in force without the patent owner's consent. These include:

- where it is a product and the person disposes of or uses or imports the product or keeps it for disposal or otherwise;
- where it is a process and the person disposes of it or offers to dispose it or imports any product directly by that process or keeps it for disposal or otherwise;
- where it is a process and the person uses the process or offers it to others for use in the UK or it is obvious to a reasonable person that using it would constitute an infringement.

It is also an infringement to provide another person with the means to work a patent when you know, or it would be obvious to a reasonable person to know, that it would introduce the use of the invention into the UK.

Remedies for infringement

Where there is an infringement of a patent, the owner of the patent can raise a civil court action seeking an injunction to prevent further abuse, to obtain an account of any profits and claim damages.

Statutory defences

Under s60(5) of the Patents Act 1977 there are six situations where a patented invention can be used without infringement. These are where the patent is used:

- for private purposes;
- for experimental purposes;
- in the preparation of a prescription provided by a registered doctor or dentist for an individual;

- exclusively for ships which have accidentally entered internal or territorial waters of the UK;
- in the process or operation of aircraft, hovercraft or vehicle which has accidentally entered or is crossing over UK;
- in exempted aircraft which have lawfully entered or crossing the UK.

EU position

Certain EU rules promote free movement of goods and trade between member states and to enable this patent owners rights have been exhausted. You have already looked at competition in the study of European Law in study session 16. For patents there is a body of case law decided by the European Court of Justice which addresses the balance between promoting free competition and protecting the rights of the patent owner. The general principle of exhaustion of rights was summarised in the case of *Zino Davidoff SA* v *A & G Imports* [2000]. In this case, where an article with a patent is put into one member state market with the consent of the patent owner, that owner cannot prevent the import of goods into another member state or prevent them being sold there. The principle of exhaustion of rights was established in the case of *Centrafarm BV* v *Sterling Drug Inc* [1975]. In this case, Sterling owned the patent to Negram (a drug). Their patent covered UK and The Netherlands. The drug had been marketed in the UK. Centrafarm bought supplies of Negram and exported them to The Netherlands where they could obtain a higher sale price. Centrafarm was the 'parallel' importer of the drugs. Sterling sued Centrafarm for patent infringement in The Netherlands. The European Court of Justice held that it would not restrict trade between member states where no such restraint was necessary to safeguard the subject matter of the patent. The reason for this was that the patent owner, Sterling, had consented by already putting the goods legally on the market.

See also the case of *Merck & Co Inc* v *Stephar BV* [1981], which approved the Centrafarm decision and affirmed that the key to the first sale in a member state is the consent of the patent owner.

Alternatives to getting a patent

Where an invention is not evident from a product it can still be protected by confidentiality law. This is discussed in study session 18.

Learning activity 17.1

For this learning activity we recommend that you search the world wide web and look for some latest inventions. You may also have watched television programmes such as *Tomorrow's World* and remember products or processes that were discussed and are now on the market. Describe two inventions and list the specific conditions that are required to submit an application for a patent.

Feedback on page 269

17

You have now studied in detail the intellectual property right called patents. Patents can motivate other people to further develop the idea. Once the patent period expires, which is up to 20 years in the UK, then anyone can use it and this benefits everyone.

Patents Act 2004

In October 2005 the latest sections of the Patent Act 2004 came into force. One of these sections was s13, which enables requests to be made to the Patent Office for a non-binding opinion on the questions of validity: that is, in respect of novelty or inventive step) or infringement of a patent.

The advantage of this opinion procedure was to provide a quick and cheap way of obtaining a non-binding expert evaluation of questions of validity and infringement. The opinion is given by a patent examiner who is neutral and therefore may prove a useful foundation for licence negotiations or may help to persuade investors of the strength of a patent. The disadvantages might be that parties will try to use this for commercial purposes and there may be a reluctance on parties to reveal their ideas in such a public procedure.

Self-assessment question 17.1

Describe when an actionable infringement of a patent arises and what action the patent owner can take.

Feedback on page 270

17.2 Trademarks

History of trademarks

Trademarks are a form of intellectual property right. They are currently governed by the Trade Marks Act 1994. The first legal framework was introduced by the Trade Marks Registration Act 1875 which established a legal register of trademarks. An entry in the register of a word or device, that is, a logo or picture, establishes the trademark and who the owneris. Registration gives the owner exclusive right to use the trademark and the right to prevent unauthorised use of it. Where there is an infringement the trademark owner can take legal action.

Trademark legislation

Until the 1994 Act trademarks remained largely unaltered even after various acts of 1883, 1905 and 1938. Other legislation was the Trade Marks (Amendment) Act 1984, which introduced registration of service marks, and the Patents, Designs and Trade Marks Act 1986; and the Copyright, Designs and Patents Act 1988, which made the forgery of a trademark a criminal offence. The Trade Marks Act 1994 (TMA) also implements the European Council Directive No. 89/104/EEC.

17

What is a trademark?

A trademark is a badge of origin. It is used so that customers recognise the product of a particular company. It can be any sign that distinguishes the goods and services of one trader from those of another trader. Signs include logos, pictures or a combination of them.

S1(1) TMA provides a non-exhaustive list of types of things that may be registered as a trademark. However, to be registered, a trademark must fulfil three criteria. It must be:

- distinctive for the goods or services being applied for;
- not deceptive or contrary to law or morality;
- not similar or identical to any earlier trademark for the same or similar goods or services.

Before the 1994 Act three-dimensional shapes were not able to be registered as trademarks. See the case of *Coca-Cola Trade Mark Applications* [1985], which concerned the distinctive Coca-Cola bottle and the case of *Reckitt & Coleman Products Ltd* v *Borden* [1980], which concerned the plastic yellow lemon in which the company supplied Jif lemon juice.

The 1994 Act reversed this position and three-dimensional shapes *can* be registered as they can be graphically represented. Other things that can be registered as trademarks include:

- specific colours and combinations if they are distinctive enough. See the case of *Smith Kline & French Laboratories Ltd* v *Stirling Winthrop Group Ltd* [1975];
- sounds such as jingles of the 'red phone' of Direct Line or the lion roar of MGM;
- tastes and smells if they are sufficiently distinctive;
- slogans such as 'have a break, have a Kit Kat' (which was previously refused under the old legislation).

Registering a trademark

The applicant identifies the class or classes that apply to their trademark. The applicant pays a fee for each class in which they wish to register. There can be multiple registrations of the same name or sign in different classes. For example, the trademark, Jif, is registered by two different companies as it falls within two separate classes. One is 'Jif', a distinctive lemon juice produced by a food company, and the other 'Jif' is a cleaning fluid. Clearly there is no confusion or association of one product with another.

For dissimilar products see the case of *Baywatch Production Co Ltd* v *The Home Video Channel* [1997]. In this case similar marks were used by each company. Baywatch was the TV show and Babewatch was for adult videos and adult TV channels. The courts held that the products were sufficiently dissimilar for there not to be any real risk of confusion.

However, in the landmark case of *Visa International Service Association* v *C A Sheimer* [1999] Visa succeeded in preventing Sheimer from registering the same name for a completely different product. Visa trademark related to financial services, particularly credit card services, whereas Sheimer's product was rubber contraceptive devices (condoms). One of the grounds on which Visa opposed the registration was that Sheimer's use of the mark would take unfair advantage of or be detrimental to the distinctive character or repute of the earlier mark, that is, registration was contrary to s5(3) TMA. The difference between this case and that of *Ever Ready RM (Oasis Stores Ltd's Application)* [1998] lies in the repute of the name, which is a matter of degree, and the likelihood of the public associating its use on an unrelated product with the well-known brand. Visa was considered a more famous mark than Ever Ready.

Classes of registration

There are currently 45 classes. Classes 1–34 refer to goods; classes 35–45 apply to services. When applying to register a trademark you must remember that it has to fulfil the three criteria referred to above. The main questions you should consider are:

- Does your trademark clearly identify your goods or services from those of other traders?
- Has a trademark already been registered or is in process of being registered which is similar to yours for the same goods or services or sounds the same if it is a jingle?

If the answer is yes to the above questions then the trademark examiner will object to your mark.

Trademark duration

Registration of a trademark lasts for 10 years from the date of registration. The Trade Mark Registry write to the owner of the trademark a few months before the end of the10 year period to ask if they wish to renew the trademark for a further 10 years. As with initial registration, there is a fee for renewal of the trademark. The fee applies to each class.

After the application for registration but before registration, the letters 'TM' can be used on the trademark. Once registered the symbol which is used is ® or the abbreviation RTM. These symbols are not compulsory.

Trademark examiner objections

The examiner will object to words, logos, pictures or other signs that are unlikely to be seen as a trademark by the public. Some examples include:

- marks that describe the quality or quantity of your goods or services (see below);
- marks that have become customary in your line of trade (for example, aspirin and linoleum);
- are not distinctive; or
- a combination of the above.

Practical examples of objections

- The one for you (as this is used often in trade); or
- Buy one get one free (this relates to value of goods or services); or

17

- Tastydrinks (as this describes quality); or
- Tea Shop (this is not distinctive);
- Same day delivery (as this refers to time of production of goods or services).

A useful tip is to use made-up words that are normally distinctive unless they have become customary to your line of trade.

Of course, marks that fall into the above practical examples may be registerable if they have become distinctive upon use. See the case of *Proctor & Gamble v OHIM (Baby-Dry) [2000]* where the case related to disposable nappies. The European Court of Justice (ECJ) implied a wider category of descriptive marks than had been considered before. The UK Registry may adopt a more generous approach to distinctive marks in the future.

It is also possible for a trade association to obtain a trademark for what are known as certification marks, which denote a quality certification or means of manufacture: for example, British Standards Kitemark.

Trademark search

Of course, you may think of something made up but someone else has registered it first. To find out if this has happened the examiner searches the Trade Mark Register containing UK marks, international marks relating to the UK and European Community marks.

Learning activity 17.2

Consider some familiar trademarks or jingles. Describe the function of a trademark and what criteria require to be fulfilled for it to be accepted for registration.

Feedback on page 270

Trademark infringement

The owner of a trademark has certain rights in the event of infringement. These rights come into existence from the date of registration, which is the date of filing of the application for registration.

Infringement occurs where there is use of an identical sign for identical goods or services or use on identical goods or services. Such use constitutes infringement where the public is likely to be confused about the origin of the goods or services or is likely to assume that there is an association with the registered mark,

Infringement also occurs where there is use of a mark similar for dissimilar goods or services where such use takes unfair advantage of, or is detrimental to, the distinctive character or reputation of the registered trademark.

S10 TMA provided for contributory infringement where a person who applies a trademark to certain materials has actual or constructive knowledge that the use of the trademark is unauthorised. The provision under s10 of the 1994 Act extends down the supply chain. However, printers, publishers and manufacturers may avoid liability in practice by inserting suitable standard contractual terms in their contracts with their clients.

Defences to infringement

Comparative advertising: Before the TMA comparative advertising was considered an infringement. However, since the 1994 Act comparative advertising is allowed provided it is honest and not detrimental to or takes unfair advantage of the distinctive character or reputation of the trademark. See the case of *British Airways Plc* v *Ryanair* [2001] where British Airways brought an action for trademark infringement against Ryanair for publishing two Ryanair advertisements comparing Ryanair fares with those of British Airways. The courts held that this was allowed and considered that although the advertisements may have caused offence they were not dishonest and the price comparisons were not significantly unfair.

Exhaustion: This occurs where the owner of the trademark consents to putting the goods bearing the trademark on the European market. For example, once a trademark owner consents to their goods being marketed in France, trademark rights cannot be used to prevent these goods from being resold in the UK unless there are legitimate reasons for this under s12 TMA. Goods resold in this way are known as parallel imports or grey imports.

Remedies for infringement

The remedies available for trademark infringement include:

*   damages (s14(2) TMA);
*   account of profits (s14(2) TMA);
*   injunction (s14(2) TMA);
*   erasure of the offending sign (s15 TMA);
*   delivery up of the sign (s16 TMA);
*   destruction or forfeiting of the infringing goods (s19 TMA).

Some offences under the Trade Descriptions Act 1968 and Consumer Protection Act 1987 which carry criminal sanctions may be applicable to trademarks.

In a recent case relating to a famous trademark it was suggested by some commentators that the decision will result in lower protection for such famous marks. See the case of *Picasso* v *Picaro* [2006] where the court rejected the opposition of the Picasso Estate (owners of the trademark Picasso) to the registration of the mark Picaro for vehicles and vehicle parts and omnibuses in class 12. The court rejected the opposition as it found no likelihood of confusion between Picasso and Picaro. It has been long established that the greater the distinctive character of a mark the broader the protection it enjoys. A mark can possess significant distinctive character either by its inherent qualities or through its reputation in the market place as in the case of Coca-Cola (see above).

17

The European route

If you want trademark protection in countries that are members of the European Union then you apply for a Community Trade Mark through the Office for Harmonisation in the Internal Market (OHIM), based in Alicante, Spain. There is a registration fee.

The International route

Where you wish to register your trademark in countries which are party to the Madrid Protocol then application for international registration is through the World Intellectual Property Organisation (WIPO), based in Geneva, Switzerland. There is also a fee for this registration.

Outside the UK

Where you want to use your trademark in countries other than the UK you can make a single application by using the above European or international routes, which means one application which can be less costly and faster. Or you can apply direct to the Trade Mark Office in each of the countries in which you wish to register.

Self-assessment question 17.2

Explain the process that would protect the logo for a new business.

Feedback on page 270

17.3 Unregisterable rights of design rights and copyright

Unregisterable rights

In this section you will be looking at unregistered rights. These include copyrights and unregistered design rights.

Traditionally copyright was an important source of protection in the design field. However, as you will see in the section below, a separate system of registered design was developed to protect aesthetic designs.

Copyright definition and duration

Copyright is a property right that subsists in certain works. There are different categories of works. It is a statutory right that gives the owner certain exclusive rights in relation to their works. These rights include a right to make copies of their work, to sell the copies to the public or the right to give public performances of their work.

Copyright comes into existence automatically where a person creates a work that is original and tangible. There is no copyright in ideas.

Copyright lasts for the life of the creator plus 70 years.

To establish copyright all that is required is proof that you created the work and the date of that creation.

Copyright history

The first Act of Parliament to provide protection for copyright in books and other writings was the Statute of Anne 1709. Before this, any dispute over the rights of publishing of books was enforced by common law.

The main UK statute now relating to copyright is the Copyright Designs and Patents Act 1988 (CDPA).

Categories of copyright

The categories are subdivided into two: primary or authorial, and secondary or entrepreneurial. The definitions for the categories are contained in ss3–8 CDPA.

The authorial or primary division includes: literary works; dramatic works; musical works and artistic works. For example under s3(1) CDPA literary works include any work that can be expressed in print, irrespective of its quality. See the case of *University of London Press* v *University Tutorial Press* [1916]. In this case the court decided that LDMA, that is, literary works, dramatic works, musical works and artistic works, must be original in the sense that they originate with the author. This is a minimal requirement. Original works need not be inventive or original and a wide range of works have been held to be original. Within this division are computer programs and databases. Under European Directive on legal protection of databases (Directive 96/9/EC) and Computer Directive (Directive 91/250/EEC) both computer programs and databases must be original: that is, they must be the author's own intellectual creation.

The entrepreneurial or secondary division includes: sound recordings; broadcasts; films; cable programmes and typographical arrangement of published editions.

Learning activity 17.3

Describe and define copyright. List items that would be considered as copyright works and give some examples.

Feedback on page 271

17

Ownership of copyright

The basic rule is that the person who created the work is the owner of the copyright. There is an exception to this rule under s11(2) CDPA. This section provides that where a person creates a work in the course of employment the employer is the first owner of any copyright subject to any agreement to the contrary. Such an agreement can be written, oral or implied.

To identify whether an individual is an employee or not it is important to distinguish between a contract of service and a contract for services. Individuals who are contracted as consultants or commissioned to produce copyright works are not employees. They do not fall within s11(2) as mentioned above. It is important to clarify the position of ownership of copyright within the contract. Any transfer of copyright must be in writing.

Remedies for infringement of copyright

The remedies are the same as those discussed above: that is, damages, injunctions, account of profits, seizure of infringing copies, delivery up of infringing copies and criminal offences under ss107–108 CDPA.

Unregisterable design rights

As already discussed, copyright was traditionally an important source of protection in the design field. Before 1980 one had a choice of applying for a registered design or relying on copyright to protect your design. The advantage of relying on copyright was that it was automatic, there was no fee and there was a longer term of protection. However, in some cases copyright was abused in the design field. See the case of *Dorling* v *Honnor Marine* [1964], which related to non-aesthetic designs. This case dealt with whether a copyright existed in plans for a boat design. The court held that where the design of an article was not 'registerable' under the Registered Design Act 1949 as being functional rather than ornamental, it still enjoyed copyright protection. As a result of abuse and in response to European developments, reforms were introduced that relate to unregistered and registered design rights.

Summary of protection routes for a design

You can protect a design by one or more routes. These include:

- design rights under CDPA ss213–264 Part III;
- copyright under CDPA ss51–53;
- registered designs under Registered Designs Act 1949 (see below).

The unregistered design right was introduced in CDPA to give protection to functional designs. Before this the courts had ruled that there was no copyright protection in respect of merely functional items designed for mass production. See the case of *BL Cars* v *Armstrong Patents* [1986] where the design of a car exhaust pipe was unique and a company that made copies of the pipe was sued by BL Cars for breaching their copyright in the drawings of the pipe. CDPA 1988 gives protection to a design right. The right gives a 15-year protection to such designs. However, it is still not a monopoly right as copyright is. The protection is limited as others may apply for a licence to produce the product after 10 years and this cannot be unreasonably refused.

There is a further restriction in that the design right does not and cannot apply to any functional items which are specifically designed spare parts or components. The CDPA 1988 refers to these items as must-match or must-fit spare parts. So generic items are protected but specifically designed ones are not.

17

Self-assessment question 17.3

Describe the forms of protection that a designer can use to protect the intellectual property.

Feedback on page 271

17.4 Distinction between registerable and non registerable rights

In the previous sections of this study session you have looked at the different types of intellectual property rights, including those that are automatic and therefore not registered, namely, copyright and design right, and those that are registered which include patents and trademarks. The matter of registered design rights will be looked at in more depth below.

It is recommended that you review the previous sections on the different intellectual property rights before attempting the learning activity.

Learning activity 17.4

Distinguish between registerable and unregisterable intellectual property rights and describe the registered rights of Patents and Trade Marks and the unregistered intellectual property rights of Copyright and Design right. Refer to the appropriate statutes.

Feedback on page 271

In the above information you have already looked at registerable and unregisterable intellectual property rights, with the exception of registered design right. This is going to be discussed now.

Design rights: routes to protection

Remember from the above information that there are three routes to protecting design rights. These are:

- design right under CDPA ss213–264 Part III (unregisterable);
- copyright under CDPA ss51–53 (unregisterable);
- registered designs under Registered Designs Act 1949 (registerable).

In this section we discuss those design rights that are registered under the Registered Designs Act 1949 (as amended). The law underwent substantial reform in 2001/2002 when the Directive on the Legal Protection of Designs (Directive 98/71/EC) was implemented. This Directive was to harmonise the laws of EU member states and pave the way for further Community harmonisation.

17

Registered design rights

These are monopoly rights that protect a design. The right can be for all or part of a product resulting from the features of the product or its decoration. The features include:

- lines;
- contours;
- colours;
- shape;
- texture or;
- materials.

The design may be the shape of a product, the decoration applied to a product or both. You must remember that it is the design that is protected.

When applying to register a design it must fulfil two criteria:

- it must be new which means that it must not be the same as any design already made available to the public;
- it must have individual character which means that the overall impression must be different from that of any previous design.

You can register a design for up to 25 years but to do this you must renew it every five years from the date of your application.

Design rights are valuable intellectual property rights and you can license other people to use them and sell them to someone else.

An infringement occurs when someone uses a design in the UK that is identical or similar to your registered design. You must remember that registering your design in the UK does not give you protection abroad. If you want protection in other countries then you can apply through a single application or separately in each country. We recommend you revisit the section on trademarks for the European and international routes for registration.

Benefits of design registration

When you register a design you get exclusive right to make, import, export, use or stock any product to which the design has been applied in the UK (see above for European and International routes to registration).

You obtain the right to take legal action against others who infringe the design and to claim damages.

As you have seen above, design rights are a valuable asset and you therefore you have a financial asset that could increase in value.

17

Self-assessment question 17.4

Read the following short scenario and describe what remedies are available.

(continued on next page)

Self-assessment question 17.4 *(continued)*

Lelio have designed a new functional product and want to develop it. Unfortunately they do not have the facilities to do this. They have not applied for any intellectual property rights protection such as a patent or trademark or design rights. They have entered into a contract with Kenyth to manufacture the product. Lelio will provide the mouldings for the manufacture of the product. Lelio later discover that a pirate version of their product is on the market and that Kenyth have been making and marketing it through Zylon, a wholesaler. Describe what remedies, if any, Lelio have and against whom.

Feedback on page 272

Revision question

Now try the revision question for this session on page 315.

Summary

In this study session you have been looking at intellectual property rights (IPRs). You now know that this term is used to describe the various rights that give protection to innovative and creative endeavours whether in words or goods. You have looked at different types of registered and unregistered property rights. You should remember that intellectual property rights are valuable assets of a company. The protection that these rights afford is very relevant to the purchasing professional and the question of retaining intellectual property rights is frequently addressed in terms and conditions of contract.

Suggested further reading

Griffiths and Griffiths (2002). You should read the chapter on intellectual property, part V, chapter 19.

Feedback on learning activities and self-assessment questions

Feedback on learning activity 17.1

In your answer you will have your own two products or processes. You might have found the same as we have. For example: Word Isolating Educational Tool is a product that assists children, adults with special needs, and foreigners to become confident with reading; Disposable Toddler Helmet is a product that provides protection for the entire upper head region and the ears, when the toddler is learning to walk, ride a toy or even if he or she has a medical condition. The 'Sandphibian' Convertible Beach Sand Chair is a foldaway chair and is the first of its kind to be patented in the USA.

Your list of specific conditions for the patent application will be the same for each of these products. The invention must be novel, which means that it must not form part of everything that has been made available to the public before the date of the application. It must involve an inventive step, which means that the invention must not be obvious from the viewpoint of a skilled person in that area of technology. Finally, it must be capable of industrial application; that is, be able to be made or used in any kind of industry.

Feedback on self-assessment question 17.1

Your answer should be in the form of a short essay. An infringement occurs when someone makes, uses or sells the invention without the permission of the patent owner. This is governed by s61(1) Patents Act 1977. You can further explain that infringement can occur whether the invention is a product or a process. A person is infringing a patent where they dispose of, use or import the product or process, or where they keep it for disposal or other purposes. It is also an infringement to provide another person with the means to work a patent when you know or it would be obvious to a reasonable person to know that it would introduce the use of the invention into the UK.

The action that can be taken by a patent owner is a civil action for an injunction. An injunction is to prevent the person from further using or disposing of the product and to obtain an account of any profit where the product has been sold and claim damages.

Feedback on learning activity 17.2

In this exercise you may identify trademarks such as McDonald's large yellow 'M' or perhaps the jingle and red telephone of Direct Line. There will be many more that you can use as examples.

The function of trademarks is to act as an indicator of the trade origin and quality and reliability of the product. This protects the consumer of branded goods from confusion or deception in the marketplace. It also enables the owner of the trademark to take action against certain acts of unfair competition.

To apply for registration of a trademark it must be distinctive for the goods or services being applied for. It must not be deceptive or contrary to law or morality. It must not be similar or identical to any earlier trademark for the same or similar goods or services.

Feedback on self-assessment question 17.2

Your answer should take the form of a short essay. You should explain that the process of registration includes identifying the class or classes (there being currently 45 classes) that apply to the particular trademark. You should also mention the criteria that the trademark requires to fulfil, namely that it is distinctive for the goods or services being applied for; it is not deceptive or contrary to law or morality and it is not similar or identical to any earlier trademark for the same or similar goods or services. Go on then to explain that the applicant will have to pay a fee for each class in which they wish to register. Explain how there can be multiple registrations of the same name or sign in different classes. You should give an example such as Jif. However, you should also mention more recent cases such as Baywatch Production Co and the landmark decision in the Visa case mentioning that the ground was based on s5(3) TMA, being unfair or detrimental to the distinctive character or repute of the earlier mark. You can distinguish between the Visa case and that of *Ever Ready RM (Oasis Stores Ltd's Application)* [1998], namely that Visa was considered a more famous mark than Ever Ready.

Feedback on learning activity 17.3

Copyright is a statutory property right that gives the owner certain exclusive rights in relation to their works. These rights include a right to make copies of their work, to sell the copies to the public or the right to give public performances of their work. It exists automatically where a person creates a work that is original and tangible. There is no copyright in ideas. Copyright lasts for the life of the creator plus 70 years.

To establish copyright all that is required is proof that you created the work and the date of that creation.

Your list of items should include:

- literary works;
- dramatic works;
- musical works;
- artistic works;
- computer-generated programs or databases;
- sound recordings;
- films;
- broadcasts.

Examples might include: Harry Potter books, *Brokeback Mountain*, Robbie Williams hits, and so on.

Feedback on self-assessment question 17.3

Your answer will include the following different routes to protection: by design right under CDPA ss213–264 Part III; by copyright under CDPA ss51–53 or by registration under Registered Designs Act 1949 (see below).

Feedback on learning activity 17.4

Your answer should be in the form of short paragraphs, firstly on the distinction between registerable and unregisterable rights, and then a brief paragraph on each of the intellectual property rights. Some examples follow.

Registered intellectual property rights are those that are registered by applying to the appropriate authority for registration. Unregistered rights arise automatically.

17

Patents are registerable rights. You apply to the Patents Office for registration. They are governed by the Patents Act 1977 and the Patents Act 2004.

Trademarks are registerable rights. Trademarks are registered by applying to the Trade Marks office. They are governed by the Trade Marks Act 1994 which brings English law in line with the EU Directive 1988.

Copyright is an unregisterable right that arises automatically. It is governed by CDPA.

Design rights can be unregisterable as well as registered. For this answer, the unregisterable design rights are protected under CDPA ss 213–264 as design rights or as copyright, under CDPA ss51–53.

Feedback on self-assessment question 17.4

As Lelio have not registered any of their intellectual property rights they cannot rely on those rights. They can only fall back on the existence of copyright or unregistered design rights or the tort of passing off (at this stage you may not have included this as it is discussed in study session 18). However, you should have mentioned the other points.

Lelio will have a copyright of the original drawings of the product. However, the scenario refers to the product being functional and therefore Lelio will not be able to rely on full copyright protection. Since CDPA 1988, products that do not have a clear aesthetic or artistic quality and are intended for mass production attract limited design right protection. This is in same way as copyright and is not the formal registered design right.

Kenyth have been making and selling the product without authorisation. They will be liable for this infringement. This can go down the supply chain and Zylon may be liable for infringement too. However, this will depend on the extent of Zylon's knowledge of the infringement. It would have benefited Lelio if they had included contractual clauses which ensure all patterns, designs and moulds and tools needed for production of the items belonged to them. Such clauses should include that the items must be returned to Lelio on completion of the contract and that Lelio would pay for them. A clause specifying the existence of intellectual property rights might have prevented Kenyth from manufacturing pirate items.

17

Confidentiality and trade secrets

'Life would be intolerable...if information could not be given or received in confidence.'
Sir John Donaldson in the Spycatcher case [1999]

Introduction

This study session links with the previous study session on intellectual property, where you learned that intellectual property is a valuable asset to a company. You will now be looking at two areas that are also of important commercial value to companies and their competitors. These areas are confidentiality and trade secrets. As part of this you will look at breach of confidence and the tort of passing off, which both provide relief against business practices that amount to 'unfair competition'. You start by looking at the tort of passing off.

Session learning objectives

After completing this session you should be able to:

18.1 Explain the tort of passing-off.
18.2 Explain breach of confidentiality.
18.3 Impact of restraint of trade clauses.

Unit content coverage

This study session covers the following topics from the official CIPS unit content document:

Learning outcome

Examine those intellectual property rights that are registerable and those that are un-registerable.

Learning objective

4.2 Explain and apply the common law rules relating to confidentiality and the protection of trade secrets in English law.
   • Tort of passing-off
   • Breach of confidence
   • Restraint of trade clauses

18

Prior knowledge

Study sessions 16 and 17.

Timing

You should set aside about 4 hours to read and complete this session, including learning activities, self-assessment questions, the suggested further reading (if any) and the revision question.

18.1 Tort of passing-off

The tort of passing off

The tort of passing off was summarised by Lord Oliver in the 'Jif Lemon' case, the proper title of which is *Reckitt & Colman Products* v *Borden Inc* [1990]. He stated that '...the law of passing off could be summarised in one short generally proposition: no man might pass off his goods as those of another'.

We remind you here that you must *not* confuse the tort of passing off with the passing of title. This often happens in examinations. Please ensure that you know the difference.

The tort of passing off offers two protections:

- it protects a trader against the unfair competition of competitors; and
- it protects consumers who would otherwise be confused about the origin of the goods or services they are offered.

Many trademark infringement cases also involve passing off issues; these two areas of the law are closely related in practice. You may wish to revisit study session 17 to refresh your memory on trademarks. If a trademark case fails then the passing off action can be a fallback position.

For an action of passing off to be successful, Lord Diplock identified five characteristics in the case of *Erven Warnink BV and Another* v *J Townend & Sons (Hull) Ltd and Another (Advocaat)* [1980] (known as the Advocaat case). However, these were reduced to three characteristics in the case of *Reckitt & Colman Products* v *Borden Inc* [1990], known as the Jif Lemon case. The test in the Jif Lemon case is simpler than the Advocaat case and is known as the classic trinity formulation as there are three elements or criteria for a successful passing off action, namely:

- the claimant must be able to demonstrate goodwill;
- there must be misrepresentation as to the goods or services offered;
- there must be actual or likely damage.

These are the criteria used in other cases. See the case of *Consorzio de Prosciutto Di Parma* v *Marks and Spencer* [1991] where damage was referred to as consequential damage.

Damage can occur in several ways, such as decrease in the claimants' goodwill through loss of sales caused by confusion, the claimant's product being confused with an inferior product.

At one point it was thought that passing off might fall by the wayside because of the relaxation in trademark registration introduced by the Trade Mark Act 1994.

However, the cases of *Re Elvis Presley Trade Mark* [1999] and *United Biscuits UK Ltd* v *Asda Stores Ltd* [1997] (also known as the Penguin/Puffin case) showed the continuing importance of passing off. In the Penguin case, Asda marketed a biscuit with similar packaging to Penguins. The claimant failed to succeed in an action for trademark infringement because the marks of the puffing and penguin were insufficiently similar. However, an injunction for passing off was successful.

Learning activity 18.1

Do not confuse this with passing of risk/title. Explain what passing off means and how it relates to intellectual property law, explaining the summary provided in the *Reckitt & Colman* [1990] Jif Lemon case.

Feedback on page 283

It is important to consider the elements of passing off mentioned above. We will look at these in order: namely, goodwill, misrepresentation and damage.

Goodwill

Goodwill is a property right. It has been concisely defined by Lord MacNaughten in the case of *The Commissioners of Inland Revenue* v *Muller & Co* [1901]. His definition was that goodwill is the attractive force that brings in custom. Goodwill is not the same as reputation. See the case of *BBC* v *Talksport* [2001]. In this case the BBC was the only UK broadcaster entitled to broadcast live Euro 2000 football matches. The BBC objected to Talksport's advertising claim that its Euro 2000 radio coverage was 'live'. Talksport used various devices and sounds to give the false impression that its radio coverage was live. The BBC failed in its claim for passing off as although the BBC had a reputation as live broadcasters of sports, the reputation for this activity did not amount to protectable goodwill.

How is goodwill created?

Goodwill is seen as a legal property right associated with business. It can be created within a short period of time. Although the idea of 'trade' is key to the concept of goodwill, it is not restricted to commercial organisations. Non-profit making organisations can benefit from passing off.

In addition to the key element of business/trade, the claimant must also demonstrate goodwill through advertising signs that are distinctive to him/her. These include marks, logos, names, images. You must remember that passing off does not protect the names, marks, logos and images but the goodwill in these.

Misrepresentation

This is the second element in a successful action for passing off. The defendant must make a false representation, usually by using the claimant's distinctive signs which misleads the public. The misrepresentation can be innocent of fraudulent but it must be material.

18

Damage

This is the third and final element in a successful action for passing off. Actual or likely damage must arise as a result of the misrepresentation. Damage includes direct loss of sales; decrease in sales; inferiority of the defendant's goods; injurious association; injury through constant confusion and loss of licensing opportunity.

Defences to an action of passing off

Defences include that the claimant has failed to establish the necessary elements as described above. The claimant has acquiesced or delayed in raising an action.

Remedies available

These have already been discussed in study session 17. We recommend that you revisit and refresh your memory. The remedies include damages, account of profits, delivering up or destruction, declaration and injunction.

Domain names

This is a growing area since the development and increasing use of the world wide web. Domain names may give rise to both passing off and trademark issues. Domain names are signs that can be registered as trademarks providing of course they satisfy the relevant criteria (see study session 17).

See the leading case of *British Telecommunications plc* v *One in a Million Ltd* [1999]. In this case One in a Million registered several well-known trademarks to sell them for profit to the brand owners and third parties. This activity is known as 'cybersquatting' and constitutes a false representation to people who visit the domain name register. Such people were led to believe that One in a Million were connected or associated with the names registered. This amounted to passing off.

Deception

According to the Jif Lemon case, deception is not a necessary element for a successful passing off action. However, in practice, deception of the public appears to be a key element to successful passing off actions.

Self-assessment question 18.1

What characteristics must be present to create a valid cause for pursuing an action for passing off?

Feedback on page 283

18.2 Breach of confidentiality

An action for breach of confidentiality is based on equity and contract. It can either be a supplementary action to another action, such as, an action for patent infringement, or an action by itself.

The law of confidentiality protects private, government and commercial confidences and trade secrets. Although most types of information can be protected by the law of confidentiality, the courts will not protect trivial tittle-tattle. See the case of *Coco* v *Clarke* [1969]. The courts will also not act as censors in cases of immorality. See the case of *A* v *B and C plc* [2002] which concerned the freedom of the *Sunday People* newspaper to publish the identity of the participants in a kiss-and-tell story.

Look back at the short attention grabber at the beginning of this study session. This is an abbreviated version of a statement on confidence made by Sir John Donaldson in the case of *Attorney-General* v *Guardian Newspapers* [1999] (also known as the Spycatcher case). Sir John said that there is an inherent public interest in individual citizens and the state having an enforceable right to the maintenance of confidence. Life would be intolerable in personal and commercial terms, if information could not be given or received in confidence and the right to have that information respected supported by the force of law.

A case concerning personal secrets was the case of *Naomi Campbell* v *Mirror Group Newspapers* [2002] where the court had to consider whether an individual's Narcotics Anonymous treatment was confidential. With introduction of the Human Rights Act 1998 English law now recognises the right to privacy in accordance with Article 8 European Convention on Human Rights. This must be balanced against Article 10 of the European Convention on Human Rights, which guarantees freedom of expression. See the case of *Douglas* v *Hello!* [2001] where the Court of Appeal noted that there are differing degrees of privacy and in this case a major part of Michael Douglas and Catherine Zeta-Jones' right to privacy in their wedding had been sold in a commercial transaction.

Trade secrets

We look again in this study session at trade secrets. You may wish to revisit study session 17 and refresh your memory on trade secrets. Trade secrets can relate to the design, the product components, the marketing strategy and manufacturing methods. You may recall that trade secrets are of commercial value to companies in relation to their competitors, and that it is important to protect them. Companies should guard their secrets and take steps to ensure that employees, former employees, other companies, suppliers and contractors with whom secrets may be shared do not breach the confidential information. A company can ensure that there is no disclosure of trade secrets either deliberately or inadvertently by employees or former employees by inserting an express term in the contract of employment. This express clause is called a restraint of trade clause, which is discussed later in this study session.

Elements required for a successful breach of confidence action

The elements are:

- quality of confidence;
- obligation of confidence;
- unauthorised use of confidential information.

Regarding the necessary quality of confidence, this means that the information must not be public property or public knowledge. In other

18

words once information is in the public domain it cannot be regarded as confidential.

An obligation of confidence arises:

- under contract where there is express contractual provision as to confidentiality;
- from an existing relationship such as commercial or employment. In the case of an employment relationship if there is no express term as to confidentiality then there is an implied term as to duty of good faith or fidelity imposed on the employee;
- from professional relationships where professional advisers owe an obligation of confidentiality to their clients;
- under statute such as Official Secrets Act 1989 and the Copyright Design Patent Act 1988.

The final element for a successful action for breach of confidence is that there must be actual or threatened use of the confidential information. There is no need for the breach to be deliberate or unconscious. See the case of *Sir Elton John & Others* v *Countess Joulebine* [2001]. In this case the claimants sought summary judgment against the defendant for breach of confidence in relation to material placed on her website relating to a court case between Sir Elton John and his accountants. The source of the material was a stolen draft advice of counsel. The website specialised in gossip and Joulebine invited the world at large to place gossip on the website via a noticeboard. The materials were therefore placed by an unknown individual on 11 March 2000. However, when it came to J's attention she placed a link on the home page so that it could easily be reached. An injunction was obtained on 27 March 2000. J's defence was that she did not know or realise that this was genuine or confidential material. She counter-claimed alleging that the claimant's actions had resulted in the closure of her website and that she had been put to expense, particularly in taking advice and representation from an American lawyer. The court held that it was quite clearly confidential information belonging to the claimants and that the test was whether Joulebine ought to have known that it was being imparted in breach of confidence. She ought to have known that there was a risk that it was being imparted in breach of confidence and therefore ought not to have continued to have it on her website and far less created a link. Joulebine did not succeed in her defence and was not entitled to costs. The court found in favour of the claimants who were entitled to summary judgment.

Remedies have already been discussed in study session 17. You should revisit that session and refresh your memory on the remedies available.

18

Learning activity 18.2

Describe the law of confidentiality and define confidence referring to case law. Explain how an employer can protect trade secrets from being disclosed by employees or former employees.

Feedback on page 284

As you have read from the above information, the law of breach of confidence is used extensively to protect sensitive commercial information and trade secrets. Employees also owe their employers a duty of confidence either by the terms of their written contract or by the implied term of loyalty and fidelity.

Professions are also subject to obligations of confidentiality. For example, lawyers and doctors must not disclose to any third party information given to them by their clients or patients.

The law of breach of confidence is a flexible doctrine, which is adapted and developed by the courts to include new situations, such as, a case in 1987 where a permanent injunction was granted against a newspaper to prevent it from publishing the names of two practising doctors who had AIDS. The courts held that the newspapers could only have obtained the information from a hospital employee who has obtained unauthorised access to the information.

Now complete the following self-assessment question.

Self-assessment question 18.2

What three elements are normally required for a breach of confidence action to succeed and what case illustrated this?

Feedback on page 285

18.3 Restraint of trade clauses

In study session 4 you studied frustration of contracts and learned what it means if a contract is void. You also learned that illegality has the effect of bringing a contract to an end. You may wish to revisit that study session and refresh your memory.

So you might be thinking what is the link with restraint of trade clauses? Well, restraint of trade clauses falls within the area of law relating to illegal and invalid contracts. The courts will refuse to enforce a contract that is illegal. See the case of *Birkett* v *Acorn Business Machines Ltd* [1999]. In this case the parties had entered into a contract which they both knew was to be used to defraud a third party finance company. When one sued the other for breach, the court refused to order the contract to be enforced as the contract was illegal.

Many different categories of contract are illegal or void. In this study session we are only concerned with restraint of trade clauses.

Restraint of trade clause

Such a clause means to restrict someone from trading. This is interfering with a person's freedom and generally would be against the public interest. However, there are certain circumstances where it may be reasonable to

18

restrict an individual's ability to trade freely. For this study session we are going to look at the following circumstances:

- the right of a new owner of a business to protect the goodwill from abuse by the previous owner (see study session 17);
- the right of an employer to protect trade business interests such as client lists, trade secrets, customer databases (see study session 17).

The other circumstances relate to competition law and are: contracts that are contrary to the Competition Act 1998 (see study session 16) and agreements where a trader restricts his sources for products or services to one manufacturer or wholesaler (see study session 16)

In study session 17 you studied the importance of goodwill to a company and that it is a valuable commercial asset. You also looked at how important it is for companies to guard trade secrets. You will now look at when restraint of trade clauses can be enforced by the courts and what criteria need to be fulfilled to be successful.

As the purpose of a restraint of trade clause is to restrict someone from trading and interfere with their freedom these clauses are prima facie void. However, if a person wants to rely on such a clause, it is up to them to show its validity.

Elements for validity of restraint of trade clauses

We are going to be looking at these elements with regard to the clauses in the above two circumstances. The validity of clauses in these two circumstances depends on:

- whether it is in the public interest;
- whether it is reasonable between the parties;
- the geographic area of the restriction;
- the time period of operation of the clause; and
- in contracts of employment, the position and role of the employee may be relevant.

Public interest: reasonableness: As we have seen from the above, restraint of trade clauses are prima facie void. It is up to the person wishing to rely on them to demonstrate validity. They can do this by showing that the clause is in the public interest and that it is reasonable between the parties.

Reasonableness: The clause must be no wider than is necessary to protect the interest involved in terms of the area and time of its operation. Remember that the matter of reasonableness is one for the courts to decide upon in all the circumstances, which include trade practices and customs. When applying the test of reasonableness the courts will take into account the factors below, namely, geographic area of restriction and the duration of the restriction as well as the position and role of an employee where the clause is within a contract of employment.

Geographic area: The validity of a restraint of trade clause will depend largely on the geographic area of restriction. The purpose of the clause is not to prevent competition. See the case of *Nordenfelt* v *Maxim Nordenfelt Guns and Ammunition Co* [1894] where the courts considered it reasonable for an

18

arms manufacturer to be bound by a restraint of trade clause whereby when he sold his business he promised not to deal in arms worldwide for a period of 25 years. See also the case of *Forster & Sons Ltd* v *Suggett* [1918] where a manager who had acquired trade secrets about the manufacture of glass was prevented from working in the glass making industry in Britain for 5 years. How large the geographic area of restriction is will depend on all the circumstances of each case.

Duration: How long a time period will be acceptable also depends on all the circumstances in each case. See the case of *M & S Draper* v *Reynolds* [1956] where the courts did not enforce a restraint of trade clause prohibiting a salesman from working for 5 years.

Employment contracts: Trade secrets, customer lists: restraint of trade clauses preventing former employees from poaching clients of the company for a given period can be enforced depending of course on all the circumstances. They can even be enforced by a subsequent purchaser of the company as in the case of *Morris, Angel & Son Ltd* v *Hollande* [1993]. In this case the purchaser of the company acquired all the rights and obligations of the company at the time of purchase. This included the right to enforce the restraint of trade clause. So when they immediately sacked the managing director they were able to enforce the restraint of trade clause in the managing director's contract. You have already looked at legal implications of outsourcing and the Transfer of Undertakings (Protection of Employment) Regulations 1981 (TUPE) in study session 15. Once again the validity or otherwise of a restraint of trade clause will depend on all the circumstances in each case. For example in, the above case the employee was a managing director so the position and role within the company would be relevant.

Vertical or solus agreements: These agreements are where a trader agrees to restrict his source of supply to one manufacturer or wholesaler. Such agreements may be valid but it will depend on whether the duration of the agreement is reasonable and the trader obtains benefit from the contract. See the case of *Esso Petroleum Co Ltd* v *Harper's Garage (Stourport) Ltd* [1967] where Harper entered into two agreements with Esso. In the first agreement they agreed to buy all the petrol for two garages from Esso. In the second agreement they agreed to keep the garages open at all reasonable hours and ensured that a purchaser of the garages would abide by the solus agreements. In return, Harper received a discount on all petrol and a loan from Esso of £7,000 by mortgaging the second garage to Esso. The agreements were to last for 4½ years for the first garage and 21 years for the second garage (this was the mortgage term). The House of Lords held that the first agreement was valid but the second one was void as being unreasonable.

18

Learning activity 18.3

Describe what elements are taken into account to establish whether a restraint of trade clause is valid.

Feedback on page 285

Before completing this study session it is worthwhile looking at the overlap between duty of fidelity and restraint of trade in contracts of employment and also the matter of 'garden leave' situations.

In contracts of employment the key principle is that if an employee competes with his employer during the existence of his contract then this will normally be regarded as a breach of duty of fidelity. A case that demonstrates the overlap of duty of fidelity and restraint of trade is the case of *Hivac Ltd* v *Park Royal Scientific Instruments* [1946]. In this case two employees of Hivac worked part-time for Park Royal, who was a competitor of Hivac. There was no evidence that the employees had passed on any secrets or confidential information or that they were in a position to do so. However, Hivac applied for an injunction restricting them from working for Park Royal. On granting the injunction, the courts took into account the right of the employee to spend his own leisure time by working if he wanted and the right of the employer to protect itself from its employees deliberately harming business.

Normally the duty of fidelity concerns competition while the contract of employment exists and restraint of trade concerns the period after the contract of employment has been terminated.

Garden leave

The key principle of garden leave is the situation where an employee who on termination of the contract of employment with the company may be restrained or restricted from working for another employer until the expiry of the period of notice, even if the company do not require the employee to attend work as long as they continue to pay the employee's salary. See the case of *Evening Standard Co Ltd* v *Henderson* [1987], where Mr Henderson's contract of employment provided for a one-year notice period to be given by either party. Henderson terminated his contract giving only 2 month's notice with the intention of working for a rival newspaper. The *Evening Standard* applied for an injunction to stop Henderson from working for the rival until the one-year notice period expired. The courts granted the injunction.

Self-assessment question 18.3

Read the short scenarios below and explain whether the restraint of trade clause would be considered valid and enforceable and why.

Harold is a technician in an engineering company. His contract of employment contains a clause restricting him from working for any competitor for a period of six years after the termination of his contract.

Archie is a skilled and specialist chemist in a UK company involved in the development of new cancer cure drugs. His contract of employment contains a clause restricting him from working for any competitor in the UK for 2 years.

18

(continued on next page)

Self-assessment question 18.3 *(continued)*

Fred is the production manager of a company involved in the competitive industry of glass making. As manager he is privy to many trade secrets. His contract of employment contains a clause restricting him from working for a competitor for a 5-year period after termination of his contract.

Feedback on page 285

Revision question

Now try the revision question for this session on page 315.

Summary

Having completed study sessions 17 and 18 you will realise that the subject matter of intellectual property is very wide and overlaps into many other areas of law. Where appropriate we have recommended that you revisit relevant study sessions to refresh your memory.

Intellectual property is a valuable commercial asset to a company. It is crucial to obtaining and maintaining competitive advantage in any commercial or industrial activity.

Suggested further reading

Griffiths and Griffiths (2002). You should read the chapters on intellectual property, part V, chapter 19.2.

Feedback on learning activities and self-assessment questions

Feedback on learning activity 18.1

Your activity should take the form of a short essay describing passing off. It should include reference to the close link between passing off and trademarks. You can provide the short definition as stated by Lord Oliver in the Jif Lemon case, namely, '...the law of passing off is where no man might pass off his goods as those of another'. Go on to explain what protection passing off offers such as the protection of a trader against unfair competition of rivals and protection of consumers who would be confused about the origin of the goods or services they are offered. Also explain the criteria required for an action of passing off to be successful which is laid down in the Jif Lemon case; that the claimant must be able to demonstrate goodwill; there must be misrepresentation about the goods or services offered; and there must be actual or likely damage which is referred to as consequential damage in the Consorzio case.

Feedback on self-assessment question 18.1

Your answer should include the three key elements decided in the Jif Lemon case. These are that the claimant must be able to demonstrate goodwill;

18

there must be misrepresentation as to the goods or services offered and there must be actual or likely damage. You should then provide a short paragraph of explanation on each of the key elements: goodwill, misrepresentation and damage. The explanations should include information from the information in this part of the study session. For example, on goodwill mention that it is a property right defined concisely in the case of *The Commissioners of Inland Revenue* v *Muller & Co* [1901]. Provide the definition that states that goodwill is the attractive force that brings in custom. Mention that goodwill is not the same as reputation and refer to the case of *BBC* v *Talksport* [2001] where the BBC failed in its claim for passing off as although the BBC had a reputation as live broadcasters of sports, the reputation for this activity did not amount to protectable goodwill. As regards misrepresentation, you can explain that it can be innocent or fraudulent. Finally, the third and final element in a successful action for passing off is that there has to be actual or likely damage resulting from the misrepresentation. Damage includes direct loss of sales; decrease in sales; inferiority of the defendant's goods; injurious association; injury through constant confusion and loss of licensing opportunity.

Feedback on learning activity 18.2

The law of confidentiality protects private, government and commercial confidences and trade secrets. Although most types of information can be protected by the law of confidentiality, the courts will not protect trivial tittle-tattle. See the case of *Coco* v *Clarke* [1969]. The courts will also not act as censors in cases of immorality. See the case of *A* v *B and C plc* [2002] which concerned the freedom of the *Sunday People* newspaper to publish the identity of the participants in a kiss-and-tell story.

A brief definition of confidence was provided by Sir John Donaldson in the case of *Attorney-General* v *Guardian Newspapers* [1999] (also known as the Spycatcher case). Sir John said that there is an inherent public interest in individual citizens and the state having an enforceable right to the maintenance of confidence. Life would be intolerable in personal and commercial terms, if information could not be given or received in confidence and the right to have that information respected supported by the force of law.

A case about personal secrets was that of *Naomi Campbell* v *Mirror Group Newspapers* [2002] where the court had to consider whether an individual's Narcotics Anonymous treatment was confidential. With introduction of the Human Rights Act 1998 English law now recognises the right to privacy in accordance with Article 8 European Convention on Human Rights. This must be balanced against Article 10 of the European Convention on Human Rights which guarantees freedom of expression. See the case of *Douglas* v *Hello!* [2001] where the Court of Appeal noted that there are differing degrees of privacy and in this case a major part of Michael Douglas and Catherine Zeta-Jones' right to privacy in their wedding had been sold in a commercial transaction.

Regarding protection of trade secrets from disclosure by employees and former employees, it is best to have an express term within the contract of employment. Where there is no express term, the law implies a duty of good faith and fidelity from an employee.

Feedback on self-assessment question 18.2

There are three elements that should be included in your short essay. The case you should refer to is the case of *Coco* v *Clarke* [1969]. Write a short paragraph on each: quality of confidence, obligation of confidence and unauthorised use. For the necessary quality of confidence you must mention that that the information must not be public property or public knowledge. In other words, once information is in the public domain it cannot be regarded as confidential. Describe the circumstances when an obligation of confidence arises including under contract, in an existing commercial or employment relationship; in a professional relationship or under statute such as the Official Secrets Act 1989 and the Copyright Design Patent Act 1988. There must also be actual or threatened use of the confidential information. There is no need for the breach to be deliberate or unconscious. See the case of *Sir Elton John & Others* v *Countess Joulebine* [2001].

Feedback on learning activity 18.3

Your answer should be in the form of a short essay starting with bullets points as a reminder of the different factors. For example, the validity of a restraint of trade clause depends on a number of factors. These include:

- whether it is in the public interest;
- whether it is reasonable between the parties;
- the geographic area of the restriction;
- the time period of operation of the clause; and
- in contracts of employment, the position and role of the employee may be relevant.

Go on to explain that a restraint of trade clause is prima facie void. However, it can be shown to be valid but this must be demonstrated by the person wanting to rely on it. This can be done by showing that the clause is in the public interest and that it is reasonable between the parties. So the clause must be no wider than is necessary to protect the interest involved in terms of the area and time of its operation. The courts will take into account the geographic area of restriction. It will depend on all the circumstances. You should cite cases such as Nordenfelt. The courts will also take account of the period of restriction in all the circumstances. Here you can cite the case of Forster, which has reference to both geographic area and time period. For the circumstances surrounding a restraint of trade clause in an employment contract, in addition to the geography and time period you should mention that the role and position of an employee may be relevant as to whether the clause is enforceable or not.

Feedback on self-assessment question 18.3

In scenario one you should explain that in his position as a technician Harold has probably no access to trade secrets, confidential information

18

285

or customer lists and therefore the restriction in a period of 6 years is not reasonable in the circumstances. Also the geographic area is not made clear and the use of the word 'any' competitor would be too wide in the circumstances. A possible case reference would be the case of *Herbert Morris Ltd* v *Saxelby* [1916] where Saxelby was an engineer whose contract contained a restraint of trade clause restricting him from working for any competitor for 7 years after the termination of his contract. The courts did not enforce the clause as they deemed it to be a restriction on Saxelby's skill and ability rather than safeguarding the company's interest.

Scenario two differs from scenario one in the position and role of Archie. As a specialist in the field the courts will take into account that he is working with and has privy to trade secrets. Being a specialist company it is possible also that they may be the only company in the UK. However, the restriction only refers to the geographic area of UK. It does not stop Archie from working abroad. Looking at all the elements required for validity, public interest, trade secrets, customer lists, role of employee, geographic area and duration, it is more than likely that the courts will enforce the clause as being reasonable in all the circumstances. A case where geographic area was considered reasonable is the case of *Fitch* v *Dewes* [1921]. In this case the employee was a solicitor's clerk working in an office in a small town. The restraint of trade clause stopped him from working in a solicitor's office within a seven mile radius of the town centre for the rest of his life. The House of Lords held that the clause was valid because of the confidential nature of the business and the relatively restricted geographical area involved.

The last scenario is the case of *Forster & Sons Ltd* v *Suggett* [1918] where Forster was a production manager in the competitive industry of glass making. He was also privy to many trade secrets. The courts held that because of the secret nature of the manufacturing processes involved and Forster's level of position and role within the company, the clause was enforceable.

18

International trade

Introduction

This study session relates to international trade, which occurs when goods cross national boundaries. You can imagine the kind of problems that arise when the seller resides in one nation state and the buyer in another. In this study session you will be studying how the challenges of international trading can be removed by the use of standard terms, in particular, the Incoterms published by the International Chamber of Commerce. Key points within the various forms relates to when the property to the goods and the risk of loss passes from seller to buyer.

The Hague, Hague-Visby and Hamburg Rules were enacted to clarify and simplify international sea carriage yet their differing approaches and legislative styles have become the main obstacle to uniformity...
adapted from Karan Hakan (2005)

Session learning objectives

After completing this session you should be able to:

19.1 Explain Incoterms and contract of carriage.
19.2 Describe Bill of Lading.
19.3 Jurisdiction issues.
19.4 Impact of the Uniform Law on International Sales Act 1967 (Hague Convention).

Unit content coverage

This study session covers the following topics from the official CIPS unit content document:

Learning outcome

Predict the legal issues that need to be addressed when entering into an international contract for the purchase of goods.

Learning objective

4.3 Predict the legal issues that need to be addressed when entering into an international contract for the purchase of goods.
  • Incoterms including CIF, FOB, EXW, DDP and FAS
  • Bill of Lading
  • Contracts of carriage
  • Jurisdiction
  • The Uniform Law on International Sales Act 1967 (Hague Convention)

Prior knowledge

Contract law sessions at Level 4, or equivalent material, and those earlier in the present course book.

Timing

You should set aside about 4 hours to read and complete this session, including learning activities, self-assessment questions, the suggested further reading (if any) and the revision question.

19.1 Incoterms and contract of carriage

Standard forms

The use of standard forms can remove the challenges which arise in international trading. As stated in the introduction, international trade occurs when the seller resides in one nation state and the buyer in another. So how are such transactions financed and how is the property in the goods and the risk passed from seller to buyer?

The question of financial risk and financing of contracts of carriage are discussed in study session 20. Later on in this study session you look at the Hague-Visby Rules and legislation governing contracts of carriage of goods by sea.

In most cases the goods in an international sale are carried by sea. Where goods leave from the UK, irrespective of their port of destination, the law that governs this is the Carriage of Goods by Sea Act 1971. This Act has been adopted by the Hague-Visby Rules, which are discussed in more detail in section 19.3 below.

In this part we look at Incoterms and some of the more common forms of international contracts, including: CIF (cost, insurance and freight); FOB (free on board); EXW (ex works); DDP (delivered duty paid); and FAS (free alongside ship).

What are Incoterms?

They are a set of rules for interpreting trade terms in international trade. They were first published in the International Chamber of Commerce (ICC) in 1936. They have been updated many times over the years.

The basic function of Incoterms is to clarify how the functions, costs and risks are divided between the buyer and the seller in connection with delivery of the goods as required under a contract of sale. The key issues relate to delivery, risks and costs. Each Incoterm clearly stipulates the responsibilities of the seller and the buyer. Incoterms are divided into four distinct groups, which are:

- Group E: where the goods are made available to the buyer at the seller's premises;

19

- Group F: where the seller must deliver the goods to a carrier appointed by the buyer;
- Group C: where the seller must contract for carriage of the goods without taking on the risk of loss or damage to the goods or additional costs due to events happening after shipment;
- Group D: where the seller has to bear all costs and risks to bring the goods to the place of destination.

In this study session we look at an Incoterm in each of these groups.

Obligations of seller and buyer

Incoterms clearly set out the obligations of the seller and the buyer. Each Incoterm contains clauses. There are clauses for the seller and ones which mirror these for the buyer. Where the parties intend protection of an Incoterm they must expressly refer to the current edition of Incoterms in the contract of sale.

CIF contracts

This Incoterm falls within Group C (main carriage paid). The letters stand for cost, insurance and freight. It is the most common form of international contract. This type of contract places responsibility on the seller to arrange for the shipment of the goods and to insure them against loss or damage during the voyage. This means that the price charged to the buyer includes these services. This is beneficial to the buyer as the seller bears the risk of increased costs of transport or insurance.

However, a CIF contract places duties on both seller and buyer. Where the contract contains a jurisdiction clause stating that the contract is governed by English law then it will comply with the statutory duties under the Sale of Goods Act 1979. You may wish to revisit and refresh your memory on the Sale of Goods Act 1979 in study sessions 7 – 9.

Seller's duties under CIF

The seller's duties under a CIF contract relate to:

- conformity: the goods must conform to the contract in description, quantity and be of satisfactory quality and fit for purpose. A breach of these is a breach of condition and entitles the party not at fault to repudiate the goods and terminate the contract;
- time is of the essence: he must deliver the goods to the correct port of loading within the specified time as time is of the essence. If delivery does not take place within the agreed time then the innocent party is entitled to terminate the contract;
- delivery: the seller must deliver the goods to correct port of destination: the seller must arrange this and ensure the vessel has appropriate facilities for the goods, for example, refrigeration should the goods be food or perishables
- insurance: the seller must arrange for insurance against loss or damage during the voyage;

19

- liability for payment of charges: the seller must pay for the freight and insurance charges;
- documentation: the seller must ensure that the appropriate documents are available and forwarded to the buyer or the bank (if appropriate – see study session 20 on letters of credit). Such documents enable the buyer to take delivery of the goods at the destination port;
- other documents: the seller must arrange any other documents where necessary, for example, export licences.

Buyer's duties under CIF contracts

The buyer's duties include those under the Sale of Goods Act 1979 as well as those included in international contracts. The duties relate to:

- taking delivery: the buyer must take delivery of the goods at the port of destination provided they comply with the contract description and statutory implied terms (see study session 7);
- accepting the Bill of Lading and paying for the goods: the buyer must accept the Bill of Lading provided it is in the proper form and pay for the goods delivered according to the Bill of Lading.

In addition to the above duties, the contract may specify other duties that the buyer must undertake. Where the contract so specifies, the buyer must fulfil them. These may relate to:

- paying additional freight or demurrage (these are costs incurred through a delay in loading at the port of loading/departure);
- arranging for transportation of goods after arrival at port of destination;
- giving sufficient notice to the seller of the date and place of destination of goods to enable the seller to make the necessary arrangements for shipping;
- arranging and paying for import licences or customs duties.

An alternative form of international contract is an FOB, which is now going to be discussed.

FOB contracts

This falls within Group F (main carriage unpaid). It is an alternative form of international contract which places the responsibility on the buyer to arrange for the shipment of the goods and to pay for insurance cover for the voyage. In an FOB contract the responsibilities of the seller stop when the goods are loaded on board the ship.

Some of the duties on the seller and buyer are similar to those in a CIF contract. The similar duties relate to delivery. The seller must deliver goods which comply with the contract and the statutory implied terms. The buyer must take delivery of the goods and the documents of carriage and pay for the goods.

Duties on the seller and buyer which differ from CIF contracts are detailed below.

Seller's duties under a FOB contract

In addition to delivering goods which comply with the contract and the statutory implied terms the seller must:

- arrange for the transportation of the goods to the port of departure;
- deliver goods to the appropriate vessel within the time agreed in the contract;
- obtain a mate's receipt once the goods are loaded and hand the receipt to the forwarding agent for handing over to the buyer (a mate's receipt is an acknowledgement that the shipowner has received the goods in the condition stated therein).

Buyer's duties under a FOB contract

In addition to taking delivery of the goods and the documents of carriage at the port of destination and paying for the goods the buyer must:

- book appropriate shipping space on a suitable ship/vessel;
- inform the seller of the port of loading, the name of the ship and the date of departure, all within sufficient time to enable the seller to make the necessary arrangements. If the buyer fails to give sufficient time for this to be done, the seller can terminate the contract;
- insure the goods against loss or damage during the voyage;
- pay freight charges.

One of the advantages to a buyer of an FOB contract is that the buyer can choose the ship or vessel. A buyer may regularly import goods and have a block insurance policy to cover this or he may have shipping contacts which enable less expensive shipping. In such situations an FOB contract is appropriate for him.

Passing of property and risk in the goods

You will recall that under s20 Sale of Goods Act 1979, risk in goods usually passes when the property in the goods passes unless there is an agreement to the contrary. You may wish to revisit study sessions 8 and 9 and refresh your memory on this topic.

However, in international trade contracts irrespective of when property in the goods passes, it is usual for there to be a provision in the contract that the risk in the goods passes to the buyer when the goods are loaded on to the ship, that is, cross over the ship's rail during loading. This means that the seller bears the responsibility for any damage occurring before the goods cross over the ship's rail.

Learning activity 19.1

Compare and contrast CIF and FOB contracts in relation to when property to the goods and the risk of loss passes from seller to buyer.

Feedback on page 298

19

The other contracts of carriage we are going to consider here are:

- EXW: ex works;
- DDP: delivery duty paid;
- FAS: free alongside.

EXW

This means ex-works and falls within Group E (departure). This term represents the minimum obligation for the seller. In this contract the seller must place the goods at the disposal of the buyer at the seller's premises or another named place which is not cleared for export and not loaded on to any vehicle. The seller fulfils his obligation to deliver when he has made the goods available to the buyer at his (the seller's) premises. The buyer bears all costs and risks involved in taking the goods from the seller's premises to the desired destination.

DDP

This means delivery duty paid and falls within Group D (arrival). In this case the seller must deliver the goods to the buyer, cleared for import and not unloaded at the named destination place. The seller fulfils his obligation to deliver when the goods have been made available to the buyer at the named place in the import country. The seller has to bear the risk and costs, including duties, taxes and charges of delivering the goods to the place of importation, and clear them for import.

FAS

This means free alongside ship and falls within Group F (main carriage unpaid). In this case the seller must place the goods, cleared for export, alongside the vessel at the named port of departure. The seller fulfils his obligation to deliver when the goods have been placed alongside the ship on the quay. This means the buyer has to bear all costs and risks of loss or damage to the goods from that moment onwards. The buyer will need to clear the goods for export.

Self-assessment question 19.1

What is the distinction between a seller's duties under an FOB contract and under a CIF contract?

Feedback on page 299

19.2 Bill of Lading

International sale contracts are considered as being contracts of sale of documents as the most important part of international contracts and contract of carriage are the documents. This is because the buyer and seller are unlikely ever to meet. So unlike the domestic contracts the documents are important evidence of the international sale contract. One of the most common forms of shipping document is the Bill of Lading, which is discussed in detail below. The Bill of Lading and another form of shipping document, the sea waybill, is discussed in study session 20.

Bill of Lading

This is one of the most common forms of shipping document. It serves three main functions which are:

- as a document of title;
- as evidence of a contract of carriage;
- as a receipt.

Document of title: When discussing the irrevocable documentary credit arrangement you will recall that the Bill of Lading enables the buyer to use this document to sell the goods even if they are still in transit. Once the buyer has possession of the Bill of Lading it gives title in the goods to the buyer. However, remember that the buyer obtains only such title as was possessed by the transferor. The title also depends on the wording of the Bill of Lading.

Evidence of a contract: You will also recall from the above that the Bill of Lading enables the buyer to claim delivery of the goods at the port. The Bill of Lading is evidence of a contract of carriage. The Bill of Lading should contain all the terms of the contract of carriage under which the goods are being transported. This should include the standard terms of carriage and any variation clauses agreed by the carrier/seller and the shipper. Where the Bill of Lading does not include all the terms of the contract and a dispute arises then the parties are governed by the main contract and the Bill of Lading will only act as evidence that a contract exists. Remember that the buyer will not be party to the contract between the shipper and the carrier. However, under s2 Carriage of Goods by Sea Act 1992 the buyer has some enforcement rights. The only contractual document that the buyer will have is the Bill of Lading.

Receipt: The Bill of Lading as a receipt is vital to the contract of carriage as it provides evidence of the identity, quantity and condition of the goods. Details of each of these must be included in a Bill of Lading where the Bill of Lading is governed by the Hague-Visby Rules.

Where the Bill of Lading is governed by the Hague-Visby Rules

The goods must be identified as those to which the Bill of Lading relates and any marks must be sufficiently permanent that they cannot disappear en route.

As the ship's master is obliged to account for the full quantity of goods to the buyer, the Bill of Lading must stipulate the quantity for which the carrier accepts responsibility. In the event of a lesser quantity being delivered the carrier will be responsible.

It is important that the Bill of Lading specifies the condition of the goods at time of loading. In the event that the buyer claims the goods are damaged or

19

not of satisfactory quality then the Bill of Lading is proof of the condition at the time of loading. Where the goods are in good condition the carrier signs the bill as 'clean'. Where there is any damage the carrier should specify the damage and the bill is then known as 'claused'. The reason for this is to enable liability for any damage to be properly allocated. For example where the bill is 'clean' and damage occurs the carrier will be liable.

Learning activity 19.2

Describe what details the Bill of Lading must provide.

Feedback on page 300

As you can see from the above discussion on the Bill of Lading the contract of carriage is between the carrier (seller) and the shipper. As the buyer is not a party to the contract of carriage, the Bill of Lading is the only document that the buyer will definitely have about the terms of the contract of carriage.

Self-assessment question 19.2

Describe the main functions of the Bill of Lading.

Feedback on page 300

19.3 Jurisdiction issues

As you will recall from the information in section 19.1 above, international trade occurs when the seller resides in one nation state and the buyer in another. This raises the question of what law is applicable to the contract. Is it the law of the country of the seller or the buyer? In this part of the study session you are going to be looking at the issues surrounding the applicable law and the choice of law clause.

Although it is not essential to have a full understanding of the laws and rules relating to the many international conventions, it is necessary to have an appreciation of the potential problems that can arise in relation to what law, which venue and how to enforce judgements.

Learning activity 19.3

Look at some of the contracts entered into by your organisation. Can you identify the clause that governs jurisdiction?

Feedback on page 300

19

One of the potential problems that can arise in international contracts relates to jurisdiction. This is because international contracts involve the transportation of goods across at least one national boundary and the seller resides in one nation state while the buyer is in another. We have seen how the buyer and seller can agree where responsibility lies and the duties and obligations under the contract by the use of Incoterms. We now look at how the parties can minimise and remove the problem of jurisdiction by choosing the applicable law. The problem is largely resolved by international conventions which are ratified into English law, and that of most other major trading nations, by domestic legislation. In the UK this is done by the Contracts (Applicable Law) Act 1990, which is discussed in more detail below.

Contracts (Applicable Law) Act 1990

In general this Act adopts a similar position to that of common law. For example it preserves the freedom of the parties at common law to use an express choice of law clause within the contract. Such a clause will be valid if the party's intention is bona fide and legal and there is no reason for avoiding the clause on grounds of public policy.

This Act deals with the choice of law problems that may arise in contract. It enabled the UK to ratify the Rome Convention on the law applicable to contractual obligations. The Rome Convention was created to harmonise choice of law rules in contract.

The Rome Convention gave force to the Brussels Protocol, which gives the European Court of Justice jurisdiction to give rulings on interpretation of the Convention but only at the request of a contracting state.

The 1990 Act applies to contracts between member states and also to situations where there is a choice between the laws of different countries whether or not the applicable law is a state within the European Community (EC). Some contracts are excluded, such as arbitration agreements, bills of exchange and negotiable instruments, wills, succession and matrimonial property rights and contracts relating to risks within the territories of the member states.

However, under Article 3 (Schedule 1) of the 1990 Act, the parties can choose the applicable law except where the mandatory rules of a country, where all the elements of the contract (except from the choice of law clause) point exclusively to that country. Mandatory rules are those which the parties are not permitted to contract out of. For example, the parties in an exclusively English contract cannot contract out of the Unfair Contract Terms Act 1977.

In the absence of an express choice of law clause the applicable law is determined by the provisions of Article 4 of the 1990 Act. The general test is that the contract shall be governed by the law of the country with which it is most closely connected. This mirrors the common law position.

The Hague-Visby Rules also established a framework of rules for contracts of carriage and the rights and liabilities of the parties to the contract, such as, carriers and cargo owners. These are discussed in the next section.

19

Self-assessment question 19.3

Explain why a jurisdiction clause is included in a contract for the international sale of goods.

Feedback on page 301

19.4 The Uniform Law on International Sales Act 1967 (Hague Convention)

You have now learned a lot about international sales contracts and the various terms which are used to minimise and remove problems. We are going to look at how the many conventions and legislation have attempted to bring uniformity to international sales law.

Learning activity 19.4

What must be stipulated in a Bill of Lading that is governed by the Hague-Visby Rules?

Feedback on page 301

A contract of sale used for domestic sales is not adequate for international contracts of sale. In an endeavour to bring conformity to international sale contracts rules were developed. Over the years there have been many Conventions, all intended to bring uniformity to international sales law and many labelled so.

The Hague Rules, known as the International Convention for the Unification of Certain Rules of Law relating to Bills of Lading, was a compromise arrangement adopted by seafaring nations in 1924 to allocate the risk of loss to ocean-borne cargo among the carrier, the shipper or consignee and by implication their respective insurers.

Then there was the 1964 Hague Convention Uniform Law for International Sale and Uniform Law of Formation. But this was not successful in bringing uniformity to international sales law. Legislation adopting the Hague Convention is the 1967 Act, which is discussed in more detail below.

Uniform Law on International Sales Act 1967

This Act applies to contracts of sale of goods entered into by parties whose places of business are in the territories of different contracting states. The contracts to which the Act applies are:

- where the contract involves the sale of goods which are at the time of conclusion of the contract in the course of carriage, or will be carried from the territory of one state to the territory of another state;

- where the offer and acceptance of the contract have been effected in the territories of different states;
- where delivery of the goods is to be made to a different territory from that where the contract was concluded.

After the 1967 Act there continued to be various Conventions. In 1968 there followed the Hague-Visby Rules 1968 (these were the Hague Rules as amended by the Brussels Protocol). This was a framework for contracts of carriage, which is discussed in more detail below.

Hague-Visby Rules

These established a framework of rules for contracts of carriage and the rights and liabilities of the parties to the contract, such as, carriers and cargo owners. There are basic criteria which require to be fulfilled before these rules will apply to any party to the contract of carriage. The criteria are:

- there must be certain documents such as a Bill of Lading or similar contract of carriage;
- the contract must be for carriage of goods between ports (formerly ports in two different nation states now to any port of destination);
- the contract must contain an express term that these rules or legislation adopting them will govern the contract.

The rules apply where goods leave from a UK port to another nation state or remain in coastal waters. The rules can also be adopted by documents other than bills of lading, such as sea waybills, which are discussed in study session 20.

However, it was apparent that there was a need for something more comprehensive. One of the most significant was the 1980 Convention on Contracts for International Sale of Goods (CISG) as it was uniform and had global recognition. It took years of diplomatic drafting among representatives of many nations.

However, one author, Karan Hakan, believes that the three international conventions known as Hague Rules, Hague-Visby and Hamburg Rules have become the main reason for lack of uniformity in the field of carriage of goods by sea, because of their different texts and legislative styles.

Self-assessment question 19.4

Read the following statements and provide the correct answer by circling one of the choices 1, 2 or 3.

DDP Incoterm means:

1   the seller must deliver the goods to the buyer, cleared for import, and not unloaded at the named place of destination;
2   the seller must deliver the goods at the disposal of the buyer not cleared for import on the quay at the named port of destination;
3   the seller delivers the goods, cleared for export, over the ship's rail.

19

(continued on next page)

Self-assessment question 19.4 *(continued)*

CIF Incoterm means:

1   carriage, insurance and freight;
2   cost, insurance and freight;
3   cost, import and freight.

FOB Incoterm means:

1   the seller must place the goods, cleared for export, alongside the vessel at the named port of shipment;
2   the seller must place the goods at the disposal of the buyer at the seller's premises or other named place not cleared for export and not loaded on any collecting vehicle;
3   the seller must deliver the goods, cleared for export, when they pass the ship's rail at the named port of shipment.

Contracts (Applicable Law) Act 1990:

1   enabled the UK to ratify the Rome Convention on the law applicable to contractual obligations;
2   does not apply to contracts between member states;
3   means that mandatory rules of a country can be contracted out of.

Feedback on page 301

Revision question

Now try the revision question for this session on page 315.

Summary

You have learned from this study session that international trade is a vast subject. You should now appreciate that it is more complex than domestic trade because the number of parties involved is greater and the distances, differences in business practice, culture, language and currency complicate the process. However, you have learned that Incoterms are a set of rules for interpreting the most commonly used trade terms in international trade. You know the importance of shipping documents, in particular the Bill of Lading, and that although there may be conflict of laws the parties can choose the law that will apply. You have looked at the various conventions and legislation and how they have attempted to bring uniformity to international sales law.

Suggested further reading

Griffiths and Griffiths (2002), part V, chapter 20.

Feedback on learning activities and self-assessment questions

Feedback on learning activity 19.1

Under a CIF contract where the letters stand for cost, insurance and freight responsibility is placed on the seller to arrange for the shipment of the goods and to insure them against loss or damage during the voyage. This means that the price charged to the buyer includes these services. This is beneficial to the buyer as the seller bears the risk of increased costs of transport or insurance.

A CIF contract also places duties on both seller and buyer. Where the contract contains a jurisdiction clause stating that the contract is governed by English law then the parties are bound to comply with the statutory duties under the Sale of Goods Act 1979.

An FOB contract is an alternative form of international contract, which places the responsibility on the buyer to arrange for the shipment of the goods and to pay for insurance cover for the voyage. In an FOB contract the responsibilities of the seller stop when the goods are loaded on board the ship.

Some of the duties on the seller and buyer are similar to those in a CIF contract. The similar duties relate to delivery. The seller must deliver goods which comply with the contract and the statutory implied terms. The buyer must take delivery of the goods and the documents of carriage and pay for the goods.

Feedback on self-assessment question 19.1

Under an FOB contract, the seller must deliver goods which comply with the contract in terms of description, quantity, satisfactory quality and fitness for purposes and all statutory implied terms. The seller must also arrange for the transportation of the goods to the port of departure, delivering the goods to the appropriate ship within the agreed time as stated in the contract. The seller must get a receipt from the ship's mate and hand this to a forwarding agent for onward transmission to the buyer.

Under an FOB contract the responsibility is on the buyer to arrange for the shipment of the goods and to pay for insurance cover for the voyage. In an FOB contract the responsibilities of the seller stop when the goods are loaded on board the ship.

Under a CIF contract as in an FOB contract the seller must ensure that the goods conform to the contract in relation to their description, the quantity and that they must be of satisfactory quality and fit for purpose. A breach of these is deemed to be a breach of condition and entitles the party not at fault to repudiate the goods and terminate the contract.

However, under a CIF contract the seller must deliver the goods to the correct port of loading within the specified time as time is of the essence. If delivery does not take place within the agreed time then the innocent party is entitled to terminate the contract. The seller must arrange delivery of the goods to correct port of destination and ensure the vessel has appropriate facilities for the goods, for example, refrigeration should the goods be food or perishables. The seller must also arrange for insurance against loss or damage during the voyage. He is liable for payment of freight and insurance charges. Finally he must ensure that the appropriate shipping documents are available and forwarded to the buyer or the bank and these documents

19

enable the buyer to take delivery of the goods at the destination port. Where appropriate the seller must arrange for export licences.

Feedback on learning activity 19.2

As the Bill of Lading is evidence of a contract of carriage it should contain all the terms of the contract of carriage under which the goods are being transported. These details are the standard terms of carriage and any variation clauses agreed by the carrier/seller and the shipper. Where the Bill of Lading does not include all the terms of the contract and a dispute arises then the parties are governed by the main contract and the Bill of Lading will only act as evidence that a contract exists. Remember that the buyer will not be party to the contract between the shipper and the carrier. However, under s2 Carriage of Goods by Sea Act 1992 the buyer has some enforcement rights. The only contractual document that the buyer will have is the Bill of Lading.

Where a Bill of Lading is governed by the Hague-Visby Rules then the bill must include the identity of the goods, identified by as permanent marks as possible so that they cannot disappear en route. The bill must also stipulate the quantity for which the carrier accepts responsibility. In the event of a lesser quantity being delivered the carrier will be responsible. The bill must specify the condition of the goods at time of loading as this establishes liability for any damage while in transit.

Feedback on self-assessment question 19.2

The Bill of Lading has three main functions. The first is as a document of title, the second as evidence of the contract of carriage, and finally as a receipt of the goods.

As a document of title it enables the buyer to sell the goods even if they are still in transit. Remember that the buyer's title will only be the same as that possessed by the transferor and will depend on the wording of the Bill of Lading. As evidence of the contract, the Bill of Lading will enable the buyer to claim delivery of the goods at the port. The bill should also contain all the terms of the contract of carriage under which the goods are being transported and if it does not then the agreement between the parties is governed by the main contract. Of course the buyer will not be party to the contract of carriage between the shipper and the carrier. However, under s2 Carriage of Goods by Sea Act 1992 the buyer has some enforcement rights. The only contractual document that the buyer will have is the Bill of Lading. Finally, the Bill of Lading acts as a receipt, which is vital to the contract of carriage as it provides evidence of the identity, quantity and condition of the goods.

Feedback on learning activity 19.3

You should look at some of the contracts within your organisation and try to find a clause that has wording along the lines of the following: 'this contract is governed by English law'. Such clauses usually appear towards the end of a contract and can be included in any contracts between two or

19

more parties. You may also want to search the websites for sample contracts and look at the clauses on jurisdiction.

Feedback on self-assessment question 19.3

International contracts of sale occur when goods cross national boundaries. It is more than likely that the seller and buyer never meet. Because of this, problems arise about where responsibility lies in the event of a dispute and what is the appropriate court where problems with the contract can be resolved. As the seller and buyer are in different jurisdictions it would be costly and lengthy for a seller to take action in a different jurisdiction and this applies to the buyer. Because of this it is best to consider expressly stating within a contract which jurisdiction will govern the contract. As regards the UK it would be best to state that the contract will be governed by English law. This means that from the outset both seller and buyer know which jurisdiction applies.

Feedback on learning activity 19.4

The goods must be identified as those to which the Bill of Lading relates and any marks must be sufficiently permanent so that they cannot disappear en route.

As the ship's master is obliged to account for the full quantity of goods to the buyer, the Bill of Lading must stipulate the quantity for which the carrier accepts responsibility. In the event of a lesser quantity being delivered the carrier will be responsible.

It is important that the Bill of Lading specifies the condition of the goods at time of loading. In the event that the buyer claims the goods are damaged or not of satisfactory quality then the Bill of Lading is proof of the condition at the time of loading. Where the goods are in good condition the carrier signs the bill as 'clean'. Where there is any damage the carrier should specify the damage and the bill is then known as 'claused'. The reason for this is to enable liability for any damage to be properly allocated. For example where the bill is 'clean' and damage occurs, the carrier will be liable.

Feedback on self-assessment question 19.4

DDP: answer 1 is correct.

CIF: answer 2 is correct.

FOB: answer 3 is correct.

Contracts (Applicable Law) Act 1990: answer 1 is correct.

19

International trade documents

'The problems of international trading can be removed by the use of standard terms and appropriate documentation.'

Introduction

In study session 19 you learned that international trade is a vast subject area. You also know that for examination purposes it is not essential to have a full understanding of this vast area of the law but it is necessary to have an appreciation of the potential problems that arise. In study session 19 you also studied one of the most common forms of shipping document, the Bill of Lading. In this study session you are going to be looking at some more international trade documents which help alleviate financial risk and remove difficulties.

Session learning objectives

After completing this session you should be able to:

20.1 Explain letters of credit.
20.2 Describe shipping documents required for sale of good in international context.

Unit content coverage

This study session covers the following topics from the official CIPS unit content document:

Learning outcome

Predict the legal issues that need to be addressed when entering into an international contract for the purchase of goods.

Learning objective

4.4 Propose the most appropriate means of payment and explain the appropriate documentation involved in a transaction for the sale of goods in an international context.
   • Letters of credit (or documentary credits)
   • Shipping documents

Prior knowledge

Study session 19.

20

Timing

You should set aside about 2 hours to read and complete this session, including learning activities, self-assessment questions, the suggested further reading (if any) and the revision question.

20.1 Letters of credit

Learning activity 20.1

Explain the difficulties that can arise in international trade contracts, and what rules were introduced to govern such contracts.

Feedback on page 308

Documentary credits or letters of credit

These have been developed to minimise the risk faced by both parties in an international sale contract. Letters of credit allow the sale to be completed through the use of two banks, one in the buyer's country and one in the seller's country. Figure 20.1 shows an irrevocable banker's commentary credit arrangement.

Figure 20.1: Irrevocable banker's commentary credit arrangement

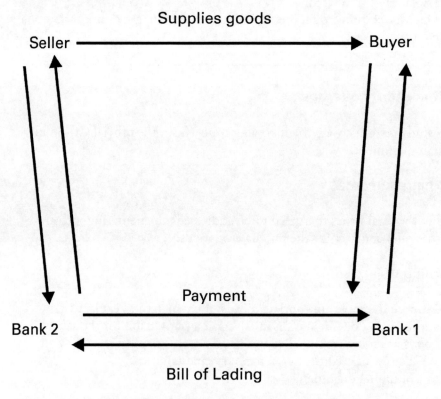

Figure 20.1 shows how documentary credit arrangements remove one of the difficulties with international sale contracts, that is, payment of the goods.

You can imagine that a seller will be reluctant to part with goods in the event that they are not paid for. The seller will also be worried about what happens if the goods are sent to the buyer and the buyer fails to pay for them. The seller would then need to sue the buyer who is in a different nation state and then enforce it in a foreign jurisdiction. This is likely to be lengthy and costly.

You can see from the from figure 20.1 that both the document (Bill of Lading or other shipping document) and the payment for the goods pass through the hands of both banks. While this is happening the goods are sent directly from the seller to the buyer.

The documentary credit process

This starts after the contract terms have been agreed between the parties. First, the buyer instructs the bank to issue an irrevocable documentary credit in favour of the seller. The buyer's bank confirms this to the seller who then sends the goods to the buyer in the knowledge that payment will be made. The buyer's bank instructs the seller's bank that the credit document has been issued and the seller's bank confirms the arrangement.

The seller can safely ship the goods as he will have possession of the Bill of Lading, which is presented to his bank. The bank will check and accept the papers and pay the seller. The seller's bank will then present the papers to the buyer's bank and receive payment. The buyer's bank will hand the documents to the buyer, which will enable him to take delivery of the goods at the port on presentation of the appropriate Bill of Lading or shipping documents the port.

As you can see, the above process is advantageous to both seller and buyer. In short, if there is a breakdown in the arrangement, whether it is the seller or buyer, the irrevocable documentary credit arrangement means enables the parties to deal with the difficulties within their own jurisdiction.

You can see from the above the importance of the Bill of Lading or other shipping documents which have been discussed already in the previous study session. You may wish to revisit and refresh your memory on these. More about shipping documents is discussed below.

In summary, the seller is assured of payment as the documentary credit is irrevocable and the Bill of Lading enables the buyer to claim delivery of the goods at the port. The buyer can also use the Bill of Lading to sell the goods even while they are still in transit.

Self-assessment question 20.1

Draw a diagram showing the irrevocable banker's documentary credit arrangement and briefly explain the advantages of these arrangements for both seller and buyer.

Feedback on page 308

Civil Jurisdiction and Judgments Act 1982

You have now learned that difficulties and problems can arise in international sale contracts as there may be conflicts as to which law will govern the contract and where the seller and buyer are in foreign jurisdictions. You also know the advantages to both seller and buyer by using the irrevocable documentary credit arrangement.

Now we will look at the situation where both seller and buyer are in different EU member states. The 1982 Act governs this situation. This Act allows judgments to be enforced through the EU but only where the buyer is in another EU member state. However, this is still a lengthy and costly situation, which a seller would wish to avoid. The seller will be worried about sending goods not knowing whether he will be paid for them or not. The buyer will not want to part with his money until he receives and inspects the goods. Also both parties may not know each other having had no past dealings and will be wary of contracting with someone who is beyond the jurisdiction of the courts. For these reasons the irrevocable documentary credit arrangement was developed with advantages for both parties.

20.2 Shipping documents

This is in part covered under study session 19 and section 20.1 above; other documents are numerous and include: invoices, marine insurance certificates, import/export licences, and bills of exchange.

Learning activity 20.2

Consider a CIF transaction and make a list of the documents associated with this.

Feedback on page 309

Shipping Documents

You studied bills of lading in detail in study session 19. We repeat the three main functions of a Bill of Lading below. However, we recommend that you revisit study session 19 to refresh your memory on Bills of Lading.

Bill of Lading

This is one of the most common forms of shipping document. It serves three main functions which are:

- as a document of title
- as evidence of a contract of carriage
- as a receipt.

You are now going to look at another shipping document, the sea waybill.

Sea waybills

These are not suitable in all trading situations. However, they have been developed to meet increasing demands for efficiency and productivity in international trade contracts.

It fulfils one of the similar functions of the Bill of Lading in that it is a receipt for goods that is evidence of a contract of carriage with a shipping company. It enables automatic delivery of the goods to the nominated consignee on proof of identity.

However, a sea waybill is not a document of title. It does not have to be sent to the destination port to act as evidence of ownership of the goods.

The advantage of a sea waybill is that there is less administration and it can be either a paper document or an electronic communication.

Situations that benefit from a sea waybill are where shipments are between related companies, payments are made under open account, or there is high degree of trust between the importers and exporters.

The way ahead may lie in the development of an electronic Bill of Lading, but this could be expensive and involve a complicated process. At present, it is possible to use each document, that is, a Bill of Lading and a sea waybill, side by side, whichever is the most appropriate in all the circumstances.

Self-assessment question 20.2

Explain the main functions of a Bill of Lading.

Feedback on page 309

Revision question

Now try the revision question for this session on page 316.

Summary

Having completed study sessions 19 and 20 you have now learned about international trade contracts and the difficulties that can arise. You also know how such difficulties can be minimised and resolved by the development of international conventions such as the Hague-Visby Rules and Hamburg Rules. You have learned about and know the importance of two of the most common forms of shipping documents: Bills of Lading and sea waybills and their main functions.

Remember that although international trade contracts are carried out on terms similar to domestic contracts, specialist payment methods have been developed to cover uncertainties. It is also probably far more essential to insist upon inserting a clause governing the law and jurisdiction that will apply in the event of a dispute arising out of the contract. Such a clause states that the contract shall be governed and construed by English law and each party agrees to submit to the exclusive jurisdiction of the English courts.

Remember that international law is a vast subject; although it is not essential to have a full understanding of the laws and rules relating to the many international conventions, it is necessary to have an appreciation of the potential problems that can arise and how these can be minimised and removed.

20

Suggested further reading

Griffiths and Griffiths (2002), part V, chapter 20.

Feedback on learning activities and self-assessment questions

Feedback on learning activity 20.1

You should explain that international trade contracts arise where the seller resides in one nation state and the buyer in another. Difficulties therefore arise as to the transfer of title, the difficulty in inspecting goods and how payment can be guaranteed.

The rules governing such contracts are covered by the Carriage of Goods by Sea Act 1971. This was adopted by the Hague-Visby Rules which are an amendment of the Hague Rules. You should include the criteria required for the rules to apply. The criticism of the Hague-Visby Rules is that they are more in favour of the carrier and this led to the introduction of the Hamburg Rules. However, although these were introduced to simplify and clarify the situation, because of their different styles they have not fulfilled this purpose. It is best when dealing in international trade contracts to expressly state that the contract will be governed by English law.

Feedback on self-assessment question 20.1

The diagram is shown in figure 20.2.

Figure 20.2

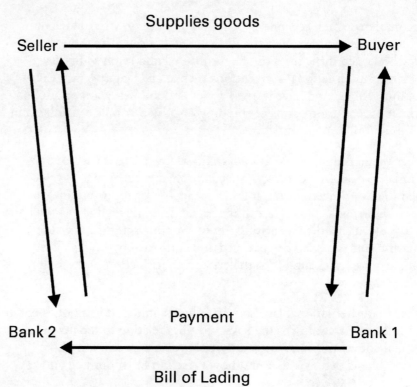

The seller is assured of payment as the documentary credit is irrevocable while the buyer has the Bill of Lading, which enables him to claim delivery of the goods at the port or sell the goods even while still in transit. Both also have the advantage of dealing with any difficulties that arise within their own jurisdiction.

Feedback on learning activity 20.2

CIF stands for cost, insurance and freight. Under a CIF contract, title to the goods passes when the seller delivers the shipping documents to the buyer. This usually occurs some time before actual delivery of the goods. Once the Bill of Lading is presented along with the contract of carriage, the insurance policy or insurance certificate and invoice the seller's responsibility ends. On delivery of these documents, the buyer is under an obligation to pay for the goods. The buyer cannot defer payment to enable him to inspect the goods.

Feedback on self-assessment question 20.2

You should provide a short paragraph on each of the three functions: namely, as a document of title, as evidence of a contract of carriage and as a receipt.

Describe how the buyer can use the Bill of Lading to sell the goods even while they are still in transit. The buyer also only gets the same title as possessed by the transferor.

The Bill of Lading also enables the buyer to claim delivery of the goods at the port. It is evidence of a contract of carriage. It should also contain all the terms of the contract of carriage under which the goods are being transported. If it does not and a dispute arises then the agreement between the parties will be governed by the main contract. The Bill of Lading is only evidence that such a contract exists.

The Bill of Lading acts as a receipt and is vital to the contract of carriage because it is evidence of the identity, quantity and condition of the goods. Details of each of these must be included in a Bill of Lading, which is governed by the Hague-Visby Rules.

20

Revision questions

Revision question for study session 1

1   New-build Ltd (N) request some suppliers to supply written *quotations* for the supply of a quantity of plasterboard sheeting. They advise that the order needs to be delivered in instalments of 100 sheets per month for the next six months. New-build include full technical specifications and a copy of their standard terms and conditions. The most satisfactory quote in relation to price comes from Plastersheet Ltd (P). Their quotation contains their standard terms and conditions of business. After some negotiation, N is satisfied as to the quality of P's plasterboard sheeting and N places an *order* on its own standard terms and conditions by faxing a standard order form to P. This standard order form repeats N's terms and conditions of business. It also requires that P fax their *acceptance* to N. P fax back their acceptance with *only the front page* of their acknowledgement form. Later they post the whole acknowledgement form which has on the reverse side P's standard terms and conditions of business.
Analyse the legal position of the two parties and determine whose standard terms legally bind the contract.

2   Toys4U advertise the latest robotic toy on their website. The in-house price is £40 but by mistake the price on their website is £4. Orders start coming in via the website but Toys4U refuse to honour the orders. Advise Toys4U of their legal position.

Feedback on page 317

Revision question for study session 2

1   Foodstores Ltd (F) require supplies of cheese to be delivered in 12 instalments. They enter into a contract with Cheese Wholesale plc (C). The contract is on C's terms and conditions. C included clause 4 in the contract as follows:

> Clause 4 – the seller shall not be liable whatsoever for non-performance in whole or in part of its obligations under the contract due to causes beyond its reasonable control. Such causes might include but are not limited to war, strikes, government actions, supplier delays or any acts of God.

Before the third instalment could be delivered, a strike in Holland restricted the supply of cheese. This meant that C could not meet the fourth delivery date and F had to source cheese elsewhere.

Evaluate whether or not C can rely on clause 6.

2 Describe a Romalpa clause.
3 Explain how the Unfair Contract Terms Act 1977 restricts the right to exclude or limit liability for breaches of commercial contracts.

Feedback on page 318

Revision question for study session 3

1 Explain what it means to vitiate a contract and what the difference is between void and voidable.
2 Petspecial (P) is a small company who provides pet food to their largest customer, Animalworld (A), a national retailer. P contracts with Express Inc. (E) to deliver cartons of the pet food to A's stores throughout the UK. They agree a rate of £50 per carton with an anticipated load of at least 400 cartons. However, the first load was only 200 cartons and E refuse to deliver any more until P agree to pay £100 per carton. P cannot find alternative transport and are worried about losing the contract with their largest customer, Animalworld. They agree to pay the new rate. P are now refusing to pay E. Advise P.
3 Remedies for misrepresentation depend on the type of misrepresentation. Discuss this statement.

Feedback on page 318

Revision question for study session 4

Printfine (P) enters into a contract with Quickrepair (Q) to repair one of its printing machines at a cost of £400. Q's employee negligently reassembles the printing machine incorrectly. This results in the drive shaft breaking when it is used for the first time after the repair. The machine is now beyond repair. The cost of replacing the printing machine is £10,000. P cannot obtain a replacement for four weeks. During this period they estimate that the lack of the machine has reduced their profit by £800 per week. P also miss out on a lucrative contract worth £20,000. Advise P as to the damages it can claim for Q's breach of contract.

Feedback on page 320

Revision question for study session 5

Constructquick have entered into a contract with Rooflite to install the roofing at their development of 20 new units. If a dispute arises they do not want to be involved in a long court battle. Explain adjudication as the alternative dispute resolution which is available.

Feedback on page 320

Revision question for study session 6

1 Provide examples of contracts that would fall within the Sale of Goods Act 1979 and those which fall within the Supply of Goods and Services Act 1982.
2 Anne needs a new ball gown from her local shop for the charity event the next evening. She visits her local shop and while there she sees that

they have extended their services to include laundry/cleaning services. She knows her dress size and does not try the dress on. She pays for the ball gown and takes it home. She returns to the shop later with a suit and coat for cleaning. When getting ready for the charity event she notices that the ball gown has some stains and she is unable to wear it. She returns to the shop the next day to return the gown and pick up her cleaning. The shop apologise but refuse to give her a refund. To make matters worse they have ruined her suit and coat in the cleaning. Explain which Act governs the two contractual situations.

Feedback on page 321

Revision question for study session 7

1 Describe the circumstances in which the courts are prepared to amend an existing contract by inserting implied terms.
2 Describe the terms implied into contracts under the Sale of Goods Act 1979.

Feedback on page 321

Revision question for study session 8

Xeran place an order with Anco for 10 tons of grain to be delivered at 9 am on 10 June at Xeran's place of business. A tanker containing the grain arrived at Xeran's premises at 4 pm on 9 June. Xeran could not take delivery of the grain at that time and requested that the tanker park overnight at Xeran's premises. The tanker contained 30 tons of grain, 10 tons for Xeran and 20 tons for another customer. During the night the tanker was stolen. Anco are claiming the price of the grain claiming that they had delivered the grain to Xeran as it was on their premises. The contract made no mention of when title and risk would pass.

Feedback on page 322

Revision question for study session 9

A person cannot pass to another person property they do not own. Discuss the exceptions to this rule.

Feedback on page 322

Revision question for study session 10

1 Gregor Construction (GC) enter into a contract with Woodsupplies (W) to build two dwellinghouses. W subcontract the building work to ConstructionUK. Explain the circumstances when it is possible to sue the subcontractor.
2 Jameson Ltd (JL) purchased mechanical toys from Robots Wholesalers (RW). RW imported these from manufacturers in China. Jane purchased one for her son Alex aged three. Alex was injured while playing with the toy. The safety instructions were in Chinese and only when translated did they realise that the toy should not have been given

to a three-year-old. Advise Jane of any legal claim she has and against whom.

Feedback on page 323

Revision question for study session 11

Geothermals engages an agent to source certain products in Poland. The agency contract is subject to English law. The agent enters into a contract on behalf of Geothermals with Polenski, a Polish supplier. Geothermals later discovers that the agent had taken a secret payment from Polenski in return for the award of the contract. Examine the remedies available to Geothermals against both the agent and Polenski.

Feedback on page 323

Revision question for study session 12

Clough Council (CC) is a public sector body operating in the UK. CC want to outsource their office cleaning service. CC decided to invite tenders for the cleaning contract. The estimated value is £1,000,000. CC placed the invite for competitive tendering on its website and included downloads of a prequalifying questionnaire. After evaluation of the submitted questionnaires three suppliers who met the initial criteria were invited to submit tenders. The tenders had to be returned by 12 noon on 10 June to room 177 of CC's offices. Each supplier submitted the tender on time. CC rejected all three tenders. CC approached one of the tenderers, DD, to negotiate some issues. After some discussion DD resubmitted their tender and were awarded the contract. EE was one of the three tenderers whose bid was rejected. EE are unhappy about the preferential treatment given to DD. Analyse whether or not EE have a legal claim against CC.

Feedback on page 324

Revision question for study session 13

Describe what procurement procedure should be followed by a public authority when embarking on a tendering process, taking into account the EU directives.

Feedback on page 324

Revision question for study session 14

Explain the public interest test for non-disclosure under the Freedom of Information Act 2000.

Feedback on page 325

Revision question for study session 15

Cookieland employs 40 staff as lorry drivers to deliver products across the UK. The directors have decided to outsource the delivery service to ExpressDeliver. They are specialists in deliveries and are based near the offices of Cookieland. ExpressDeliver can offer employment to only 25 of

Cookieland drivers. Explain how the legal rights of the deployed staff from Cookieland are protected.

Feedback on page 325

Revision question for study session 16

1   Tudorfabrics Ltd is a large manufacturer of curtain material with markets in the UK and in Europe. It has subsidiaries in France and Italy. It is now considering a partnership with a German competitor. Under this partnership they both agree not to compete in certain products that they both manufactured previously. Describe the UK and European competition law implications of this proposal.
2   Outline the main provisions of the Enterprise Act 2002.

Feedback on page 325

Revision question for study session 17

Anders is developing a new range of sportswear in partnership with a manufacturer. Anders is keen to protect their intellectual property rights. The sportswear includes special running shoes with a unique 'spring' action in the sole. The unique spring action sole can be used in other training shoes. Describe the forms of intellectual property rights available to provide Anders with protection for its exclusive range of sportswear, its shoe design and the unique spring sole that it has developed for use in training shoes.

Feedback on page 326

Revision question for study session 18

Please note that there is often confusion by candidates as to the meaning of 'passing-off'. Students often give an answer on 'passing of title'! Please ensure your understanding of this topic by reading study session 17 and attempting the following question.

Explain the legal requirements necessary to succeed in an action for passing off.

Feedback on page 326

Revision question for study session 19

Blackstone Ltd purchased 100 tons of tea to be shipped from South America to London on a nominated ship. The contract was CIF and the seller, Americano, acting as the buyer's agent, arranged for the freight contract and insurance cover. The contract specified that it was governed by English law. The tea was shipped on the due date on the nominated ship but the whole cargo was lost at sea due to an uninsurable risk. Prior to this loss, Americano had delivered the relevant shipping documents to Blackstone. Blackstone refuse to pay, claiming that the goods have not been delivered. Advise Americano of their rights under English law.

Feedback on page 326

Revision question for study session 20

Describe the purpose that a Bill of Lading serves.

Feedback on page 327

Feedback on revision questions

Feedback on revision question for study session 1

1   The case study scenario is all about the chain of documents in terms of the legal status. What you could do is highlight the different documents so that you do not miss any (these are shown in capitals in the question). You should unravel this chain by looking at each of the documents in the chain.

The first point to consider is the request for quotations. This is just a request for information and is not an offer. The next document to consider is the quotation. If the quotation received is precise then it may amount to an offer to trade on specified terms and in this case the terms would be on P's terms and conditions which were contained within their quotation. You may decide that the quotation did not have precise information and is also a request for more information. Either of these answers is acceptable.

The next document is the order form placed by N. Depending on what you have said about the quotation, the order form is either a counter-offer to the offer or an offer if you have decided that the quotation is just a request for more information. This order form repeats N's terms and conditions, therefore at this stage the contract is on N's terms. P conforms to the request and faxes back their acceptance on their acknowledgement form. However, the important point here is that they only fax back the front page of the acknowledgement form. This means that their acceptance is on N's terms and conditions. The contract is formed at this stage and on N's terms. So the fact that the whole acknowledgement form was sent later and contained P's terms on the reverse does not matter. The contract is legally binding on N's terms and conditions of business.

2   If you have been researching the internet you may have discovered the case of *Argos* [2003] who advertised televisions on their website for £3 instead of £300. When orders started coming in they refused to honour them. However, this case never reached the courts as the cost to the consumer was too great. So this was not tested in the courts. However, you should mention that the essential elements of a contract apply to e-contracts. You should mention that it depends on whether the contract is bilateral or unilateral (that is, open to the whole wide world to accept), as in the case of *Carlill* v *Carbolic Smoke Ball Co.* [1893]. In that case the court decided that an advertisement promising £100 to anyone who caught influenza after using the advertiser's smoke ball was an offer.

Feedback on revision question for study session 2

1   You should first of all identify that clause 4 is a force majeure clause. You should explain the purpose of such a clause. Such a clause is an attempt by the contracting parties to stipulate what will happen if some event beyond their control interferes with the performance of the contract. Typical force majeure clauses include acts of God, delays in manufacture and problems with subcontractors. You should examine the wording of the clause and mention that the failure to meet the next delivery date was due to a strike and that this is included within clause 4. So C had accounted for the possibility of their being a strike. As the contract is on C's terms and conditions they can rely on clause 4. However, you must also mention that as a force majeure clause is an exclusion clause it is subject to the reasonableness test as defined in the Unfair Contracts Terms Act 1977 (UCTA 1977). A good answer will include identification of the appropriate sections of this Act, namely section 3, section 11 and Schedule 2 to the Act, which are the key provisions to be applied. Schedule 2 lays down five criteria to be considered in relation to liability. These include the bargaining power of the contracting parties; whether the party received an inducement to accept the term; whether the party ought to have known of the existence of the term; where the clause excludes liability for non-compliance with a contractual term, whether such compliance is practical; and where goods were manufactured, processed or adapted to special order if it is reasonable for the supplier to exclude liability for fitness for purpose.

2   A Romalpa clause is also known as retention of title clause. You should explain how it came to be called Romalpa. A retention of title clause was recognised by the Court of Appeal in the case of *Aluminium Industrie Vaasen BV* v *Romalpa Aluminium* [1976]. Since that case retention of title clauses are quite usual in commercial contracts. A retention of title clause protects the seller against the liquidation of the buyer and gives the seller preferential treatment over other creditors. It means that the seller allows for retention of title until some condition of the contract is fulfilled.

3   You should explain that a contract cannot restrict or limit liability for negligence if the negligence causes death or personal injury. If the negligence causes other loss or damage then the clause must satisfy the reasonableness test under UCTA 1977, which includes taking into account the bargaining power of the contracting parties; whether the party received an inducement to accept the term; whether the party ought to have known of the existence of the term; where the clause excludes liability for non-compliance with a contractual term, whether such compliance is practical; and where goods were manufactured, processed or adapted to special order if it is reasonable for the supplier to exclude liability for fitness for purpose.

Feedback on revision question for study session 3

1   Vitiate means to render the contract defective. When a contract is rendered defective then it may be considered void or voidable. You should explain the difference between void and voidable. Void means that the contract will be considered as if it had never existed. Neither party acquire rights or incur liability and the contracting parties are

returned to the position they were in before the contract was concluded. Voidable means that the contract remains legal and enforceable until such time as it is avoided by the innocent party.

2   This scenario is based on the case of *Atlas Express Ltd* v *Kafco (Importers and Distributors) Ltd* [1989] and is about the effects of economic duress on a contract. The *Atlas* case firmly established the concept of economic duress. In the *Atlas* case the court held that the pressure applied by Atlas to force Kafco to renegotiate the contract was economic duress and this vitiated the contract. You should also mention that there are two criteria which must be satisfied for duress to be actionable. First of all the victim must complain at the time, and secondly did the victim intend to repudiate the contract? Go on to explain that duress consists of two elements – there must be coercion and the pressure must be illegitimate.

3   You should first of all describe the three types of misrepresentation: innocent, negligent and fraudulent. Innocent misrepresentation occurs when the misrepresentation was made without any fault. Negligent misrepresentation occurs when a false statement is made by a person having a duty of care. Some relationship must exist between the parties to a contract. You can mention here the case of *Hedley Byrne* v *Heller* [1963] which affirmed the rule that an action for damages for negligence lies in tort provided the false statement is made negligently. This case related to a banker's reference about a potential customer. It turned out that the customer was not creditworthy. An action was raised claiming the bankers had been negligent. However, in this particular case the bankers had included a disclaimer in the reference stating that 'it is given in confidence and without responsibility on our part'. The court held that the disclaimer was adequate in this case. However, in the absence of such a disclaimer the circumstances would have given rise to a duty of care. Finally describe fraudulent misrepresentation which occurs when a party makes a false statement without believing it to be true. It may be deliberate or reckless. You could refer to *Derry* v *Peek* [1889] which was based on fraudulent misrepresentation. However, the action in deceit failed as Derry honestly believed that they would get the consent from the Board of Trade.

Now go on to describe that rescission is available for all three types of misrepresentation unless it is prevented by undue lapse of time, or it is impossible to restore the parties to their original positions or where third party rights are involved. If the misrepresentation is entirely innocent then there is no remedy. If the misrepresentation is negligent or fraudulent, a remedy in damages is available. For negligent misrepresentation the remedy is provided by the Misrepresentation Act 1967. This applies where the person making the statement cannot show that they had reason able grounds for believing it to be true. Fraudulent misrepresentation is governed by the tort of deceit. You should describe the remedy of rescission. Rescission means to set aside the contract. The aim is to put the parties back to their original position as if the contract had never been made. Under the Misrepresentation Act 1976 rescission is at the discretion of the court. In fraudulent misrepresentation the claim for damages is based on the tort of deceit. The purpose of damages is to restore the victim to the position they were in before the representation was made. You should also mention the test of remoteness in deceit. This is that the injured party may recover all the direct loss incurred as a result of the misrepresentation.

Feedback on revision question for study session 4

This question relates to the issue of remoteness of damages. You should outline the principle from *Hadley* v *Baxendale* [1854]. P will be able to recover the cost of replacement and some lost profits, but the main issue is whether missing out on a lucrative contract can be taken into account. If Q has knowledge of this or it is within their reasonable contemplation then the issue is one of assessing the value to be placed on the lost opportunity. Q are clearly in breach of contract as a result of their employee's negligence and P can seek damages. What the courts have to achieve is to put the innocent party (P) into the position they would have been in had the contract been performed properly. P also have a duty to minimise their loss. They should take reasonable steps to obtain the cheapest replacement machine as quickly as possible. If they have done this then the assumption is that £10,000 is the best deal and Q will be liable to pay this amount.

Now you should look at the losses which follow from the breach, namely the loss of profits. You must mention that such losses are recoverable but they must be caused by the breach and not be too remote. The contractual rules of remoteness are set out in *Hadley* v *Baxendale*. This case was about a delay in the delivery of a drive shaft. The principle set out by the court was that the defendant was liable for all losses which flowed from the breach in the natural course of events as well as those which may reasonably be in the contemplation of the parties at the time the contract was made. You can mention *Victoria Laundry (Windsor)* v *Newman* [1949] and *The Heron II* [1969]. These cases really show that there is one test, namely, given the parties' state of knowledge at the time the contract is made, was the loss one which they should reasonably have contemplated would have occurred because of the breach. So in this case study, if Q had known that P did not have a spare drive shaft they would be liable for loss of profits as a result of the breach.

Feedback on revision question for study session 5

This question requires you to provide a brief explanation of adjudication and its advantages. You should explain that it was introduced by the Housing Grants, Construction and Regeneration Act 1996 as being a faster and significantly cheaper way of resolving disputes. It is widely used in commerce, especially construction contracts. However, although it was introduced as being cheaper, parties involved in adjudication are using the services of lawyers more and more, therefore in practice the cost is increasing. The contract will contain a clause stating that in the event of a dispute arising between the parties, the dispute will be referred to adjudication. There are various nominating bodies within the UK. The process starts with the nomination and selection of an adjudicator. The adjudicator must confirm that there is no conflict of interest. The adjudicator sets out the deadlines, seeking clarification of any representatives and advising the parties of the appointment. Jurisdiction of the adjudicator is governed by the Housing Grants, Construction and Regeneration Act 1996 and associate Scheme for Contraction contracts or within the contract. The process involves referral notice, responses and submissions. The adjudicator may convene a meeting to establish the facts. The meeting is not for the purpose of arguing the law. The adjudicator can seek independent specialist advice. The object of adjudication is to reach a decision. One disadvantage is that the parties may still end up in court.

Feedback on revision question for study session 6

1   You should identify goods as animals, cleaning materials which fall within SGA 1979 whereas energy supplies and office cleaning services fall within Supply of Goods and Services Act 1982 (SOGAS 1982).

2   You should firstly identify the different types of contract. The purchase of the ball gown is governed by the Sale of Goods Act 1979 and the laundry/cleaning services are governed by the Supply of Goods and Services Act 1982. The purchase of the ball gown is a contract for sale of goods by the shop to Anne. The cleaning of the suit is a contract for the supply of services from the shop to Anne. She has rights under both of these statutes. In particular you can refer to the section 14 SGA 1979, fitness for purpose and satisfactory quality, and for the ruin of her suit and coat she can claim under the SOGAS 1982 for damages for her loss.

Feedback on revision question for study session 7

1   You should explain that the function of the courts is to give effect to what the parties to the contract intended. This means that the court will not enhance a contract. The courts will not imply a term that would be inconsistent with an express term. However, the courts may imply a term into a contract where it is necessary to give business efficacy to it. The court may imply a term into a contract if it is the custom of a particular trade or profession or if it is necessary by law. You should refer to the case of *The Moorcock* [1889]. In this case a ship was moored for loading. Both parties realised that when the tide was out the ship would rest on the river bed. The ship, *The Moorcock*, sustained damage when she ceased to float on the water. Although no warranty was given, the court held that there was an implied warranty that the place was safe for the ship to lie. Another case you could refer to is *Liverpool City Council* v *Irwin* [1977] where the court held there was an implied term in a lease of a flat in a block of properties owned by the Council that the landlord (the Council) should maintain the properties in a reasonable state of repair. From this case we see that the court will imply a term into a contract under the officious bystander rule. This means that the court will imply a term into a contract which was so obvious to the parties that it was not worth stating it expressly. The circumstances for implying such a term is rare. It must be so obvious that it would not occur to the parties to state it.

2   You should explain that the terms implied by the Sale of Goods Act 1979 fall within sections 12–15. Provide a short paragraph explaining each section. Section 12 relates to implied conditions as to title or right to sell. You should explain that unless the circumstances

indicate differently, there is an implied condition that in a contract of sale the seller has a right to sell the goods, and in an agreement to sell the seller will have the right to sell the goods at the time when the property is to pass to the buyer. Section 13 relates to sale by description and provides that there is an implied condition that the goods will correspond with the description. Section 14 relates to satisfactory quality and fitness for purpose, but only to sales 'in the course of business' and not to private sales. Finally, section 15 governs both private and business sales. It provides that the bulk will correspond in quality with the sample, and the goods will be free from any defect which would be apparent on examination of the sample.

Feedback on revision question for study session 8

This case concerns the issue of when the parties intended ownership to pass. You are required to identify the Sale of Goods Act 1979 and in particular section 17 which states that ownership passes when the parties intend it to pass and this general rule relates to specific goods. In order to determine the intention of the parties you must consider the conduct of the parties and the circumstances of the case. It is helpful to look at the types of categories into which goods fall, such as existing goods, future goods, specific goods, unascertained goods and ascertained goods. Now look at the case study and identify into which category the grain would fall. You should identify that the grain falls into the category of unascertained goods. Where there is no reference in the contract to when title and risk pass, the courts will look to section 18 of the SGA 1979. Knowing that the grain falls within unascertained goods you can identify the appropriate rule, namely rule 5 of section 18 SGA 1979. Rule 5 applies in a contract for the sale of unascertained goods. No property passes until the goods are ascertained. Ownership will only pass once the goods have become ascertained and unconditionally appropriated to the contract. In this case study the goods have not been ascertained or unconditionally appropriated, and therefore ownership still rests with Anco who will have to bear the loss.

You could also mention the case of *Healey* v *Howlett & Sons* [1917] and provide a brief explanation of the case. Howlett were fish dealers in Ireland and they supplied fish to English customers. All fish was sent to an agent in Holyhead. Healey was a fish salesman in London and he ordered 20 boxes of mackerel from Howlett; 122 boxes were sent to the agent in Holyhead to fulfil the order for the London fish salesman. The agent selected 20 boxes for dispatch but due to delays the fish was found to be bad on arrival in London. The fault was not due to Howlett. Healey refused to pay Howlett and Howlett sued for the full price, claiming that property had passed in the fish as they had sent 122 boxes to their agent. The court held that property would not pass until the agent had earmarked the 20 boxes for Healey and therefore the fish was still at Howlett's risk. Healey did not need to pay.

Feedback on revision question for study session 9

This refers to the *nemo dat* rule. Under section 21 of the SGA 1979, where a buyer has no title to the goods then they must be returned on demand to the true owner or face an action of tort. Of course the buyer can recover damages from the seller for breach of section 12 which is the section of the SGA 1979 relating to title. In practice this may be difficult as the seller may have absconded. This would be very harsh on the buyer and this is why there are exceptions to the *nemo dat* rule. The exceptions are estoppel, sale under a voidable title, sale by seller in possession, sale by buyer in possession, Hire Purchase Act 1974, sale by bailee, sale by mercantile agent and sale by court order. Provide a short paragraph on each of these.

Feedback on revision question for study session 10

1 This question refers to privity of contract and you must define privity of contract. You should then explain the varying ways of getting round the privity of contract rule. Your answer should include explanations of collateral contracts, negligence, expressed warranties, indemnity clauses and the Contract (Rights of Third Parties) Act 1999.
Under common law of England, privity of contract means that only the parties to a contract can acquire rights under it and be bound by it. This of course means that third parties cannot acquire any rights in a contract between two other parties and these two parties cannot of course impose obligations on a third party who is not a party to the contract.
You should refer to the case of *Dunlop Pneumatic Tyre Co. Ltd* v *Selfridge & Co. Ltd* [1915] which laid down fundamental principles of privity of contract. Privity is an obstacle in certain situations and there are statutory and common law exceptions. Statutory exceptions are under insurance law and road traffic legislation as well as the Contracts (Rights of Third Parties) Act 1999. Common law exceptions are agency, joint parties, contracting on behalf of a group, assignment, tort of negligence and collateral contracts. Collateral contracts are separate contracts related to the main contract as in the case of *Shanklin Pier Ltd* v *Detel Products Ltd* [1951]. The principles of tort of negligence were laid down by *Donoghue* v *Stevenson* [1932]. The principles include that a duty of care exists between parties, the duty has been breached and loss or damage has resulted from the breach. Manufacturers are also liable, as seen in the *Shanklin Pier* case.

2 This question relates to the Consumer Protection Act 1987. This is often missed by students. First of all you should identify words in the question such as 'toy', 'manufacturer', and immediately identify this with the 1987 Act. You should explain that a claim must be over £275 and that Jane would only succeed if the product is defective and the defect caused the injury. You should also explain that a product can be defective if the instructions are inadequate, which seems to be the case here as they could not be read by the consumer. You should go on to explain who is liable – this includes the manufacturers, the importers into the EU, any people who own the brand, the supplier – and that liability is joint and several. You should also explain that liability cannot be excluded.

Feedback on revision question for study session 11

You should first of all identify that this relates to agency and that Geothermals is the principal and Polenski the third party. You should outline the duties of an agent which include carrying out lawful instructions, exercising reasonable care and skill, acting in good faith, avoiding conflicts of interest, not misusing confidential information and not taking secret payments or bribes. So clearly we have the agent in this case abusing his duty. Geothermal can take action against the agent to recover any secret profit, refuse to pay any commission to the agent and dismiss him without notice. Geothermals can also take action against Polenski to rescind the contract with Polenski. You should also mention that both the agent and Polenski have committed criminal offences under English law. However, enforcement is unlikely.

Feedback on revision question for study session 12

This question relates to tendering and you are required to discuss the tendering process and contractual obligations under such a process. You should include that there is a contractual right for a bid to be considered as long as it satisfies the bid criteria. We see from the above case that all three suppliers met the initial criteria, that is, including EE. The whole tendering process must be conducted in good faith. There is an obligation to treat all tenderers fairly until the contract is actually awarded. This did not happen in this case. DD were treated with preference, having been given the opportunity to resubmit. You should refer to the case of *R* v *National Lottery Commission ex parte Camelot* [2000]. This case is very similar to the case study. All bidders should have been given an equal opportunity to be reconsidered prior to the contract award. CC have breached this duty and EE would be entitled to ask for an injunction to stop the process. If the contract has already commenced then EE may claim damages. Damages will be restricted to the cost of presenting and submitting the bid.

Feedback on revision question for study session 13

You should explain that the public authority must consider the threshold levels set by the EU public procurement directives. They should follow the rules preventing discrimination against companies from any Member State. There must be free movement of goods and services. You should mention that the directives set out clear standards which are based on fairness, openness, non-discrimination and competition.

The public authority must also consider the types of contract, whether one-off purchases of a particular product or service by a specific date or the purchase of goods and services over a period of time, or whether they are considering a framework agreement over a period of time.

They will have to make decisions on advertising, deadlines, prequalification stages and evaluation information.

You should mention that the aim is to award the contract to the supplier who provides the most economically advantageous tender based on price and quality. Other issues you can include are invoices, payment, health and safety issues.

Feedback on revision question for study session 14

You should explain that not all information must be disclosed by public authorities under the 2000 Act. One of these exemptions is the public interest test where public authorities can withhold information which is commercially sensitive. They can only do this where withholding the information in the public interest outweighs the public interest in disclosing it.

Feedback on revision question for study session 15

For this answer you need to identify that the deployed staff that go from Cookieland to ExpressDeliver are protected by the Transfer of Undertakings (Protection of Employment) Regulations 1981 (TUPE 1981). You should include a definition of a relevant transfer as TUPE regulations apply when a business is transferred to a new owner as a going concern. Staff who are transferred to ExpressDeliver retain all their rights and are entitled to an automatic transfer of rights and obligations. They are employed on the same terms and conditions as they were at Cookieland. This relates to continuity of employment and pay but does not include pension rights. You should also mention that employees must be consulted. Any staff who are dismissed at the time of the transfer are deemed unfairly dismissed unless the dismissal is for economic, technical or organisational (eto) reasons, in which case they are deemed redundant.

Feedback on revision question for study session 16

1   This requires you to outline UK and European competition law particularly Articles 81 and 82 of the EC Treaty. An in-depth answer is required.
    You should include the Competition Act 1988 and why it was created, namely to simplify the law in relation to EC legal and business environments. You should go on to describe that it is designed to prohibit anti-competitive practices and abuse of monopoly situations in a given market. You should then describe Article 18 of the EC Treaty which prohibits anti-competitive agreements which may prevent, restrict or distort competition in the single market. Article 82 relates to the dominant position and you should provide a definition of dominant position, that is, when an undertaking behaves to an appreciable extent independently of its competitors and customers and ultimately of consumers when making commercial decisions. You should list some types of conduct which would be prohibited.

2   You should explain that the 2002 Act introduced a stricter regime into competition law. You should explain the possibility of class actions brought by consumer groups, known as super complaints, the stop-now provisions. It created the body called Office of Fair Trading (OFT) and increased its powers. The OFT has taken over the role previously undertaken by the Director General of Fair Trading (DGFT). It created the Competition Appeal Tribunal (CAT). Also, an independent body makes decisions on mergers and markets. The Act also introduced

criminal sanctions for cartels who operate agreements to fix prices, share markets and limit production or rig bids.

Feedback on revision question for study session 17

You should first of all identify the different products, such as sportswear (this could include t-shirts and shorts), shoes, spring action sole. Once you think of each of these you can go on to describe the different intellectual property rights. Copyright would be applicable for the sportswear, and if they are branding the product then trade marking the brand/name under the Trade Marks Act 1994 would be applicable. The design of the sportswear could be registered under the Registered Designs Act 1949 which gives 25-year protection.

The unique spring sole might attract a patent right if it is novel, involves an inventive step and is capable of industrial application.

Feedback on revision question for study session 18

First of all you must recognise that passing off is a common law right rather than a statutory right. It is designed to protect the goodwill of a business. You should explain the criteria required for an action of passing off to be successful. The criteria was laid down in *Erven Warnink BV* v *J Townend & Sons (Hull) Ltd* [1979] (the *Advocaat* case) but reduced and summarised in *Reckitt & Coleman Products Ltd* v *Borden* [1990] (the *Jif Lemon* case) as no man might pass off his goods as those of another. The tort of passing off provides two protections in that it protects a trader against the unfair competition of competitors and it protects consumers who would otherwise be confused as to the origin of the goods or services they are offered. Trade mark infringement cases often involve passing off issues as these two areas are closely related. According to the *Jif Lemon* case the claimant must be able to demonstrate goodwill, there must be misrepresentation as to the goods or services offered and there must be actual or likely damage.

Feedback on revision question for study session 19

You should explain the main features of a CIF contract (which stands for cost, insurance and freight). In a CIF contract, once the shipping documents are sent to the buyer the goods must be paid for whether or not the goods arrive. This is the situation here so the seller, Americano, has a duty as the buyer's agent to ensure that he obtains the freight and insurance contract on the best terms possible for the buyer. When you are asked about a case study relating to CIF do not give explanations of all other types of shipping contract! You can explain that the use of standard forms removes the challenges which arise in international trading. CIF is the most common form of international contract. It places the responsibility on the seller to arrange for the shipment of the goods and to insure them against loss or damage during the voyage. This means that the price charged to the buyer includes such services. CIF is beneficial to the buyer as the seller bears the risk of increased costs of transport or insurance.

Feedback on revision question for study session 20

You should explain that a Bill of Lading is one of the most common forms of shipping document and it serves three main functions: it acts as a document of title, it is evidence of a contract of carriage and it acts as a receipt.

References and bibliography

This section contains a complete A-Z listing of all publications, materials or websites referred to in this course book. Books, articles and research are listed under the first author's (or in some cases the editor's) surname. Where no author name has been given, the publication is listed under the name of the organisation that published it. Websites are listed under the name of the organisation providing the website.

Department of Trade & Industry: http://www.dti.gov.uk.

Dobson, P (1997) *Charlesworth's Business Law,* 16th edition, London: Sweet & Maxwell.

Griffiths, M and I Griffiths (2002) *Law for Purchasing and Supply,* Harlow: FT Prentice Hall.

IDeA: http://www.idea-knowledge.gov.uk.

Longdin, I (2005) *Legal Aspects of Purchasing and Supply Chain Management* Liverpool Academic Press

Mills, R (2005) *Construction Adjudication* Coventry: RICS Books.

Office of Government Commerce: http://www.ogc.gov.uk.

Smith, K and D Keenan (2003) *Law for business* Harlow: Pearson Longman.

Stone, R (2000) *Principles of Contract Law*, 4th edition. London: Cavendish.

UK Patent Office: http://www.patent.gov.uk.

Waring, M (2006) *Commercial Dispute Resolution*, London: Jordan Publishing

Index